PRAISE FOR

FEATURE FILMMAKING AT USED-CAR PRICES

"An intriguing book that takes on Hollywood with a healthy, 'do-it-yourself' attitude."

—*Cineaste*

"It's as much an inspirational book as a step-by-step guide to the process of making 'no-budget movies.' "

—John Hartl, film critic, *The Seattle Times*

"I wish I could have read this book thirty-five years ago, before I made my first low-budget features,"

—Vilmos Zsigmond, cinematographer, *Deliverance*, *The Deer Hunter*, *Close Encounters of the Third Kind*, *The Crossing Guard*

"Rick Schmidt is the only person on Earth who could shoot an entire feature film *inside* a used car . . . and then sell the film (and car) for a profit."

—Nicholas Kazan, screenwriter, *At Close Range*, *Reversal of Fortune*, *Patty Hearst*, *Dream Lover* (also directed), *Fallen*

"An indie's A to Z . . . If you want to jump on in, Rick'll get you rolling."

—Jon Jost, feature filmmaker, *Speaking Directly*, *Last Chants For a Slow Dance*, *Frame Up*, *Sure Fire*, *All the Vermeers in New York*

PENGUIN BOOKS

FEATURE FILMMAKING AT USED-CAR PRICES

Rick Schmidt has spent over twenty-five years writing, directing, and producing low-budget feature films that have received national and international recognition. He began in 1973 with his first feature, *A Man, a Woman, and a Killer*, which was co-directed with his roommate, Wayne Wang (*Chan Is Missing*, *The Joy Luck Club*, *Smoke*, etc.). This feature premiered at the Bleecker Street Cinema in New York City and won Directors' Choice at the Ann Arbor Film Festival.

His second and third features, *1988—The Remake* and *Emerald Cities*, completed his trilogy about the American dream.

Schmidt's fourth feature, *Morgan's Cake*, made on a $15,000 budget, was selected by the Sundance Film Festival for its Dramatic Competition (1989), and was also presented at the Berlin Film Festival (Panorama), San Francisco International, AFI/LA, and at New Directors/New Films, where critic Janet Maslin of *The New York Times* called it "a delight."

In 1992 his fifth feature, *American Orpheus*, premiered at the Rotterdam and Seattle International Film Festivals, and won a Gold Award at Houston International for Best Low-Budget Theatrical Feature of the year.

Since the release of *Blues for the Avatar* in 1995 (Slamdance, Figueira da Foz), Schmidt and his son Morgan Schmidt-Feng have co-produced several 16-mm and Pro-DVCAM features (*someone like me*, *Welcome to Serendipity*, *Loneliness Is Soul*, *Maisy's Garden*, *Crash My Funeral*, *Sun and Moon*, *Chetzmoka's Curse,* etc.) with writer-directors who collaborate with them at Feature Workshops.

PENGUIN BOOKS

Feature Filmmaking at Used-Car Prices

HOW TO WRITE, PRODUCE, DIRECT, SHOOT, EDIT, AND PROMOTE A FEATURE-LENGTH MOVIE FOR LESS THAN $15,000

THIRD EDITION

RICK SCHMIDT

PENGUIN BOOKS
Published by the Penguin Group
Penguin Putnam Inc., 375 Hudson Street,
New York, New York 10014, U.S.A.
Penguin Books Ltd, 27 Wrights Lane,
London W8 5TZ, England
Penguin Books Australia Ltd, Ringwood,
Victoria, Australia
Penguin Books Canada Ltd, 10 Alcorn Avenue,
Toronto, Ontario, Canada M4V 3B2
Penguin Books (N.Z.) Ltd, 182–190 Wairau Road,
Auckland 10, New Zealand

Penguin Books Ltd, Registered Offices:
Harmondsworth, Middlesex, England

First published in the United States of America in hardcover and paperback
editions by Viking Penguin Inc. 1988
Second edition published in Penguin Books 1995
This third edition published 2000

1 2 3 4 5 6 7 8 9 10

LIBRARY OF CONGRESS CATALOGING IN PUBLICATION DATA
Schmidt, Rick.
Feature filmmaking at used-car prices: how to write, produce, direct, shoot, edit, and promote a feature-length movie for less than $15,000 / Rick Schmidt.
p. cm.
Includes index.
ISBN 0 14 02.9184 9
1. Motion pictures—Production and direction. 2. Low budget motion pictures. I. Title.
PN1995.9.P7 S34 2000
791.43′023—dc21 99-053296

Printed in the United States of America
Set in Garamond
Designed by Deborah Kerner

for Julie

I read recently that Americans are buying used cars for an average of $12,000 and I thought, Why don't they take the bus to work and make a feature film instead?*

—Rick Schmidt

*(*Yes, basically* double *the $6,000 average cost of used cars when I first wrote this book in 1988! And I just learned on the Internet*
<www.isd.net/msp00050/driving.html>
that it costs approximately $6,100 more per year out-of-pocket to keep that car on the road, counting monthly payments, insurance, maintenance, gas, etc.!)

A Preamble for the 2000 Edition

Welcome to Edition 2000. (Don't you love how everything has been tagged with a 2000!) While it may be a little hard to deal with the hype of the new millennium, there is no problem acknowledging the effusion of new digital technology upon us—the main reason for this new revision. Surely you've seen the ads in magazines, watched demonstrations on TV, as the new flat monitor TVs are paraded out. Doesn't that make you think of the Superman movies and their flat crystal screens in which criminals were caught, their spirits impounded and sent out into space? It's beginning to feel like science fiction. And the fidelity of video images, super-high-resolution (DVCAM, DVD, HDTV, etc.), has turned television into a window of super reality, hasn't it? Now images pack more of a wallop than what we see as "everyday life," which means that movies can have a stronger impact on us. It feels as if we have more responsibility now, to center our moviemaking activities on meaningful topics instead of wasting our talents on strictly entertainment fare.

The most important development at the turn of the century is that new technology has brought digital cameras and computer editing into the affordable range, so that anyone with the will and desire can create a movie right from his or her home or office. With a wealth of information available on the Internet for selecting the latest digital camera, assembling compatible edit systems, FireWire, decks, networking, etc. (see: <www.dvcentral.org>, <www.digital-filmmaking.com>, <www.dvfilmmaker.com>, <www.indieclub.com>, and others), each scriptwriter, director, film buff, videographer, or filmphile can now plan on fulfilling his/her feature moviemaking dream within the used-car price range of $5,000 to $15,000. Or you may want to entirely bypass buying your own editing software and rent a membership in an Internet multimedia site such as **<www.videofarm.com>** that supplies anyone who has a personal computer and standard Web browser with the ability to edit their movies *online.* (Yes, you heard right! Make your movie on the Internet!) After you assemble your full-service digital video production company (even if it takes some credit card debt to buy that initial gear of camera and computer editing system—see **<www.fetching.com/bihari/cc.html>** for an overview), you will have the freedom to carry on your quest with an outlay of just a couple of hundred dollars per feature-length movie (a box of five one-hour Mini-DVCAM video cassettes costs about $50 each).

Have I forsaken shooting in *film?* No. Not exactly. But if you are self-financing your own first movie, whether scripting "by the book" or experimenting with new, noncommercial forms, why risk all your hard-earned money on a first feature and then leave your future in the hands of self-appointed "experts," directors of programming at "important" film festivals, TV buyers from the U.S. and Europe, and the like, who may fail to see the value of your cutting-edge work? It is my hope that we will soon see the recent tide ebbing of one-shot feature filmmakers, the generation that watched in horror as their little miracle films failed to reach any festivals, screens, or critical acclaim.

Once you sever your economic dependence from that system of selection, when you finally take control of your own artistic future by creating features electronically (by affordable means), you'll be surprised at the leap of imagination your mind will take. Suddenly, you'll be focused on spiritual and emotional topics of great personal concern instead of trying to play the Hollywood game. You'll shoot differently, edit with abandon. We filmmakers have for too long censored ourselves in subtle ways, traded in our creativity to follow the "correct" moviemaking model, which we believed offered the best promise for distribution up the road. Pardon my heresy, but forget plot points, dramatic arc, 120 pages of script, three acts. Forget just about everything you've learned, heard, or read about filmmaking (see Ray Carney's "Open Letter to the Next Generation of American Filmmakers" on page xxi). And while you're at it, dismiss some of this book as well (no guide is perfect for everyone). What's important is that this new digital age has finally handed over the means of production of images *to the people* (that's you and me), and it's up to us to throw off our shackles and reinvent this art form. Good luck on having the courage to try.

R.S.
PORT TOWNSEND, WA

Contents

Appendices 341

FOREWORD

How (and How Not) to Do It: An Open Letter to the Next Generation of American Filmmakers

BY RAY CARNEY

Author's Note: Those who have enjoyed Ray Carney in the past, either in his gritty essays or in a series of widely publicized interviews crusading for indie film (and lambasting fake, Hollywoodized indie knockoffs), will be equally entranced by this latest contribution. Carney is professor of Film and American Studies, and head of the Film Studies Program at Boston University, as well as author of more than ten books, including the critically acclaimed *The Films of John Cassavetes* and *The Films of Mike Leigh*, both published by Cambridge University Press. (Check out the Website <http://people.bu.edu/rcarney> for further essays, articles, interviews, publication updates, etc.) The following ten "anti-rule" rules of filmmaking from Carney run counter to almost every conventionally held belief regarding the "correct" way to make movies. When I recently met Belgian film critic Alfons Engelen, another proponent of creativity in filmmaking, he reminded me that Carney wasn't alone in his approach. "Cinema is only one hundred years old. So only a dozen letters of the film alphabet are known," said Engelen while we awaited the next screening at Figueira da Foz International Film Festival in Portugal. "Therefore, look for something new, never done before. As a filmmaker, cameraman, actor or actress, editor, *make* something new, never done before . . . fresh." I want to thank Ray Carney for his permission to include this letter to filmmakers in my new edition. —R. S.

In response to several interviews I have given attacking Hollywood filmmaking, a number of readers have asked me if I could provide a more positive statement. In a word, now that I've hatchet-murdered the studios, could I offer a few rules on how to do it *right?* I hesitated at first, since as far as I am concerned, rules are the problem with most of the movies we now see. The shortcoming of Hollywood is that its confections are whipped up from recipes (you know: a dash of romance blended into a cup of suspense with a dollop of social relevance thrown on top to create the perfect post-dinner entertainment). I had no desire to offer my services as a French pastry-chef of independent cinema. Real art is not created from formulas. No matter how fancy the name we give them ("story structure," "creating a character," the "three-act screenplay"), rules and formulas are ways of avoiding what art is really about. That's why I initially thought a how-to-do-it essay was a bad idea, but after mulling it over, I decided that maybe there was something worth saying. So, for anyone who is interested, I hereby offer ten anti-rule rules:

1. Accept no imitations. Imitate no one and nothing. I teach university film courses. Most of them are devoted to screening and discussing cinematic masterworks: Renoir's *Rules of the Game*, Dreyer's *Ordet*, Ozu's *Tokyo Story*, De Sica's *Bicycle Thief*, Rossellini's *Voyage in Italy.* But sometimes I wonder if seeing these films doesn't do more harm than good to the young filmmakers who are my students. The problem is that too many of them seem to take the wrong lesson away from the courses. They think I show them classics so that they can go off and make movies that look like the ones I screen. They think I want them to weave spaces and bodies together the way Renoir does in *Rules of the Game*; or to keep looking around and behind their characters, through windows, into doorways, and around corners, the way De Sica does in *Bicycle Thief*; or to slow events down, silence the characters, and induce meditative states the way Ozu does in *Tokyo Story.* The right lesson, of course, is precisely the opposite one. I show masterpieces not to persuade students to look like *these* movies, but to inspire them to dare to look utterly and completely like *themselves.* That's the lesson all great art teaches us. De Sica, Dreyer, Renoir, and Ozu didn't get to be great artists by imitating someone else, by making movies that resembled the ones they had seen, but by being brave enough to break all of the then-established rules in order to express their own distinctive, unique, personal visions of life. They teach us the value not of imitation, but of resisting influences, even their own. And they teach us how hard it is to do that—how hard it is to create a style that will be true to our own vision of life, and how bizarre and idiosyncratic such a style will always look (at least at first blush). Audiences jeered these masterworks when they were first screened.

2. Film what you really are. One of the reasons Hollywood films can get away with being so fraudulent is that most of them are set on a fantasy island populated with characters who bear no resemblance to anyone who ever lived on planet Earth. Dare to make a movie about yourself. It doesn't, of course, have to be true to the superficial details of your life (though that wouldn't hurt), but at least make it deeply true to your honest feelings and beliefs, your genuine doubts and uncertainties, your actual interests and fears. Dare to film what you really are, what you really feel, what you really see around you. Don't be afraid of being too personal. Your most private emotions, most secret puzzlements, most idiosyncratic obsessions are the only legitimate subject of your art. That's another lesson the masterworks teach us.

A further reason to hold tight to your actual experiences and feelings is to avoid the clichés that lurk everywhere waiting to entrap you and your characters. As soon as you take one step away from your actual life, your work is in danger of turning into a cartoon or a soap opera. It's easy for Spielberg to slide into sentimental pieties when he presents what other people, in another country, felt and suffered fifty years ago. What would keep him honest would be to show what he himself actually feels like when he goes to lunch to close a big deal, or how he treats his wife and children that evening if it falls through. The Hemingway-patented bullshit detector is that much more sensitive if your characters and situations are close to your own life. It's just too easy to fool yourself, to cheat or exaggerate for effect, if your movie takes place in a galaxy far away. Make sure there is no "them" in your movie. It should be all "you." Make sure you are as kind to your characters (or as hard on them) as you would be on yourself. Make sure they are as interesting and complex (and self-justifyingly self-deluded) as you are. Let them never think they are doing anything wrong, just as you never do.

A corollary is that your characters should be at least as intelligent and self-aware as you are. Half the movies in Hollywood would evaporate if a character simply asked himself why he is behaving in such an idiotic way. Every character ever played by Schwarzenegger or Stallone would stop dead in his tracks and sign up for counseling if he were allowed to have one second of normal self-awareness. Why am I lugging this bazooka around anyway? Why do I feel such anger toward everyone? What did my parents do to me to make me feel this way? These are, of course, Neanderthal examples. But why do characters even in movies by allegedly highbrow directors (Woody Allen, Mike Nichols, Steven Soderbergh) invariably understand less about themselves and their true situations than the audience does? Why are they all so limited? It's time we had a few characters who were smarter, more sensitive, more morally complex than the average viewer is. Why do we need movies that make us feel superior? It's time we had a few characters who humble or chasten us, who don't yield to trashy journalistic understandings of what makes us tick. Look at Rossellini's *General della Rovere* or Dreyer's *Gertrud* for illustrations.

3. Film what you don't know. Does not contradict the preceding; though if it did, it wouldn't really make any difference. I only mean that there is no point in writing, casting, directing, and editing a film if you know in advance where you are going to come out, how you feel about your characters and events, and what it all means. If you can storyboard your film, save your time (and that of your actors and crew), skip the shooting, and publish the storyboard. There is no need to make the movie. If you don't learn anything, no one else will either. If you don't change your feelings about your characters and events as you go along, your audience won't either. If your mind isn't twisted into pretzels, theirs won't be either. If your heart isn't torn and conflicted by the situations your characters are in, you haven't created complicated enough situations. You've reduced life to the "lite" experiences television or the newspapers give us.

Your movie should help viewers see things about their lives that they didn't realize before they went into it. Of course, learning something, being forced out of your mental and emotional ruts, is precisely what never happens in Hollywood films. Movies like *Pulp Fiction, L.A.*

Confidential, and *Wild Things* represent a button-pushing sense of art where the only goal is to force the viewer to jump through a set of preprogrammed emotional hoops. Art becomes a game of emotional tiddlywinks where you're judged not on whether anybody actually got anything valuable out of the whole experience, but on finesse points—on how well you keep the nonsense moving right along. The director and producers decide what points they are going to make before they begin. They cast, shoot, and edit the movie so as to be sure to make them. The audience goes in and "gets" them. Then the critics come along and assign marks for how well they did it all. The reviews of these movies remind me of the chestnut about the comedian's convention: A comedian calls out number 43 and everybody laughs. Another gets up and calls out number 12; there is even louder laughter. A third calls out number 37; nobody laughs. Explanation: Some people just don't know how to tell a joke.

The experiences in these films are canned. Nobody involved in them—from the writer and director to the actors and editors—actually learns anything new. No one changes his mind. No one is forced out of his or her old patterns of understanding. They are vast emotional recycling operations. You put clichés in; you get clichés out. The only sermons the director or his viewers stumble on are the ones he's already cleverly hidden under his own stones when he began. It's the difference between the way Picasso painted and filling in the outlines in a coloring book.

That's not art. That's not even good conversation. All valuable acts of expression are acts of exploration. (Even a minor one like writing this piece. Why would I waste my time doing it if I already knew in advance where my argument would take me?) Film the parts of your life you don't understand in order to try to understand them. Film the aspects of your dealings with others where you don't know what went wrong (or whether anything went wrong). Use film to blaze a trail through the emotional jungle we all live in. Consciousness cannot precede expression. Every movie Tarkovsky and Cassavetes ever made was an attempt to understand a part of their experience that they didn't understand before they began it. Along with spoken language, art is one of the greatest inventions in the history of the universe for discovering the meaning of our lives, our times, our culture.

A corollary: Dare to fail—abysmally on occasion. If you function as a genuine explorer, you can never know in advance where you'll come out (or if you'll come out anywhere valuable). It's always safer to cook from a recipe, and always risky to throw the book away, but that is the only way you'll ever make anything new. Like any other mass-produced product, if Hollywood films never rise above a certain average level of achievement, by the same virtue they never fall very far below it either. With a non-standardized approach, nothing is guaranteed. Your film may be a disaster. It may not work out. But that is the case with all truly creative experiments—Charlie Parker's solos, Paul Taylor's dances, Einstein's late theorems. Working the way a documentary filmmaker does, discovering your purposes and meanings as you go along, necessarily means performing without a safety net. But the greatest art is always made by taking the greatest chances. The road not taken is the only path along which real discoveries can be made (which is why imitating yourself is as deadly as imitating someone else).

4. A movie should be at least as strange as life. I don't know about everyone else's experiences, but the emotional lives of myself and the people I know are stranger and more complex than anything I've ever seen in Hollywood films. Their characters are too logical, knowing, and articulate by half. They have clear motives and intentions and act in accordance with them. If they have problems, they know what they are, and have game plans for dealing with them. They execute complex courses of action in pursuit of a definite goal. I don't know anyone in life who is this clear about things—including myself. I don't have intentions, motives, and goals in this way. I don't know what I really want most of the time. I don't understand my emotions. I don't know why I do or feel most of the things I do. When I am in real emotional trouble, I am the last one to realize it. Having a *real* problem is *not* knowing you have it. (Think of your former boyfriend or girlfriend for confirmation of this.) I don't have a road map for where I'm going. I usually don't even know where I have gotten to until long after I've arrived. The people I know (including myself) are more mixed up, more contradictory in their behavior, more changing in their feelings than characters ever are in the movies. Who of us is a character in the Hollywood way? (Dear reader, what is your character?) Even the most ordinary life is stranger and less rational than these movies assume.

When Hollywood wants to present a character who behaves less "normally," it gives us a hockey-masked slasher, has Jack Nicholson turn into the Joker or a Wolfman, or has Jim Carrey do one of his wild and crazy impersonations. But these characters separate the weirdness from everyday life too much. They make it seem too exceptional and rare and fleeting. They imagine our strangeness too externally and superficially. Our casual remarks cut more deeply than Freddy Krueger's razor-fingers. The masks we wear are much scarier than Jason's—and not removable. Our animal natures can be far more savage and unpredictable than a wolf's. Our emotional lives are much spookier and more mysterious than anything in a John Carpenter movie. You can't pound a stake through this aspect of experience. You can't lock it up at the end of the movie. Everyone I have ever known—landlords, bosses, businessmen, parents, lovers, and friends—has an interior life that is knottier and more out of control than Hannibal Lecter's. Capture some of the real strangeness of our emotional lives. If you don't think it can be done, look at a tape of Cassavetes's *Faces* or Tom Noonan's *The Wife*. The kinks and twists in their characters' psyches put a horror movie's to shame.

5. Leave the 'toons to Disney. It's a truism that most American feature films and the performances in them are indistinguishable from cartoons. But the problem is deeper than our cultural infatuation with superheroes or the cults that have grown up around Robert De Niro's or Sharon Stone's cartoon versions of acting. Even most so-called serious movies (from *Easy Rider* to *Thelma & Louise*, *Malcolm X*, and *Schindler's List*) are dumbed down to the level of comic books. Characters are generic; situations are archetypal and representative; and the morality is as black-and-white as a children's book. The actors might as well wear signs around their necks telling us how we are supposed to interpret them. The audience is more or less told what to know and how to feel every step of the way.

American film needs to move beyond the Boy's Book and Harlequin romance stage. We need films where characters are not generalizations and stereotypes, but particular, prickly individuals. We need figures who are neither good nor bad, neither heroes nor villains, whose motives are impure and mixed. We need films where the drama is not premised on external conflicts, but on internal confusions and ambivalences. Why can't we have movies about characters that viewers will not be able to figure out and situations they will not be able to make up their minds about? We need movies that go into the gray and fuzzy places—movies that capture the murky irresolution of life as it is actually lived. We need scenes that explore the in-between places of life, where there is no clear problem and no clear solution. We need scenes that are pitched at tonal in-between places, scenes that don't allow the audience the luxury of figuring them out too easily or settling back into a simple relationship to them. If you think it can't be done, check out a competent stage production of any of Chekhov's plays. He made a career of doing it.

6. Make adult movies. Another way to put the preceding is to say that it's time we recapture the "adult movie" category from the pornographers. There are enough movies for teenagers. It's high time we had some genuine adult films—movies made by adults, about adults, for adults, where there is more on the characters' minds than getting laid or stoned or shot. One way to go about making adult movies would simply be to leave out everything that is there strictly to suck in teenage boys (the nudity, sex, car chases, tough-guy theatrics, shoot-outs, thriller plots) or girls (the lovey-dovey romance stuff, dating game comedy, mood-music melodrama, and soap operatics).

The standard reply is that a movie that lacks these sorts of things wouldn't be "entertaining" enough to sell tickets. But it's a circular argument: what is being invoked to justify childish movies is a child's definition of entertainment. We need to forget about being entertaining in this sense, and redefine entertainment to include sophisticated adult interests. Complex adult social interactions, the play of adult emotions, the difficulties of a difficult life are the most interesting things in the world for someone with an adult perspective.

Our movies are too simple, too obvious, too easy, and ultimately too boring. An adult movie will necessarily be hard and challenging, just as all real adult relationships are. Kids may want things easy, but an adult knows that no important experience (or person) yields up its meanings casually or lightly, and that the more it resists you or forces you out of your habitual patterns, the more exciting and valuable it is. That's as true in art as it is in life. Great works necessarily make demands on us; they test us; because they force us to enter into new states of awareness, new ways of knowing. You can't experience a really great work of art in a relaxed or passive way. You can't listen to Bach on your back. He forces you to answer his energies with your own. He rouses you to activity. That state of tension, engagement, and activity is not an accidental side-effect of a great work, but the very heart and soul of what all important art does.

The moral of the story is that there is no reason to apologize if a viewer has to see your movie two, three, or more times, or to struggle for months or years to work through it emotionally. I've seen Tarkovsky's *The Sacrifice* and *Stalker* at least ten times each, and still can't get comfortable with them, am still puzzled and mystified by aspects of them. That's not what's wrong with them, but what's right—like the best, most challenging, exciting experiences and people we come up against in life. Even if it's not true in aerobics, in art (as in life) "no pain, no gain" really is a reality. New experiences, fresh insights, new points of view are going to leave your emotional muscles a little sore at first. They'll have you panting to keep up with them. It has to do with the way our brains are wired. Our emotions are inertial. Our hearts always rest on the last experience. Every genuinely new way of seeing and feeling is disorienting—because it does brain surgery on us.

Of course, given our channel-surfing, easy-listening culture, many people will still prefer Happy Meal movies. They may storm out of your film muttering about its incomprehensibility; but what if they do? You are better off without them. If people aren't willing to exert themselves to the degree the work demands, they can't have the experience you want them to have even if you physically chain them to their seats (or psychologically chain them by adding sex scenes, shootouts, and suspense). If they are determined to lie on their backs, they are not going to hear Bach anyhow. If you play Beethoven to the supermarket crowd, you succeed only in turning the Ninth Symphony into Muzak. You can't make someone have an experience they aren't ready to have. You can't give someone an emotional gift they are not mature enough to receive. They may need to grow up some more, live a little more, or fall in love before they are ready for your film. And, of course, they may never be ready for it; but that is their loss, not yours. Don't dumb it down in an attempt to reach everyone, or you will lose the very viewers you should most care about reaching.

7. Forget sets, props, locations, costumes. Insides are where it's at. Hollywood spends hundreds of millions of dollars every year getting the cars, furniture, haircuts, and period music right. Spielberg thinks nothing of constructing an entire city block or a country estate in order to re-create a past era. Unfortunately, in his obsession with the authenticity of objects and events, he overlooks the fact that the only thing that matters is emotional reality. The people who make these movies are clearly more comfortable dealing with props and costumes than feelings, which is why they will fuss over the most minute details of the sets, but don't see the emotional fraudulence of the scenes that take place in them.

Take sex scenes as an example. I've seen hundreds of them in Hollywood movies, but I don't think there has been even one where the woman was embarrassed by the size or shape of her breasts or hips or where the man was anxious about his ability to perform. I've seen scores of depictions of one-night stands, but I've never seen a single film where the two strangers express a profound sense of emptiness, regret, shame, or violation after making love. I shouldn't even use the word *love*. There is lots of glycerin, lust, and infatuation in these movies of course, but where is the trust, admiration, devotion, self-sacrifice, or deep emotional vulnerability that constitutes real adult love?

What is true of romantic attraction is true of the other feelings in these works. They are cheap, plastic knockoffs of real emotions—with only the faintest, superficial resemblance to the actual ones. (It doesn't take a Hamlet to make us realize that even reptilian emotions like anger and revenge are more complicated than the Hollywood versions of them—more tangled up in double- and triple-thinking.) The feelings in these films are as clichéd and unreal as the plots or the mood music on their sound tracks. The characters bear about as much resemblance to humans as computer animations do.

Ninety-nine percent of the American movies released in a given year simply recycle five or ten of these fake emotions over and over again—canned, condensed, instant anger, revenge, lust, fear, romance, and a few others. They are like well-worn counterfeit coins passed from hand to hand, from film to film, as promissory notes for the real thing. The very fact that we can assign these emotions names at all proves their fraudulence. Our emotional life never comes to us in such simple bundles. It can never be labeled like this (since it is not static, but a continuous flowing and melting transformation). Most of the feelings we have every day of our lives are utterly unnameable and indescribable. We aren't even conscious of most of them.

All of this, needless to say, represents a great opportunity for independent filmmakers. The artist moves beyond the known world of clichés, exploring the emotional wildernesses that are not on our charts. He or she moves into the "here there be dragons" sections of our souls and maps the true emotional geography of the present, reporting back his or her findings for the benefit of the rest of us.

8. Plot—not. One of the most limiting aspects of American film is that the plot is all that matters at virtually every stage of the process. Movies are pitched, scripted, and budgeted on the basis of the cleverness of their plots. In the directing and editing process, characterization, emotional nuance, mood, and psychology are thrown to the winds to keep the plot zipping along from event to event. Filmmakers like Spielberg actually pride themselves on "telling a good story" in this children's-book sense of the phrase. The great works of literature—*Huckleberry Finn*, *Paradise Lost*, Shakespeare's plays—are not reducible to their plots; only hacks like O. Henry and Agatha Christie confused narrative art with "telling a good story" in Spielberg's sense. No one ever sat through the classics of cinema for their plots. Who ever watched *The Passion of Joan of Arc* for its plot? Reduced to their plots, Ozu's movies are hokey melodramas. Plot has almost nothing to do with a great film's complex pleasures.

What capitalistic, materialistic myth have we enslaved ourselves to? Why do we think life is about achieving something or attaining a goal? Why do we think it is about getting somewhere or doing something? Why do we make movies about actions and events? Whose life is reducible to its events? Whose soul can be summed up by its actions? What we *are* is infinitely more interesting than what we *do*. Dare to make a film that shows that people are more interesting than the trivial events taking place around them. Show how what we do *to ourselves* emotionally is more interesting than anything anyone else does *to us*. Dare to push the pause button on the narrative and let your actors actually interact with each other. This is different from merely turning them loose to chew up the scenery in the Meryl Streep, Harvey Keitel, or Nick Cage way. Interaction is subtle, nuanced, and responsive; not flamboyant, ostentatious, and scene-stealing. Dare to make a movie where everything is not all tied up narratively with pink ribbons in the final scenes. Why does everything have to be resolved and explained? Make a movie that is narratively inconclusive or open to different interpretations.

A strictly personal request: make a tragic film. America is the culture that invented the sitcom and the happy face, and we seem to have lost sight of the enormous expressive power—and truth—of tragedy. Tragedy has almost disappeared as a cinematic form in America. Suffering and loss reveal things about our hearts and souls that no happy ending ever can. In rewarding their central characters with money, power, fame, and success at their ends, our films tell us a lie about life. Why deny your own emotional experience—your endless frustrations and setbacks—this way? These films define life's value too economically, too externally, too materialistically. In its deepest wellsprings, life is not about attaining rewards (or punishments), but about testing our spirits, deepening our souls, and enriching our consciousnesses. Make a film about that—a film in which a character may lose the world but gain her soul.

9. Why should your movie look like a movie? Who says you have to use master shots or shot-reverse shots or close-ups or music on the soundtrack or anything else that other films have? It's another occupational hazard of being a film teacher that after I spend a few weeks with students teaching them some of the possibilities of cinematic syntax, many of them think that I am telling them that they should shoot their films like Hitchcock, light them like Sternberg, edit them like Eisenstein, or score them like Bernard Herrmann. What I'm actually trying to teach them is the lesson a novelist or poet presumably learns from reading great writers: to invent new forms of language to express *their own* particular thoughts and feelings. Don't hesitate to bend the forms past the breaking point if it will allow you to catch the little wiggle in life that only you see and feel. No more than there is a right way to paint a painting or score a symphony is there a correct way to light or shoot a movie, a best way to edit it, a right or wrong way it should look. Hollywood has brainwashed us by flooding the market with movies that look, sound, and feel almost identical. But the question to ask is why would anyone want their movie to look like a Hollywood one? Why would you want your handcrafted personal expression to look like it rolled off an assembly line? It's the uniqueness of our voices that makes us interesting; the most boring voices in the world are those of professionally trained radio announcers. Let your own squeaky, twitchy, nervous voice emerge; don't polish and smooth the roughness away.

A filmmaker friend of mine, Robert Kramer, made a movie called *Starting Place.* There are many amazing and powerful moments in it, most of which represent completely new imaginings of the possibilities of what you can say on film. There is an extended conversation in which Kramer repeatedly cuts away from the principal figure's face to show views of his feet and hands (and not as a twitchy indication of guilt in the pseudo-Freudian cliché *60 Minutes* employs). There is another conversation in which Kramer intercuts tight close-ups of a woman's eyebrows and hairline and ears rather than showing her whole face. What Kramer does is simply what every artist does: he gets us to see with fresh eyes, to think and feel in new ways. But to do that, he has to fracture and dislocate conventional cinematic forms of presentation. He must reinvent language to make it capable of carrying the meanings he wants it to bear. It's a question of who is the master, and the true artist is always the master of the forms he uses. And make no mistake about it: If you don't use the forms, they will use you. If you don't twist and torture them, and beat them up, they will twist and torture you and beat you up. If you don't ride them, they will ride you. They will homogenize and blandify your ideas. They will bend and flatten your eccentric wiggles and curves into their own cookie-cutter shapes and mass-produced meanings.

10. Who's afraid of the dark? Why do movies have establishing shots? Why does mood music tell us what characters are thinking and feeling? Why are characters' goals and intentions made visible? Why must everything be explained? Life isn't like this. I don't know what people I talk to are thinking. I can't see inside their hearts and read their minds. Why do we expect to be able to do that in our movies?

In fear of losing viewers, Hollywood explains more or less everything. The goal is not to leave viewers in the dark for a single minute. It's why most Hollywood movies are improved by catching them on television a half-hour or so after they have begun. Characters and events become much more fascinating when we can't figure them out. Why do we want things in our movies to be clear? Why do we want actions, events, and outcomes to be logical and rational (since so much of life is not this way)? Why do we insist on knowing, knowing, knowing so much about everyone and everything? Life is full of mysteries, darkness, unknowns, randomness. What we are is, of course, the greatest mystery of all.

A little dark would be preferable to this blinding insight. Make a movie where people's surfaces are as opaque, their insides as invisible, as they are in life. Make a movie where people don't progress step by step toward goals. Make a movie where the ending does not clear everything up. Read *The Sacred Fount* or *The Awkward Age* if you want to see it done in words. Cherish the mystery of experience. Respect what can never be known—even about those closest to you: friends, relatives, and lovers. In a word, honor life.

That's ten, and as good a place as any to stop. The perceptive reader will have detected long before now that these ten rules are really only one rule repeated ten times: Tell the truth, the whole truth, and nothing but the truth. Which leads to one meta-rule that overrides all of the others: Violate any of these rules rather than betray the truth.

Preface

Hello, independent filmmaker, film student, film buff, video maker, and other media enthusiasts who have always wanted to direct and produce a feature-length movie. With the help of this step-by-step guide to low-budget production, and the money it would cost to buy a used car (approximately $12,000), your dream is now within your reach.

Feature Filmmaking at Used-Car Prices has been written to teach the process of producing a "no-budget" movie in the simplest and cheapest way possible. As you read through the chapters, from "Story Concept" to "Scriptwriting for No-Budget Features," to chapters on preproduction, filming/directing, editing, and promotion, you will learn from my experiences in filmmaking during the production of my various features: *A Man, a Woman, and a Killer* (co-directed with Wayne Wang), *1988–The Remake*, *Emerald Cities*, *Morgan's Cake*, and *American Orpheus*, along with recent explorations into producing features in 16:9 digital video (Pro-DVCAM) at my Feature Workshops. Also included is valuable information from the production of *The Last Roommate*, created in a three-month collaboration with students at the California College of Arts and Crafts (Oakland, California).

You will learn how to select your story so that you can succeed in producing your feature within a strict low budget. You will be shown how to rally your filmmaking team around you through the use of "the contract," using deferred payment and percentage points of profit in your film instead of cash to pay all those people who help you complete your project. You will be taught my Fifteen Rules for Shooting No-Budget Features (Rule #14—"Get as many charge cards as you can *before* you start making a feature!"). You will learn how to finally overcome your fear of equipment, how to operate even the most complicated 16-mm camera by pushing just one button, or how to videotape with the latest cutting-edge digital video cameras. My "secrets of editing" will be revealed—secrets that will help you turn your filming "mistakes" into an innovative and original style. By reading how to promote your feature you'll understand how to use your first feature to help produce your second (you're hooked by now). Most important, this book is dedicated to helping you survive the difficult process of low-budget feature filmmaking and to create films that are original and meaningful as well as entertaining.

You may ask, "How do I go from what I'm used to doing [being a housewife, salesman, student, engineer, fry cook, artist, businessman, teacher, computer programmer] into being a film director/producer?" I'm not sure how *you* will do it, but I got into making films quite by accident. My story really begins when I was a dropout from the engineering program at the University of Arizona. I had married a woman with two children and was working as a fry cook at a local hamburger chain in Tucson. One day my first wife brought home some notes she had taken at the library about a college named the California College of Arts and Crafts (CCAC). She thought I might like to study industrial design, since I liked to make things with my hands and had taken engineering classes. Disgusted with life in general, I quickly crumpled up the paper and threw it on the floor. About an hour later, alone in the room, I got up and retrieved the notes. Calling CCAC the next day, I heard to my amazement that they would accept me "on probation" with my C− average. When they told me that tuition was $387 per semester (1966), that settled it, and we moved to California the following month.

At CCAC I found myself immersed in the world of professional art terminology—*form, texture, line, content*—with hotshot art students who had learned all the words in high school. Floundering and scared, I would have quit college again if it hadn't been for several teachers who took an interest in me. My first teacher, Marie Murelius, worked extra hard with me, helping me understand her assignments so that I had a chance to succeed. A later teacher, Charlie Simonds, taught me to ask two important questions of an artwork: (1) "What is it trying to say?" and (2) "Is the message worth saying?" Charlie also reminded his students that if something had already been expressed in art, and expressed well, there was no reason to try to say it again.

My immersion into media came one day when teacher Phil Makanna decided to invite several painters and sculptors to take his experimental video class (1971). The thought of cameras, lights, and the harsh glare of examination was frightening to me, and I offered my place in class to another sculptor, who seemed happy to accept. After he took a few steps down the sidewalk toward registration I called him back, telling him I'd reconsidered and would take the class myself. I had just barely enough self-confidence to give video a try.

After I shot my first video with an early-model Sony portapak camera and recording deck, Phil suggested that I edit the footage. But since CCAC didn't have any video-editing equipment at that time, he told me I needed to transfer the video to film. For a couple of hundred dollars I transferred the video to 16-mm and was handed an "original" copy, a "work print" (a low-quality contact print made from the original for editing purposes), and a "mag track" (sound track for editing). After asking a few questions of the employees at the lab, I found out that I needed to "sync up" the picture work print and sound track so that the picture would line up with its corresponding sounds. I rented a small editing cubicle and asked another employee to show me how to use the equipment, to make a "splice." Since I had rented an editing space that was generally used for cutting together original film for printing (a process called "conforming"), he assumed (wrongly) that that was my objective, and proceeded to show me how to use a "hot" splicer with glue that cut off a frame with every cut. The right tool would have been a "tape" splicer, which allows editing experimentation and reassembly without loss of frames of film. Screening my "rough cut," Phil was shocked to see glue splices, and thought that I had been so sure of myself that I had made permanent splices on my film. What a joke! But I was hooked . . .

My little seven-minute black-and-white video film entitled *The Legal Operation* didn't show at any film festivals or win any awards (I never entered it), but I was thrilled to be able to put it on a projector and rain down the thunder of sound and images on my friends at school. It felt great to be able to shoot something very personal to me and then reveal it in such an immediate way to fellow humans. The process of video filmmaking seemed to connect me in some way to the rest of the world. I didn't consider myself a "director" or even a filmmaker at that time. I was just an artist who'd made a video film. I had no idea to what extent imagemaking would take over my life.

How did I go from making a seven-minute video (edited on film) to becoming a feature filmmaker? Certainly not through planning. It happened naturally as I shot longer videos, and then took the next step of shooting directly on film. About six months after graduation from CCAC, during which time I hadn't produced anything, I began to feel desperate to get back to work. While standing in front of a booth at the Alameda Flea Market on a Sunday morning, I made the decision to break my deadlock by just picking up a magazine, any magazine from the box at my feet, and shooting "a film." I didn't know what story I might pick and certainly had no idea how to get my hands on film equipment or even how to use it, but I felt I had to do something. I had also been stymied by the admonition of teacher Charlie Simonds to "say something worthwhile," because I didn't have any good ideas! I reached down into the box and pulled out a *True Confessions* magazine from 1933. Closing my eyes, I flipped open the magazine, then I opened my eyes to an article titled "What Flirting Cost Me." For the next six months I shot the film on weekends, using CCAC film equipment that my friends Wayne Wang and George Chang checked out for me when available. Each time I shot a scene I would simply hand the one copy of the magazine to the actors, Willie Boy Walker and Linda Egar, who would memorize their lines while I set up the camera and lights. Different friends helped me load the camera, take light readings, and record "sync" sound on location. On one evening I found myself without help, doing everything myself, from setting up lights and loading film, to blindly working the knobs on the Nagra sound-recording machine until I finally got it to record. The film ended with Willie reading the caption at the end of the *True Confessions* article: "to be continued . . ."

After a month of editing, the thirty-minute *What Flirting Cost Me* was completed, and with urging from Willie I entered it in the Marin

Film Festival, where it was a prizewinner. Actor Bob Cummings presented the awards. My friend Wayne Wang said he had been surprised that I could edit a good film out of what he assumed to be a lost cause, and on that basis we collaborated on a short film with actor Bruce Parry. By the time our fourteen-minute film, *1944*, had won a first place at the Ann Arbor Film Festival (1973), Wayne and I were sharing an apartment and talking a lot about feature filmmaking.

While I was in art school I had inherited some money, which had mostly gone to supporting my wife and kids. I was now separated from them, baby-sitting the youngest ones—Heather, Morgan, and Bowbay—each Friday night to Monday morning; the two oldest daughters, Kathy and Lisa, stayed with their mother in Berkeley. I still had about $11,000 left when Wayne and I decided to go for it: to make a feature. Another friend, Dick Richardson, who had loved *1944*, joined us as a collaborator on the film. It was decided that we would write for two weeks and then film during the following two weeks, the entire process to be completed in one month's time.

I paid both Wayne and Dick $250 at the beginning of each week of writing, to assure all of us that the project was really happening. And during that period I ordered filmstock from Kodak, hired a soundperson with an assistant, helped select actors, drew up a profit-sharing contract with the help of an attorney, reserved equipment, arranged baby-sitting, did everything necessary to be prepared for the shoot. At the end of the month, I had spent a total of $5,900 and had shot my first feature film (July 1973).

Of course, I didn't realize that once the film was shot the problems of production were only just beginning. During the next year and a half of what seemed to be insurmountable editing problems, I ran out of money and was very thankful that my mother decided to invest in the film in return for a small percentage of the hoped-for profits. Every weekend I would take care of my little kids and every Monday I would return to my rented editing room and go back to work. I was fortunate that the lab where I was editing allowed me to charge the editing room ($320 a month) as well as other editing costs (splicing tape, some sound recording for narrations, shooting and processing titles). At one point I had gone almost six months without making a payment. On the home front, my kindly landlord also let me go several months without paying rent ($100 a month), and the corner store gave me thirty days to pay for groceries. Although my life was in a complete financial mess, the inspiration I derived from working with the footage kept my spirits afloat through those difficult times.

In December 1974 I held the finished projection print ("answer print") in my hands and was thrilled when I showed it to friends at the Pacific Film Archive theater, which I had rented for $60. The excitement generated from the screening helped me overcome my exhaustion and gave me the energy to take the print to New York, spending my last few hundred dollars to try to sell the film, get a distributor and a showing, and find some way to pay the lab the remaining $4,000 I had charged to complete *A Man, a Woman, and a Killer* (75 minutes, color/B&W).

Each day in New York I dropped off a print at some distributor or showcase, and after each rejection I tried another possibility. The film was rejected by the Whitney Museum, the Museum of Modern Art, New Directors/New Films, Film Forum, Cinema 5, New Line Cinema, New Yorker Films, etc. When I arrived at the Bleecker Street Cinema and was asked by programmer Marc Weiss what other response had been to my film, I listed all the rejections. He screened the film and said he wanted to give it a show in March (1975). Anne Wehrer, at whose loft in the Bowery I had been staying, had gotten herself drunk in order to tell me that I would fail to get a New York screening with my film. She was dumbfounded when I told her about the coming "world premiere." I didn't think much of it, since it didn't appear to solve my immediate money problems, but at the time I didn't know how difficult it was to get *any* showing in New York. And considering that the independent film program at the Bleecker Street Cinema folded a month after my premiere, I had been exceedingly lucky to get any show at all.

Returning home to Oakland, I resumed the baby-sitting of my little kids Friday night to Monday morning, trying to keep up with feeding them properly and taking care of them (Heather was eight, Morgan was six, and Bowbay was three), and mostly lying on my bed, exhausted, watching TV and worrying about my avalanche of unpaid bills. What saved my spirit was the knowledge of the coming Bleecker

Street show. I had also entered the film in the Ann Arbor Film Festival and looked forward to any positive results.

Around this time my filmmaker friend Bill Farley was applying for the American Film Institute independent filmmaker's production grant of $10,000 and kept insisting that I write up a proposal. I resisted, having little energy to expend, but he kept on my case, saying, "You have a feature film to use as an example of your film work [needed with the application]. . . . *You have to apply!*" I tried for several days to think up a good concept for a new film and finally, under pressure of the coming deadline, I thought up *Showboat 1988*, about my librarian friend Ed Nylund (an actor from *A Man, a Woman, and a Killer*) who sells his house when he finds out he has cancer and uses the money to give an audition for the classic American musical *Show Boat.*

Ed had always bad-mouthed the musical format to me, saying it was phony, and he said he wanted to bring the "stench of death" to the musical comedy. Ed's real life had been a series of "almosts." He had almost been a doctor, having had the distinction of being accepted twice at top medical schools during the 1930s before dropping out. He had also gotten close to receiving his master's in musicology from the Manhattan School of Music before his marriage broke up, destroying this second career. I liked the idea of Ed finally making a dream come true by staging the audition for *Show Boat*, at the same time giving all the troopers who performed the chance to "be a star" before the cameras. After I typed out the proposal I couldn't even afford the sixty cents of postage to mail it, and Bill Farley jammed the needed coins into my hand.

In March (1975) *A Man, a Woman, and a Killer* opened for a five-day run at the Bleecker Street Cinema during some of the worst weather New York City had ever experienced (hailstones, etc.), showing every day at 4:00 P.M. to a few scattered survivors and several critics the programmer had worked very hard to get to the theater. A review came out in *The New York Times* with the headline "FILM: 3 Interlocked Lives." Under that there was a caption: " 'A Man, Woman, Killer' Is Mildly Interesting." In the New York *Daily News* we did better, with critic Jerry Oster giving the film two and a half stars and calling it "one of the most absorbing films I've seen of what is generally called the independent film movement." A week later I heard that our feature had won Directors' Choice at the Ann Arbor Film Festival, and I was thrilled. On the film tour the festival sponsors yearly, the film won several first places in competition, earning me a couple of $100 checks, which seemed like a million dollars to me in my tough economic situation.

One day in early April, as I rounded the corner to my apartment, I met my roommate Wayne Wang on the sidewalk, and with excitement in his voice he said, "Congratulations . . . you deserve it . . . you earned it." I had no idea what he was talking about. At the door I saw a telegram stuck into the crack. It was from the American Film Institute announcing that a panel of four, including King Vidor, had decided to award me $9,918 to make my next film, *Showboat 1988.*

I had been saved! For the first time in months, I relaxed, not fully realizing the strain I had been living under. I was deliriously happy, relieved that I could now tell all those people to whom I owed money that I would soon be able to pay them back. All of a sudden everything was OK—great, in fact! But what was the difference between this week and last week? I still didn't have any cash in my hand. The difference was the *idea* of money coming. I wished that I could have just thought "Money" and received all the energy that the idea of winning the grant had supplied.

By the time I received the production grant money, I was eight months behind in my rent. I promptly paid it off. And at the lab they agreed to let me charge my processing and work printing on *Showboat 1988* if I cleared my account. Although I wasn't really fully recovered from the workout of the first feature, with renewed energy and a full bank account I moved into production.

At this point the reader may ask what would have happened to me if I hadn't been lucky enough to receive the grant. After all, only ten such grants were given out from hundreds of applications. Well, since I was still in my late twenties and still had some youthful energy, I imagine I would finally have found some sort of job and begun slowly to pay off my bills. And of course any normal person who worked a regular job and used vacation time to shoot a feature would be able to return to work and pay off their accrued lab bills just that way. But I had begun without a safety net of any kind, and that added intensity affected my life and filmmaking in both negative and positive ways. For over a year I had spent much of my time desperately needing money for my film and living expenses. But, to paraphrase Mick Jagger, you can always get what you need. Somehow the fact that my life depended on getting help to live through my filmmaking process actually helped me overcome certain obstacles of shyness and reticence, enabling me to ask relatives, friends, even bankers, for their assistance in my struggle. And since I knew that I had only one "tool" with which to pull myself out of my difficult situation—the finished feature film—I was able to devote my constant attention to the project until it was completed. Of course, I probably would have done this if I *didn't* have a money problem, but I was certainly less apt to quit editing the difficult body of footage knowing that it was the only way to turn my economic situation around.

My friends and I had discovered early in our filmmaking careers that it seemed as difficult to make a five-minute film as a seventy-minute film, and it was often just as hard to get $200 as $2,000. The difference was that with a feature you had at least a chance to sell it somewhere and make some money back. The investment in months and years also made much more sense if the project had feature-length status. So although I hadn't been fully conscious of all the new editing skills I would have to learn to finally edit a feature to completion, I knew that taking the risk was the only really sensible step to take for my filmmaking career.

With the production of my second feature, *Showboat 1988*, I again ran into economic difficulties. Part of the problem was that I had needed to use part of the grant monies to clear up the past debt from *A Man, a Woman, and a Killer*, giving the lab $4,000 off the top of my budget. The next problem was that the *Showboat* audition grew so large that I shot over forty-five 400′ rolls of filmstock to accommodate the filming of all the auditioners who crossed the large stage at California Hall in San Francisco, which I rented for three consecutive nights at a cost of $1,100. The grant money was eaten up with the production of posters and PR material, the hiring of lights for the large hall and "gaffers" to operate them, catered lunches for the fifteen friends who helped run the audition, a full video crew who interviewed each act as they walked off the stage, and a rented dolly for smooth camera shots for my rented Eclair camera. Once involved with the concept, I felt it was necessary to support the idea by supplying everything necessary to insure the highest-quality production possible. Luckily, art patron Jim Newman rescued the last night of filming by giving me enough money for the additional filmstock needed to complete the shoot. But by the time I held the processed original, work print, and mag track in my hands, I was at least $4,000 in debt to the lab.

Once again I was faced with the problem of being broke. Overcoming the fear of rejection and embarrassment, I called my uncle to ask for financial assistance to live on and to finish my film. On the phone he told me that once when he was a young man he had asked his father for $10,000 to start a small electronics store, and had been turned down. He decided to help me. Again I had put my life on the line and again I had been rescued by an understanding relative. Why had I done this to myself again? Was I a masochist? I knew I had the burning desire to create the best images, record the best sound, make the best film that I could in support of all the people who had given their time and energy to the project. I felt it was my responsibility to do the best job possible regardless of the limitations. And for that reason it was necessary to withstand the pressures of raising more money and occasionally being broke.

And it got worse before it got better. I suppose the lowest moment in trying to survive came when I found myself borrowing money from my daughter Heather's piggy bank. At the time my mother was sending me a check for $20 each week to make sure that I could feed myself and my kids (I was continuing to charge everything at the lab). Somehow I got $20 behind. With Heather's agreement to accept a 50-cent interest on the loan, I would borrow her savings each Monday, live on it until the weekend came, and then return the twelve silver dollars, several quarters, dollar bills, and other change after cashing the check. This happened repeatedly. Finally, the teller at the bank asked why I always asked for the same amount of silver dollars and change. When I told her, she looked at me with disgust. A month later I received word that I had won a grant of $7,500 from the National Endowment for the Arts to complete *Showboat 1988.*

At another point of desperation, early 1977, I got a call from the programmer at the Bleecker Street Cinema saying that Hubert Bals, the director of the Rotterdam Film Festival, wanted to present *A Man, a Woman, and a Killer*, show my new feature, *Showboat 1988*, and fly me to the Netherlands. Somehow, with the help of my miracle-working friend Lela Smith, I was able to get a print in two weeks due to her night-and-day conforming of original (AB rolling) while I completed the edit and prompted the lab to meet my deadline. Suddenly I was jetted out of my Oakland apartment into the world of European international film festivals. At the festival I met Dennis Hopper in the hallway. "*Showboat* is a great film," he said. Being slightly delirious from exhaustion, I asked, "You mean the original?" "No, *yours!*" Hopper quickly returned.

And the struggle continued from there. After I completed the final version of *Showboat 1988* (in 1978), I was threatened with legal action by MGM concerning my supposed copyright infringement of the "Showboat" title and changed it to *1988—The Remake* to avoid a costly court battle. Fortunately, I was still able to earn about $6,000 on tour with the film and sold it for $13,000 to Channel Four in England after it had a successful showing at the London Film Festival. All this money—together with a second NEA grant, money from the sale of my 1939 Dodge pickup, and timely loans from friends—helped me pay off lab bills and shoot my third feature, *Emerald Cities*, the final film of the trilogy.

By 1986 I was back in serious debt with the lab ($10,000), immobilized at home while my wife, Julie, went off to work each day and I took care of our infant son, Marlon. It was then that I started to write about no-budget feature filmmaking, hoping to somehow sell the results and dig myself out of the economic pit again. Looking back at that time I see certain similarities to the tired old cliché of the criminal in his cell on death row, painstakingly penning his memoirs, racing against his predetermined appointment with the guillotine. But instead of racing the specter of death, I was trying to avoid destitution. Julie was in a dead-end job (she supplied us with the monthly "nut" of food and shelter), looking more tired and irritated each evening when she got home, and I couldn't figure out how to earn a living, much less shoot another "no-budget" feature. Fortunately, the book did sell, allowing her to quit her job while I was inspired to keep making films, completing *Morgan's Cake* (1988) and *American Orpheus* (1992), plus a bunch of new DV features made in collaboration with participants from my Feature Workshops.

There are many ways to alter your life in order to make your feature film. Perhaps your way won't be as stressful as what I put myself through. Maybe by having read my story you can get your feature production started on a firmer economic foundation, having a better overall plan for slow payback of lab bills from the money you earn at your job. It is my wish that in the following pages I'm able not only to supply you with the necessary skills to create an affordable low-budget feature but also to impart the feeling that regardless of your particular economic situation there is nothing that can stop you from making your dream come true. Happy moviemaking, and see you on the Web!

RICK SCHMIDT
lightvideo@aol.com
www.lightvideo.com

Acknowledgments

Special thanks for the help I received in writing this book must first go to my wife, Julie Schachter, who continued to bring in the family paycheck while I toiled at home, at the same time taking care of our infant son, Marlon. It was definitely a team effort. And great thanks must be given to Jayne Walker, editor and agent, who first believed in *Feature Filmmaking at Used-Car Prices* when it was only a title and a loose collection of writings. She brought the project up to professional standards, encouraged me throughout the rewrites, taught me the basics of good writing, and gave me my first taste of what a great difference excellent editing can mean to a manuscript. Thank you, Gary Thorp, for bringing us together. Special thanks must also go to my first editor at Viking Penguin, Lisa Kaufman, for her belief that the book should be published, and for her inspired final edit that brought the manuscript to fruition. Thank you, Lisa, for that vital quality of yours: to be excited by and open to new ideas. And thank you, Caroline White, the editor of both this revised version and the previous 1995 update, for your generous assistance and care with my latest manuscript additions. You helped make this complicated process of revision a real pleasure. Also thanks to my agent, Carol Mann, who was indispensable in turning my work of writing into a second occupation.

I must also give thanks to the people who have helped me with my first occupation—filmmaking. My mother, Lura Janda, invested in my films and constantly offered her spiritual support throughout the rough times. And my uncle David Strawn deserves much thanks for his timely loans to my *1988* production during a period when I was basically homeless. Thank you, both, for your love and kindness.

None of my features could have been made without the help and full commitment of many talented and creative artists and technicians, who took time off from their own projects to see me through. Thank you, Wayne Wang, for sharing with me the first flush of independent low-budget feature filmmaking. Thanks to the cast of my feature trilogy, Carolyn Zaremba, Ed Nylund, and Dick Richardson, for putting up with ten years of my filmmaking with little or no pay. Thank you, Neelon Crawford, for showing me how great location sound can be recorded, and thank you, Nick Bertoni, for also delivering excellent recordings during the turmoil of low-budget production. Thank you, Kathleen Beeler, for giving me the gift of professional lighting during the production of *The Last Roommate* and *Morgan's Cake.* Bill Farley deserves special mention because he always seemed to have the right ideas for whatever film concept I was trying to work out and was always there to help me make my work better. Other friends, Lowell Darling, Willie Boy Walker, Ted Falconi, Phillip Hofstetter, Mike Church, Chris Reece, John Vargo, Henry Bean, and Nick Kazan, helped me script my ideas in spite of my own reluctance to give up any control. A special thank you to Lela Smith for AB rolling on my features, helping to meet my impossible deadlines. Thank you, all, for making such a big difference.

Other actors and technicians were also vital to my most recent films, each person a link in the chain of production. Thank you, Kyle Bergersen, cinematographer on *American Orpheus*, for your enormous energy, skill, and determination, helping me shoot the complicated full-color film in only ten days, even bringing in steadicam genius Troy Peterson for final "underworld" shots. And again thanks to Neelon Crawford, soundman, who came out of retirement to supply me with top-quality tracks. Paul Baker deserves thanks not only for his strenuous work as boom man, but for composing, arranging, and performing fourteen original and hauntingly beautiful songs for the sound track (and in recent years gracing many Feature Workshop movies with his original music). And thank you, Diane Witherspoon, for composing and singing the exquisite title song, "Thanking You," and granting its use in the film, with additional permission from the record's producer, Art Maxwell, of Tonal Gravity Records (Berkeley). Jody Esther, lead actress in *American Orpheus*, has earned my highest admiration for her guts-out performance in the lead role as Fay. And Willie Boy Walker, a star in both *Morgan's Cake* and *American Orpheus*, deserves highest compliments for equally fine performances in both comedy and drama. Curtis Imrie must be greatly thanked for his excellent rendering of the risky role of an abusive husband, along with other fine performances by Karen Rodriguez, Jasmine Carver, Deborah Daubner, Tom Taylor, Katrina Eggert, Betsy Newman, Aaron Carver, Al Newman, Debi Hinton, Adrian Pike, Jan Burr—everyone who helped me pull off *American Orpheus.*

My son Morgan Schmidt-Feng deserves a most special thank you, for not only delivering a superb performance in the lead of *Morgan's Cake*, but assisting me with the production of that film and appearing in and helping me produce *American Orpheus.*

Thanks must go to my collaborators on *The Last Roommate*, Peter Boza, Tinnee Lee, and Mark Yellen, for believing that we could make a feature in three months using a college course film class (at the California College of Arts and Crafts) as our base. And thank you, David Heintz, Ian Turner, Jaime Oria, Ray Berry, and actors Jean Mitchell, Bruce Parry, Anita Forbus, Sarah Mann, and Marlene Ryan, for your help.

And thanks to my collaborators on the first Feature Workshop film *Blues for the Avatar* (1995)—Eric Magun, Barry Norman, Anthony Pesce, Michelle Kulstad, and Trudie Dearinger, with help from cinematographer Kyle Bergersen, grip Karen Rodriguez, and soundman Mat Monroe—for proving that we could actually shoot and edit a feature in ten days. Thank you, J. Cheyenne Wilbur, Mary Jane Knecht, Jane Holloway, Judy Goulder, Patrik and Tess Barr, their avatar baby Chyna, Stafford Decker, Tasha Roth McCormick, Donn Trethewey, Joe Calabrese, and Etta Roth, for acting and supplying locations for this breakneck production.

I'm very fortunate to have made many new friends and associates while making Feature Workshop movies in the late 1990s. But before I thank anyone in particular, my son Morgan Schmidt-Feng again deserves my heartiest praise and appreciation, thanks for co-producing the workshop movies with me. Without his gung ho efforts of recruiting his talented friends (most of the actors and crew members listed below), budgeting the shoots, securing locations, sharing story concepts, performing the demanding tasks of director of photography, and (as if that weren't enough!) co-writing and co-directing scenes with me and collaborators on location, none of these movies would have got made. I'm a supremely grateful and proud dad.

For our 1997 workshop movie, *someone like me* (16-mm, color), I want to thank our top-notch crew, Gary Rohan (director of photography), and Greg von Buchau (sound recordist). Thanks to you both for making this difficult shoot so professional and organized, giving *me* faith that we could pull it off! And Brad Marshland, our assistant director (AD), knows that he "saved the shoot," so any expression of thanks is inadequate given his huge contribution. But I'll try. Thanks, Brad, for just doing your job so incredibly well (and good luck with your own low-budget indie feature, *Liar's Dice*). Our Avid editor Gabriel Rhodes, who went one hundred plus hours in six days to cut our movie from two and a half hours of footage, was a miracle worker of the highest order (thanks again, Gabe, for making us a movie!!!). Thank you, Mary and Margaret Craig (twins), for acting in the movie, letting your lives be taken over by the filmmaking process. And thanks to actors Finn Curtin and Craig Strong, terrific as their respective boyfriends. Thanks again, guys, for bringing such a high level of professionalism to our shoot. And thank you, Brandi Smith, for jumping into our production on a moment's notice, performing your femme fatale to perfection. Our large band of co-writer/co-director collaborators deserves great thanks for their hard work and determination, so thank you, Doreen Alexander, Ned Barth, Mark Fogarty, Greg Gerson, Steve Heffner, Andrew Hettinger, Virginia Saenz McCarthy, James O'Brien, Mark Toscani, and Robert J. Weythman, for all your fine work.

Our January 1998 Death Valley production, *Welcome to Serendipity*, was the first DVCAM digital video workshop feature with Morgan aboard as director of photography, as well as co-writer/co-director (and co-producer again). Thank you, Barry Green and Karen Gloyd (Fiercely Independent Films, **<www.fiercely-independent.com>**), for your invaluable co-producing help, plus all your contributions as co-writer/co-directors, actors, and editors. Thanks for such a total effort! And thank you, Marta Becket (famed as painter, performer, and creator of plays at the Amargosa Opera House), for your kind permission to shoot in your town of Death Valley Junction. Thanks also to our other co-writer/co-director collaborators, Irene Barnett (who also did a great job of performing the lead female role) and Robert Black, for helping us to create such a beautiful movie!

For our April 1998 movie, *Loneliness Is Soul*, thanks must first go to Avid editor/co-writer/co-director Mike Rogers, whose mind-boggling achievement of finding the final cut on this movie in less than eight days (culled from seven hours of beautiful DVCAM footage shot by Morgan) will continue to amaze me. Thank you, Mike. You're a wizard! And thank you, yahn soon, for co-writing/co-directing, performing your beautiful song "Cataloging Fears" (the movie's title found in the lyrics), and sharing your amazing, real-life "mushroom story" (good luck getting your own first feature, *Learning to Crawl* into festivals). Thank you, actresses Jessica Heidt, Meeka Schmalle, and Marla Schmalle, for your terrific performances, giving the movie its wonderful energy. And thanks to Jay Coakley, for dropping your usual Hollywood gigs (all that money!) to light our scenes to gorgeous perfection (and for your fine co-writing/co-directing as well!). We were also blessed with the use of the "Fly Crane" for exciting aerial and crane shots, and give huge thanks to Todd Horrisberger and Kira Stoll for those wonderful big-budget effects! And while I've already thanked musician Paul Baker earlier, I want to reiterate my appreciation for his fine musical score for this movie, the use of his recording studio as a location, and his appearance on-screen. Thanks for everything, Paul. And thank you, co-writer/co-director collaborators Hal Croasmun and Alexander Marchand, for your great ideas, scene building, and wonderful performances in the movie.

For *Maisy's Garden*, our August 1998 DVCAM production (Morgan again making a major contribution as co-producer, co-writer/co-director, and DP . . . THANKS, MORGAN!!!), attorney Michael Bolgatz gave us use of his house, his personal stories, his writing/directing talents, his terrific lead performance, availability of his young daughter Maisy for scenes, *every* consideration. Thank you, Mike!!! And our fabulous lead actress, Jill Pixley, outstanding as his movie wife, deserves huge thanks for her great acting work. Thanks, Jill, for giving a full-out performance! And thank you, *Loneliness* actress Jessica Heidt, for again gracing our set with your superb talent and professionalism. Hope to see you (and Jill) again on future productions! And once again, yahn soon added a special, positive force field to our set. Thanks, yahn, for your incredibly fine acting and ideas, and another great song (written and performed during the shoot). And thank you, Doreen Alexander (August 1997 Feature Workshop), for joining us again, and acting in a supporting role. And our other Mike, editor/co-writer/co-director extraordinaire Mike Rogers, pulled off his miracle again, somehow roping down a great cut in just a week of Avid craziness, selecting from over *twelve* hours of Morgan's great shots. Thanks, Mike, for basically doing the impossible again! And thanks, Paul, for supplying us with a DAT full of original Paul Baker songs (your great music saved us again in the editing room!). And thank you, co-writer/co-director collaborators Carlos R. Acuna, Peter Aris, Grace Eng, Jon Jennings, and Whit Wagner (also acting in a lead role), who helped create this movie.

Many other people have helped me on my films, and I thank you again for this assistance. Thank you, Michael Mideke, Kelly Brock Boen, Skip Covington, Lee Serie, Joe DiVincenzo, Mary Garstang, Jim Newman, Phyllis Richardson, Terrel Seltzer, Alan Shulman, Jim Summers, Bobby Weinstein, Fran Hawkins, Julie Schachter, Bill Kimberlin, Jim Mayer, Gary Coates, Flipper, The Mutants, Joe Rees, Liz Sher, Phil Schnayerson, M. Louise Stanley, Lee Chapman, Leon Kenin, Rachel Pond, John Claudio, F. Paul Hocking, Sara Rosin, Bob Arnold, Peter O'Halligan, Peter Buchanan, Judy Newman, Ben Goon, Bill Palmer, Brad Wright, Swain Wolfe, Bob and Judy Pest, Vic Skolnick, Charlotte Sky and Dylan, Fred Padula, Linda Egar, Jane Egar, Jim Maher, Gary Thorp, Lucile Fjoslien, John Corso, Murray Korngold, Elliot Rosenblatt, Alex Prisadsky, Anne Wehrer, Alex Feng, Johanna Feng, Gail Fisher, Katherine Sherwood, Leon Hayes, Billy Hiebert, George Manupelli, Bob Zagone, and Mary Ashley, every one of whom has helped me along the way.

Lastly, I want to thank Boston University professor Ray Carney, Cassavetes expert and author, for reminding us that our struggle to make personal movies is a worthy and vital contribution to society.

Introduction to Low-Budget Feature Filmmaking

If you've looked over the table of contents, with its extensive chronology of the steps needed to create a feature on film or DV (digital video), you may feel a bit frightened by the seeming complexity of the process. And if you don't consider yourself a "technical" person, you may also have become worried that you don't have the necessary skills for making a movie. This book, like other books that must include some technical information, may appear at first glance to be over the head of the novice who has always just had a *feeling* about making movies. But in this case that isn't true. Making something even as complex as a feature can be accomplished if the process is undertaken in a thorough, step-by-step fashion. Each step in the process of production is carefully outlined and explained in the following chapters of this book. And each step flows naturally to the next step, the final result being the creation of a motion picture for under $15,000.

Perhaps you don't even have an idea about what your feature would be about. If you just have a *feeling* that you would love to make movies, that is enough purpose with which to begin your project. In chapter 1—"Story Concept"—you will be taught how to discover ideas in your own life as well as in outside news events that can be the subject of your work. Most people don't place enough value on their own experiences, overlooking the incredible possibilities for feature film concepts relating to real life. By the end of the chapter, you will have been taught how to expand your idea into a one-page "treatment" that can be registered with the Writers Guild for copyright protection.

In chapter 2 you will learn how to script your idea, whether it be a conventional story or a series of images and sounds that tells a different type of narrative. The emphasis of this book is on each person's striving to create his or her own original vision on film or video. If you don't consider yourself a writer, you will learn alternative scripting techniques that help you create a "menu" from which you can detail your shooting ideas.

Once you have formed a script or outline for shooting, chapter 3 explains how to write out a contract for the production, paying cast and crew mostly with hoped-for percents of profit or deferred salaries from money to be earned from the feature. You will learn how to follow the strict $12,000 budget, understanding the limitations of your low-budget enterprise. There is also information on raising money from investors and applying for grants.

In chapter 4, on preproduction, you will be taught how to collect the people, places, and things necessary to shoot your movie. You will be shown how to locate the needed members of your cast and crew, find locations, and get the best deal on camera rentals, lighting kits, and other essential pieces of equipment. Different types of filming will be discussed, some that require only natural light to illuminate interiors, avoiding complex lighting systems by using faster filmstocks. At every turn you will be taught ways to save additional money on your production. By using the preshoot lists outlined at the end of the chapter, you will know when you are fully prepared for the next step in production—the actual shooting of your feature.

Chapter 5—on production—begins by telling you my Fifteen Rules for Shooting No-Budget Features. There really aren't any hard-and-fast rules to creative work, but I think you'll enjoy the food for thought. Once again the chapter is constructed in a step-by-step fashion, discussing each facet of shooting a movie, from picking up cast and crew members to loading your rented camera—or just how to shoot it if you have been able to afford a camera assistant who can technically maintain the equipment for you. Here I encourage you to overcome your fears and just begin shooting, trusting intuition and honest intentions to help create an original and meaningful product. I've outlined steps that teach you how to set up lights and take a light reading, and I also offer suggestions for types of shots and techniques for shooting that save money and add originality. You will learn how to shoot titles on location and save hundreds of dollars. At the end of the chapter, you are taught how to deal with the lab regarding processing and work printing of your footage, and how to check your film and sound for quality before completing the filming.

After the movie is shot and the on-location sound has been recorded, the real alchemy of editing your footage into a feature begins. Each step in the editing process is presented in chapter 6, from syncing up the picture and sound track so that the words spoken are lined up with the image of the mouth moving on screen, through finding the best order of shots, refining the scenes, testing your edit, using music and sound effects to improve your cut, and adding needed pieces of narration or photos to complete your ideas. Once the final pacing and tightening have taken place, you are shown how to prepare your sound rolls for the "mix," in which every volume and tone is controlled in support of your story. You are also shown how to cut your original footage for printing at the lab, "conforming" the original using the identical images on the work print as your guide. Doing this process yourself can save you thousands of dollars. I discuss how to order your print, making sure that the lab has the full, clearly stated instructions necessary for making a good first print ("answer print") on the first try. And finally you're shown how to assemble your feature and screen it for eager members of cast and crew.

Next comes chapter 7, on promotion, your lifeline to hopefully earning some of your production monies back, attending some glamorous film festivals in the U.S. and Europe, and getting your chance to make your second feature. I show how to make your own pressbook, creating graphics (posters, letterhead) that will help sell your product. There is much information on how to enter film festivals in the United States and Europe, including Websites and addresses, and a listing of possible buyers for TV. Distribution is discussed along with alternative forms of getting your movie into theaters or viewed as streaming video on the Web. The final word in this chapter is to enjoy your accomplishment regardless of the acceptance or rejection of your final product.

Next comes a dose of reality check, chapter 8, to help give the moviemaker a sense of purpose for making feature number two.

For those writer/directors who found it impossible to raise even the no-budget amount of $12,000 for a first feature attempt, chapter 9 offers the radical alternative of making super-low-budget features by collaboration: Ten people share the financial burden and create a feature-length film or digital video for as little as $750 each. And if you have already survived the hardships of producing that first feature, but were not fortunate in producing one of the few films that became critical and financial successes, then this chapter offers you a viable option for extending that one-shot feature attempt into a moviemaking career, by helping you afford to produce new works.

Chapter 10 is devoted to the possibility of shooting your feature in "old format" video. With the advent of cheaper video equipment at broadcast quality, video is now certainly a viable means for producing indie features.

Chapter 11 reviews everything from DV cameras to NLE (nonlinear editing) systems, DV-to-film transfers, and promotional Websites, explaining how all filmmaking, from Hollywood big-budgets to no-budget feature filmmaking, will be affected by advances in digital technology. For the first time, no-budget moviemakers can purchase their entire movie studio (DV camera, computer, and editing software) for the cost of a used car (under $12,000), so that their subsequent movies can be shot for just the cost of the recording tape or disks. From digital correction of a sound track thought to be ruined by excessive camera noise (the whirring sound of a camera can be totally removed without affecting the sound quality!), to digital editing (speeding up assembly and fine cutting, which allows a hundred hours of rough footage to be reduced to a finished cut in just weeks), this technology is now becoming more affordable in its numerous applications.

Chapter 12 is about the future of DV and film technology, how HDTV (high definition TV) will affect the shape (and even content) of all future broadcasting and theatrical motion picture presentations. And some of the new technology is already here, with companies like Nagra and Sony offering sound recorders and cameras, respectively, that record to PCMCIA sticks instead of tape (the Nagra Ares-C recorder has *no moving parts*). I discuss the battle for trying to reach a standard "univisium" viewing format (1:2) for both TV and movies, and how the moviemaker should weigh the option of shooting in 16:9 so that his/her movie(s) will remain broadcastable into the new millennium (whether by satellite, Web TV, Internet, or . . .). But regardless of the new technology or methods of production, what's most important is that each person take responsibility for making his or her feature filmmaking dreams come true.

1 Story Concept

To create a high-quality, low-budget, feature-length motion picture, the moviemaker must think of a film concept that not only excites his or her imagination, but that also can be made on, and that stands a chance of actually benefiting from, the severe restrictions of a used-car budget.

After each of my students and I had written treatments of possible feature film concepts for one of our collaborative efforts at the California College of Arts and Crafts (1984), I began the final selection process for choosing the one concept for our no-budget feature by withdrawing my own idea because it was obviously too big for our tiny budget. After two out of the three students also withdrew their story concepts, we were left with the one workable idea, which recounted the story of a woman in her thirties, living alone, who rents out a room to a male roommate (*The Last Roommate*). The story was about their relationship and how it developed with regard to the male partner's insane jealousy and her need to make a decision about aborting her pregnancy. This concept offered us (1) one basic location—her apartment, (2) only two main characters, (3) a straightforward narrative flow, and (4) a chance to discuss the timely issue of abortion. And by finding an actress who would be willing to let us use her apartment as the location for our movie, we would be able to save the cost of location rentals and benefit from filming in her private living quarters, which would undoubtedly reveal real aspects of her personality. The monetary restrictions actually inspired us to enhance our concept by including the extra touch of reality.

My first feature, *A Man, a Woman, and a Killer*, also benefited from the severe shooting budget of $5,900. Wayne Wang, Dick Richardson, and I designed a story that included three main characters: a young gangster holed up in a house with his girlfriend, and an older man who wanders into their lives and is mistaken for the hit man they are expecting. For the filming I was able to rent a house on the Mendocino, California, shore for two weeks, which accommodated our nine-person cast and crew. Because it was economically necessary for us all to live together during the shoot, we were quickly transformed from a group of perfect strangers into a commune whose members shared their most intimate secrets. One of the most original things about the film is that it interweaves the real love affair between Dick and actress Carolyn Zaremba with the scripted affair portrayed in the story. So in this case the budgetary limitations not only enhanced the concept but expanded it and ultimately redesigned the entire structure of the film.

While budgetary restrictions may be a determining factor in choosing a film concept for production, the first step for the filmmaker is to begin searching for ideas, and defining personal attitudes, that will gel into an intriguing feature film concept.

Where Do Ideas Come From?

Each person's life is filled with unrecognized stories and ideas that could be used to create fantastic feature-length movies. Because we all get caught up in daily routines that camouflage the real dramas of just being a living human, it's easy to be unaware of the truly great stories each of us already knows. The concept for *The Last Roommate* came to us because a friend of student Peter Boza told him the true story of how her jealous roommate terrorized her, becoming so crazy that he ended up in her backyard pruning her trees while completely nude to embarrass her with the neighbors. Although your life may not include this graphic an episode, if you closely examine your life you may be surprised to find you hold within your memory an important story that should be told on film.

Perhaps there is a good story in how your parents or relatives immigrated to America. There have been a lot of films made that deal with a person's overcoming overwhelming odds to survive and win (*Rocky* and *Rocky II*, *III*, *IV*, and *V*, to name a few), and maybe you or someone you know falls into this category. I personally think that more films should be made that celebrate the silent heroism of people with disabilities, who must strive each day just to function, and that every Vietnam veteran has a moving story to tell. Everyone's life is heroic if placed in a proper dramatic structure. The play *Death of a Salesman* by Arthur Miller is a heroic story about an American salesman near retirement age who has exhausted himself in pursuit of financial success. Maybe your job offers some interesting filmatic possibilities for stories. The story line of Kevin Smith's hit movie *Clerks* (<www.viewaskew.com>) centered around a convenience store where he worked and included characters inspired by the odd customers and clerks who assembled there each day. If you've been mind-boggled by continual car crashes and murders on nightly TV, it's hard to see the simple, yet immensely vital, stories each of us lives out in our quiet ways. These stories are the ones that the independent filmmaker should tell.

Many good films have been based on newspaper articles some scriptwriter noticed while in search of divine inspiration. Nick Kazan, a co-scriptwriter on my second feature, *1988*, based his screenplay for *At Close Range* on a series of newspaper articles about the father of a crime family who was turned in for murder by his son. For several weeks before deciding to produce *The Last Roommate*, my students and I had worked on developing a story based on a newspaper article about a bully who terrorized a small midwestern town and was ultimately shot to death, with the entire town refusing to divulge the identity of the killer. If you read your hometown newspaper every day, from front to back for two weeks, I'm sure you'll spot a story that sparks your interest. (Most major newspapers can now be accessed on the WWW by typing their names in a search engine slot.)

Sometimes an idea for a movie comes to you in one line, or in a single flash of inspiration. My film *Emerald Cities* began with the single thought: What would it be like to watch the events of the modern world in 1984 on TV from a shack in the middle of the desert? It then occurred to me that maybe the TV would be an early color console in disrepair, that could only transmit green images. Comic Steve Martin has said that the premise for his first film, *The Jerk*, came from a line in one of his routines: "I grew up as a simple white boy born into a Negro family."

Ideas can also arise out of those things you most value or enjoy. Frank Capra's movie *It's a Wonderful Life* presented the premise that each person's life is vitally important to all others it touches. If you feel that no one should go hungry in an affluent society like America, maybe you can expand this attitude into a full-fledged feature film concept. Maybe you can make a film that sheds some light on the modern victims of economic depression, as John Ford did with his film of John Steinbeck's book *The Grapes of Wrath.* The other day I saw a film on TV about South Sea island pearl divers and thought this would be the perfect topic for an independent filmmaker who enjoys scuba diving and likes to travel.

But before making a movie that explores your particular hobby or preoccupation, carefully check in a reference book to make sure there aren't films already made that sufficiently explore what you are interested in. The impact of your film depends to a great extent on the originality of your subject matter, and the power of your story will be diffused if it's too similar to an already-existing film. One good way to check out your idea for a feature is to read through a book such as Leonard Maltin's *Movie & Video Guide*. Reading a short synopsis on each film not only lets you know what's been done, it also gives you a better understanding of the ideas behind the films you've seen. Reading the weekly reviews in *Variety* (**<www.variety.com>**)—an entertainment industry magazine—would give you the most current selection of movie concepts. Of course, even if you attempted to copy the story line of an existing Hollywood film, it's quite doubtful that anyone could recognize the similarity between your $12,000 effort and a big-budget movie with millions of dollars' worth of production values. One of the greatest virtues of low-budget features is that most of them appear to be unquestionably original.

Not all ideas for low-budget features need to fall within the guidelines of traditional narrative structure. Many interesting movies that challenge the way we see our world through the media of film and television have been made by avant-garde artists. James Benning made a feature film constructed only of one-minute static shots of industrial sites. Pop artist Andy Warhol made an eight-hour film that included only one continuous image of the Empire State Building over the course of a single day. Many film artists have used the essay format to speak about their world through personal observations. If you select this format for your feature production, you would first choose the theme of your work and then script the text for your narration and the images to illuminate your ideas. Some artists such as Bruce Conner and Craig Baldwin (*Spectres of the Spectrum*), have used "found footage"—acquired film footage shot by others—and edited the pieces into new, original works.

Whether you choose narrative storytelling or more abstract means of speaking through media, I believe it's most important to respect your intuition and follow your instincts so that the final result of your efforts will ring with a personal truth and originality.

Selecting the Right Concept

After you have thought of several ideas that appeal to you as concepts for your low-budget movie, each idea must be analyzed in terms of feasibility within the severe restrictions of a used-car budget. In my earlier discussion of production on *The Last Roommate* and *A Man, a Woman, and a Killer*, I mentioned how each film made use of a few main characters and one central location. If your movie concept demands the use of many characters, such as our "bully" story did for the class production, it may be too expensive for the meager resources you have available. With a budget of only $12,000, there is little money to pay actors, and only a certain amount of percentage points of profits that you can give away as enticements (see chapter 3). And since you are also very limited in funds for transportation to various locations, and cannot afford the additional days of shooting, with increased equipment rental rates and salaries that multiple locations would require, ideas that require such treatment must be withdrawn from consideration.

When examining potential choices of ideas for your feature production at used-car prices, you must also evaluate all areas of your concept for costs that would be apt to destroy your chances for success. Does your concept require a great deal of voice-over narration or sound effects at costs that would exceed allotted funds for sound transfers to mag stock and sound studio time (see "Budget," chapter 3)? If you can't figure out a means of shooting your extensive credits as part of the on-location shoot (see chapter 5), just this one extra expenditure could rob your production of precious production monies. And don't plan a low-budget *American Graffiti* around scores of popular songs for which you can't possibly afford expensive music rights. Obviously, don't consider making a low-budget "period" costume epic either, unless you have free access to the wardrobe of an opera company. Any deviation from the strictest limitations of story, location, and number of characters has the possibility of ruining your chances for completion of your production.

Eleven Essential Qualities of a No-Budget Movie

Before making any final decisions with regard to your movie concept/idea, consider its potential in terms of the eleven qualities listed below.

- ☐ *Originality*
  Have similar movies been made?
- ☐ *Feasibility*
  Is your concept possible to produce given budget limitations (see chapter 3)?
- ☐ *Drama*
  Does your story have the possibility of human drama that will touch the audience's heart?
- ☐ *Responsibility*
  Does your movie concept add meaning or understanding, in a personal or universal way, to our lives?
- ☐ *Interest*
  Will the audience be interested in the story you are telling?

- ☐ *Screenplay potential*
  Will your idea continue to grow into a feature-length script, or dry up in less than thirty pages?
- ☐ *Personal choice*
  Is this the kind of movie you would go to see in a theater?
- ☐ *Notoriety*
  Is this the kind of production for which you'd like to be known?
- ☐ *Richness and complexity*
  Is this a feature that can be viewed more than once—that becomes *more,* not less, when seen again?
- ☐ *Timeliness*
  Will your work quickly become outdated?
- ☐ *Critical response*
  What is the best—and worst—review your movie could receive?

note: To avoid possible legal problems, it is vital that, as a moviemaker, you get written permission from an individual whose story you've derived from a newspaper article (e.g., the Teena Brandon story upon which Kimberly Pierce based her hit movie, *Boys Don't Cry*). If you use a newspaper story only as inspiration, changing the names and incidents into unrecognizable form, this permission is no longer necessary. For our production of *The Last Roommate*, we gave the real person upon whose story our film was based 1 percent of the hoped-for profits as payment for her idea. It is not wise to base your feature film idea on a published or unpublished book unless you are able to clear the legal rights with the help of a lawyer. And since the legal fees and "option payment" usually required for using such material may easily cost more than your entire used-car budget, it's best to avoid all these legal problems by thinking up an original idea derived from your own unique experience.

Writing Your Concept in One Sentence

It is an old Hollywood adage that the head of a major studio will ask the producer who is pitching the idea for a new feature to "give me your idea in one sentence!" While it is not our intention to sell our idea to a studio, and certainly not necessary since we have the wealth and power to send our own idea into production (at used-car prices), it's definitely worth the time it takes to define an idea in the strongest sentence possible. Not only should this exercise bring about an increased awareness of the foundation of your story, but it gives you a chance to begin writing your movie. Below you will find several examples of how my class and I tried to define our idea for our "bully" movie in one sentence:

The Bully is a film about a small town that is terrorized by a bully, and then destroys him.

The Bully is a film about a group of townspeople who are terrorized by the town bully, and the moral dilemma they are confronted with of what to do about him.

The Bully is a film about the rise of a small-town bully whose victims reach their limits and take action to end the torment.

The Bully is about a bully who terrorizes a small American town and is killed by town consensus, the whole town refusing to reveal who actually killed him.

The Bully is a film about a town that worked collectively to kill a bully and then refused to reveal the individual responsible.

The Bully is a film about a group of townspeople who, after being terrorized by a bully, take revenge on him and hide the crime.

The Bully is a film about a group of townspeople who are being victimized by a bully, and the violent action they are forced to take after the legal system fails.

While each sentence describes basically the same story, the subtle shift in emphasis could account for seven different films made from the same idea. In some descriptions the grammar or use of words is poor and the idea loses energy. What do I mean by "energy"? If you read over the descriptions again, you should find that each one has a different ability to gain your interest. Most likely the description with the most punch will be the one that is structurally correct in grammar and concise in its use of words, giving it the "energy" to grab your attention. By beginning your project with a sense of accuracy with regard to each word expressed, you are putting into motion the necessary care needed at every stage of production. Whether you are writing your script, ordering filmstock (videotape, DVDs, etc.), renting equipment, directing actors, or editing your footage, the end result of all your labors will depend on your ability to communicate your ideas to others as concisely as possible. So by writing and rewriting your one-sentence description of your movie concept until the words are at their best, you will clarify your ideas to yourself and initiate a standard of quality that will affect all aspects of your feature production.

In a recent interview with Gavin Smith in *Film Comment* magazine (<**www.filmlinc.com/fcm/fcm.htm**>), director Mike Nichols discussed the power of "the central metaphor" of a work. He said basically that if the story you select to produce (your movie) has purpose, some compelling ingredient (that metaphor . . .), then you'll have a powerful creation that can hold an audience. Nichols says, "An audience is a ruthless, heartless, and unruly monster . . . and if it doesn't sense purpose then get out of its way, because it's going to be difficult. But when your purpose is high and strong an audience can sense it." The key is that the audience members must somehow understand why they're sitting there, spending a couple hours of their precious lives watching your play or film. If that one sentence you've used to describe your movie indicates a bigger experience than the mere collection of words you used to describe it, then maybe it's worth spending four years of your life scrambling for funds to pull a feature-length movie together from scratch. The process of *choosing a story to make into a movie* must include this question of the "central metaphor."

Expanding Your Idea into a One-Page Treatment

Once you have settled on the one sentence that best describes the movie you want to make, the next step is expanding your idea into a one-page "treatment." Below are two examples of treatments written by students at CCAC for *The Bully* concept. You'll notice that each student renamed the film, coming up with the following titles: *The Round of Justice* and *Thou Shall Not Kill.* Although neither of these titles is really dynamic enough to be a final choice, at least an attempt was made to create an original title. Using their imaginations, the students developed the bully as a character in their stories, inventing his past, his size and shape, his attitudes and motivation. And each person tried his or her best to come up with a beginning introduction, a middle development, and a suitable ending to the drama.

> The Round of Justice
>
> The Round of Justice is a film about a group of townspeople who are being victimized by a bully and the violent action they are forced to take after the legal system fails.
>
> The people of the town pride themselves on being a self-sufficient entity. The desire for a quiet life is something they share. Their tolerance and helpful concern for each other give them productive and useful lives. They all know why they are there; not because they are bitter fugitives from the outside world, but because they want to be in control of their lives.
>
> Tobias Young, the catalyst of the action, a large-boned hulk of a man, is from a farm near the town. He served as an army supply sergeant in some recent war, where he developed a taste for personal power and dabbled in black-market goods. Now he works in a gas station by the

highway. He needs respect, but doesn't know how to earn it until he discovers fear will get him what he wants. He uses his physical size to intimidate the townspeople. He stops paying for coffee, then for clothes; soon he pays for nothing, and when they complain, he breaks up their stores. After he has beaten up several people, one of the townspeople tries to teach him a lesson by burning his big pickup truck, but Tobias catches him and beats him nearly to death.

Tobias is arrested, and in the trial at the county seat he gets a minimal sentence for a first offense. When he returns from jail a few months later he shoots one of the men who testified against him. The town has a meeting to try to decide what to do. They know that even if they get him put in jail again he'll return as soon as he gets out. The next day they see his pickup truck approaching the town and gather in a crowd around him. A shot rings out and he falls dead.

The bully has been killed in a crowd of townspeople who all say they didn't see who did it. The state can't decide whom to prosecute. The town has gotten away with murder. They realize they have to live with their guilt. Have they lost what was good in the town? Have they gotten rid of the encroachment of the outside world or have they brought it even deeper into the town themselves like a Trojan horse?

Although the basic story is outlined in the above treatment, it's hard to get a specific feeling for the characters involved. Missing from this treatment are the little details about people and places that give life to the words. And there are some unanswered questions—such as what the bully Tobias was like as a kid, some history of his family that would account for his need for self-respect at all costs. Also, what was decided at the town meeting with regard to the bully? Did they *decide* to kill him? How have the townspeople been affected by the death? Will the whole town be prosecuted? These details must be filled in to complete the story and fulfill the needs of the treatment.

Thou Shall Not Kill

This feature-length motion picture is a film about a group of townspeople who are being victimized by a bully, and the violent action they are forced to take after the legal system fails.

The bully has been getting away with terrorizing a small town for the last two years, since he returned from a job as a supply sergeant in the army. It seems his self-esteem fell very low after returning to the town he grew up in and discovered there was no job waiting for him. In the military he dealt with selling black-market goods, special favors, etc., and he enjoyed the power that went along with his position. But back home he was a failure, a three-hundred-pound "nothing."

His mother, with whom he lived, was unable to offer any positive support for his rage other than her nightly reading from the Bible, and soon he directed his anger and frustration on the town at large. In the initial stages he was fueled by an incident where he refused to pay for his coffee after being angered by an inattentive waitress. Getting away with the free coffee, he soon turned to helping himself to free clothes in the town's best men's store, bullying his way into the barbershop for a free haircut, free meals at the cafe. Everyone, including the one local peace officer, looked the other way as this bullying increased like a type of fission. Everyone tried to understand.

Finally, a well-liked member of the community, eighty-five-year-old Mr. Ferguson, made a formal legal complaint to law officers in Judson, the town twenty miles east. The bully was brought to court and Mr. Ferguson testified against him. Through a technicality the bully was released and, returning to the town, shot Mr. Ferguson in the leg with a .38-caliber revolver. The bully also broke several windows, cleaned out the clothing store, and threatened several locals with injury. It seemed nothing could stop him.

The townspeople decided to protect themselves, and fearing that the local justice system would not help them in their defense, they decided they must destroy the bully. The next time he drives his mother in to church they (a group of thirty to forty people) circle his car, and a shot rings out. When the crowd clears he is found dead.

Questioned by authorities in Judson, the entire town refuses to talk about the killing. This film ends with the possibility of the whole town's being tried for murder and the changes that take place in the townspeople who were forced to take justice into their own hands.

Once again, the treatment does not quite meet the major requirements of storytelling. We are given a slightly more detailed description of the bully (a three-hundred-pound "nothing") and now know that his mother reads the Bible, but what about his father? What were the ingredients of his childhood that prompted his behavior? It helps to see how a small incident such as "an inattentive waitress" began his reign of terror, and it is much more convincing to believe that he got off easy for wounding an old man than for almost killing him, as is stated in the treatment of *The Round of Justice*, but the treatment is not nearly as gripping as it should be, given the basic premise. Since the story must rely on the development of the bully's personality, it is vital that we learn about him through the use of "the characterization."

Improving a Treatment Through Detailed Characterization

To write a treatment that seems to describe a flesh-and-blood character, it is essential to understand the life of that character, from childhood through adult years. An example of the characterization of "Greg" from *The Last Roommate* is shown below. By understanding the physical attributes, education, social life, and work history of Greg, we were able to understand clearly how his character would relate to any given situation. Not only did this help to fuel additional scenes for scripting, it also aided the direction of actor Bruce Parry, helping him to attain a believable performance as the Greg character.

Greg

Physically:

Trim, well built, stands around 5′11″, 175 lbs.; athletic-looking, brown hair, clean-cut. No physical defects. Goes jogging, eats health foods, but smokes grass and drinks.

Family Background:

He grew up in a small town in New Jersey. His home life was rather unhappy due to father dying of cancer at an early age. Mother then remarried to a man who disliked Greg, and eventually also died of cancer. Greg's mother had a difficult time raising Greg and his brother. In school Greg did well because he spent most of his time after school at home working on cars or studying. Did not date girls, although there was some interest in a girl who lived nearby. Most of the time if he went out, it was with the boys. His family was lower middle class, and lived in a modest home. The absence of his father caused him to withdraw some, especially with the arrival of his stepfather. Greg valued the old-fashioned family unit and rituals his father practiced (togetherness at dinner table, respect for elders, family cooperation).

Education:

Graduated from high school with good grades. Attended college two years before going into the marines for a tour of Vietnam. He is well read; as a matter of fact, reading is a passion for him. Social subjects fascinate him. He is somewhat concerned with the struggle of poor people and the American drive to make money. He feels society has lost its ideals. He gradually becomes anticapitalist in his beliefs. Vietnam was a shocking experience for him, one that became especially difficult upon returning to American society.

Social Life:
Greg has always been single, one of those individuals who felt more comfortable with others of the same sex. Not much on dating, he spent most of his time working on cars with other friends, or hitting the books. There was one female interest he saw at random. She was a neighborhood girl who took more of an interest in him than he in her. She turned out to be his senior prom date. The two years he spent in college were more socially active with girls, but still mostly with the boys and drinking. As an adult, Greg still was not well adjusted with women, though he became more outgoing. Insecurity plagued him and the relationships he had. He has old-fashioned beliefs that run afoul in his encounters with the modern woman. Because of this his last relationship ended when his girl walked out on him due to jealousy. He has tried unsuccessfully to come to grips with this problem.

Work History:
Steady and reliable since he was a kid, Greg has had a good job background. As a teenager he worked part-time in a gas station as a mechanic's helper, doing tune-ups and other small jobs from which he picked up enough knowledge to work on his own car. While in college he held another part-time job in an auto-parts store. After returning from Vietnam he taught for a while, but the lack of good pay forced him to turn to private business. Since starting a new position placing executives with corporations, he has had difficulty adjusting to the aggressiveness of private business.

Reading the characterization for Greg, you should have the feeling that you know him as you would a relative or close friend. With this type of solid background, writing a treatment and script comes much more naturally. Here's another treatment for *The Bully*, entitled *A Time for Justice*, that benefited from the student's writing a short history of the "Ned" character, and then using the psychological and physical descriptions from his characterization to better understand Ned's motivation.

<u>A Time for Justice</u>

<u>Synopsis:</u>

This feature film is about a group of townspeople who are being victimized by a bully, and the violent action they are forced to take after the legal system fails.

<u>Outline:</u>

The town of Eden is a small community symbolic of small-town America. It is a town that prides itself on being self-sufficient enough to control its own destiny and not be ravaged by progress. The old values that founded this country, independence, justice, religious freedom, hard work, and respect for your fellow man, are traditions that give Eden its character. Tolerance and concern for each other are virtues the townspeople practice. Pursuit of the quiet life is something they share. That is, until Ned returns.

Ned Tobias once was a teenager in Eden with a reputation as an occasional hell-raiser whose trespasses were taken as nothing more than growing pains. If anything, the townspeople ignored him. He reveres his mother, Hilda, a Bible-reading disciple, who tried to guide him, but could not control him after his father's death. His closest companion had always been old Billy, the retarded cartman who cleans up the town in his own way. Now things are different. Ned has returned from the service—the Marines, to be exact—a different man. For one thing, he's grown into a massive 6′2″, 240-lb. man who's very aware of his strength. Attuned to power and manipulation, something he learned as a supply sergeant dealing in the black market, special favors, and simply getting whatever he wanted through intimidation, he's someone to reckon with. Since returning, his life has taken a turn for the worse. There is no job waiting for him except as a gas station attendant. The means to power and respect he found in the Marine Corps don't exist in Eden. His self-esteem reached bottom until he employed intimidation to get what he wanted.

It all started with an incident that took place his first day back. Feeling proud and worldly-wise upon returning to Eden, Ned walked into the coffee shop to have a cup of coffee as well as to be seen by the people there. Expecting clamor and attention, he was instead ignored. Resentful, he grabbed the waitress by the wrist and made a pass at her. When she pulled her hand away she accidentally spilled the coffee onto his lap and the uniform he proudly wore. Incensed and insulted, he used the moment to vent his anger at being ignored by breaking dishes and turning over the table before leaving. In time, one incident led to another as Ned gained strength from the fear he struck within the community. He manipulated the town through anger, threats, and violence. He interpreted their impotence as the respect he deserved. It became standard for him not to pay for meals, clothes, drinks, etc., if he chose not to. He beat up Kevin Kern, the town barber, for standing up to him. When Lyle Swanson refused him credit, Ned took all the clothes he wanted and vandalized the store. He disrupted church services. Finally, a well-liked member of the town, seventy-five-year-old Sam Ferguson, tried to teach him a lesson for stealing groceries by filing charges. But Ned got a suspended sentence and the sheriff was powerless to stop Ned from returning to town.

This final incident compelled the townspeople to meet. They realized that the sheriff was old and useless and the justice system ineffective. They knew that if Ned were jailed again, when released he'd return with greater vengeance. They tried to understand what had become of their lives and community. They discussed various solutions to the problem that gave rise to moral conflict amongst them. But their fears were great, and they finally reached a conclusion.

The next day, a Sunday, Ned drove into town for a drink. As he pulled up to the local bar in his pickup truck, a group of townspeople surrounded him. A shot rang out from the mob. The crowd then dispersed to the church for the Sunday service. After a moment, Ned's body slumped forward onto the steering wheel, setting off the horn in a final outburst of anger. There was no trace of the anonymous killer.

The state tried to prosecute, but there were no witnesses. The town maintained a silence over the incident. Their problem was gone, but will life be the same in Eden?

This treatment succeeds because it involves the reader in the drama, gives numerous details that enhance the story, and concludes the action. And, most important, the story is told with the necessary energy to indicate the larger script that must flow from this beginning concept. The material seems to be begging for expansion. So it is worth the extra effort of writing a well-thought-out treatment in order to give yourself the best start possible for your feature project. Even with projects that don't depend on either character development or story—more abstract features that can't easily be defined—it's worth the effort to write out your concept and title in order to have the opportunity to protect your original work by registering it with the Writers Guild.

Registering Your Treatment

After you have written the best treatment possible for your project, and thought of the most appropriate title for the movie, you will want to legally protect your work by registering the treatment with the Writers Guild of America. (<**www.wga.org**>). A title page form must accompany your writing. Once your treatment is registered, you will have legal grounds for a lawsuit if someone tries to produce a movie with either an identical story line or title after your registration date. It's even possible that you may be approached by Hollywood producers who wish to purchase your registered title for their big-budget project (registration with the Writers Guild does not protect your title, but someone may learn your movie's name through their database). Filmmaker Jon Jost sold the rights to his film title *Angel City* for several thousand dollars when approached by agents who needed the title for their movie.

To establish the ownership of your concept, send a check or money order for $20, along with your treatment and title page, to Writers Guild of America, West, Inc., 7000 West Third Street, Los Angeles, CA 90048, (323) 782-4500. There is no limit on the amount of pages you can submit, so if your treatment has run to fifty pages, that amount of writing can still be registered for the $20 fee. Within a month you will receive a slip of paper from the Writers Guild that shows your date of registration and your registration number. This information should be transferred to the title page of your treatment for future reference. Once the moviemaker has written a treatment that not only conforms to the rigid demands of a used-car budget, but also excites the imagination, the next step is to expand the concept into a full-fledged shooting script.

Use this title page format when registering your treatment with the Writers Guild:

THE LAST ROOMMATE

Feature-length Motion Picture Treatment
by Peter Boza, Tinnee Lee,
Rick Schmidt, and Mark Yellen.
Copyright 1984.

(Registered by Writers Guild of America, West, Inc.,
on this date ____________, registration # ___________.)

2

Scriptwriting for No-Budget Features

If this is your first moviemaking venture, you may be quite surprised to find yourself confronted with the task of writing a feature-length script. Maybe you found it exceedingly difficult to arrive at a one-sentence description of your concept, and took weeks just to write a one-page treatment for your story. Maybe during this time you kept repeating to yourself: "I'm not a writer . . . I'm not a writer . . . I'm not a writer . . ."

It's true that not everyone is a writer in the grandest sense of the word. Not everyone can use words to bring ideas and characters to life. But almost anyone can write out a recipe for chocolate chip cookies and list the ingredients that must be purchased from the store. A script is like that recipe. The simplest form of a script could be a list of scenes, or just shots and accompanying sound track, that are the desired ingredients for your movie.

INTERIOR—JEAN'S HOUSE—DAY.

1. (Wide shot)

   JEAN enters house and locks front door. (CUT TO)

2. (Wide shot)

   JEAN walking away from camera down hallway toward the dining room. She notices a trail of clothes leading from GREG's bedroom entrance to the kitchen. She stops at bedroom door:

   JEAN (knocks on door)

Greg?

Getting no response, she opens the door and looks in.

(CUT TO)

INTERIOR—GREG'S BEDROOM—DAY.

1. (Wide shot)

From inside GREG's bedroom we see JEAN open the door and look in.

JEAN (looking about)

Greg . . .?

(CUT TO) . . .

A more complex version of a script might include pages filled with thoughts, essays written in loose form, with none of the speakers of the lines identified, as was the case for *A Man, a Woman, and a Killer*:

"What do you want?" I asked.

"You mean you want me to lay you," I said.

"No, I don't want you to lay me. I just want you to love me."

"Yeah. But what do you want me to do?" I said.

"I want to be happy."

"Tell me what to do and I'll do it."

"I want you to take care of me." she said (pause).

Long still shot   fade out

Thanks to my professional scriptwriting collaborators Nick Kazan, Henry Bean, and filmmaker Bill Farley, I was supplied with writing for my feature *1988* that closely resembled the traditional form of Hollywood scripts, as seen on the next page.

Just as each person is able to think up original feature film concepts, each filmmaker will be able to arrive at a scriptwriting format that best suits his or her needs and the needs of the project. Since you are producing your own feature film at used-car prices, you don't have to conform your filmatic recipe to standard script format, which would normally be necessary for acquiring major studio funding. You can structure your script so that it best helps you prepare for shooting your

ED

I don't want big names. i don't want Zanuck and I don't want Bette Davis. Hollywood would poison this film. I want a sidewalk Showboat.

SKIP shakes his head helplessly; he tries to impress ED with realities.

SKIP (SLOWLY)

Do you want a movie, Ed? Or do you want to sit around this ridiculous hotel suite and pretend for another couple of days until they throw us out. LOOK...

(HE TAKES SOME MONEY OUT OF HIS POCKET)

I've got about six bucks. You want it? Here.

(HE PUTS IT ON THE TABLE)

That's not enough for the breakfast! You're making a movie, Sweetheart.

ED

Skip, I'm going to have ten thousand dollars by lunch.

SKIP

Where from?

ED holds up a hand telling SKIP not to ask.

ED

We're going to make this with our own money. I want a film that comes out of America, a film America gives to herself, instead of buying one pre-fab from Hollywood. I'm going to give the means of image production back to the people.

The phone rings. SKIP answers and begins talking in a low voice. ED goes on talking to DICK or, perhaps, just to the room.

SKIP (background)

Hi, yeah, great. (laughter). Right. I think it'll be very hot word-of-mouth. We open in colleges and the cities, score the hip-liberal press, then sell to Corman or somebody. Right. Yeah. We forget the the south, Midwest, the hicks. Yeah four-walling is a posso, but...right. But you figure the budget's under a hundred, and we spend raisents on promo. No, we want twenty-five grand minimum investment for twelve and a half percent. Right

ED (foreground)

Everyone - Every <u>one</u> is a star, and I'm going to give them a chance to show it and find out for themselves. I'm going to let them write their fantasies in celluloid. My producer tells me it's impossible. My assistant director tells me it's impossible, and the money men say I'm out of my mind. And that convinces <u>me,</u> that it is not only possible -- it's <u>necessary</u>.

Page of script from *1988—The Remake.*

film. Although it is generally considered taboo to include instructions for camera angles in a "professional" script, any notation you decide to add to your script is entirely appropriate if it helps you realize your goals. Even if you aren't a writer, it should at least be possible to list the ingredients (scenes) of your film, and then describe the action that takes place with regard to your story.

If you are still hesitant about trying to script your movie, one possible way to break the "block" is to speak about your story into a tape recorder. Once you have described your concept and talked about the characters, location(s) you envision, and mood you'd like to achieve, remembering to give your story a beginning, middle, and end, spend $50 to have a typist transcribe your words on paper. When the typist hands you twenty pages of rough "scripting," you will realize that you can create a recipe for your feature-length movie.

Writing Scenes on Index Cards

Writing for a feature is done in stages, each new stage bringing the ideas of the film more into focus. After writing one sentence that best described your concept, you expanded the idea into a treatment, adding some character development while envisioning your central theme. The next step toward completing a shooting script is to once again expand the writing, using the treatment as a source of inspiration for thinking up as many scenes as you can for your feature. A method that's worked for me in creating scenes is to change the size of the writing surface from 8½″-by-11″ paper to 4″-by-6″ index cards, using one card per scene (both Movie Magic and Final Cut scriptwriting software products offer print-out to index cards, with option to re-merge that info back into full script form). This format helps me overcome my fear of large blank pages and gives more presence to the one-sentence scene descriptions written on each card.

After you've written down as many scenes as you can, read the cards in order and see if you get a complete feeling from your story. It should be easy to determine where scenes are missing. By being sensitive to the flow of your story, you should have the ability to create new scenes that will make transitions between the scenes you've already written. By filling in these structural holes, you can quickly add many new scenes to the movie.

Expanding Cards into Scripted Scenes

The final stage of writing the first draft of your script is to expand the idea on each card into a living scene. This means that you need to describe the location where the action is taking place, perhaps provide some background information on the emotional mood of the characters, and actually create the dialogue spoken. Let me mention once again that it isn't necessary to write your scenes in any particular professional scriptwriting format. What's most important is that you are continuing to develop your ideas and concepts as freely as possible. And if you have any confusion about the structure of your story, it may help to list your scene ideas on a single piece of paper and then shift them around to get a renewed sense of the beginning, middle, and end you are trying to achieve. Here's how we listed our scenes (out of order) for *The Last Roommate*:

Scenes for The Last Roommate

1. First dinner Greg & Jean/dishwashing/begin romance.
2. Jogging . . . Jean meets Greg . . . surprise.
3. Jogging . . . Greg's jealousy of Jean's jogger friend.
4. Jogging glimpses . . . sound effects, breathing, steps.
5. Jogging . . . Jean's fear that she is being followed.
6. Bookstore . . . jealousy . . . Jean leaves before Greg jealous.
7. Interviews with selection of roommates at restaurant.
8. First meeting of Nancy with her girlfriend (about new roommate).
9. Second girlfriend meeting (Greg real possessive, etc.).
10. Third girlfriend meeting (Jean is scared).

11. Jean moves into girlfriend's house.
12. Abortion clinic sequence.
13. Driving (Jean) from SF to clinic (credits?).
14. Ride home from clinic.
15. Greg moves in (boxes, etc.).
16. Answering service jealousy (in bed).
17. Answering service messages from Greg.
18. Greg nude in backyard.
19. Jean gardening.
20. Greg . . . drugs . . . drunk.
21. Greg moves back into his room (after argument).
22. Greg cries (Jean watches?).
23. Jean back home after abortion (catharsis?).
24. Billy and computer.
25. Typing and bulletin board.
26. Greg complains about money, job, etc.
27. Greg goes through Jean's purse.
28. Greg punches holes in diaphragm.
29. Greg gets angry and breaks something.
30. Greg shows up outside Jean's girlfriend's house.
31. Police scene . . . evict Greg.
32. Jean alone . . . Greg bangs on door (night).
33. Jean reads letter about Greg wrecking diaphragm.
34. Greg and Jean have a good time.
35. 4th of July fireworks.
36. Lovemaking collage Greg and Jean night to morning.

Some books on scriptwriting, such as Syd Field's excellent *Screenplay* (Dell Books, 1984, see **<www.amazon.com>** for discounts on this and other helpful moviemaking books), discuss the concept of "plot points," which are special scenes that drive your story into higher drama. These scenes, occurring at the tail of the beginning section of your film, and just before the start of your film's ending section, should throw a monkey wrench into the regular flow of events, adding new spice to propel the story forward. Something unusual should happen, something ironic or surprising that changes the basic way in which the audience perceives the story. A film may have many plot points, each one shifting the context and energizing the audience's interest. As Field says, every movie has plot points or the audience would probably walk out from boredom. In your list of scenes you may already have created moments in scenes that are, in fact, plot points. Look over your most exciting and interesting scenes. Do these high points generate a rebirth of interest in your story? Do they twist the story around, adding new insight into your characters?

Field says that the first plot point usually occurs about twenty minutes into the action. In our film the first plot point is probably in the abortion sequence, when Jean discusses abortion with a nurse at the clinic. This scene fills in the gaps of information from the beginning flashback, and propels the film forward as Jean is prompted to tell her story. Another plot point occurs when Jean discovers her roommate Greg standing nude in the backyard, pruning plants. This scene signals to the viewer that Jean's moody boyfriend is perhaps also a psychopath. As Jean runs out of the house, terrified by Greg's erratic behavior, the film jumps to a higher dramatic level. Relating with the character Jean as she tells about her problems with Greg, the audience now is doubly frightened for her, and doubly interested in what happens next. The next time you watch a movie, look for the plot points. How many plot points are there in *Citizen Kane*?

While Field's book on scriptwriting is mainly directed toward the writer whose primary goal is probably to script a commercial feature, his advice regarding the structural creation and plot points of a script is also of great interest to the independent filmmaker and avant-gardist. *Screenplay* would be a worthy addition to your reference library. And Field's $79 two-video VHS Screenwriting Workshop tapes (also available on audiocassette) from Final Draft software may be the best money you ever spend toward achieving your moviemaking goals ([800] 231-4055, <www.finaldraft.com>).

If you continue to have a problem writing your scenes, sit back and try to identify what's wrong. If you're having problems breathing life into your imaginary characters, it may help to think of real people you have known, writing some real events and observations into your scenes. Or maybe you've been working too hard writing your script, and desperately need to give yourself a break. Take a week off in search of rest and new inspiration. See three movies in a row, or read a good book from cover to cover. If, on the other hand, you have been lazy and sluggish, it may be time to apply the needed pressure of a deadline on your writing. On our production of *A Man, a Woman, and a Killer*, we decided that the only way to actually produce a feature film, given all the daily pressures of just living, was to work within the strict deadlines of writing for two weeks and then filming the next two weeks. All systems for the shooting of the feature were set into motion at the same moment that the scripting began. We made the commitment to film with whatever we had at the end of two weeks, with added writing completed during the shoot. *The Last Roommate* was mostly scripted from index cards during the shoot, with each collaborator often writing into the night for those scenes to be shot and directed the following day.

If you're in the enviable position of having thought up a great feature film concept, and find that you still can't begin scripting no matter what approach you take, it is probably time to consider working with a collaborator.

Scripting by Collaboration

If you are able to remind yourself that all movies are a collaboration in some capacity, dependent on cast and crew working together toward a common goal, it shouldn't be difficult to imagine the possibility of sharing the job of scripting your feature with a friend or professional writer who believes in your concept. Although it will be necessary to pay your co-scriptwriter with either money (if available) or percentage points of future profit in the film, as well as share the glory if the film is successful, you'll quickly discover that the price you pay a collaborator is small compared to the overview he or she will offer. Once you have decided that you absolutely can't do it alone, you will want to carefully begin your search for a co-scriptwriter.

One of the most serious and wide-ranging decisions you will ever make in your creative life is whom you choose for a collaborator on your project. This decision can make, or break, your movie. Not only must you exercise extreme business acumen, but you must intuitively select a talented individual who will enhance your original concept without trying to own it, at the same time freely giving the best of his or her abilities toward your project. You want to pick a person who is as different from you as possible, with different experiences and insights, and who is at the same time compatible with you and your story. If you select someone outside of your small group of friends or associates, what you're basically doing is creatively marrying someone you know only from appearances and a few conversations. If you have a friend, male or female, who is not only very sympathetic to your concept, but also talented and available, you must still use extreme caution in making your final selection. If you fail in *any* way to define any aspect of your relationship, from amount of potential payment if the film succeeds to which name appears first on the film poster or credits, you stand a good chance of losing that friend during or after the production process. Before you choose a collaborator just because he or she is a friend and available, you may want to make an attempt to stretch your limits—by considering the possibility of working with a professional.

If you are a member of Film Arts Foundation (346 Ninth Street, 2nd Floor, San Francisco, CA 94103, [415] 552-8760, **<www.filmarts.org>**) and have paid your $35 yearly dues, you are eligible to place three small ads in their *Release Print* newsletter for free during the period of one year. It is not unusual to see ads from filmmakers who wish to collaborate on scripting of feature productions. You may want to advertise for a few months in order to see if you can meet a compatible scriptwriter by this means. FAF also offers an extensive file of filmmakers and their various skills, which you may want to review in search of potential collaborators.

911 Media Arts Center in Seattle (117 Yale Avenue North, Seattle, WA 98109, [206] 682-6552, **<www.911media.org>**) also offers its members free listings in the extensive resource guide they put out each month. So if you are searching for a collaborator, rustling up filmmaking equipment (or selling it), ready to enter film festivals with a completed film, or interested in a wide variety of workshops and screenings, give them a call and join up ($35 per year). You will also be eligible for discounts at many Seattle-area media companies and labs, quickly earning back your membership fee if you are actively making films.

On the East Coast, the Association of Independent Video and Filmmakers (AIVF) publishes a magazine called *Independent Film and Video Monthly* (304 Hudson Street, 6th Floor, New York, NY 10013, [212] 807-1400, **<www.aivf.org>**), which offers advertising for "Freelancers" and "Opportunities—Gigs" in its classified section. Your ad in this magazine for scriptwriting assistance would surely reach someone who would enjoy collaborating on a feature-length project. And if you don't live on either coast, you might try advertising in your local alternative newspaper or local film society newsletter. Another approach is to check out some Websites on the Internet that offer free postings of jobs and opportunities. Try **<www.mandy.com/1/filmtvjobs.cfm>**, or **<www.101hollywood.com/wwwboard.html>** (there are lots of these Internet posting sites!). Maybe you'll be lucky enough to spot an ad placed by someone who, like yourself, wants to be part of a scriptwriting collaboration.

Once you are satisfied that you have found a co-scriptwriter who will satisfy your needs both spiritually and technically, you will want to write out a simple contract that clearly states the facts of the collaboration. Appendix A shows a contract I wrote for my script collaboration with Mike Church on *The Attraction.* In this case Mike approached me with a body of essays he had written with my style of filmmaking in mind. I liked the writing very much and decided that the best way to proceed with a collaboration on scripting a feature film from the writings was to pay him a small option payment that I could afford ($100 a year) as his salary for the work he had already done. I also stipulated that an additional payment would be given to him if the film was produced, with a sliding scale of increased payment depending on the final shooting budget. I then outlined how our names would read on the credits ("Script by Michael Church and Richard R. Schmidt") and that he would receive an additional credit for his initial writing ("Original story by Michael Church"). In the last paragraph of the contract, I stated that Mike would receive 10 percent of the profits of the film if I was producer, outlined when each option payment would be paid, and stated clearly that I had purchased the right to direct, film, edit, and produce the film (originally titled *The Monopole Verification Experiments*) without restriction. With our signatures legally binding our collaboration, we wrote together for a year before completing the script at 118 pages. I greatly enjoyed receiving Mike's latest writing breakthroughs in the mail (you'll get yours by e-mail . . .), working with the new ideas, and then sending him my new writing. And whenever I was creatively stymied, Mike was able to resuscitate the script and vice versa. If you have emerged from a shared writing venture with a finished script, and your friendship is still intact, then you can definitely consider your collaboration a success.

Scripting with Software

For most of us who now use computers for writing (editing, e-mails, accounting, searching the WWW . . .), there are several great scriptwriting software products designed to make our lives easier with regard to formatting, creating reoccurring headings for settings and naming characters, and adjusting each page for ultimate readability and print-out. Movie Magic Screenwriter (cost around $300 from Screenplay Systems, Inc., [818] 843-6557, **<www.screenplay.com>**) not only helps you write in several different formats (film, sitcom, plays, and multimedia), but it also has a built-in electronic card system that allows you to build your script the old fashioned index card way and then reincorporate the actual writing back into the script-in-progress. And as you reshuffle your "cards," the scenes in your script are automatically changed as well. Screenplay Systems also offers an amazing writing software program called Dramatica Pro (priced around $400) that runs the user through a grid of questions and tasks that help the writer thrash out the story, characters, dramatic thrust of a script (or novel). It's fun to be bossed around by your software, following threads of plot and character development that suddenly and surprisingly lead to a completed piece (and everything you create can be imported directly into your Movie Magic formatted screenplay!). Screenplay Systems also offers cutting-edge software for Scheduling your movie ($899), and Budgeting ($899), but for most no-budget moviemakers there isn't much advantage to spending this kind of money to learn what you already know (you don't have enough time or enough money . . . what you need is to get crazy enough to go for it!).

Another great choice for ease of scriptwriting on your computer is

Movie Magic Screenwriter is a powerful writing tool when integrated with its companion software, Dramatica Pro (excellent for thrashing out story and characters for either scripts or novels).

Final Draft software ($299 from Final Draft, Inc., [800] 231-4055, **<www.finaldraft.com>**, with discounts available for educators and film students/inquire), which is the choice of top screenwriters like Syd Field, Lawrence Kasdan (*Body Heat*, *Grand Canyon*, *The Empire Strikes Back*, etc.), Christopher McQuarrie (*The Usual Suspects*), Sydney Pollack (*Three Days of the Condor*, *Out of Africa*, etc.), and also actor Tom Hanks. Final Draft's interface is extremely easy to understand and use, so that as soon as I installed the software and jumped in, I got the results I expected (character names and scene descriptions where they belonged, quick switches between tabs, fun without computer-style confusion). Final Draft also offers an Index Card and Outlining feature that lets the writer view his/her script interactively, check out scenes in the script, outline, or on simulated index cards. The Scene Navigator automatically upgrades any changes you make on the cards or in the out-

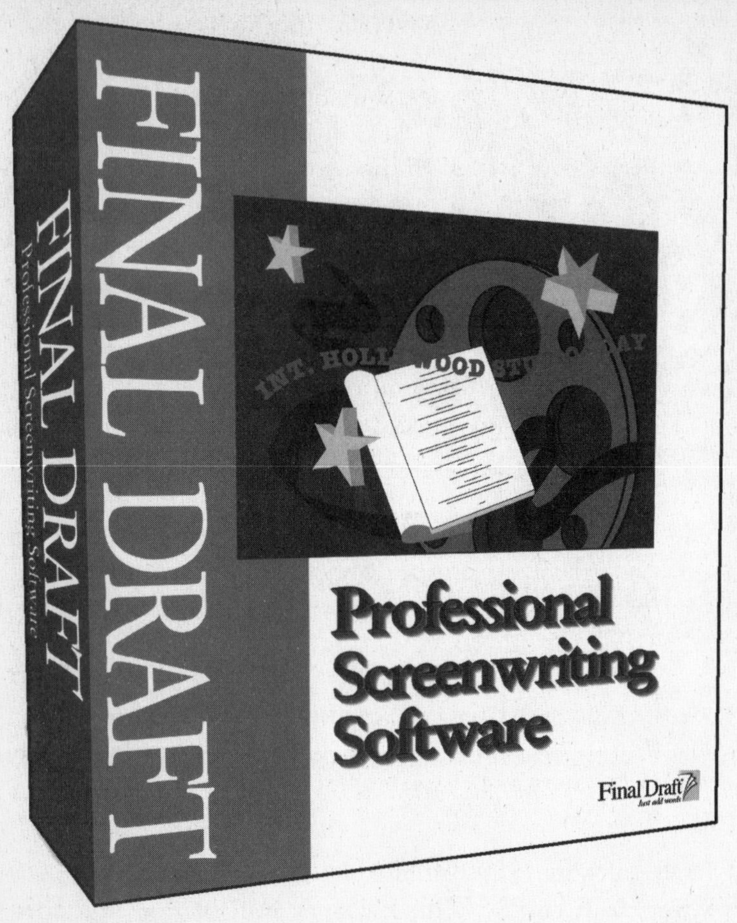

Final Draft Professional Screenwriting Software, an amazingly straightforward program for writing and compiling your script into a presentable package.

line, moving or adding scenes within the full script form. And you can print out the cards on laser-perforated index cards and pin them to your wall for an overview of your ever-shifting scriptwriting process.

If you don't have the deep pockets to invest part of your hard-earned no-budget monies on scriptwriting software, then you may be able to make use of a free writing template download off the Web.

Apotheosis Pictures (**<www.execpc.com/~jesser/>**) offers a free template for scriptwriting called Screen Forge. Or check out the Sophocles Screenwriting download at **<www.sophocles.net>**, which offers a very creative and useful interface for developing characters and dialogue, shifting scenes around to improve story structure.

Maybe you require a last minute aesthetic shock to the system before you launch into scripting, and need to be reminded about some of the common mistakes made by film students on their first movies. Go to **<www.filmmaker.com/dumps/>** for a heads-up moment of sobriety about all the pitfalls of your quest (as the Webmaster bluntly states it, "a very specific list of common mistakes and trends which we've seen in crappy student films again and again, at screening after screening"). This Website can save you a few years of meaningless debt and confusion.

And while we're discussing various software products that can aid the no-budget writer/director, it seems appropriate to recommend a fantastic new three-CD-ROM software product, *How to Make Your Movie* ($89.95, [614] 221-5626, **<www.interactivefilmschool. com>**), which gives an actual taste of what the filmmaking process is all about. With imaginative computer-enhanced visuals, QuickTime movies, and voice-overs, this inventive software (written, directed, and produced by noted filmmaker Rajko Grlić of Ohio University, with assistance from Electronic Vision) presents a seemingly deserted filmmaking facility in which various rooms represent different parts of the process. As you click your way up four flights of stairs, you find doors with signs that read RESEARCH ROOM, PRE-PRODUCTION ROOM, SCRIPT ROOM, PRODUCTION ROOM, POST-PRODUCTION ROOM, SCREENING ROOM, FILM GRAMMAR, EQUIPMENT ROOM, FILM HISTORY ROOM AND LIBRARY, FESTIVAL ROOM, basically all the facets of making movies. Wherever you click your mouse the screen comes alive; letters fly out of envelopes, film posters talk, QuickTime movies roll, files open to reveal a cascade of valuable information along with a cache of the basic filmmaking forms (location release, actor's release—all available for print-out). Also included in this dazzling display of computer fanfare are some contemplative moments, questions about life and art, that enhance this interactive experience.

Out of the hundreds of e-mails I've received since the 1995 revised

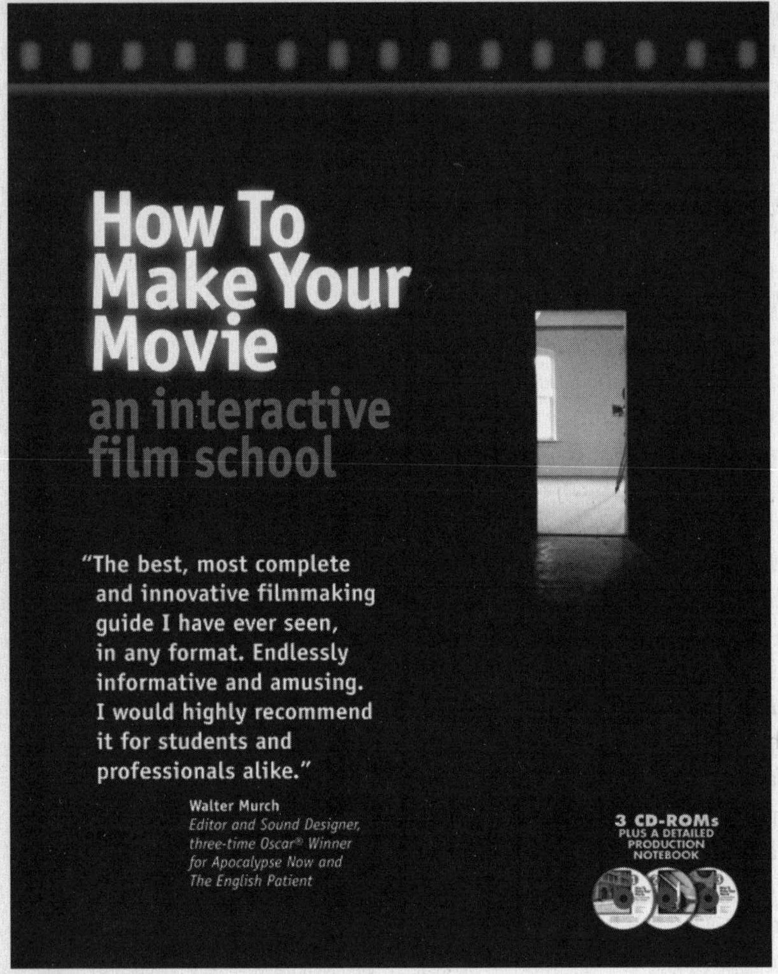

How To
Make Your
Movie
an interactive
film school
"The best, most complete and innovative filmmaking guide I have ever seen, in any format. Endlessly informative and amusing. I would highly recommend it for students and professionals alike."
Walter Murch
Editor and Sound Designer, three-time Oscar® Winner for Apocalypse Now and The English Patient
3 CD-ROMs
PLUS A DETAILED PRODUCTION NOTEBOOK

A three-CD-ROM software program, "How To Make Your Movie"—the perfect primer for anyone who's considering attending film school.

edition of *Feature Filmmaking . . .*, a good portion of the aspiring filmmakers have asked me whether or not they should bother to attend film school. My usual answer has been that by attending even one semester of some film classes they will at least make a few friends who can help them pull together their no-budget feature (and vice versa). Short of that, *How to Make Your Movie* is guaranteed to deliver a realistic first taste of the film school experience and inspire anybody considering a writing/directing career.

Finalizing Your Script

Often a commercial scriptwriter must rewrite his or her script several times until it satisfies his producer, agent, and possible stars of the production. But when you write for a feature that you will produce (at used-car prices), the only one you have to satisfy is yourself. Since you will continually be able to make contributions to your movie throughout the shooting and editing, your script need not be complete in every detail. If you have been honest in your feelings toward your subject matter, and truthful to your intuition while writing, you probably have created at least a viable outline from which to shoot your feature.

After you have completed the first draft of your script, place it aside for a few days and give yourself some distance from the material. Then read it over with an eye toward possible improvements you could make to increase the power and clarity of what you've already written. During this review process you may also think up new scenes, but your main focus is on finalizing your script.

If you are not a professional scriptwriter, it's probably not worth having someone else read your work at this point, since your writing most likely only reveals a tapestry of your ideas and feelings that will be made complete during the remainder of the production process. If, on the other hand, you desire to create a fully commercial script, incorporating all elements of dialogue and story necessary to fulfill a reader's needs, then you must understand that you have actually embarked on the career of a scriptwriter instead of that of a filmmaker. You may see the years slip by as you change a line here, a word there, fine-tuning your script into oblivion. Don't let the writer in you forsake the need to shoot the movie. If you are the rare individual who can not only write a commercial script over a several-year period but also take the chance of shooting the script on a hairline budget, then I applaud you. What usually happens, though, is that the several years of scripting somehow work to convince the filmmaker that he or she must go for a bigger production budget. I've seen friends spend several years trying to sell their commercial script, even getting their project to the point of being listed for the next year's production by a major studio, only to see their title erased from the blackboard when their contact at the studio is fired. While creating a finished script in any form is quite an accomplishment, it is important to withhold some measure of self-satisfaction until the feature has actually been produced.

Strangely enough, at this final stage of writing a script, you also need to ask yourself the same question that readers at major film studios ask: "Do I love this script enough to recommend it for actual production?" Certainly, most no-budget scripts written in unique styles, with "no story," wouldn't seem appropriate for production at a major studio whose audience must be drawn from a huge cross section of America. Someone at the studio has to love the script being considered for production, love its potential for monetary success. In your case, as a no-budget feature filmmaker, you must be much purer in your demands on the scripted materials. You should love the story, dialogue, characters, locations, the way that the writing touches upon important truths that you want to share with the world. You can love your script because it is uniquely funny or fascinating. You can even love it because it will lead you into new worlds of people and places where access wouldn't normally be granted if you weren't shooting a movie. But as a final verification, to make sure that you didn't write your script for the wrong reasons, read over your writing to see if it truly comes from your heart.

In parts of East Africa, when people see each other on the street, they grasp hands and give the familiar greeting, "Do you love yourself today?" If one answers "No," then the other person keeps a firm grip on his or her hand and asks a laundry list of questions. "Is it your husband or wife? Your children? Money? Health?" The questioner holds tight until he or she gets a suitable response. So ask yourself, "*Do you love your script today?*" If not, why not? Is there something wrong with your choice of story? Is the dialogue clunky? Did you write it with a conviction worthy enough to put yourself and your family through the hell (and expense) of production? Now's the time to face your work and make sure that your writing is worth rendering into film (or DV). Even if what you've written isn't, in itself, great, you may have a strong enough personal motive for making the movie that your drive to express these feelings will override any and all logical reasons for abandoning the project. If that is the case, I say, "Go for it." Only doubt yourself if your intention is just to earn money or to elevate your status to that of "film director." Tell the truth. I'm holding your hand firmly in mine. Soon we'll be past this uncomfortable moment. Do you love your script today?

The Shooting Script

The final step toward more completely visualizing your script as a movie is to add instructions for the shoot. You will want to add notes regarding camera angles and movement, possible cuts, needed sound effects, anything that will help you make these important decisions during production. Don't worry if you aren't experienced enough as a moviemaker to be able to write this information down at one sitting. Not all directors can totally visualize their entire feature before they shoot. The process of developing the shooting script can take several months as you work in preproduction to find locations and select actors. Rumor has it that Orson Welles screened John Ford's movie *Stagecoach* fifty times before going into production with *Citizen Kane.* We all need inspiration for our work, so if you don't have any idea of how or what to shoot, start by seeing some of the classic movies that are available on videotape. Go to your nearest video store and rent films such as *Grand Illusion*, *L'Atalante*, *Zero for Conduct*, *Le Testament d'Orphée*, *Modern Times*, *Metropolis*, *8½*, *The Battle of Algiers*, *Wild Strawberries*, *Citizen Kane*, *À Bout de Souffle* (*Breathless*), and any film by John Cassavetes. Or rent (buy!) an early NO-budget feature by filmmaker Jon Jost, in particular one entitled *Last Chants for a Slow Dance* (available at: Facets Multimedia, 1517 West Fullerton Avenue, Chicago, IL 60614, [800] 331–6197, <**www.facets.org**>), if you want to (1) see a great, true indie feature (not the "low-budget" *The English Patient*–type indie that cost millions . . .), (2) be enveloped by a movie made up of just eight set-piece scenes, long takes that deliver great drama and magic (see "The Long Take," chapter 5), (3) witness a movie that was shot virtually 1:1 (he shot just *eight* 400′ rolls of 16-mm footage), (4) understand how wonderful and inventive a film can be that cost only around $3,500 to produce (he edited without a work print, spliced the long takes of original together and printed!). And check out the gritty realism of veteran indie filmmaker Rob Nilsson's *Chalk* (<**www.chalkfilm.org**>), made in collaboration with his Tenderloin Action Group. Or see Christopher E. Brown's breakthrough feature *Metal* (<**adryenn@21stcentury.org**>), which film scholar Ray Carney has called "one of the best films in the last ten years." A different Chris Brown of the Bay Area has also made an important indie feature, *Daughters* (<**cbrown@infinex.com**>), that shows the power of "small" human moments told sparingly with much heart and filmmaking expertise. And don't miss *A Little Stiff* by Greg Watkins and Caveh Zahedi (<**cavehz@earthlink.net**>), a true no-budget comedy of high invention and glorious revelations. Another must-see is yahn soon's *Learning to Crawl* (<**yahnsoon@earthlink.net**>), which should put to rest anyone's doubt as to the viability of shooting a visually gripping and touching B&W no-budget feature on DVCAM. Watch the use of the camera, the framing, the cuts. Listen for the sounds and music that create the atmosphere for the stories to unfold. With inspiration high, it's time to move into the world of production.

note: Your final script or creative outline should also be registered with the Writers Guild of America, West, Inc. (<**www.wga.org**>), for copyright protection. Cost for script registration is $20. As with the treatment registration, you should include a title page listing the title of the script, author(s), and blanks for registration date and number.

3 Beginning

In the world of big-budget feature filmmaking, only a few of the many hundreds of scripts optioned each year by film companies are chosen for actual production. In 1998 the Writers Guild of America, West, Inc., received more than 37,000 treatments/concepts/scripts to register for copyright protection. Given the fact that fewer than 500 commercial feature films are usually produced in the United States each year, one can see that the odds are very high that most scripts will remain only scripts. Instead of fighting these nearly impossible odds, the low-budget independent filmmaker has the power to take a script or outline right into production, without anyone else's approval. For the price of a used car—plus enormous amounts of determination, hard work, and enthusiasm—you can make your idea for a feature film into a reality.

For the low-budget filmmaker, the first and most crucial step is telling yourself and your friends that you are going to make a feature film. Because the idea of making a film always generates excitement, you'll probably find that people around you will respond with laughter, amazement, and then great enthusiasm. For a while, you may feel that your friends believe in your movie more strongly than you do, but as you go on talking about it, the project will start taking on a life of its own. When people start volunteering to become involved in your production, you'll realize that by wishing out loud, you've already come a long way toward willing your feature into existence. At that point you'll need to do a little reality check.

Defining Your Production Limitations

Is it really this easy to begin your movie? The answer is yes—as long as your concept and script are tailored to the limitations of a used-car budget (see chapter 1) and both you and everyone involved in the project are prepared to work within the special constraints of a super-low-budget production.

If you're making a feature film at used-car prices, almost all of your budget will be eaten up by the irreducible costs of renting equipment and purchasing and processing enough filmstock to produce at least seventy minutes of usable footage. Even with every price break imaginable from the lab, you shouldn't expect to be able to shoot more than fourteen 400′ rolls of film (of course with a DV production [see chapter 11] the low cost of videocassettes allows for almost unlimited shooting capabilities). This means that you will be able to shoot two and a half hours of film, out of which you will cut a feature somewhere between seventy and ninety minutes long. Because of this two-to-one shooting ratio, you must attempt to shoot every scene right on the first try and then move on to the next shot. If there is a technical problem or a disastrous mistake by actors, then and *only* then can you afford to reshoot the scene. You and everyone who works with you must be prepared, both psychologically and practically, to do the best possible job with this nerve-racking shooting ratio.

To be able to afford to rent a high-quality 16-mm camera (Eclair, Aaton, Arriflex, CP-16) that delivers the sharp and consistent image necessary for potential sales or possible blowup to 35-mm, you'll probably have to do most of your filming on weekends when special rates are available. Many equipment-rental outfits will offer weekend rentals (from Friday afternoon to Monday noon) for a one-day rental price. If you're shooting on weekends, your location must be easily accessible to all the people involved with the production. And you'll have to use your shooting time on location very efficiently to minimize the costs of travel, food, and equipment rental.

Even with all these economies, you'll have very little (if any) money in your budget to pay actors or a production crew. Is this an insurmountable problem? Not at all. But it does require some careful planning—and some powerful incentives—from the beginning.

note: Keep in mind, as you read on, that unless you're willing to go to the wall with your own financial resources and physical capabilities, performing a slew of filmmaking tasks yourself (from writer to production manager, location scout, casting director, cinematographer, director, editor, and publicist, etc.), and are ready to give up the lion's share of profit points by contract for when the movie sells, you shouldn't even consider asking others to participate in your "no-budget" venture.

The most minimal crew for a feature film that requires lighting and sound recording will have to include the filmmaker/cameraman (and after reading chapter 5, you should have gained enough confidence to shoot your film yourself), a good soundperson with sound-recording equipment, and a camera assistant to help the filmmaker place lights and take light readings, sync up scenes with a clapboard, load and clean the camera between takes, and cope with dozens of other production chores. The sound recordist is usually the most expensive member of a low-budget crew, and he or she shouldn't be expected to work on anything except getting the best possible sound. It would be nice to be able to afford a production manager to organize all the details of the shoot for you, but in this super-low-budget situation, you'll have to do this yourself, perhaps with the help of your camera assistant. You'll also have to edit your feature yourself, with some input from other people you invite to view and critique your rough cut.

Fortunately, many professional actors, as well as most amateurs, are willing to do almost anything, including paying their own expenses, to star in a feature film of any budget—as long as they respect the story and the filmmaker. Still, it's wise to pay each of the cast members, as well as every member of the crew, at least a small daily stipend of $20 or so to help insure that they will take the production seriously enough to show up on time every day, with their equipment or costumes, ready to work hard for the production.

This small daily stipend, which doesn't even approach the minimum wage, will not in itself be enough to convince expert cast and crew members that they should give all their energy to your production. You'll have to give them a share in the potential profits of the feature so that they'll at least have the assurance of being well paid if the movie is a success.

Profit Sharing

Profit sharing is the most powerful persuasive tool of the filmmaker whose budget lacks the vital ingredient of ready cash. Once you realize that the only way you can make your film is with the help of talented people you can't afford to pay, you should be able to give away a large percentage of your potential profits and feel good about it. If you are receiving all or most of your small budget from one or more investors who have demanded 50 percent of the profits from the film, you may have to give away half or more of your remaining 50 percent. But if this is what it takes to make your feature, you should have no qualms about doing it. Profit sharing is the only financial incentive you have to offer potential cast and crew members.

And it can be a powerful one. When I assigned my soundman friend Neelon Crawford 5 percent of the profits of *1988—The Remake*, he was very impressed, because he'd never heard of a soundman receiving even 1 percent of the profits of a feature. And I felt good about promising him a generous share of the film because I knew I would have to depend heavily upon his expert sound recording for that production.

It's fun to be generous with numbers on a piece of paper, but keep in mind that low-budget features have been known to earn millions of dollars. If yours is next year's big hit, all those points of profit will turn into cash. My friend Wayne Wang gave most of the profit points from his hit feature *Chan Is Missing* to the cast and crew, leaving himself with under 20 percent of his own film. Be careful! But if you are the kind of filmmaker/director who believes in working your cast and crew until they are ready to drop, you had better be prepared to give away a lion's share.

Deferred Payment

Some professional cast and crew members may request that you pay them their usual high salary in the form of a "deferred payment," so that they will be guaranteed their salary from first monies received from the finished film (see appendix C, deal memorandum for *Morgan's Cake*). Contracts vary as to exactly when the deferred payments will be forthcoming. The best and most honorable way for a producer to regard these payments is as real debts of the film, to be paid out of first monies received by the film company, without any deductions subtracted for various distribution or operating costs. If the producer/director has worked for free alongside everyone else, he or she would not want to spend weekends writing checks for everyone while sitting penniless wondering how to pay the rent, and must include his or her own deferred salary in the contract. Once the schedule of payments is agreed upon, and it is written in the contract that your soundman/woman will receive $750 per day for on-location recording (the going rate for top soundpeople), the cameraman/woman $1,200 per day, and so on, you should be able to afford the best technicians and actors that money (or, in this case, lack of money) can buy.

Sometimes you will want to write a contract that includes a combination of deferred salary and profit percents as incentives for working on your production. Looking over the contract for *Emerald Cities* (appendix B), you will notice that not only is there a list of percents to be paid in the event that the film is profitable, but also that deferred cash salaries are indicated for some members of cast and crew. Had I not been able to pay less than half of the camera rental fee up front to Bill Kimberlin, I couldn't have afforded to shoot on location in Death Valley. And in some cases, like the deferred salary for soundman Nick Bertoni, the small amount of payment reflects my need to give him a monetary "gift," not the actual salary he could command on another production. He was helping me out of his love for a friend, and money was never an issue. At best, the writing of your contract will be an outpouring of love and thanks in the form of monetary rewards for those people who help you make your film become a reality.

Some film producers would rather not deal with the idea of being caught in a situation of paying percents of profit from their film, writing checks quarterly, and at times getting phone calls in the middle of the night from workers wondering when they will be paid again. If you don't like the idea of being the focus of cast and crew members for the rest of your life (if your film is a hit), then assign "top dollar" amounts for their deferred payments, and honor these production debts from first monies earned by the finished feature.

The Contract

The best tool I know for beginning the process of willing your feature film into existence is the contract. Writing a contract forces the filmmaker to start making the kind of decisions that will result in a concrete plan of action. What will be the name of the production company (under what title will you be doing business)? How much will the film cost to shoot on location? What will be the total budget, including editing and print costs? What cast and crew members will I need and what payment will they receive, in cash or percentage points, for their participation?

By thinking seriously enough about all these issues to be able to draft a contract, you will be forced to develop a detailed plan for organizing your film project. And once it is written, the contract will become a powerful force for conjuring the film into existence. By transforming your hopes and dreams into a legal document, the contract will help generate the momentum that will carry your film through to completion. Here's an example: When I wrote the contract for *Emerald Cities*, I didn't actually have the $5,000 I'd committed myself to raising in order to begin production with a five-day shoot starting on or about December 15, 1979. As this date approached and the pressure on me increased, I worked harder and harder to raise that money, asking everyone I could think of for help, even selling my used car (a 1939 Dodge pickup) to force a cash flow. Amazingly, a series of minor miracles eventually brought me the money I needed to begin production by the deadline. Without the self-created but very real pressure exerted by that contract, *Emerald Cities* might have remained only a dream.

Besides serving as a powerful incentive for the filmmaker himself, the contract is also a very effective device for persuading other people, from potential investors to prospective cast and crew members, that the film is a viable project, not merely an idle fantasy. When I showed up at the first class of my CCAC "Feature Filmmaking at Used-Car Prices" workshop with a contract that every class member was to sign, it immediately convinced them that, although we were meeting as a class, we were actually agreeing to collaborate in the serious endeavor of creating a feature film (see appendix D). A carefully drafted contract will have the same effect on all the people you'll need to help you make your film.

Each contract for a feature film must be carefully designed to fit the particular needs of the production. For a low-budget film, the contract should be simplified to be as straightforward as the production itself. Although each contract will reflect a different set of production needs, all have a number of important features in common.

Contract Checklist

- ☐ The contract uses legal terms that are universally accepted.
- ☐ The filmmaker is identified as *doing business as* a "film company" for the production of a feature-length movie *tentatively entitled* ______________ (*name of film here*).
- ☐ The movie is described as 16-mm gauge (or other applicable format), color or black-and-white, and as a feature-length motion picture film (or video if you go the DV route).
- ☐ Everyone who will participate in the production of the movie is listed by name and job title, and the amount of payment to each person is clearly stated.
- ☐ The contract stipulates that those people working on the production will *not* receive any payment unless they complete their jobs.
- ☐ Usually, the length of the shooting schedule is declared and identified by dates, as is the total amount of time needed to complete the project. It is important to state this timetable so that members of the cast and crew will know when their participation is required, and it's also important to any investors who must know the (tenta-

tive) release date of your feature for tax purposes. The word *approximate* is used when describing these dates so that the moviemaker is legally protected from being overly optimistic.

☐ Each person who commits to becoming involved in the production has signed the contract on the line with his or her name printed below, and has written the date and location of signature.

☐ The contract lists the order of payback to investors, lab, cast and crew, etc.

The most important words in a contract are *upon completion of services* and the terms *gross* or *net.* You must include a clause stating that if the work isn't completed, then the person who fails to do the work will not share in the rewards. And if your cast and crew are to receive a percentage of the *gross* profits, they will receive their money from the total amount of dollars earned, before any is spent on overhead costs and other expenses. If your helpers receive a portion of the *net* profits from your film, then they receive their percent of profits after you deduct reasonable expenses for such things as limited promotion and advertising, travel to a few film festivals, and replacement print costs.

If, as I've suggested, you are drawing up a contract as your first major step in the filmmaking process, your first draft will have to approximate some entries such as the length of the shoot and the budget for the movie. You will probably begin with a list of job descriptions and rates of pay for cast and crew members, with blanks left for the names of the people you will later find to fill these roles in your production. If you decide to use my contracts as models for your feature, you should still consult with a lawyer who is knowledgeable in entertainment law. Tell him the amount of your budget and ask if he can help you draw up a very basic contract. Or at least let him review the contract you draw up on your own using my examples. Because a contract must stand up to the possibility that a movie might earn hundreds of thousands of dollars, it is very important that every point accurately reflects your wishes.

The contracts for my first two features were drawn up by a lawyer in San Francisco, Peter Buchanan, who specialized in motion picture law. When I first went to him and announced that I was planning to produce a feature film for $11,000, he was shocked, saying that he had never heard of such a low budget. He then helped me with the contract, for a token fee of $100 (a portion of his hourly rate).

Budget

After you have drawn up your contract, the next step is to prepare a detailed budget, so that you will be able to plan exactly how much you can do—and how many corners you will have to cut—to produce your film with the amount of money you have or can raise. To help you see how to fine-tune the budget for your own film, I'll take you through the various steps that will empower you to do your feature within a $12,000 budget.

Film production prices are continually subject to change, but one thing never changes: To create a feature film at used-car prices, you *must* get the maximum price break from your lab. To do this low-budget filming, you must let people know you are making a feature film for the same price as the average American used car—$12,000. After they stop laughing, they will probably do everything in their power to help you succeed.

Filming Costs

As I've mentioned in earlier chapters, most of your used-car budget will be eaten up by irreducible costs: equipment rentals, minimum salaries, food and transportation costs, and filmstock, with the biggest bite out of your budget coming from lab expenses. While filmstock may be purchased from the lab, a large savings can be made by dealing directly with the distributor (Kodak, Fuji, etc.) unless the lab offers a blanket deal on all lab costs for your project (discussed later in this chapter). After the lab develops your footage, charging you the "processing" fee of so many cents per foot, you will probably need to have them print another copy of your film, a low-quality "work print" from which you can edit your feature without the risk of scratching or damaging your precious original footage. Because the lab must supply filmstock, make a contact print from your original, and process the results, the work print is very expensive.

There is also some expenditure required for the production of a high-quality sound track. After the soundperson records your location "sync" sound on ¼″ tape using the high-quality Nagra recorder, these tapes must be "transferred" to 16-mm gauge sound track ("mag track") for editing purposes.

Here's our first estimate for the filming costs alone.*

16-mm Shooting Budget (Film Edit)

14 rolls (400′) Kodak Color #7277 ($151.91/roll)	$2,126.74
14 rolls 1/4″ sound recording tape ($7/roll)	$ 98.00
Camera rental package (2 weekends @ $350 ea.) (includes camera, magazines, battery belt, lights, light meter, lenses, power cables, tripod, everything needed to shoot)	$ 700.00
Soundperson with Nagra recorder ($250/weekend)	$ 500.00
Camera assistant ($100/weekend)	$ 200.00
Actors' fees ($100/weekend for 2 actors)	$ 400.00
Food for 2 weekends for cast and crew (60 meals)	$ 250.00
Transportation (gas)	$ 30.00
Processing of filmstock ($.15/ft.) 5,600′	$ 840.00
16-mm work print for editing ($.32/ft.) 5,600′	$1,792.00
Transfer cost from 1/4″ tape to mag track ($50/hr.)	$ 150.00
5 1,200′ rolls mag track for 1/4″ transfer ($50/roll)	$ 250.00
	$7,336.74

Just to complete our two-weekend shoot and process the results we would have already spent $7,336.74 of our $12,000 budget. And we haven't begun to budget editing and determine final projection print

**Prices quoted in shooting and editing budgets vary greatly from lab to lab. It's up to the filmmaker to negotiate with his or her hometown lab (Monaco {San Francisco}, Duart {New York City}, or?) to get these prices reduced down to the lowest cost possible. Taxes also vary state to state and have not been included in this budget, or those that follow.*

cost, which usually alone runs above $3,000. Even with actors handling their own makeup, costumes, and props, we are at least a couple of thousand dollars over our budget even before we add in editing costs.

Could we retrieve the $1,100 total we assigned for the sound person, camera assistant, and actors and still have a production? Only by deferring these salaries could we hope to complete such a low-budget feature film. And if each person ate breakfast before leaving home for the filming, so the production only paid for a good lunch and beverages ($30) on location, we could probably reduce the food budget to four lunches for five people (twenty meals) at a cost of $6 per meal and save $100. Each person who worked on the production could still receive a $20-a-day salary so that at least the filming wouldn't cost them money out of their own pockets. For the four days of filming, that would cost the production $80 per person. Two actors, a soundperson, and a camera assistant would then cost the production only $320 for two weeks, saving $780 from the $1,100 originally allotted for salaries. With this savings of cash from the salaries and food costs ($780 + $100 = $880) plus the remaining funds up to our full $12,000 budget ($4,663.26), we would still have only $5,543.26 remaining, barely enough to edit and complete the film (funds will be needed for editing on flatbed, shooting titles, mixing sound, conforming original for printing, and final print costs!).

If each person in the cast and crew was generous enough to forfeit his or her salary and work for the $20-per-day stipend, then they would each deserve to share in the profits of the film. Each of my features abounds in examples of this type of profit sharing, and I'm sure the reader will be able to offer his or her helpers a generous share of the pie. I gave 60 percent away on *A Man, a Woman, and a Killer*, 82 percent on *1988—The Remake*, and 75 percent on *Emerald Cities.* Without my friends' help, I would not have been able to even begin these projects.

With lab and filmstock costs rising all the time, it's obvious that the first-time no-budget feature filmmaker can't really afford to shoot in color. With Kodak 7222 black-and-white negative stock ($77.30/400′ roll), the cost of fourteen rolls is reduced from $2,126.74 (color negative #7277) to $1,082.20, saving the production a crucial

$1,044.54 (lab fees of processing and work printing are relatively identical for black-and-white or color). This raises our sum of available funds to $6,537.80, at least within range of our editing costs.

Another possible way to reduce our budget is to forgo our work print, saving $1,792 (5,600′ @ 32 cents/ft.). If your film will be made up of several long takes, which reduces the actual handling of the negative film, this option could be seriously considered. (Because long takes can be pieced together into a film without the considerable handling that short takes require, there is less risk of damage.) But if your first-time effort will require a lot of editing to overcome the vast quantity of unknowns you will most certainly face, then you should spend the money on a work print to avoid damaging the original footage. Another possibility is to make your work print only after you've eliminated all the original footage you know is unusable. This could save close to a third of the work print budget. Using this projection, we could add another $597 ($1,792 ÷ 3) to our production budget, giving us up to $7,134.80 for editing and final print costs of a black-and-white feature.

Shooting Budget (for Computer Edit)

For those of you who are determined to edit your movie with the new computer software tools now available, including Adobe Premiere, Final Cut Pro, Canopus DVRex, Avid Xpress and Showcase, EditDV, etc. (see chapter 11), here's a budget that reflects the lab expenditures for producing a time-code/key-code video work print from your film original (NOTE: this budget retains its full salary costs for actors and technicians, plus a full food budget, and does not include tax).

16-mm Shooting Budget (for Computer Edit)

14 rolls Kodak Color #7277 ($151.91/roll)	$2,126.74
14 rolls 1/4″ sound recording tape ($7/roll)	$ 98.00
Camera package (2 weekends @ $350 ea.)	$ 700.00
Sound person with Nagra, mikes, mixer $250/weekend)	$ 500.00

Camera assistant/gaffer ($100/weekend)	$ 200.00
Actors' fees ($100/weekend for 2 actors)	$ 400.00
Food for 2 weekends (60 meals total for cast and crew)	$ 250.00
Transportation (gas)	$ 30.00
Lighting package (various lights, reflectors, dolly, etc.)	$ 400.00
Processing filmstock ($.15/ft. [5,600′] plus tax)	$ 840.00
Prepare film original for video work print transfer ($.025/ft.)	$ 147.56
Cue rolls for Edge-Write (included)	0
Betacam SP MOS (silent) transfer ($185/hr. × 8.5)	$1,572.50
Syncing 1/4″ sound to Betacam SP masters ($90/hr. × 9.75)	$ 877.50
Betacam SP stock (4 60-min. tapes/$46.20 ea. and tax)	$ 184.80
	$8,327.10

Editing Costs

Once you have in your hands the work print and mag track from your film (videotape or DVD work print!), you should feel confident that it will be possible to edit your feature together regardless of the obstacles that lack of money can present. After you learn how to make a tape splice and are able to "sync up" your picture and sound track (see chapter 6 on editing), you should have identification numbers printed on your sync rolls ("edge numbers") to insure that you can't lose your sync during editing. With a number at each foot of synced-up film and corresponding mag track, you have the capability of shifting footage without worry. Unless you have shot your film in long takes that require little or no editing, I recommend spending this money for your peace of mind. Another expense of editing may be the rental of a flatbed editing machine. This machine shows your film on a screen and plays your sound track, so that you can see how your edit is progressing. Once your film has been edited into the most cohesive and dynamic form possible, you will need to "mix" your sound track, adjusting the volume (sound level) and tone (equalization) of every shot. This procedure can also become very expensive, but with the help of this book you should accomplish the mix in eight to twelve hours for a feature-length film. Your mix prepares the sound track for your *projection print,* referred to by the lab as your "answer print." The picture is prepared for printing by matching your original footage to each piece of edited work print and splicing the original together in a "checkerboard" pattern on two separate "A" and "B" rolls, using black leader between shots (see the section entitled "Conforming Original for Printing" in chapter 6). The answer print is the final result of your best picture and sound quality, ready for projection, and is usually the largest lab expense.

Now that you are somewhat familiar with the terms used for editing procedures, let's look at editing costs we would normally encounter after shooting is completed:

Editing Budget (16-mm)

Edge number 5,600′ picture, 5,600′ mag track ($.015/ft.)	$ 168.00
Flatbed editing machine ($600/month for 3 months)	$ 1,800.00
Titles (if not shot on location while filming)	$ 500.00
Editing tape (10 rolls picture tape @ $11.50/roll)	$ 115.00
(10 rolls sound tape @ $10.50/roll)	$ 105.00
Sound mix (10 hrs. @ $185/hr., plus $150 for mag)	$ 2,000.00
Conforming (matching original to work print 90 hrs. @ $30/hr.)	$ 2,700.00
Black leader (3,000′ for conforming "AB" rolls)	$ 300.00
Answer print ("A" and "B" rolls, sound, 80 min., 2,880′ B&W @ $1.30/ft.)	$ 3,744.00
	$11,432.00

Again it is all too obvious that we are way over budget. And while there is no way to erase the cost of our answer print, there are, fortunately, ways to reduce some of the other editing costs.

We really can't afford to pay $1,800 for the rent of a flatbed editing machine for a solid three months. One way of reducing this cost might be to edit at a nearby art school or college film department by enrolling in a class. Hopefully, you will be able to complete your feature film by editing on the school's flatbed machine after hours while, at the same time, getting college credit to satisfy parents' or career demands. You may be able to book time at "alternative" editing facilities such as the Film Arts Foundation in San Francisco ([415] 552–6350), where you could edit on a flatbed for a half day (twelve hours of day or night) for a fee of $35 if you're an FAF member ($50 for 24 hours, or $140 for a full week). By grabbing small amounts of affordable editing time, you would be able to constantly refine your film as your budget permits.

Build an Editing Bench

Another possible solution is to build an editing bench in your house for a cost of about $150. The drawing on page 61 shows the dimensions of an editing bench I built to fit in a space usually reserved for a washer and dryer. This 64″-long editing bench represents the shortest-length bench possible that can still accommodate the largest 2,000′ reels along with editing equipment (synchronizer, Moviescope, sound reader). The simplest way I found to build my bench is to make careful measurements of the space it will occupy and have the 2″-by-4″ structural boards precut at the lumberyard. (Make sure your measurements are, if anything, 1/8″ larger than the space, to insure a tight fit. If your editing bench isn't enclosed by two walls, you will need to add a support leg; see photo on page 60. After the boards are cut, lay them on the ground as they will be nailed together, to check them for overall measurements and to make sure that boards with the same length are cut correctly. Once home, you can nail your 2 × 4s together with glue on each joint and nail the whole structure to the walls. If you set the height of the 2 × 4 structure at around 34″, then your countertop will be about 38″ from the floor. This has been a good position for me (at 6′ tall) for either sitting on a stool or standing at the editing bench.

Once your 2 × 4 structure is nailed into place, the next step is to

Turn a washer/dryer alcove into an editing workstation.

2″-by-4″ wood structure for "do-it-yourself" editing bench.

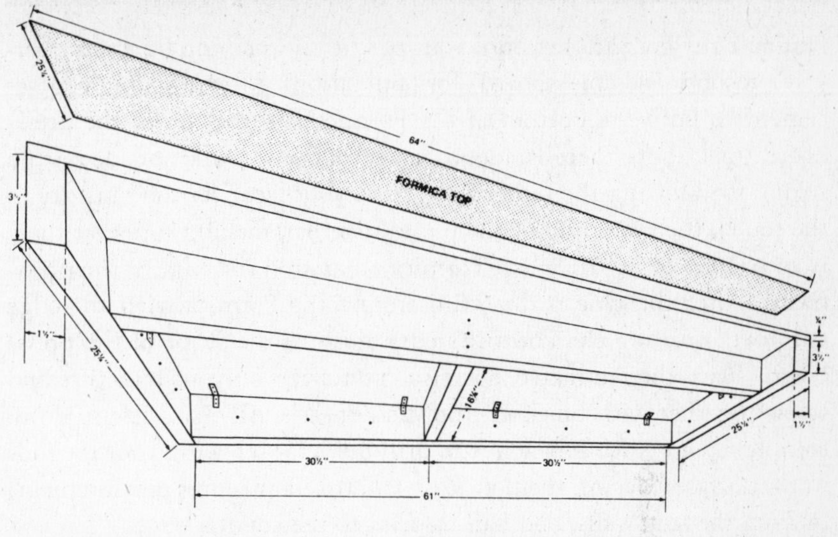

Editing bench plans.

Sound speaker, Moviescope and sound reader, synchronizer, rewinds—everything you need to edit movies with film work print and mag track.

laminate the Formica top onto your precut plywood top (most lumberyards recommend "pressboard" for lamination). After applying contact cement to both the bottom of the Formica and the top of the pressboard (make sure there is adequate ventilation—work outside with a strong fan blowing the fumes away from your face), let the glue dry to the touch, then carefully fit the pieces together, making sure that there is an overlap of 1/4″ to 1/2″ of Formica all around the edge of the pressboard. After the glue is dry, trim around the Formica with an "edge trimmer," making the Formica's edge flush to the shape of the pressboard. Place the laminated Formica countertop on your structure and screw together with brackets from underneath. All that's left to do to complete your editing bench is to drill holes for screwing your rewinds to the surface, placing them at least 10″ (to their center measurement) in from the side walls, and nail on trim to the counter edge.

List of Materials (Editing Bench)

1 ¾″ pressboard sheet, 25¼″ × 64″
Board lumber (no. 2 and better grade):
- 2 2″ × 4″ × 61″
- 2 2″ × 4″ × 25¼″
- 1 2″ × 4″ × 16¼″

1 Formica sheet (white), 26″ × 65″ (trim to pressboard)
Contact cement (1 quart), cheap brush
"Edge trimmer" (cost approx. $35) for Formica
3½″ nails, white glue, brackets for top
1 ½″ × 1½″ × 64″ (wooden trim for front of counter)
1″ finishing nails and filler for nail holes
1 pint white acrylic paint for trim and 2″ × 4″ structure

If you don't like carpentry, then perhaps you could purchase a sturdy table that would satisfy these needs. To edit with this kind of arrangement, you would need to purchase (or rent) rewinds to reel the film from head to tail; a Moviescope to view the images on a small, 4″ screen; a sound reader and small speaker to hear the sound from your mag track; a "synchronizer" to keep picture and sound track synced up; reels to hold the film and mag track; locks to keep the reels together while rewinding; spacers between reels; a tape splicer; and small accessories such as a marker pen, grease pencil, and a razor blade. I edited my first two features with this basic equipment, screening the footage as often as possible to check my results. You should be able to purchase the equipment listed above, in used condition, for about $400 to $600. Check ads in film newsletters and magazines (*Release Print, Independent Film and Video Monthly*), on bulletin boards at your lab, nearby film school, FAF, AIVF, or 911 Media Center in Seattle, and on the WWW to find the best deal on equipment.

Total Used-Car Budget (Film Edit)

As far as reducing other editing cost goes, the sound mix is an expense that is almost impossible to avoid. I've found that sometimes the cheapest mixing can end up costing you more money and aggravation in the long run. I'll discuss this whole topic more fully in the editing chapter, but for now I want to emphasize that a high-quality sound mix is vital to the film you are producing. Sometimes it is possible to gain access to a mixing studio in a film school, but without the help of a skilled technician, your results will surely be disappointing.

One large cost that we *can* radically reduce is the $2,700 budgeted for conforming the original for printing. Although cutting the original film and splicing it together for printing is a task that requires careful attention to detail, and usually takes a couple of weeks to accomplish for a feature-length film, it is certainly within each person's reach to learn the process. In the editing chapter I'll show you how to do it yourself—and save almost $3,000.

Working within our total used-car budget of $12,000, even with the reductions of cost in flatbed editing and conforming, the $6,932 remaining ($11,432 – $1,800 – $2,700) for editing our film (see page 58) barely covers the cost of a sound mix and one answer print. It's time to take another look at the total budget, including the cost of the shoot, to determine what other reductions we can make without jeopardizing the success of our project. If we only shot twelve 400′ rolls of B&W film instead of the fourteen rolls of color as budgeted on page 54, the savings from less filmstock, processing, and work printing would be $1,589.14. And with this twenty-two-minute reduction in footage we could cut back on mag track needed for transfer from ¼″ sound rolls, saving another $50. Some money would be saved from edge numbering cost, now that there would be less work print and mag stock. Also, if we budgeted only one roll each of picture and sound splicing tape ($22) instead of listing the total ten rolls (purchased tape as needed), we would release $198 to the overall budget. And while it's almost impossible to edit a feature in a couple of weeks, let's budget some twelve-hour "half days" on a flatbed machine, giving the opportunity for syncing up and rough assembly of the footage. One final saving can be made if we reduce the length of our answer print from eighty minutes to seventy-five minutes, the minimum length most film festivals regard as "feature length."

Although these savings can't help us to afford the full price of an expensive, high-quality sound mix, the little bits of added cash should supply an "emergency cash fund" during the shoot, using cash that remains as a savings for the mix or additional flatbed editing time. What's important is that the budget allows the filmmaker to shoot the film and reach a point in the editing where the rough assemblage can generate the necessary inspiration needed to combat financial and creative problems ahead.

At this point let's take a look at our reworked budget:

Shooting/Editing Budget (16-mm)

12 rolls B&W Negative 7222 stock (4,800′)
@ $77.30 . . . . $ 927.60
Processing/work printing ¾ of the stock (3,600′)
@ $.47/ft. . . . . $ 1,692.00
12 rolls of ¼″ sound tape (1 roll per filmstock) . . $ 84.00
4 rolls (1,200′ ea.) of mag track . . . . $ 200.00
Camera package rental (lights, etc.), 2 weekends . $ 500.00
Soundperson with Nagra recorder/mikes
(daily stipend) . . . . $ 80.00
2 actors' fees (daily stipend) . . . . $ 160.00
Camera assistant (daily stipend) . . . . $ 80.00
Food (4 lunches for 5 people) . . . . $ 120.00

Transportation (gas)	$ 30.00
Edge numbers (3,600′ work print, 3,600′ mag track)	$ 108.00
Flatbed editing machine rental (10 12-hr. sessions)	$ 350.00
Editing tape (1 roll picture tape, 1 roll sound tape)	$ 22.00
Titles (shot on location)	$ 0
Black leader for conforming	$ 300.00
Conforming (done by filmmaker)	$ 0
B&W answer print (75 min./2,700′ @ $1.30/ft.	$ 3,510
	$ 8,163.60
Sound mix (10 hr. @ $185/hr. + stock [$150])	$ 2,000.00
Miscellaneous costs, (taxes, sound internegative*, etc.)	$ 1,836.40
	$12,000.00

The creative filmmaker/scavenger should be able to reduce this pared-down budget even more by gaining free access to needed film equipment (camera, Nagra, lights, mag transfer machine, flatbed machine, splicer, etc.) that sits unused 95 percent of the time in film schools, art schools, in closets of individual owners. If one of your collaborators is currently enrolled in a school or college that offers film classes, then it's a good bet that you can shave another $1,000 off your budget. At our CCAC Feature Film Workshop, we were fortunate to have the use of an Eclair camera with extra magazine, 12–120 lens, Lowel lights, Tota kit lights, Nagra recorder and microphones, transfer machine for resolving ¼″ sound tape to mag sound track, Showchron flatbed for editing, and free help from fellow collaborators. CCAC also supplied us with free mag track and ¼″ sound tape, splicing tape for editing picture/sound, screening facilities, and conference room. Although the students had to pay a hefty tuition and a $650 lab deposit for the project, there was an obvious advantage to collaborating on a feature at a well-supplied film department such as CCAC's.

**Occasionally the filmmaker will be required to purchase an expensive sound internegative when informed that the lab cannot supply an adequate-quality 16-mm optical sound track for the print without one.*

16-mm Shooting/Editing Budget (Computer Cut)

For comparing the finalized, pared-down $12,000 16-mm "flatbed editing" budget to the "computer cut" discussed earlier, you'll want to add the $8,327.10 we arrived at (on page 57) to the cost of completing a digital cut. Consider either editing on Avid (by the week) at a facility like FAF in San Francisco (or at some other facility such as The Green Room in Berkeley, [510] 644–3641, that offers supercompetitive discounts for true "no-budget indies"), or purchasing your own computer and software (Adobe Premiere, EditDV, Final Cut Pro, etc., on a Pentium or G-4 Macintosh platform), plus final print costs. If the computer system you purchase is powerful, you'll also be able to mix your sound digitally in the computer, forgoing the cost of a sound mix. That leaves the expense of black leader for conforming the originals yourself (see chapter 6), and the cost of an "answer print."

The damage: $8,327.10 (16-mm shooting budget for computer editing) + $5,000 (Avid/3 weeks, or purchase of computer + editing software), + $2,000 (for either sound mix at a postproduction facility, or for purchase of "Pro-Tools"-type sound-manipulating software), + $300 for black leader + $3,510 for a color/B&W 75-minute (2,700′) answer print = $19,137.10.

If you evaluate the difference between this amount and the $12,000 "flatbed" budget, you'll see that you're basically trading $7,000–$9,000 for speed of electronic computer editing (more than half the budget increase accounts for Avid time/your computer purchase, the rest being mostly the initial costs of your time-code/key-code video work print Betacam SP masters). But if you plan to make additional features (have a feature filmmaking career . . .), and invest wisely in your own top-end computer system and editing software, this $9,000 or so will be recouped down the road, as you continue to shoot and edit features at your own postproduction facility. Whatever your circumstances, the important thing is to get a good start on your feature with whatever funds you can raise initially and take each stage of the production as it comes.

Raising Money for Your Feature

After you have a clear idea of the financial needs of your project, you may want to start looking for some investors. When you ask people to invest money in your feature film at used-car prices, usually it takes a few moments for the laughter to stop and the questions to begin. Is it a *real* film? It's so low-budget! How will your film earn money? When will I get my money back? If it *is* good, will I get my name in the credits? And so on. I've found that the best policy is *the truth.* Yes, it's a *real* film. No big stars, no expensive car crashes, but a sincere attempt to portray something important on film. The film may earn some money by being shown at the several film showcases and museums across America (see lists in chapter 7). And if we're very fortunate, the film will be shown at European film festivals and will then stand a chance of being purchased by more progressive television programmers such as those at Channel Four in London. Yes, we'll be happy to put your name in the credits if you invest a major amount of the needed budget.

Any prospective investor should be reminded that filmmaking is, and always has been, a form of gambling. There is no way to know ahead of time if a film will be a financial success or not, but even if it fails, at least they'll come out with a tax deduction. For family members and friends, a more important point is that they are helping you create a unique film that may help expand the understanding of people on this planet. You are willing to perform the service of producing a film with minimal resources, and you are asking them (your parents, friends, guardian angels) for their support.

If you are approached by a serious investor, that backer will want to know what he or she will get in return for financial risk. If the investor gives you the entire budget for your film, the usual agreement is that he or she receives one half of the profit points (50 percent) in the film as well as being paid back for the investment plus 10 percent interest per annum. For investments of less than the full amount, it is up to the filmmaker/producer to set a price for each percentage point of the profits. For smaller investors such as family members and friends, you can give 1 percent of the film away for each $500 invested and only spend 24 percent to get your $12,000.

If an investor wants to put up the entire budget of your used-car production, then it is important to add back into the budget the salaries of the actors, soundperson, cinematographer, camera assistant, and probably yourself. Otherwise, if the investor gets half of the percentage points, you could be left with few points after you've paid your cast and crew with points instead of cash. If an investor is receiving 50 percent of the profits of your super-low-budget feature, you would have to raise the budget amount to at least the $25,000 to $35,000 range to pay everybody something and still have 25 percent of the profits for yourself.

For our film *The Last Roommate*, we set a price of $650 for each percentage point of profits. Since the four directors were splitting whatever points were not given away to the cast and crew, there were very few points left to sell (see appendix D). We were all working for free and the students were investing lab fees of $650 in the project, so it was necessary that each person be given a suitable amount of percentage points for his or her labors.

If you have drawn up a professional contract, worded properly, that clearly states your plans to produce a feature film, family, friends, or other interested investors will look at this document and see that you are serious and businesslike. You should also meet with someone at your lab and have him or her write out a commitment to an estimate of prices for your film. This price quote from the lab will give the interested parties the impression that you are moving ahead on the project, with or without them—and they will be right. You may also want to take pictures of your prospective actors and use these photos, along with a copy of your script, contract, lab quote, projection of earnings from showcases and possible TV sales, and background information on qualifications of key members of cast and crew (yourself included) as part of your "presentation package." With Adobe Photoshop software (**<www.adobe.com>**) and a good 1440 dpi printer, you can produce an expensive-looking printed cover with eye-catching graphics for a presentation folder. All these things help to give the impression that you are a professional, so don't show anyone poorly typed pages or out-of-focus photos. Make sure that everything you present is absolutely as impressive as you can possibly make it. If you are able to present your film project as a legitimate business venture, an investor might be able to write off a trip to a European film festival where your feature is being presented and recover some of his or her small investment in tax deductions.

The most essential principle of making a feature film at used-car prices is that lack of money shouldn't be able to stop your production. If you can afford to drive a car, you should be able to make a feature film. By persuading friends or relatives to part with a couple of $500 investments, perhaps selling your car and taking the bus or car pool to work, and sprinkling money toward the project from your salary over the next year, you should be able to produce your feature cheaply, with your own resources. And don't worry about not having the entire budget in your hands when beginning the project. Once you have a work print—something concrete that you can show to potential investors (relatives, friends)—you'll probably find it much easier to raise the money you need to complete the film. Also, by making a high-quality video copy of your work print and synced sound track or computer cut (see chapter 7), you could apply for grants, enter competitions that offer completion funds, or even enter film festivals.

note: For even feature film projects at used-car prices, investors may require a "limited partnership agreement," that includes "purchase offer" papers, so that you and your film attorney can supply him or her with a K-1 form at tax time. While it will cost the filmmaker around $100 to file the partnership papers, and up to $700 for a certified public accountant knowledgeable in film law to prepare the tax returns each year for the partnership (based on your declared costs of the film and any money earned over the years), you should save thousands of dollars by making a copy of the California limited partnership papers provided in this book (see appendices H and I). Just adjust "number of units" and "cost per unit" to fit your movie's particular financial needs. Be cautioned that the partnership and purchase offer papers *must* be revised by a lawyer in order to conform to current federal and state requirements, and should only be used as a timesaving model for the lawyer to follow when drawing up new agreements for your particular project.

Grants

Many organizations offer grants for production of independent films. These funding bodies usually require a sample of your previous film work, or at least a script of the proposed project. Check out your local and national filmmaking magazines (the *Independent Film and Video Monthly*, FAF's *Release Print, 911* in Seattle) for lists of foundations that fund independent works, and apply to as many as possible. And there are a lot of grant-type sites on the Web these days, including everything from government funding for the arts, to small, dedicated, regional organizations. You might want to start at **<http://www.ipdg.org/academy/funding.htm>**, with its numerous links to grant sites for filmmakers, videographers, artists, etc. It lists the National Endowment for the Arts (the address for this site is: **<http://arts.endow.gov/>**); the American Academy in Rome, **<www.aarome.org/>** (maybe you'll end up studying and shooting a movie in Rome!); Djerassi Resident Artists, **<http://www.djerassi.org/>** (a California residency program that includes an online application); A.N.E.W. (Artists Now Exhibiting Work), **<www.anew.org/>** ("a non-profit foundation for the arts providing financial and other assistance to professional artists from all disciplines, as well as to various organizations and institutions who support fine art"); the John Simon Guggenheim Foundation, **<www.gf.org/>** (filmmakers like Jon Jost have been the recipients of their generous five-figure grants), etc. You can certainly spend a week at multiple-link sites like this one. And **<http://rtuh.com/adl>** has a great Art Deadlines list, along with other arts-related links of interest.

ITVS (Independent Television Service), at **<www.itvs.org>**, is another granting organization for film and video producers. It was mandated by Congress "to fund and present programming that involves creative risks and addresses the needs of underserved audiences." You should click to their Website and get on their mailing list in case you have a film or video that falls within their guidelines.

In the Seattle area there is a highly motivated support site for film- and videomakers called Wiggly World (**<www.wigglyworld.org>**) that offers studio space, editing facilities, screenings for indie features, and even occasionally funds no-budget features that they subsequently present at their independent Grand Illusion theater. If you can't locate a support group for imagemakers in your own town, then maybe you can become inspired by great organizations like Wiggly World and start one up yourself!

Since there are new granting links appearing on the Web weekly, just head over to your favorite search engine (Yahoo, Starting Point, Webcrawler, HotBot, Lycos, Alta Vista, InfoSeek, etc.) every so often and type in the word "grants." Maybe you'll be the lucky one. At any rate, I highly recommend checking what sources of funds are available. But be careful that you don't become a professional grant applicant instead of a moviemaker. Apply, and then continue to battle your low-budget feature into existence with your own resources.

Emergency Self-Funding

note: If you are the type of super-logical filmmaker (film buff, scriptwriter, producer-to-be) who can now talk yourself out of your "used car" feature filmmaking fantasies because the whole idea seems just too complex and expensive (even $12,000 is a big chunk of money), you may want to override the negativity and jump-start your production now by following the steps listed below:

Step #1: Phone Kodak "Film Center" at (800) 874-6867 (or check their Website, **<www.filmcenter.com>**, for current prices).

Step #2: Order twelve 400′ rolls of Kodak 7222 B&W Negative filmstock (Kodak offers delivery of filmstock by 10:00 A.M. the following day for all orders charged by phone before 4:00 P.M. Eastern time. While stock and shipping costs are more expensive, make the call for FedEx delivery if it helps to overcome inertia).

Step #3: When the shipment of filmstock arrives, immediately place the rolls in your refrigerator to assure cool storage, and place a note on the outside of the refrigerator with the date, one year hence, inscribed in bold letters.

Step #4: Before the stock spoils (Kodak guarantees stock for one year), get an idea, write a script, round up a cameraperson, sound recordist, and actors, select locations, confirm shooting dates. You *will* shoot your feature before the expiration of that filmstock. (No logical person would ever allow almost $1,000 worth of filmstock to go to waste!)

4

Preproduction: Preparing to Shoot

Preproduction begins the period of time when the moviemaker turns his or her *idea* of making a feature into a *reality.* While most Hollywood productions can afford to spend many months in preparation for their expensive productions, the independent, no-budget producer must gather all necessary components for the shoot in a matter of weeks. The activities of preproduction include, but are not limited to, the following: final selection of cast and crew, signing the contract for profit sharing, rewriting and rehearsing the script or improvisational outline, reserving all equipment (camera, sound gear, lights, etc.), purchasing filmstock, scouting and selecting locations, gathering props and other production accessories, cementing the schedule for shooting, last-minute money raising, and making sure that *everything* you need to make your movie is in your hands by the morning of the shoot. All these details of the filming must be nailed down within a short period of time so that you will be able to shoot your feature before the talented members of your cast and crew are lured away from your production by "real" jobs (jobs that pay). If your actors and technicians are crazy enough to have already agreed to work on the deferred-payment plan, then maybe there is hope that they will also be crazy enough to turn down a good paying job to help you shoot your movie . . . but I wouldn't bet on it. The indie producer who is attempting to make a feature on very little money must limit the period of preproduction to a month at most, so that his or her intensity of purpose keeps all the core members of the production interested in the project. It is also through this intensity and desperation in light of a quickly approaching deadline that the filmmaker is best able to create the miracles of preproduction that are necessary to every no-budget feature.

Each one of my feature projects has benefited from last-minute miracles that occurred during the month of preproduction. On my first feature, *A Man, a Woman, and a Killer*, my collaborators, Wayne Wang and Dick Richardson, and I found no houses available for rent in Mendocino, California, where we planned to shoot. I had already spent half of our shooting budget of $5,900 paying Wayne and Dick $500 each for two weeks of scripting, purchasing forty-five 400′ rolls of Plus-X Reversal filmstock, and making a deposit to soundman Neelon Crawford and his assistant, Lee Serie, and felt desperate to secure this location with only a week to go before shooting. I suggested we drive to the ocean side of town and look for FOR RENT signs. As we passed a red-and-white, two-story Victorian house at the edge of town, I told Dick to stop the car. In my intense state I decided to just approach the people on the porch and try to rent their house for our movie. To make sure they wouldn't think "Hollywood" when I mentioned we were making a feature film, I told them we had attended the California College of Arts and Crafts. Hearing this, the owner said she had taken a class there once, and agreed to rent the house for two weeks for $450 if I would pay for her hotel room during production ($280 for two weeks). The moviemaker must be incredibly persuasive during this stage of preproduction, able to convince anybody to do (or give) anything he or she needs for the upcoming shoot.

During preproduction of my second feature, *1988—The Remake,* the entire scope of the concept changed drastically. I had originally envisioned conducting a small audition as part of my movie, perhaps renting a small stage at a recreation center. But my art director friend Joe DiVincenzo offered to design a poster if I would pay him $1,000. I had a $10,000 grant from the American Film Institute and decided to pay Joe for the graphic promotion. While I was searching for a suitable location for the audition, someone recommended California Hall on Polk Street in San Francisco. I ended up renting the large hall, complete with a fifty-foot-wide stage that included several hand-painted scenery backdrops. And with every new decision, the event of the audition leaped to a grander scale. Friend Bill Farley insisted I hire his two scriptwriting friends (and himself) to help me write my script. These friends—Nick Kazan and Henry Bean—have since scripted major Hollywood movies. When Joe's designed poster, letterhead, and press release reached the press, the audition became a hot item on two network nightly news shows. My filmed audition for *1988—The Remake* became one of the largest ever held in the history of San Francisco. In this case preproduction completely reshaped the filming and final film result.

Preproduction for *Emerald Cities* was accomplished totally by phone, since there was little money for the shoot. Without much of a budget, all I could do was call previous members of my cast and crew to see if they could afford to work without salary for five days. Actors Ed Nylund and Carolyn Zaremba agreed to help me complete the film trilogy, with Ed offering me a loan for the production. After a friend convinced me that my idea of camping out for the five-day shoot would be a mistake for morale and creature comforts, I looked up motels in Trona, Death Valley, at the library (the extent of my "location scouting") and called to reserve four rooms sight unseen. With each phone call I was able to make the production more real to myself, adding fuel to the idea that it was really going to happen.

As soon as you make a *real* commitment to shoot your feature, you will discover that you have the power to solve all the needs of your upcoming production. These needs for the shoot fall into three major categories: *people, places,* and *things.*

People

It is almost impossible to create a feature without some help from fellow humans. Most stories need actors to play out the roles, and most filmmakers need at least a few helpers to light their scenes and record their location sound. Some exceptionally gifted artists are able to do everything themselves, shooting the camera while recording sound with a microphone either attached to the camera body or placed near the actors. But in terms of the most minimal low-budget crew for a feature that requires lighting and sound sync recording, you will usually have to hire a soundperson and an assistant, someone who can help set up lights, take light readings, "clack" the clapboard, carry equipment, do errands, maybe load the camera and keep it clean, and other things. Without this assistant you would need to have a great deal of stamina to keep up with all the physical work required to shoot on location. Often through listings at film-schools and organizations such as FAF in San Francisco and AIVF in New York (check Internet bulletin boards) you can locate an eager assistant for your shoot who will work for free just for the experience of getting his or her name in the credits of a feature film. Since the full burden of organizing all aspects of the shoot is on the shoulders of the moviemaker, "hiring" someone to help with errands and heavy equipment is the least you can do for yourself. You may also be able to locate a production manager and even a soundperson who would be willing to work on your production for the experience, but usually these professionals can't afford to work without at least a minimum salary and some profit sharing. While you look over every man and woman you pass on the street, wondering if they might be suitable actors for your story, the first concrete step you should take is rounding up the crew for your production.

Casting the Crew

It is very important to know you have a crew who will help make the film a reality. **<www.crew-net.com>** will not only help you secure a crew, but offers free fill-in slots so you can add your résumé to their database for opportunities to earn money and experience working for other low/no-budget productions. After you have met with some prospective sound people and possible production assistants and been shown either examples of their technical abilities or résumés of their past achievements, you will want to ask yourself if you feel you can get along with their particular personalities on a shoot. It is vital that you don't feel extra pressure from your technicians during filming, even if they know more than you about how to make a film. Explain to them that this is your first feature (if it is) and that you will appreciate any help they can give you, but that they may need to exercise some patience as you feel your way along. When selecting the people you will be working with and depending upon to make your movie (while spending all your money), it is critical that you find people with whom you can get along.

When you have made your final selection of soundperson and production technician, you will want to have them sign your contract to confirm that they will indeed be part of your production. Since the contract clearly states the amount of deferred salary and percentage points of profit for each job, with the stipulation that these crew members will receive nothing if their jobs aren't completed, the act of signing clarifies the business of making your movie. After the crew members have signed the contract, you should feel the added energy that comes with knowing that you are a major step closer to shooting. The next step, once the crew is set, is to begin the search for your "stars."

Casting "Real" Actors

For some types of low-budget stories, you will want to cast trained actors who can be depended upon to deliver the same high-quality performances on each take. There are always many unemployed actors who are excellent at their craft, but who don't fit the mold of whatever Hollywood film is casting at present. If you can afford the time and money to search for your actors, maybe the best way to proceed is by putting a notice in *Back Stage* magazine (<**www.backstage.com**>), describing the parts available. For between $50 and $100 you should be able to reach a large pool of talent in this way. Talent agencies may also be able to supply you with photos and résumés of actors and actresses who fit your bill, but there is usually a fee for this service. Without much money it is impossible to conduct an audition for your cast, so your next best way of scouting for professional actors is by going to plays in your town and watching the actors. And acting schools or theater departments at local colleges and universities may have bulletin boards that advertise actors looking for work. Or try *Casting*

Daily (<www.castingnet.com>, $9.95 introductory price for first week), a low-cost way to cast your movie, reviewing head shots on your computer screen.

When you interview prospective thespians for a part in your movie, let them know immediately that you are producing your feature at used-car prices. And if there is no money for salaries, let them know that you'll be paying per diem stipends (if this is possible) so the shoot won't cost them money. Explain to them that you will be sharing the profit points with the cast and crew. They may respect your story, your low-budget daring, and agree to perform in your movie on these terms.

Before a highly trained, highly professional actor agrees to perform in your low-budget "first time" feature, it is also important to inform him or her that you have no training in "traditional" directorial techniques (if this is true). In a large sense you will be depending on the actor's ability to "self-direct," to control his or her own performance. You believe this person is right for the part in your movie, and to a certain extent you will be able to spot the moment when he or she fails to act the role in an honest and believable way during the shoot. But because you are responsible for many facets of the production (shooting, directing, managing the details), you will have to depend heavily on the actors' ability to create their own performances. Some actors demand constant pampering, "directing," and need several takes to get "warmed up." If you select this type of actor by mistake, you will waste at least your first roll of film, if not sink your entire production. A good rule of thumb is that if the actor is down-to-earth, without affectations, likable and enthusiastic, and can talk intelligently about your story, then perhaps he or she might also be right for the part. Observe the actors carefully when you mention your intended super-low shooting ratio of one take per scene, with few retakes. If this small shooting ratio scares them (and why shouldn't it?), there is no real comfort you can supply. You must be able to depend on your actors to *at least* complete the filming so that you have a chance of creatively editing away their, and your, hopefully few mistakes. Sometimes it is actually easier to shoot one-to-one using untrained nonactors.

Casting Nonactors

The essence of the performance of a nonactor in a movie is the natural, raw quality that he or she is able to project on the screen. And, obviously, with each repeated take the naturalness diminishes. So it is the job of the director to catch the fleeting moment of the nonactor's best performance on the first or second try. Since most nonactors are not trained to memorize pages of dialogue and instruction, it is not even worth trying to proceed in this manner. An intelligent nonactor (like the best actors) can often take the concept of a scene and explode it into dazzling runs of dialogue you could never write in a lifetime. For most of my feature productions, I have used nonactors with great success, selecting people who *are* my characters. And many of the scenes in which they perform are scripted directly from some story or event I have observed or been told about that actually occurred in their real lives. What I'm really asking them to do is relive part of their lives before the camera. Or I may place them in a certain situation that is new to their experience and record them reacting in an honest way.

I still can't help laughing when I think of the expressions on actor Dick Richardson's face when I shot scenes for *Emerald Cities* of Dick pulling off a rubber Martian mask, sitting next to Ed Nylund in a Santa Claus outfit, and being past-life hypnotized by Freuda Morris in front of her real class of future hypnotists in Berkeley. No writer could script, and no actor could duplicate, the looks of puzzlement, suspicion, disbelief, and fear that crossed Dick's face during these scenes.

While your mind is totally set in search for your needed actors, you might spot someone on the street who perfectly resembles your mental picture of one or another of your characters. Don't let these people get away! Overcome your shyness and approach them, being as polite as possible while you explain your problem. Tell them that you only have a few weeks left to find your actors for your low-budget feature and you think that they may be right for one of the parts. If they respond positively to the idea of being in a movie, let them know just how low-budget your production is, and see how they react. If they enjoy the idea of acting and have the time to accommodate your shooting schedule, you may have hit a jackpot. We found our actress Jean Mitchell for

The Last Roommate in the cafeteria at the California College of Arts and Crafts around eight in the morning while my group of collaborators (Mark Yellen, Peter Boza, Tinnee Lee) and I were worrying about finding actors for the upcoming production.

Occasionally, a location will supply you with additional actors, when you make use of the people who live and work there. When we needed a "hit man" for the final scene in *A Man, a Woman, and a Killer*, Wayne Wang, Dick Richardson, and I drove into the town of Mendocino, California, to find someone we could ask to play the part. We spotted a large man dressed in white slacks, white shoes, sort of a "Las Vegas" look. He agreed to drive up in his station wagon, pull his rifle out of the backseat, get out of the car, and aim it at Dick, who would be standing on the porch. After he did the scene for us, he told us he was a deputy sheriff from Nevada and showed his badge. We were very lucky that the nonactor we chose for the part was an expert in firearms, because that authenticity carried to the screen. And during the filming of *Emerald Cities*, the owner of the motel we stayed at for three days unlocked the church next door and with his wife became an audience of two while Ed Nylund rehearsed the upcoming Christmas pageant. Using local nonactors in your movie always brings an added richness to your production.

note: Whether using actors or nonactors, remember to get releases from all performers *before* shooting their scenes (see release form, appendix E). Even if a clerk in a store speaks only one line of dialogue for your movie, you must have him or her sign a release. And if the actor or "extra" is under eighteen, the release form must be signed by his or her parent or legal guardian as well. Your lead actors with whom you are profit sharing must sign a contract *and* a release before the shoot.

Places

To shoot your feature you need special places called "locations" where you will bring your story to life. Often Hollywood films spend months "scouting locations," but with your nonbudget (and probably little gas money) you need to be much more inventive than the usual Hollywood production. Maybe your overgrown backyard will double for the African wilds. Maybe not. But there may be suitable locations within a few miles of your house that might work perfectly for your story. Within twenty miles of my former home in Point Richmond, California, I had access to ocean, beaches, San Francisco, Oakland, hills, country, desert, swamps, islands, Berkeley street people, the University of California, punk music, outdoor concerts, and so forth. Perhaps a friend's apartment, or the house of your actor or actress (or their parents' house), would be right for your story. If you need a restaurant or other public place for some scenes you must once again overcome any shyness and just *ask.* Most people will be happy to have been chosen for the honor of being involved in a movie. And if you experience resistance from the location's manager or owner, try to offer a small sum of money ($20 to $50) and maybe that will change his or her mind.

While shooting *Emerald Cities*, I encountered a desk clerk who would absolutely not let us film a scene in the driveway of his motel, where I had just spent $100 putting the production up for the night. I begged, I offered money, I explained that our movie was ultra-low-budget. Nothing seemed to change his mind. Finally, I told him that making movies was, for me, the same as working on his car might be for him. It was my hobby, my love. And here I finally hit the right button. He said he worked on his car and understood, and told me to go ahead and shoot my scene. The moral: If you feel your blood rush at the sight of a great location, don't give up when someone first says No. At least don't give up until you've explained who you are and why you need to film at that location. If possible, get a commitment in advance for your filming at a location.

To shoot on location without a snag demands that the moviemaker think like the genius-production-manager he or she can't afford to hire. You must anticipate problems before they happen. During my shoot of scripted scenes for *1988—The Remake*, I had rented a hotel room to film a banquet scene. At the last minute I was told by the management that I couldn't bring the already cooked (and paid for) catered meal for the shot into my room. Luckily, my production manager, Bobby Weinstein, who was working for me for three days at a salary of $250, was able to get around this problem by working out a deal with the kitchen to use their plates and silverware (at a nominal cost) with our food, thus conforming to hotel regulations. This creative solution not only saved the $150 worth of elegantly prepared food created by culinary expert Ruth Reichl, but also saved the momentum of the filming. It's always best to review any plans you have for a certain location with the owner or manager before the day of the shoot so that this kind of problem doesn't arise. And if you sense resistance during your discussion, it is probably best to change locations.

As a low-budget producer you can't really play by the same rules as Hollywood when securing locations. City regulations in most large cities such as San Francisco require a filming permit to film on their streets. I know many people who have never paid such a fee and don't intend to in the future. They have just gone ahead and shot at these locations, and have succeeded in getting great scenes without being bothered. Some risks will be necessary when shooting your low-budget feature on location, but try to nail everything down that you can. The Internet may help again, with <www.scout911.com> supplying thousands of location images of the greater Los Angeles area (includes Death Valley sand dunes, etc.)

note: The safe moviemaker will get a location release signed at each location, so that when he or she has a big hit on his or her hands the choice will not have to be made of either paying an unreasonable fee for the image of someone else's property or refilming. (See location release form, appendix F.)

Storyboarding

Once you have a firm commitment from a particular location you may want to finalize your vision by making a sketch of how you see your actors in the scene. This drawing, detailing how the camera will frame the shot, including size and position of actors and specific background elements, is called a storyboard. An average-length feature would require hundreds of such drawings, one for each cut. I'm sure that some filmmakers swear by the process of knowing every shot down to its exact composition, as did director Alfred Hitchcock. But I believe that the moviemaker is wisest if he or she is able to enter the set with both eyes open, feeling special inter-relationships, inventing ways of shooting based on the emotional network of the moment. I believe in placing the camera in the spot that feels right instead of trying to determine that special location for the camera beforehand. Also, the obvious fact is that without any real budget the moviemaker can't completely control all the facets of shooting and must be able to take advantage of unexpected moments and events.

Long-Distance Locations

When Wayne Wang and I planned the shoot for our first feature, *A Man, a Woman, and a Killer*, in 1973, it was clear to us that if we could get our cast and crew out of the familiar surroundings of our hometown (Oakland), we would have a better chance of making a good film. We had learned on shoots for shorter films that a great deal of effort is spent just rounding up all the members of cast and crew and equipment for a day's shoot. Also, if you are able to bring your cast and crew to some new place to live together as a sort of "film family," there is a "high" created that stays with you for years after the production has ended. This special emotional energy created by the teamwork of making a film on location always adds something special to what you see on the screen. If your movie demands an exotic location, as did my *Emerald Cities*, feature which was partly shot in Death Valley, it is important to be true to your concept and somehow raise the additional funds to travel and live at that special place.

Often the availability of a free mountain cabin or other type of housing will help the low-budget filmmaker get the inspiration for a story he or she wants to shoot. The only problem is that a small production can barely afford transporting the cast and crew to the location (gas credit cards) and feeding everyone during filming. While shooting *A Man, a Woman, and a Killer* in Mendocino, I paid for breakfast at a restaurant each morning for nine members of the cast and crew, supplied cold cuts for lunch, and gave each person an "allowance" of $4 for dinner. I actually handed out four $1 bills to each person on the production, which was the price of the basic dinner offered by the Mendocino Inn (in 1973). Only if you are making a feature at used-luxury-car prices can you afford today's prices for food and shelter for weeks on location. But if you limit your long-distance shooting to a five-day trip with three days for actual filming, as I did on *Emerald Cities*, you may be able to afford the special images that come from such an adventure. Carefully budget your food money and call ahead to a motel, making a deposit if necessary to give yourself the security of shelter during the few-days' shoot you will attempt. You may find that food prices are greatly reduced from what you expect to pay in cities such as San Francisco and New York City, when you travel to rural settings. The air is fresher, the food is home-cooked, new vistas await the daring no-budget filmmaker who takes his or her show on the road.

Things

Things for the production include every piece of equipment (camera, lenses, sound recorder, light meter, lights, batteries, power cables, tripod, etc.) as well as props, food, clothes or costumes, filmstock, sound tape, and all the accessories that you will need to have on location. It is very important to decide what items you need for the shoot and either reserve them for renting or purchase them in advance. Since you can't afford to hire a production manager whose job it would be to make absolutely sure you had everything when you needed it, you must keep a notebook (check out pocket-size computer datebooks, Palm Pilots, etc.) to organize these needs. As the date of the filming approaches, each day will add new things to the list. Part of the list will indicate members of the cast and crew you must call by phone to discuss shooting schedules, e-mail with revised script concepts, and so on. The other part of the list will reflect which pieces of equipment are needed, when and where they must be picked up for the shoot, with additional notes on food and transportation—everything the moviemaker must remember if the shoot is to be successful.

Camera Equipment

One of the most vital pieces of equipment (as well as the most expensive) that you must acquire for the shoot is a camera. Although we have chosen to shoot our feature in 16-mm instead of 35-mm for the obvious reasons that 35-mm filmstock and Panavision equipment are many times more expensive than our used-car budget could afford, we are still committed to producing the sharpest images possible, to insure the potential for blow-up to 35-mm in case our film is theatrically distributed. And while 8-mm film and equipment are much cheaper than 16-mm, the smaller-gauge film offers an image only half the size of 16-mm, causing much more grain buildup when quadrupled in size for 35-mm blow-up. To protect your own investment of time and money, not to mention investors' dollars, it is essential to the production that you shoot your film with the best 16-mm camera and optics available. A high-quality 16-mm camera (Eclair, CP-16, Aaton, Arriflex) usually rents for between $70 and $275 per day. Each filmmaker must get the feel of these cameras in his or her hands and choose the one that seems best and is affordable according to the budget of their feature. The rental price on each should include a battery belt or some type of battery power, two film magazines, power cables, crystal sync motor, lenses, and a camera case. Most rental houses carefully check their equipment after each rental before sending it out again, and this should insure a smoothly running camera for your shoot. If you decide to rent your camera from a rental house, ask them if they have checked the magazines for quiet running. Ask them if the lens has been calibrated lately. Look at the camera and get an impression of how new or old it is. It should look clean instead of banged up. You will want to reserve the equipment as early as possible, phoning at least two weeks in advance to set your reservation for the camera, sound gear, and lights you will need. And if you have decided to shoot on weekends, then make sure you request the special weekend rate (if available) of one day's cost for a Friday-night-to-Monday-morning rental. It is worth spending the few extra dollars for equipment insurance when renting your gear (most rental houses require

Arriflex 16SR-3 camera and quick-release tripod. Photo courtesy of Arriflex Corporation.

CP-16R/A camera with hand grip, including standard 12X Viewfinder, PLC-4A Magazine, and *Ultra T* 9-mm Prime Lens-T1.35. Photo courtesy of Cinema Productions Corporation.

insurance and include it in the rental price), since you are legally responsible for damage and loss when you sign the rental agreement.

It is possible to save money by renting a good camera from someone who has advertised equipment for rent on a bulletin board, in a moviemaking magazine (like FAF's *Release Print*), or on the Internet. The owner may refuse to rent precious equipment to you unless he or she is present at the shoot (with an extra fee included), but this may be to your advantage if the person knows the camera and can help load it and clean it between shots. I rented a camera and sound gear for my *Emerald Cities* shoot from a friend who greatly reduced my workload with his attention to the camera duties. As the digital video revolution gathers steam, I imagine that more and more filmmakers who invested heavily in expensive 16-mm cameras will be anxious to rent their equipment on feature projects whenever possible. Even if their rental price is the same as that of a rental house, if the price includes their help, you are getting a good deal. Just make sure they aren't the type that will bully you or intimidate you on location. You will want to make your own decisions, shoot your own movie, with their assistance.

Which Lenses?

If you are renting your camera from a rental house, you will need to choose the high-quality lenses that are best for your shoot. The 12–120 Angenieux zoom lens ($80 per day) and the wide-angle 9.5–57 Angenieux lens ($50 per day) are both excellent choices because from wherever you place your camera you can zoom in to select your framing of the shot. The Angenieux 9.5–57 is a good choice for shooting wide angle since its lens allows for very close-up, in-focus shots. And this lens is indispensable for keeping all your titles in focus if you use the low-budget method of shooting titles made with stick-on letters on clear acetate placed in front of a lit scene (see chapter 5). To insure that the on-location filmmaker still has the wide-angle capability with either choice, I recommend renting the 9.5–57 lens, or a 9-mm or 10-mm wide-angle lens ($50 per day) along with your 12–120 lens for the shoot.

note: When you talk to technicians (like Ken at White House Audio Visuals in Newbury Park, California, [805] 498-4177, <www.whitehouseav.com>), you'll find that what they recommend beyond using "the best 16-mm camera" is using "*THE BEST LENSES.*" Ken is the guy who cleans and calibrates lenses, and can lead you to a good Angenieux 12–120 zoom lens (like the one I used with the Eclair NPR on my first feature, *A Man, a Woman, and a Killer* with Wayne Wang back in 1973). If you want to shoot the sharpest images possible, talk to Ken, or someone like him, and get the professional help you deserve!

Sound Gear

Usually, a good soundperson will have his or her own Nagra sound recorder, which he or she will have pampered by resoldering any loose connections over weekends. This type of soundperson is most certainly out of reach financially for the low-budget or no-budget filmmaker, unless he or she has such a sound expert as a best friend. You will probably have to hire a soundperson and rent the necessary sound equipment for filming. There is no question that the Nagra is the best-quality workhorse recorder for on-location sync sound, and it usually rents for around $50 a day. Rents are higher for newer Nagras that record time code on audio tracks for eventual transfer to video, but if you intend to complete your production on video, editing on digital equipment, then you must obtain this special Nagra T recorder with SMPTE time code ($70 a day). You will also need to rent microphones, which will add another $60 per day to the cost. The Sennheiser #416 is a high-quality mike ($20 per day) that is very sensitive to sound and must be used with a very quiet-running camera at an equally quiet location. This mike can literally hear through walls. (While I was filming a scene in a restaurant the soundman informed me that his #416 was picking up the motor sounds of what was probably the refrigerator of the store next door.) For outside recording you will want to have

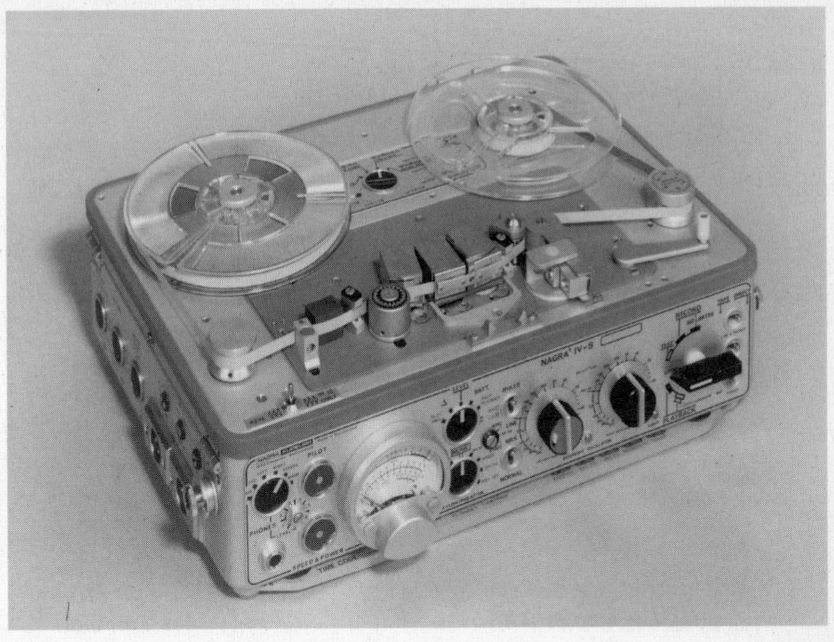

Nagra IV-S time-code recorder. Photo courtesy Nagra Recorders, Inc.

rented a Sennheiser #816 shotgun mike ($25 a day). This directional mike allows the soundperson to pick dialogue out of the mouths of your actors without recording all the interruptive outdoor sounds nearby. And if a large portion of the filming involves dialogue between several actors in different parts of the room, you will probably need to rent several wireless lavaliere mikes ($75 per day), which pin onto the inside of a shirt (like those seen on TV newscasters). For sound recording on location there will also be the need for several recording "accessories," such as a 4′ to 15′ fold-up extension boom pole with shock mount, which gives the soundperson the ability to hold the mike high above the actors, or low below the frame line of the shot, for the best possible position for recording (well worth $20 a day).

As you can see, when renting sound or camera gear, all the necessary "extras" quickly raise the overall price per day to a barely afford-

Filmmaker Jon Jost's CP-16 film camera (he loaned it to director Greg Araki, who shot his breakthrough feature, *The Living End*). Includes a custom handle, 400′ magazine, highly portable Sony Walkman Pro sound recorder (60-cycle sync pulse generator box plugged into channel-2), and directional mike.

able rate. So once again it might be to the moviemaker's great advantage to hire someone with his or her own equipment. Some rental houses will also require that you buy the $25-worth of batteries needed to power the Nagra, which easily brings the total rental price for the Nagra into the range of $100 a day. If you can hire a soundperson for $200 (including equipment) for the weekend, you are doing very well. Check the lab bulletin boards, FAF listings, and WWW filmmaking message boards for a reasonable sound package with perhaps a soundperson attached to the deal.

Another option, if you need sync sound recording on location, may be to purchase a Sony Walkman Professional recorder. It is possible to buy this recorder, which tests very close in quality to the $12,000 Nagra, for under $500. My soundman expert, Neelon Crawford, checked the Sony recorder against his state-of-the-art Nagra and found that it was quite comparable in fidelity. By hooking up a special box of electronics (about the size of a pack of cigarettes) that supplies one channel with a 60-cycle sync pulse, and connecting a high-quality mike to the other channel, one can record excellent sync sound onto audiocassettes with this lightweight, compact recorder. The Sony TCD-5 recorder is also excellent for on-location recording, but this model is about twice as expensive ($900) and not pocket-size. So if your Nagra rental will be more than $500 for your shoot, you should definitely consider the purchase of one of these Sony recorders (an external 60 hz crystal sync generator can be purchased for around $240 from the Film Group, **<www.members.aol.com/fmgp>**, P.O. Box 290009, Wethersfield, CT 06129, [860] 529-1877).

Lighting Kits

Unless you have chosen very fast filmstock, you will need to rent some sort of lighting kit for your shoot. These kits range from the diffused lighting of Lowell "soft lights" ($20 each per day) to the more hard-edged lighting of Tota kits ($45 a day) and "spots" ($25 a day). The rental of lights must also be accompanied by the rental of necessary accessories to make each type of lighting effective. Soft lights need only what comes in their cases (stands, diffusion cloth backing, bulbs, electrical cords with on-off switches). Other types of lighting will require support gear such as stands, "C" clamps, "scrims," "barn doors," "snoots," expensive color gels, diffusion "cotton," reflectors, etc. And for any set of lights, a rental "must" is at least three 50′ extension cords ($1.50 each per day) so that you can avoid blowing fuses on location by plugging lights into different outlets around the house.

Before committing yourself to a certain type of lighting, you should add up the total cost of various lighting concepts, taking into consideration the extra difficulty and time required by each process versus the desired results. For each of my features I have tried to simplify as much as possible the process of lighting my indoor scenes.

Examples of Lighting on Rick Schmidt Features

In my earlier features a very direct, improvisational method was used to light the scenes. In *A Man, a Woman, and a Killer* all our lighting was supplied by three 1,500-watt Lowell soft lights. George Manupelli, who ran (and founded) the Ann Arbor Film Festival in Michigan, and who has directed/produced five features himself, had told me about the soft-light method just before we were to shoot. Without really looking into the subject, I just took his recommendation and rented two soft lights. Fortunately, our grip, Jim Mayer (now a video producer in San Francisco), brought a third soft light along for the shoot. By aiming the diffused light from our three soft lights directly at the actors, and underexposing ½ stop for our black-and-white filmstock, we were able to achieve a very luminous quality for the film. (We used a filmstock called Plus-X Reversal [Kodak 7276], with very fine grain due to its low 50 ASA, which was capable of producing very rich blacks.) And so this first feature had a feeling that many foreign films have—dramatic images that are very beautiful to watch.

My second feature, *1988—The Remake*, was also shot on Plus-X Reversal using soft lights in combination with diffused lighting for large areas in the audition hall. Grip Jeff Gilliam brought large banks of lights to California Hall (San Francisco), where the audition was conducted, and these, combined with the illumination from the stage floodlights, were able to achieve the desired lighting. For smaller, scripted scenes, soft lights were once again used to diffuse the light on the characters.

Emerald Cities, my third feature, was shot on Color Negative stock (Kodak 7291). This color sort of bursts at the seams, with very bright colors, no grain, and super definition. Not all films can handle the almost cartoony color of this stock, but for *Emerald Cities* it was perfect. For the interior scenes I bounced some light off the ceiling until I got an f-stop reading between 2.8 and 4. This approach worked well for the subject matter, and instead of spending many hours lighting each scene, I was able to move quickly, set up the lights, and get good improvisational performances. Using a "Lowell D kit," which consisted of four 1,000-watt lights with "barn doors" (metal flaps that fit in slots in front of the lights, used to control the "edge of the lighting" and the brightness, $50 a day), along with a soft light for fill ($20 a day), I was easily able to reach a good f-stop, even when I had to light a large stage area in a church.

For *The Last Roommate*, Color Negative stock was again used, mainly at the prompting of Monaco Lab in San Francisco, where the manager sweetened our lab deal by offering us the stock at their cost. Kathleen Beeler, bi-city cinematographer (LA/Bay Area), signed on as our director of photography, and applied her techniques of lighting to the shoot. This was a big departure for me, having to wait an hour or more between shots while the lights were set up and tuned. Also, because of the difficulty and added amount of time it took for each lighting setup, it was necessary to shoot all the scenes that took place at that location at the same time. This made it necessary to shoot some scenes out of the natural order of the story, as it is usually done in Hollywood. It is always my desire to shoot a dramatic story in order so that the actors (or nonactors) can live through the drama in a realistic progression of events. But because of this attitude I have often settled for less-than-adequate lighting. In my features I have created my moods through the improvisational power of catching special moments of light and shadow while I film. For each filmmaker a balance has to be struck between improvisation and carefully crafted lighting.

Selecting Your Lighting

Occasionally, the low-budget feature filmmaker will attempt to give a big-budget Hollywood look to his or her film. The commitment to this idea must be very strong, because to effectively use these techniques requires many hours of setting up hot lights, much less improvisational flow for the actors, and quite a bit more expense due to an extended shooting schedule. Although it is very difficult to imagine a no-budget filmmaker being able to convince a cast and crew to abide by the extra days this type of lighting will require, it is possible that a filmmaker collaborating with a highly skilled director of photography might consider the possibility. I include some in-depth information about the Hollywood system of lighting as used by Kathleen Beeler for our production so that the reader can make a wise decision with regard to lighting his or her feature. I also include information on shooting without any lights at all, making use of fast filmstock. Since the entire schedule for shooting a feature depends on what approach the filmmaker takes in terms of lighting, this decision must take place in the preproduction period. With no lights, or few lights, a filmmaker can shoot a film in under a week. With Hollywood lighting, the filmmaker would be working night and day to complete the feature within a two-week period, at least doubling the cost of the shoot.

Hollywood Lighting

The basic groups of lights used by Kathleen Beeler for *The Last Roommate* were as follows:

1. **Tota kit (Lowell), which included three 650-watt lamp heads.**
2. **Two baby spots, each with 1,000 watts (1-K) of light.**
3. **Two 200-watt midget spots used for pinpointing light on objects or actors.**

These lights are used in combination: to cover the light directed toward the actors, the background light, and the highlights. By bouncing light from a baby spot off a piece of white foamcore board onto the actors at a 45-degree angle, the filmmaker can achieve a beautiful diffused light (as is created by the use of soft lights). During the filming of *The Last Roommate*, we often used orange gels (called CTOs) on the lights, which gave a warm, fresh glow to the actors. And we used blue gels (CTBs) for the background to visually pop the actors forward, giving them a more 3-D look. This is the type of lighting structure used on Hollywood pictures by cinematographer Vilmos Zsigmond, and it gives a coral color and fresh ocean feel to each scene.

To give a "natural" feel to a scene set next to a window, the Hollywood cinematographer would light his or her scene in such a way as to direct the main light source from the window's direction. The "key light" would be set on the side of the room near the light source (window) aimed at the actors. Then a light reading would be taken by aiming the white bulb of the meter toward the camera position. This incident reading would represent the average light reading. Using the focusable spots as "key" and umbrellas (umbrella-shaped reflectors) as "fill," we complete the lighting by adding a "back" or "rim" light to the subject. This gives a 3-D feeling to the image. Gels and diffusion materials would be held in front of the lights using clothespins to clamp them on the barn doors. Especially bright bulbs, called "practicals," might be screwed into a lamp fixture to give additional illumination to the existing amount of light in the room. For this "natural" look, the Hollywood cinematographer would also usually tone down a plain white wall, adding color to avoid the starkness. And an "85 gel" would be used to cover the glass of the window, filtering out the blue color that would occur on the tungsten balanced filmstock without such protection. Just like the 85 filter used for outside filming, the 85 gel balances the color difference.

The essence of the "Hollywood look" is the concept of "painting with light." Have you ever seen an Edward Hopper painting? Look at the values of light and the different colors that collide on his canvases. For some cinematographers, such as Kathleen Beeler, Hopper is a prime example of what they would like to achieve in their lighting of scenes. By using a spot meter, the cinematographer can check the density of light in each area of the scene, adjusting the illumination until all the values are as rich as he or she desires. Black and white areas are checked so that details aren't lost because of either extreme darkness or hot highlights.

note: If you decide to go the full lighting route, you'll want to rent a "lighting package" that includes lights, c-stands, reflectors, sound blankets, apple boxes and sandbags, doorway dolly and rails, perhaps even a grip truck. If you approach top professional equipment rental facilities in your area, like Freyer Lighting of Berkeley, California, ([510] 704-1250), and let them know you're a true indie (you're paying for your own shoot at used-car prices!), you'll be surprised by their level of helpfulness and low-cost options.

Lighting for Low Budgets

Many low-budget moviemakers tend to reject Hollywood-style lighting, preferring to invent their own lighting style. By using the stark colors of reality, white highlights and deep shadow blacks, the filmmaker can "paint with light" by how he or she selects compositions with the camera. By shooting fast and spontaneous scenes with minimum lighting interference, one can create scenes of great dramatic power, with a greatly reduced rental cost.

For a first low-budget feature film, I recommend using either fast ASA 800 color film with minimum lighting and natural light or shooting black-and-white Plus-X or Tri-X stock and lighting with three 1,500-watt Lowell soft lights for diffused light, to avoid the problems of color balance and grain buildup. If you must shoot color film, then use Color Negative stock, but without worrying about achieving a Hollywood look. Because there are so many details for the filmmaker to juggle on location, it's especially important to reduce problems associated with lighting.

Natural Lighting with ASA 800 Filmstock

One way to shoot scenes inside and maintain the highest degree of improvisational energy with your actors is by using a high-speed filmstock that doesn't require artificial lighting. Although these fast stocks often add to the amount of grain visible when your film is projected, they sometimes allow you to shoot interior scenes with just the available natural lighting. Both Fuji and Kodak now offer ASA 800 color filmstocks in 16-mm, each claiming to have scientifically reduced unwanted grain buildup in images produced by these ultra-fast stocks. The filmmaker must test these stocks to determine which nuance of color and texture works best for his or her project. If you call the Fuji representative ([800] 326-0800) and let him know you are considering using Fuji stock for your feature, he may be able to send you both a 200′ roll of ASA 250 Color Negative and a 200′ roll of ASA 800 Color Negative for you to "test." Of course, with your small budget, it is necessary to treat this free stock as potential footage for your film, and shoot it carefully as part of your movie.

You must place your actors in advantageous natural light situations to get the best results from this method, and you may need to supplement nature with one soft light and a few 250-watt practical lightbulbs to get a suitable f-stop for interior filming. If your actors are placed near a sunlit window, the natural light should be sufficient to shoot them, creating a very interesting lighting mood. And the ability to move the actors from one emotional sequence to the next without lighting-change interruptions will give you much more control over the performances. Instead of spending an hour setting up each scene with artificial lights, you will be able to film your movie four times as fast—meaning you will save money, time, and energy. If the mood of your film is enhanced by this natural lighting, and won't suffer with the addition of a grainy image, then I highly recommend shooting without lights using fast film.

While working carefully to use dramatic areas of light and shadow for your shots, it is important that you continue to keep your main focus on the actors and the story you are trying to tell. For a first feature it may be wise to use black-and-white film to eliminate the problems with color under low-light conditions.

note: To make sure that a "fast" stock is correct for your movie concept, it would be a good idea to shoot a couple of 100′ rolls of film using the stock you are considering. Since this is just a test, borrow a friend's Bolex camera and shoot test lengths of perhaps ten seconds at those locations you have selected. Get the film processed and project the results under good screening conditions. If the feeling of the stock appeals to you, then you have been blessed with the ability to shoot your film in the easiest, most straightforward manner.

Soft Lights

The most basic way to light with soft lights is to place one light on each side of the camera, aimed directly at your actors, using a third light to add illumination to the actors and background, and then take a light reading. Using your Spectra light meter with inserts for each ASA, you aim the white cone back at the camera from where the actors are located to measure the incident light. (See chapter 5 for more information on using the light meter.) If you are shooting Plus-X Reversal black-and-white film, and want a rich, luminous, European look, underexpose ½ stop (as an example, close down the exposure from f-4 to a setting between f-4 and f-5.6) and have the lab print it as normal, without timing changes. With three soft lights you won't blow fuses as long as you use your 50′ extension cords to plug into outlets in different locations in the house where you are filming. If you can light your scenes to get your f-stop readings between 4 and 5.6, you should be able to shoot quickly with elegant results.

Saving Money on Filmstock and Sound Track

Sometimes, if you check the bulletin boards at the labs or look through ads in moviemaking newsletters (check the Internet!), you can find an offer for inexpensive filmstock or "ends." The price may be greatly reduced because the filmmaker needs money back for stock that wasn't shot on location, or because the filmstock is outdated. In either case it would be extremely unwise to purchase any large quantities of stock until you shoot a short test (20′) to see if it's OK. And check with your local lab to see if they still process the type of stock you are considering. In the last few years many beautiful and interesting filmstocks such as Kodachrome 2-A have been discontinued, and soon it seems only Color Negative stock will be available. Perhaps the video revolution will push the entire 16-mm film industry into the drink, but for now the filmmaker can take advantage of lowered prices, unused equipment, cheap editing "packages," and unwanted stock to complete his or her low-budget features.

If you buy your filmstock directly from a lab, make sure that your price for the stock included in the overall deal you cut with that lab (for stock, processing, answer print cost, sound mix if possible, film or video work print) approaches what the stock would cost you if purchased directly from Kodak or Fuji. And to insure consistent color values, you must request all rolls of stock be from the same batch of emulsion numbers. (This will be apparent when you examine the cans of filmstock and see that the numbers on the labels are the same.) If you weren't able to make a package deal with the lab for all your processing and printing needs, then definitely purchase your twelve or more rolls of stock directly from the Kodak or Fuji distributor in your area, since this (small) bulk purchase will save you several dollars on each roll.

It is not worth purchasing either ¼″ recording stock for your Nagra, or sound cassettes for your Sony Walkman Professional recorder, from individuals at "discount." The regular prices are low enough, so the filmmaker should make sure he or she gets top-quality tape for on-location sound recording.

For each low-budget feature production, the filmmaker should purchase a case of ten 1,200′ rolls of mag track directly from the supplier. This purchase will save you more than a hundred dollars. Phone Quantegy in Burbank ([800] 752-0732) and order your case of sound track a few weeks in advance of the shoot. This mag track will be used for sound transfers from ¼″ recording tape from your on-location recordings, as well as for all other needed sound transfers, including sound effects, music, narrations, dubs, and possibly the final sound mix.

Renting Equipment

When it comes to a question of whether to buy or rent equipment, a moviemaker should consider the technical support that comes along with renting equipment from a top-quality facility. Some film equipment rental houses, like Armanda Costanza, Inc., of Nashville (<**www.acincnashville.com**>, [800] 937-2774), will go to the wall to insure that their clients' productions run smoothly. Robert Costanza prides himself on working closely with filmmakers to help them fit their equipment costs (and filmstock expenditures) within a preexisting budget. If a first-time feature filmmaker says he or she has $3,000 per week to spend, then Costanza will personally design their equipment list to maintain quality and affordability, even for a production as far away as Tucson, Arizona. Because of their great working relationship with Southwest Airlines, their rental house can get your equipment delivered for 55 cents per pound (wherever Southwest flies), and it will be a Costanza who takes your equipment to the airport . . . so you can depend on whatever schedule of delivery they commit to by phone! And if you need an assistant cameraperson, they have a "beeper" list of people ready to oblige (ACs come virtually free since the presence of a certified operator defrays the 8.75 percent sales tax bite, at least in Tennessee!). Plus, they usually have a million dollars' worth of filmstock on hand and can cut incredible deals for features (cases of 800 ASA Kodak Vision stock are ready to ship for your next rockumentary!). Costanza's can take a filmstock order at midnight and have it delivered to your set that morning by 9:00 A.M. (Kodak has discontinued such "hotline" service.) Given the high level of attention they devote to productions seeking their services, they virtually become an unnamed "associate producer" for those features. When you're ready to shoot, talk to Robert or one of the other Costanza family members who run this incredible facility.

Support Equipment

Various other pieces of equipment must also be rented or obtained for the successful on-location shoot. A tripod will be needed to support and smoothly move the camera. I recommend the Miller Pro fluid head tripod ($35 per day), and for shots that require a lower vantage point you will want to rent "Baby Legs" ($10 a day), with their shorter tripod legs. To keep the tripod legs from slipping on a slick floor, a "spreader" is essential ($5 per day). A changing bag ($15 per day) will be needed to load and unload the filmstock in the camera magazine. And if you plan to shoot over four 400′ rolls of film each day, you will need an additional battery belt ($15 a day) to keep the camera running. Sandbags ($1.50 a day) are helpful to weigh down the base of the tripod or light stands, but not all rental facilities have these in stock. Of course, if the filmmaker has some idle time and lives near the coastline, he can fill up some durable cloth or plastic bags with sand from the beach and save some money. Also, apple boxes ($2.50 a day), sturdy wooden boxes about one foot tall, are excellent for standing on while working at high tripod settings when shooting the camera, for adjusting lights set high, or recording sound from above the actors' heads. Reinforced orange crates or plastic milk crates may do the job without the cost. To insure that good, clean sound is recorded on location, the noise from a running camera must be silenced with a "barney" ($10 per day), which surrounds the camera with sound-resistant padding. And several filters, including an 85 filter for outside filming, and a polarizer filter to avoid glares and enhance clouds, must be rented ($4 each day) for the camera. You will need a clapboard ($5 a day) for striking sync before each scene, and a light meter (Spectra or Luna-Pro) is a must for setting f-stops ($15 a day).

It will also be necessary to purchase "shooting aids" such as gaffer's tape (large roll, $25), which you will quickly discover is indispensable for securing tripod legs, sealing up camera magazines, holding lights, repairing costumes—the list goes on. You will need a bottle of compressed air for cleaning out the camera magazines after shooting each roll of film ($8), and some orange sticks to scrape out dirt from the camera aperture ($1). Lens tissue is a must ($3), and a few Sharpie permanent marker ink pens ($1) will be needed to identify magazines shot, etc. If there will be a lot of setting up of lights then some sort of work gloves ($7) will be necessary to protect your hands from the hot light heads. And if you will be doing a lot of painting with light, you'll need to purchase a collection of different gels, which could easily run you over $100 for an assortment. All these costs add up quickly, but if the low-budget feature filmmaker is able to simplify his concepts of lighting (leaving "Hollywood" lighting to Hollywood), he or she can afford these prices.

Equipment Checklist

☐ Camera body
☐ Batteries and battery pack
☐ Extra magazines
☐ Power cables
☐ Lens mounts
☐ Lenses

- ☐ Filmstock
- ☐ Barney
- ☐ Light meters
- ☐ Tripod
- ☐ Baby legs
- ☐ Hi-Hat (tripod mount to shoot from tabletop, other surfaces)
- ☐ Spreader
- ☐ Spreader dolly
- ☐ Wheelchair (for no-budget dolly shots)
- ☐ Apple boxes
- ☐ Sandbags
- ☐ Ladder
- ☐ Gloves
- ☐ Plug-in electrical boxes with four outlets
- ☐ 3-prong adapters/3 50′ extension cords
- ☐ Foamcore board (for reflecting light)
- ☐ Reflectors
- ☐ 1-K baby spots (including scrims, barn doors, snoots, to aim light)
- ☐ Midget spot
- ☐ Stands and clamps for lights
- ☐ Tota kit
- ☐ Soft lights
- ☐ Gels, diffusion
- ☐ Orange curtain, neutral density curtain, black cloth, black backdrop, other lighting accessories
- ☐ Changing bag
- ☐ Accessories for unloading camera (small cores, reels and black bags, empty cans)
- ☐ Compressed air, orange sticks for cleaning camera
- ☐ Gaffer's tape, camera tape
- ☐ Filters, filter rings/85, diffusion, polarizer
- ☐ Clapboard
- ☐ Marking pens, chalk
- ☐ Powder pad for makeup

Paperwork/Errands/Lists

The four weeks of preproduction are like being on a roller coaster, cranking up the large first hill before being released toward the dips and curves ahead. As you continue to try to remember everything important for the shoot, the juggling of so much information makes you feel like an overworked computer. Even in your sleep the wheels continue to spin. Small details merge with major concerns. Each morning you must rely on your large organizational calendar to keep the shoot in perspective and in control. This wall calendar is made out of 4″-by-6″ index cards Scotch-taped together, each card representing one day, a countdown until filming is completed. With deadlines for reserving equipment, meetings with actors and technicians, other production details, you will watch the calendar fill up as the shooting deadline approaches. Or you may prefer to watch your production develop on the screen of your laptop computer, juggling budget and schedule, other details, right up until (and during) the shoot.

In the last two weeks before the shoot, there will be many small errands to run. You will need to make copies of your revised script/outline and mail them (e-mail, fax) out to the cast. And you will need to make copies of your release form for the actors or anyone who happens to appear in your movie. Searching for props, costumes, locations, maybe even lead actors, will keep you constantly on the move. On your calendar you need to remind yourself to keep in touch with the key members of your cast and crew, keeping their energy high for the upcoming shoot. Every day you will make lists on your calendar of things to do, and every night you will cross off what you've accomplished, along with putting an *X* across the day that has been spent. You will need to write a schedule of what scenes will be filmed, at what locations, on what day, with which actors in attendance (for large indie productions you may want to purchase scheduling software, like Movie Magic Scheduling, $899, [800]-84-STORY, **<www.screenplay.com>**). As you do this last-minute schedule, you may find that you need to write more scenes to complete the transitions. Working under pressure always seems to open up new thoughts and ideas. When you hand out the shooting schedule to your cast and crew a few days before the shoot, they will get the feeling that you do, indeed, have everything under control.

It is very difficult to be responsible for everything connected to making a feature-length movie, but this is what every person who has attempted such a low-budget project has endured. Soon the air will clear, and even though the next phase of production—*the shoot*—is the most intense, it will be a relief to be able to just focus on actors, camera work, and constructing scenes that tell your story. Before we begin the tasks of directing and filming on location, let's review what must be readied for the shoot.

Preproduction Checklist

- ☐ Reserve all equipment at least two weeks in advance, after first checking with the rental agency to find out when they recommend you make your reservation. Inquire about the special rate for weekend shooting if applicable, or request a "camera package" rate for shoots that run longer than two days. In either case make sure the lens has been, or will be, calibrated for sharp focus. Review your equipment checklist to make sure you will have everything you need for the shoot.
- ☐ Select the cast and crew as soon as possible and have them sign contracts (and releases for actors) before the shoot. Hire as good a soundperson as you can convince to work on your project.
- ☐ Order filmstock from the lab (as part of your "lab deal") at least two weeks before the shoot, requesting all rolls be from the same batch of emulsion. Or purchase rolls directly from the Kodak or Fuji supplier. Keep rolls cool and dry.
- ☐ Buy sound tape (¼″ or sound cassettes) and order a case of mag track.
- ☐ Select locations for filming and, whenever possible, nail down agreements with responsible parties to insure no last-minute snags, getting signed location releases in advance.
- ☐ If you have decided to purchase your filmstock from the lab, make sure that you talk to the manager about a "lab deal" involving their best price breaks on stock, processing, work printing (of usable

scenes), sound transferring from ¼″ tape or sound cassettes to mag track, final answer print cost—after making them aware that you are producing a feature film at used-car prices.

- ☐ Budget your money for the shoot ahead, making sure that there is enough cash for equipment, accessories of the filming, small per diem salaries, and food that will be provided by the production. Have at least an extra few hundred dollars in your wallet (if possible) for unexpected needs during shooting.
- ☐ Spend as much time as possible going over your story, thinking hard about what you will film, what you are trying to say.
- ☐ Give a copy of the script or outline to the actors.
- ☐ Talk to your cast and crew members occasionally during the last week before filming, keeping their energy and commitment high, making sure everything is still "go."
- ☐ Schedule the scenes to be filmed, at which locations, involving which members of the cast and crew.
- ☐ Organize transportation for the cast and crew to the locations of the shoot.
- ☐ Mentally prepare yourself for the jump into the unknown of filming; ready yourself to work to exhaustion (and convince others to do the same) until the filming is completed.
- ☐ Try to plan your production day to run approximately ten to twelve hours, to avoid burning out cast and crew for the long haul (starting your shoot with a ruinous eighteen-hour day is courting disaster for your feature).
- ☐ Get some exercise (swimming, running, or just walking), eat some good food, and grab some rest, to prepare yourself for the hard work ahead. Good luck!

5

Production: Filming and Directing

Although lack of money is generally thought of as the major problem for not getting a movie into production, I believe *fear of the unknown* is the primary reason why so many productions collapse just before the shooting is scheduled to begin. And the biggest unknown is: Will it be any good? No one wants to be associated with a failure—neither a Hollywood studio nor an independent producer. At this point in production, everyone realizes that his or her self-esteem is on the line. Last-minute doubts flutter in the face of the moviemaker. He or she wonders: Can I really shoot a feature? Is my story really worth telling? Will my actors (or nonactors) be convincing? Can I direct? Will I have enough money to finish my movie and also pay my rent? Will I fail? You are certainly aware that all your friends are watching, with attitudes that range from scorn, jealousy, and disbelief to pride, encouragement, and love. Everyone will be waiting for the results of your "folly," and although you are trying your best to ignore the negativity, you must admit you have your own (well-hidden) doubts. You can still back out, cancel the equipment rentals with a phone call, call the cast and crew and tell them that the production is "temporarily" postponed until . . . The fear of failure has reigned supreme. Or has it?

To overcome the gut-ache panic of taking this last step of commitment to your feature-length project, it is important to remember the role fear plays in the creation of art. This final bout with the fear trapped inside the gut of any self-respecting filmmaker is no different from the last-minute butterflies most of the best actors feel before they walk onstage. It is this fear that fuels greatness. As every cell in your body becomes aware of the intensity of the risk you feel you are taking, your focus narrows down to meet the challenges of the production. Your energy is stronger, your creative powers never better. The complexity of being an adult has been replaced by the simplicity of single-minded purpose. You're scared, but also excited. Instead of being bothered on a daily basis by mundane worries, bills, small talk, lightweight games and hobbies, you are on the threshold of taking back some control over your life.

Just before shooting was to begin on *The Last Roommate*, my collaborators experienced a severe case of last-minute jitters. They couldn't believe that I was serious about shooting with "no script" (we had only completed five pages of scripting, but had a very clear outline, detailing the incidents of our story). I convinced them to just jump in and begin, scripting each night as we shot the film. After they saw the beautiful results from the first 400 feet of footage, the doubts vanished and the work carried us through. To successfully shoot a feature, it is important to open yourself up to the possibilities, as expressed in my Fifteen Rules for no-budget moviemaking.

Fifteen Rules for Shooting No-Budget Features

1. Script . . . but go with the flow.
2. Don't overlook miracles around you.
3. Use available people you know (actors, technicians, extras).
4. Use all problems to *benefit* the production.
5. Try to pay people who work for you *some* money so you won't be embarrassed when you take control of their lives for a movie.
6. Contractualize everything.
7. Don't skimp on getting good recorded sound.
8. Rent the best camera (or hire a cinematographer who has one).
9. Be creative and original while shooting; find your own way of seeing.

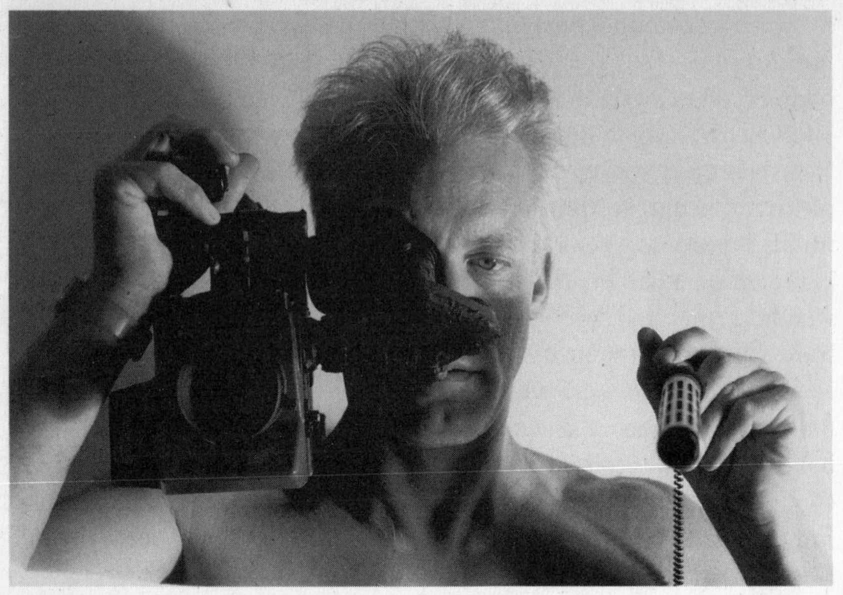

Jon Jost—a crew of one—shooting CP-16 and recording sync sound for a feature.

10. Don't get discouraged. You can fix it in the editing (even if some say you can't).
11. Don't turn your back on the ideas and resources of your actors (change the script instead).
12. Say something with your movie—action is not enough!
13. Pick a location that offers great visual possibilities.
14. Get as many charge cards as you can *before* you start making a feature (use them *only* as a last resort).*
15. If you don't quit, you *can* finish your no-budget feature before you die.

**The filmmaker/videomaker who racks up more than $20,000 in credit card charges for his/her movie must expect to face extremely high monthly payments, probably equaling several times what they currently pay for rent (and rents are high enough!). I've gone this route a few times (not fun) and hope that the moviemaker of the twenty-first century will have a better chance of bringing economic balance to his or her life, holding down a good-paying job, saving up a* used-car *production budget before jumping into the fray.*

Because it is such a complex task to film/direct a feature-length movie (especially with no money), it is absolutely vital that the low-budget producer simplify, as much as possible, the problems of the shoot. When I was a sophomore in engineering at the University of Arizona (Tucson, 1964), I took a course called "Statics and Dynamics." This course was designed to confuse, discourage, and weed out the uncommitted engineers, and it did just that. The class started out with a hundred students coming to lectures, and after the teacher filled four large blackboards with mathematical equations in vector calculus (which none of us knew anything about), only eighteen students bothered to show up for the following session. I tried to do the twenty problems assigned at the end of each chapter we studied, but after spending eight hours on one problem and not getting the answer, I gave up. I doubted if there were enough hours in a month to complete the weekly assignment. So I decided to spend my time trying to understand the one sample problem of each chapter (though it still took hours and hours). I would go over the mathematics and keep checking myself against the numbers in the sample. When I took the final exam for the class (having done only twelve problems in the book), I achieved a 33 percent—which was graded on the curve as a solid C—and passed. So what I'd like to do in this chapter is give a "sample" of how to film/direct with actors, shoot the camera, record sound, and light the scene. Hopefully, with the strong foundation created by this sample shoot, the reader can apply this knowledge to his own situations of low-budget feature filmmaking.

Picking Up Rental Equipment

Rental equipment will usually be picked up either late in the afternoon on Friday, for the special reduced weekend rate of a one-day rental, or on the morning of the shoot. The moviemaker carefully checks his or her list for the pieces of equipment that have been set aside for the rental package. He or she is most careful that nothing vital to the shoot is missing, double-checking for the power cables that run the camera and making sure the extension cords are equipped with three-prong adapters for plugging into household outlets. After all pieces of equipment have been accounted for, he or she packs everything carefully into the car, making sure *never* to leave it unattended, even for the few seconds it takes to go back into the rental agency for the next load. Then, with the Nagra recorder specially cushioned on a seat where it can't be damaged by bumpy driving conditions, the moviemaker either drives the equipment to the location for filming or drives it home, to wait for the next morning's early call.

Morning of the Shoot

You get up around six, shower to wake up, get something to eat, and go over your script for that day's filming one last time before facing your cast and crew. Perhaps, under the pressure of knowing you will be shooting in a few hours, you think of some new dialogue to add, or maybe cut some extra dialogue out. The pressure of actual filming will generate new ideas and crystallize ideas that needed to be improved. On your front door you notice the note in large print that says DON'T FORGET BATTERY BELT, and you unplug it from the outlet where it has been charging overnight. If the folks from the rental house had already charged it, they probably recommended that you give it a quick charge for about an hour before shooting. It is always worth posting this note to remember the battery belt, since the morning will be filled with distractions. You were, of course, smart enough to carry all the heavy equipment into your house for security overnight. You knew it wasn't worth risking having $35,000 worth of equipment stolen from your car by someone with a coat hanger. And now it's time to load it back in again.

Loading Equipment, Picking Up Actors and Crew

It is now eight in the morning and you've valiantly resisted checking your e-mail, a drain you don't need on this special day (you've already alerted cast and crew members that your e-mail is "off" during the shoot). No message is more important than the quiet sense-of-purpose you need to maintain right from the very start. The ONLY reason to turn on your computer, aside from reprinting a portion of the script, is to log onto the Website, <www.zip2.com>, that offers street directions between any two points in your metropolitan area (just click on "Get Directions"). Type in your address and that of the cast or crew member needing a ride, and you'll receive step-by-step instructions for driving right to their door. It's bad enough having easy access to the cell phone lying next to your script (remember to *turn it off* while on the set, and instruct cast and crew members to do the same—real-world distractions like phone call interruptions will surely diminish the quality of your movie!).

Heading out the door at 8:00 A.M. will give you twenty minutes to lift the heavy equipment into the car before leaving to pick up your actors and crew members at the prearranged times. Either you have a garage, or live in a safe neighborhood and have no fear that the equipment already loaded in your car will be stolen between trips back into the house for the next item. Or maybe you have hired a production assistant to help pack and guard your car. The last pieces of equipment you load should be the camera and the Nagra recorder, being careful to strap the Nagra on a cushioned seat with a seat belt holding the delicate machine tightly in place. If you have a production assistant, then he or she can hold the machine on his or her lap for the ride over to the location.

You have promised to pick up the lead actor around 9:00 A.M. because his car is broken, and you arrive on time. He is still eating breakfast, saying he got up late, so you decide to review your script out in your car where you can guard the equipment. You try not to fixate on the minutes ticking by, worrying about being late for the other people you are supposed to pick up. You even call him on your cell phone to avoid walking the fifty feet to his door, and try to distinguish his words between corn flake crunches. You diplomatically mention time constraints and he promises to be right out. The word "Thanks" is expelled from your lips as you punch off the phone. When the actor finally walks out to your car, you are too relieved to scold him about tardiness, and you certainly don't want to start off on the wrong foot. But if this happens repeatedly over a couple of days, or you feel yourself losing your temper, you must tell him in clear language to knock it off. If you are already in an irritated mood, then you'd better talk to

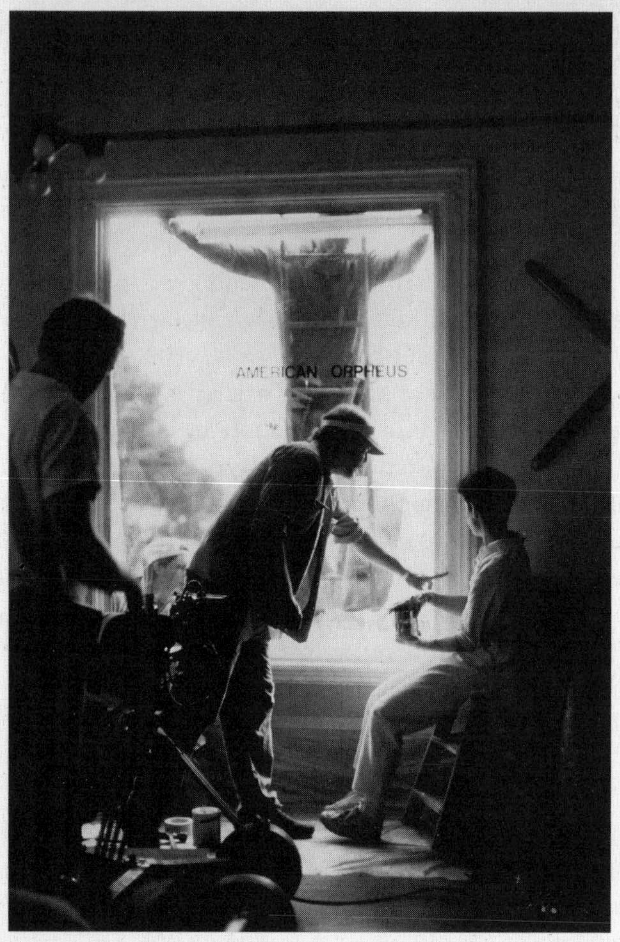

Rick Schmidt directs lead actress Jody Esther for *American Orpheus* as cinematographer Kyle Bergersen (*left*) readies camera. Photo by Julie Schachter.

him now and get it off your chest. You tell him that he has made you late for picking up the other members of the cast and crew. You tell him he must be on time tomorrow and for every deadline during the shoot. You have said this before it builds up into a big emotional thing. He says, "Sure, sorry," and everything is cool. If he has become irritated by your scolding you had better have a talk with him *now* before you waste your valuable filmstock on a problem actor. Clear it up before it gets worse.

Organization on Location

After you have picked up your cast and crew members who needed a ride (and who were able to squeeze into your car along with all the equipment) and arrive at the location, the first thing you do, if you haven't done so already, is select a small room or corner where you will bring the equipment. Pick a place that is out of the way of any shots or heavy foot traffic. This way you won't have to keep moving the equipment around the space you're using, losing valuable time for shooting. A separate room is best, since you will also use the space for loading and unloading your filmstock into the camera. It is important that you are able to concentrate on loading without outside distractions, so that you don't accidentally open up the wrong side of the film magazine, exposing the film you just shot to the light. Also, it will be very important to correctly mark each can of exposed film for the lab with your name, the number you designate for the roll, and type of stock, indicating if footage shot is either a partial or full roll. A mistake in this procedure could cost you eleven minutes of shots (one 400′ roll) and maybe demoralize the entire production.

While you load your magazines you will want each member of the cast and crew to keep busy in preparation for the shooting of the first scene. If you are lucky enough to have a director of photography, then he or she will begin to set up the lights in the room where the first shot will take place. If you must light the scenes yourself, then your assistant can unpack the lights and assemble them on their stands. The actors may also want to help set up the lights because the physical work can ease their tension before shooting begins. Or it may be necessary for them to review changes in the script. As soon as everyone knows his job, you announce that you will be loading film in the storeroom and ask them to please not come in for equipment until you are done. You may want to make up a sign that says FILM BEING LOADED—STAY OUT! Make sure everyone understands that you must be left alone, with no one bothering you with questions, until after you have unpacked the 400′ rolls of filmstock from their cans (done inside a light-tight "changing bag") and loaded the magazines. At later stages of the shoot, you may decide to load magazines with people around, but for the first attempts you need privacy.

Loading the Camera

Hopefully, the clerk at the rental agency has shown you how to load a magazine on your rented camera. And ideally you have had a chance to practice a few times. A manual for the camera you have chosen will be available as a backup guide (check places that sell motion picture cameras; or your rental agency can supply one or tell you where to find one), but no guide can replace hands-on practice using exposed film. Or maybe you rented your camera from a private individual who will load the magazines for you. When I was preparing to film *A Man, a Woman, and a Killer* in 1973, I had many doubts about my ability to use the Eclair NPR camera. All I knew was that it was a very good (and expensive) camera and that I should rent it for our eleven-day shoot. When I picked up the equipment the day before we were to leave for our location in Mendocino, California, 150 miles away, I had never even held the camera and had no idea how to load it. The manager of the rental facility pulled out a roll of exposed film and quickly gave me a five-minute lesson on how to thread the film through the magazine. I remember concentrating as hard as I absolutely could, because I knew that this was my one chance to learn the routine. After I had shot forty-five 400′ rolls of film and was preparing to return home to Oakland, my soundman, Neelon Crawford, told me that this was the first shoot he had been on where an Eclair NPR camera had not jammed at least once! I guess my constant fear of failure with regard to loading the magazines correctly prompted me to double-check each sprocket and roller for correct threading.

Don't wait until the last minute like I did. Request a demonstration on threading the film through the magazine as soon as you have selected your camera for the shoot. And if you aren't sure you know the correct procedure after one demonstration, ask for another.

As soon as you have loaded the film into your camera, your next step is to focus the eyepiece for your particular eyesight.

Focusing the Eyepiece

Before you can shoot sharp images for your movie, you need to adjust the eyepiece on the viewfinder of your camera. To accomplish this task you first need to adjust the lens to infinity and loosen a small screw on the viewfinder that locks the focus into place. Focus the eyepiece until the grain of the glass is in sharp focus and the center crosshairs are perfectly focused to your eye. Tighten down the lock-screw and you're ready for the first shot.

Shooting Wide-Screen 16:9

Given the fact that all TV sets will be rendered obsolete in 2006 by the mandated changeover to HDTV (some say the switch will take place even sooner), the filmmaker/digital videographer must seriously consider framing for the wide screen so future work isn't rendered undistributable. This means that when you frame your shot you must leave a portion of the top and bottom of the frame free of vital information. You won't want to have a close-up shot of an actor's face where the lips are near the bottom, below the cut-off point and the eyes are skimming the top of the frame. That shot would not be suitable for broadcast, or acceptable for theatrical presentation (if your 16-mm or DV was blown to 35-mm). For an HDTV cut-off (1.179), or most other wide-screen letterboxing ratios of 1:85 or 2:1, you'll need to be conscious of the framing on *each* shot, mentally evaluating what you're looking at through the film camera eyepiece, figuring out what visual information will indeed fit into a wide-screen cut-off. Of course if you're using the most recent digital video cameras, you can simply set the shots for 16:9. And several new cutting-edge 16-mm cameras, like the new Aaton, offer 16:9 ratio viewing.

Cinematographer Vittorio Storaro (*The Conformist*, *Apocalypse Now*,

The Last Emperor, *Bulworth*, etc.) is an advocate for a movement called "univisium" (see chapter 12), trying to get a consensus for shooting at a 2:1 ratio for both future HDTV and theatrical presentation so that the cinematographer's art doesn't have to adjust for different formats (as it has been chopped down for TV presentation in the past). This extreme 2:1 ratio would make it even more critical for present-day filmmakers, who would need to compose shots for this wide-screen ratio while staring through a fairly boxy 4:3 eyepiece. It might be useful to spend some time checking out one of the new DV handicam cameras that shoot 16:9 and getting a feel for this wide-screen look—you might like it! And you can test footage on computer, adjusting the viewing ratio to 1:85 if you have an editing software program that applies a "letterbox" effect. At any rate this decision of what ratio to frame your movie may be one of the most important decisions you make as you head into production.

Camera Maintenance

A final word on the camera: Don't forget to check the gate for particles of dirt that may build up on the pressure plate and aperture as you run rolls of film through the magazine. An "orange stick" should be used to scrape away any buildup of emulsion dust and dirt inside the camera. The cameraperson must also check the camera's aperture for hairs and dirt particles that would ruin the shots. A good practice is to use compressed air to blow out the camera magazines after each 400′ roll is filmed, to insure that no dust will interfere with clean images. And if just the idea of loading, unloading, assembling, and cleaning your camera has worn you out (before you've even shot a foot of film), don't worry—hire a camera assistant from a local film school who knows how to load the camera, operate it, and clean it between rolls, while you just push the button after framing your shots. Or rent a camera from someone who will help you shoot on location. Remember, your main job is to think about what you are saying in film.

Placing the Camera for Your First Shot

You must now select the placement of the camera, that spot from which your first shot will be filmed. Sometimes this decision will have already been made, drawn on a storyboard card, but for the director who works in the style of improvisation, this decision will not be finalized until he or she gets the actors together at the location and gets an intuitive feeling about the upcoming scene. Because of the heightened sense of urgency on the set, you will find that your ideas and sense of awareness about the story will seem to come into focus as never before. And with this new insight you will place your actors in the scene in a way you hadn't considered at the time you first scouted the location. It is possible that you hadn't been able to see the rooms for the filming except in late afternoon, and now you are affected by the early morning light that covers the walls and windows. And maybe the weather is different, and this also affects your decisions. Also, you may notice something different about the chemistry between your leading actors when they are together that first day and decide to shoot an unplanned scene that captures this spirit.

While the members of the cast and crew wait for you to decide the first placement of the camera, you feel the pressure that comes with being the leader of the project. Even if you are not absolutely sure, you must break the ice and make the decision of where to place the camera so that you don't stall the filming and undermine your self-confidence. Unless you are shooting with angled shots as Orson Welles did in *Touch of Evil*, either place the camera on a level surface or attach it to a tripod and level your shot by loosening the large wing nut below the mount, lining up the bubble at the center of the bubble gauge before tightening down. Look through the lens and use the zoom to (tentatively) set the framing, with your actors in their (tentative) positions. You will want to readjust this framing just before shooting, once you've observed how the lights affect the actors and background. After the camera placement has been set for the first shot, you and your helper(s) can begin to light the scene.

Tips for Lighting on Location

Whether you have chosen to light your scenes with soft lights aimed directly at your actors, Tota kits in combination with spots to create a complex zone system for painting with light, or just a couple of 250-watt Practical lightbulbs with natural light, there are similar lighting problems to watch out for during the shoot.

- ☐ Watch out for reflections in the shiny surfaces included in your shots. Look through the lens of the camera and closely examine mirrors, glass objects, and windows for reflections of cast and crew members and film equipment you might overlook during the excitement of the filming. Request that everyone behind the camera remain still during each shot; even if you have missed the reflection of a helper it probably will not be noticed if he or she doesn't move.
- ☐ While looking through the lens, check for light flares (obvious bright spots of light that will disrupt the look of your shot) on walls, edges of chairs, and on shiny surfaces. If you slightly adjust the position of your lights, most flares will disappear. Another solution may be to use black paper tape to cover reflected highlights on small areas such as metal chair tubing or edges of wooden counters. Of course, make sure that the tape isn't visible when looking through the camera.

note: With the coming of HDTV, the old standby plywood desks of network news anchors will soon have to be replaced because the new crisp-detail video reads them as just what they are—cheap makeshift sets. So you'll need to be even more careful when applying tape to cover over reflective surfaces, and with set design in general.

- ☐ Also check the faces of your actors for shiny highlights that may detract from their performances. Although the low-budget filmmaker usually doesn't have a makeup person on the set, someone should have a powder pad for this purpose.

- ☐ Always use your 50′ extension cords to plug in your lights at electrical outlets at the far corners of the house in which you are filming. This procedure guards against blowing fuses during your big scenes. And after you have checked your lights for f-stop and placement, turn them off so you don't waste the life of the bulbs. If you are unable to have all the necessary lights for your shoot turned on without blowing fuses, it is possible to "tie in" directly to the source of electricity for the house on the pole outside, but *don't attempt this without the aid of a professional gaffer.*
- ☐ Try to maintain your light as constant as possible around an f-stop of f-4 to f-8. For some reason most lenses function best in this range, giving clearest, sharpest images at that setting.
- ☐ Try not to adjust your lights between shots that you will want to cut together. If the lighting direction changes radically between a close-up and a medium shot while two people are talking, it will look pretty weird if a face goes dark on the cut. Use the same lighting to insure a consistent image.
- ☐ If lights must be placed close to ceilings and walls, tape a piece of tinfoil or other heat-resistant material to the exposed surface to prevent possible fire or heat damage. And to avoid excessively high temperatures on the set due to overheated lights, keep a door open between takes and turn off lights between shots.
- ☐ Have two light meters on the set, to occasionally double-check your light readings. Also, if one meter gets dropped during filming, you will have a backup, which is especially useful when you are hundreds of miles away from your equipment rental agency.
- ☐ It is also a good idea to have several replacement bulbs for your lights with you on location, so that if one blows you can quickly continue with the scene that is being filmed.
- ☐ Don't lift the Tota kit trunk or other heavy lights by yourself. Ask someone to help. Be careful not to lose all your creative energy by rushing the lifting and setting up of the lights.

Using a Light Meter

To take quick, accurate light readings I recommend using a Spectra meter (<www.spectracine.com>). The advantage of this meter is that if you insert a thin metal plate, one supplied for every kind of ASA, the meter is converted to give you the correct f-stop by simply reading the gauge. Other light meters are more complicated to read and require adjusting dials for each ASA.

When I'm filming I usually take what is called an "incident" light reading when shooting indoors with lights. This reading is taken from the location of the subject to be filmed (actor), toward the lens of the camera. By aiming the white plastic cone cover of the meter's eye toward the camera from where you are holding it in front of the face of your actor, you are able to get an accurate reading for the exposure of the face tones. As long as the exposure of your actor's face is correct, the scene will look correctly exposed. If you want an even light over the entire framing of your shot, you will need to check the corners of the framing with the meter and add light if necessary until you get the same light reading as for the face. But don't worry if parts of your scenes go to black or are overexposed to white because of a great difference in f-stop. As long as your actors' faces are correctly exposed, dark and light areas in a shot can often add to the dramatic punch of the scene.

When shooting outside you will remove the white cone cover and simply aim the light meter at the subject to be filmed from where you stand at the camera. This is called the "reflected" light reading. You'll then double-check the exposure for the actor's face by aiming the meter at the face from a foot or two away. Point the meter slightly down so that the meter doesn't read too much sky and falsify the true reading of the actor. Again, it is always best to expose for the actor. If you are trying to shoot a film in the style of Hollywood, you would probably want to rent some reflectors so that you could add light to an actor's face and body to even up the exposure with that of the background. After you process your first 400′ roll of film, you will want to pay special attention to your scenes with regard to their exposures. Are the scenes underexposed (too dark) because you closed down your f-stop to a smaller opening (f-11 to f-22), thinking that the scene was brighter than it really was? Your meter may have caught too much bright sky during your reading, causing your actors to look too dark. With a stock such as Color Negative, these values can be radically changed by timing corrections during printing, so all is not lost if the novice uses this three-f-stop-latitude stock. Each filmmaker gets into a rhythm of lighting and taking light readings, and by the end of the shoot, this process will be second nature to all concerned. After you see the results of the first roll, you have the option of either making a major style change with regard to lighting or continuing with what you have achieved.

What to Shoot? How to Shoot?

Even though this may be the first time you have ever shot 16-mm film (or DV), it is still quite possible to achieve original and carefully designed shots for your movie. The main thing to remember is that all the camera moves and framing decisions must be in support of the story and mood you are expressing. Don't worry about what other people have done in the past, or what other people think your film should look like. Don't worry if it will be "commercial." Concentrate on really feeling your story and the actors in front of the lens. Use your framing of the shots to convey your special connection to what is happening. Find the spot for each shot that is best, as you feel it, to place the camera. This camera location may be right because you can see the trees moving in the wind through the window behind your actors. Or it may be right because there is a blank white wall behind them. Go with your feelings and construct the shots using your intuition.

> **note:** If you are shooting 16-mm for eventual blow-up to 35-mm, I recommend you get in touch with the Du Art Film Laboratories in New York City (245 West 55th Street, New York, NY 10019, [212] 757-4580), asking to speak with the director of sales. Ask Du Art to mail you an in-depth brochure called *Shooting 16-mm or Super 16-mm for Blowup to 35-mm.*

A viable alternative to the exorbitant cost of a blowup from 16-mm to 35-mm master positive and dupe negative for multiple copies is to make just *one* 35-mm composite print, a single print to be used for the first few film festival premieres. Metropolis Film Lab, also of New York City ([212] 563-9388), offers a great deal for this "direct print method," charging approximately $9,000 for both a 35-mm print *and* a 16-mm answer print, both struck off your conformed original 16-mm negative.

The best advice I can give for choosing which type of shot to use (close-up, medium shot, wide shot) is that your film should probably have a variety of these shots so that the audience isn't put to sleep. If you are doing long takes with stationary camera setups, then have your characters approach the camera (close-up) or walk away. Anticipate the activity in the scene and allow for any movement that might take place. It's best to avoid using the zoom shot while filming, since this effect usually adds an amateurish feeling to a movie, unless it is done very carefully. Vary the level from which you shoot, get up high to shoot down, or shoot from the floor, to create a diversity of shots in support of the mood and concept of your story. Don't be afraid to come up with unusual shots and original concepts for presenting your scripted material.

Supporting Your Story with Images

The more you can tell your filmatic story with images, the more impact the material will have on the subconscious mind of the viewer. The highest compliment a film can receive is that "it stayed with me for days after the screening." That's the kind of film you want to make. In his class on directing at the California College of Arts and Crafts in Oakland, Bill Farley handed out notes to his students telling how Italian director Lina Wertmuller (*Swept Away*, *Seven Beauties*, etc.) takes a completed screenplay and rewrites every scene without any dialogue. She replaces her dialogue with visual storytelling, using images instead of words. Then she does a final draft of the script, a conglomerate of the most successful images she invented for the story (that replace dialogue now no longer necessary), along with whatever dialogue must remain for story line. In this way she insures that her films will be, first and foremost, visual experiences. Farley, a teacher and low-budget feature filmmaker (his *Of Men and Angels* showed in the Dramatic Competition at the Sundance Film Festival, 1989), wants his students to understand the power of imagery before they make their own films.

Another important advantage to "thinking visually," creating a movie with sparse dialogue, is that it will open up the potential audience for your little indie film to all the non-English-speaking countries, making it more desirable to their TV buyers.

If you're having a problem thinking visually, it might be helpful to rent some image-oriented films at your neighborhood video store. Check out some films by Godard (*Alphaville*, *Une Femme Mariée*), or Bergman (*The Seventh Seal*, *Persona*). Many silent films, from *The Last Laugh* (F. W. Murnau, 1924) to *The Cabinet of Dr. Caligari* (Robert Weine, 1919), can give you a great introduction to the graphic power of black-and-white imagery. Color films with graphic power seem harder to identify so readily, but films like *The Conformist* (Bertolucci, 1970) or *Chinatown* (Roman Polanski, 1974) reveal the power of imagery when a film is in the hands of an extremely talented director.

Another way to immerse yourself in images is to turn on your TV and leave the sound off. What you see are images that apply to your particular lifetime: talk shows, nightly news, movies made for TV. Do any of the electronic images fluttering before your face tell a story or keep your interest? Look at the choices of lighting and cuts. Do you understand the story that's being told? Are you being gripped by the images? Certainly it's easy to tell the difference between a film with images at work and a normal TV show. If an old black-and-white movie is on (that has escaped colorization!), you will probably find it has a lot more graphic power than anything else on the tube. That's the kind of imagery you want in your feature films.

The Long Take

One way to shoot a movie with great economy is to use the low-budget method of the "ten-minute take," honed to perfection by filmmakers like Jon Jost. In Jost's feature *Last Chants for a Slow Dance*, the film has been constructed mostly through beautifully crafted ten-minute takes (full 400′ rolls shot in one sequence) that are capable of telling a complex story. Jost has the ability to engineer into his long takes a great deal of narrative energy, so that although each scene is very long and without cuts, the viewer is never bored. To do what he does is very difficult, because *real* magic must be created in each long take. Every facet of the craft of filmmaking must be used to its maximum capacity: the way the shot is framed and filmed, what is said between the characters (and what is not said), the way the scene is lit, the selection of filmstock (grainy, or high-gloss color), and how the scene functions as part of the story being told. In *Last Chants for a Slow Dance*, Jost also uses some spectacular superimpositions (printing two different shots on one roll simultaneously) that are so subtle that the viewer doesn't really notice they are effects, but feels them deeply. To successfully use the long take, the filmmaker must be able to fill the frame of the shot with such a great deal of drama and magic that the audience doesn't ever feel the need for a cut. You must accomplish with this technique what must always be accomplished throughout any film, and that is to cast a spell over the viewer.

"Freeze" Method of Shooting for Cuts

If your feature will be constructed of many cuts, one method of shooting is to have the actors freeze their position at the director's command ("Freeze"), while the camera is moved to a new angle. This method designs each cut in a sequence, and the shooting is one-to-one. If the two characters in your movie are having a discussion on a couch and your first shot is wide to include the entire couch, after calling "Freeze" at an appropriate moment in the dialogue, you may want to move the camera into a closer shot of each person talking. Before the camera and sync sound recording have started up again, the actors are fed back the last few lines of dialogue, to be repeated at the next take. This gives the editor several in-points for making the cut work. A continuous sequence can be built with these changes of camera angle, so that the edited film will fit perfectly together. While Hollywood would use two cameras shooting continuously, with many takes, you are able to accomplish the same "look" shooting one-to-one with a single camera.

note: When shooting, it's best to keep the set as sparsely populated as possible, and have crew members and others avert their eyes from the scene-in-progress. It seems that actors (and especially nonactors) often have a tendency to make eye contact while the camera's rolling, with whomever they can find looking in their direction from behind the camera. And the camera can always tell when an actor has found a pair of eyes in that supposedly abandoned barn or wherever the scene is taking place, ruining the believability of the performance.

Cutaways and Pauses for Transitions

While shooting your scenes you should protect your ability to successfully edit those scenes together. In some instances a transition can be accomplished by a "cutaway," a short shot that shows either a character's reaction to dialogue said by another, or some action or object that has been part of the previous shot in wide coverage. If one of the characters was reaching for a cigarette, the camera could film a close-up of the hand as it touches the pack. This shot could be used to shorten a sequence that was running too long. Shooting a "reaction shot" of an actor's face is trickier, because without the real scene happening it's very hard for a director to create the energy of the moment, and often the result is wooden and stupid. Sometimes, in a very complicated sequence, it is worth it to shoot the scene twice, making sure that in take #1 you are on the character speaking and that in take #2 you pan over to the character responding. Any of these short little "extra" shots can save a scene in the editing room.

Also, it is important to run some footage at the beginning and end of each shot while filming, before the actors begin and after they have finished their scene, to film a "pause" that might help achieve a transition during editing. So don't say "Action" the second the clap board is pulled away, and don't call "Cut" immediately after the last word of dialogue has been spoken. Give your scenes adequate heads and tails. And after each scene is shot, it is important to record at least thirty seconds of "room tone," recorded at the same sound level at which dialogue was recorded. If changes need to be made in the sound track (words deleted or car horns removed, for example), they can be made during editing by cutting out defects and splicing in your room tone recording (which would be identical to the background sound of your shot if recorded on location directly after the take). When recording room tone you must request that actors remain in position and everyone on the crew stop moving and remain silent.

Shooting Without Sound

If you are *very* clever, and organized with regard to the structure and storyboarding of your feature, it is possible to shoot scenes without sync sound and piece in the sound later from "wild" recordings. The person off-camera delivers the lines while the camera is on the person listening, and the lines of dialogue or narration are recorded later in the sound studio. During editing, narrations and location sounds—birds, wind, babbling brook—could be added to give the scene a feeling of reality. This process opens up the possibilities of using sound as an effect, much as on radio, where sounds would expand your idea of what was actually happening. Most large-budget productions spend thousands of dollars on sound effects that fill up their twenty-four tracks for the mix. And many kung fu movies are shot without sound and are entirely dubbed later. So if the filmmaker has cheap or free access to a high-quality sound studio, this might be an option to consider.

It is also possible to reverse the process and record your sound first, editing the dialogue and effects into a tight cut, and then add the needed length of images. Once again, to use this method of filmmaking and succeed, you must be incredibly well organized in terms of every shot and sound that will make up your story.

The disadvantages of this type of filmmaking can outweigh the benefits if the method is not perfectly executed. To successfully complete the movie the filmmaker must make a large commitment to the many hours of editing such a feature will require. It will take a lot more editing to piece in the recorded dialogue and sound effects than would usually be needed to edit from the sound sync takes recorded on location. Although the production company that forgoes the cost of an on-location soundperson with gear may initially believe that it is saving money, the added expenses of creating each sound track with recorded "studio" sound, and extensive editing, may end up being more expensive and bothersome. When I have a soundperson on location, I always record sound sync for *every* shot, even if it is just a scene of someone sitting at a desk saying nothing. Then, when I sync up each take, I am saved from the aggravation of coming to a scene that has no sound, and from the worry of having to create some sound for that particular image. After the scene is shot, I have the soundperson record any sound effects that might come in handy during editing. If a man is writing a letter in a scene, I record a "wild take" of the sound of the pen moving against the paper. To avoid extra editing expenses, I make sure the soundperson has recorded a long-enough take of these sound effects to run concurrently with the sync take for which they are designed. When I finally arrive at the editing room, I find it is a great relief to know that, aside from some possible music, I have everything I need to edit my feature. So before you rule out hiring an on-location soundperson, make sure this decision is correct for the style of your film, your story, your editing process, and your budget.

High-Budget Effects

By being inventive, the low-budget filmmaker can achieve high-budget effects that will greatly enhance the possible commercial aspect of his or her film. Have you ever seen tree trimmers being hoisted up in a bucket, lifted by a hydraulic lift from the top of a truck? If you are persuasive, you can probably talk someone into loaning you his rig for the film, and use the lift for an inexpensive crane shot. Although the bucket tends to be a bit unsteady, if the camera is handheld while the bucket is raised (one person in the bucket to work the controls, one to film the shot), a beautiful effect can be achieved. If you are using powerful computer technology to edit, it's possible you can add a crane shot *after* the shoot, using the amazing Effetto Pronto software (see chapter 11).

Many filmmakers already know that a wheelchair works splendidly for dolly shots. Just set the cameraperson in the seat and roll backward or forward during the shot. You can either rent a wheelchair or, occasionally, buy one for $20 at a flea market. By the time you complete your first feature, it is quite possible that you will have invented some special apparatus or shots of your own.

Directing Actors on Location

After the camera placement has been set and the lighting properly arranged, the moviemaker/director turns his or her attention to the actors. Turning off the lights to save electricity and bulbs (not to mention lessening the uncomfortable heat), the filmmaker brings the actors onto the set and reviews their dialogue and blocking for the shot. Whether dealing with actors who have memorized the lines or with nonactors who will basically be themselves, you shouldn't spend so much time practicing the scene that all of the vital energy is expended before the camera is turned on. Although our strict budget requires basically a one-to-one shooting ratio, there is enough filmstock to do the most important shots twice if necessary. The filmmaker needs to sense the readiness of the actors and be prepared to shoot the scene before the actors have rehearsed and rehashed their performances into a lifeless state.

The most important quality an actor can convey is honesty, and it is your job to make sure that a phony performance is not in the making. The performance must be down to earth so that the movie rings true to the viewer. Often, it seems, actors (and nonactors) have pent-up energy just before a take, and when the camera rolls they talk too fast and move too fast. To protect against this recurring problem, you must slow down the shooting process. Before turning on the camera tell the

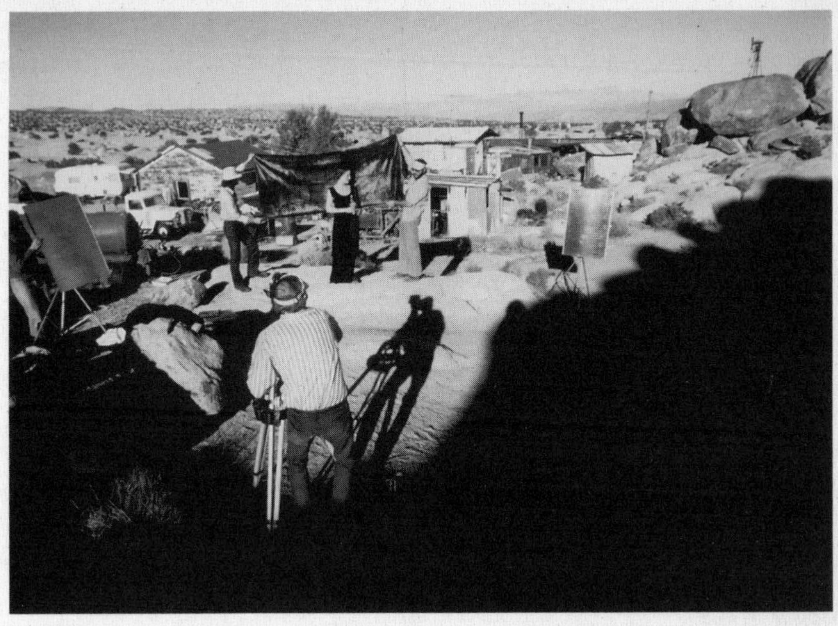

On the set for *Emerald Cities* shoot in Death Valley. Photo by Julie Schachter.

actors that you want them to give a pause before beginning. Ask them to count to five (to themselves) before speaking. It is possible that because of the pressure of the filming they will jump right on their lines the second you say "Action," at which point, camera still running, you will say "Hold it . . . pause and then start again." If the scene is still going too fast, stop the camera and start again.

Shooting one-to-one requires that actors and nonactors must somehow get their performances right on the first try. The direction given by the filmmaker of a low-budget feature is not at all like the cliché of the Hollywood director who browbeats his actors and actresses into submission. You don't have fifty takes to shoot one line from a faltering thespian. If your film has been cast correctly, then as long as your actors believe they are doing a good job, they can maintain good, consistent performances. It may be worth placing prospective actors in front of the camera before the shoot, to see if they will freeze up when you shoot a small, one-minute test. Nonactors operate best with your encouragement, and it's destructive to give them strict criticism for their "performances." Their performances *are* them, and you get who they are. In a low-budget production you only have a few chances to snap a performance into the correct groove. Sit down with an uncertain performer and explain again that you selected him or her for the part because he or she was absolutely right as the character you envisioned. Tell the person that if they would just relax things would be great. If they finally pull themselves together, the filming can move on. If not, you must bite the bullet and swiftly find a replacement. For further information on the subject of "directing actors," I'd recommend getting your hands on two great books, *Directing Actors (Creating Memorable Performances for Film and Television)*, by Judith Weston (Michael Wiese Productions, 1996), and *True and False: Heresy and Common Sense for the Actor*, by David Mamet (Pantheon Books, 1997), both available at discount from **<www.amazon.com>**.

Directing from Behind the Camera

During my productions of *Morgan's Cake* and *American Orpheus*, I developed some new techniques for directing from behind the camera; I hope that you'll find ways to apply them to your own particular situations. In the preface I discussed how my main focus in filmmaking has been on real people telling their real truths to the camera within the structure of my fictional story. That means that I've written a full script with dialogue and story development, but haven't demanded that my actors (or nonactors) recite all of my written words back to me and the camera. I'm much more interested in filming my characters speaking in their own words, using their own intelligence to complete my scenes. The technique I developed for allowing for this improvisation is to give voice commands to actors from behind the camera, speaking to them while the camera is rolling. If I'm careful and speak to them only at those moments in the scene when no one is talking (no lips moving), then I can remove my voice command from the sound track during editing, replacing the length of mag track that carries my words with other mag track that contains just room tone.

Sometimes, while shooting *American Orpheus*, I would just feed scripted lines to the five-year-old actress who played Eury (Jasmine Carver), telling her one line after another, to build a scene with dialogue which she had partially memorized with the help of her parents. By telling her what to say each time, I could control the timing of when she spoke, and make sure that what she said moved the scene forward as I had intended. Using this technique I was able to shoot a complicated scene with lead actress Jody Esther and Jasmine, where the threat of her becoming a "missing kid" was discussed from the child's point of view, and still maintain my low filming ratio. While I did have to rely on my scripting and the actual repeating of those lines by Jasmine to create this particular scene, Jody (playing her mother) did not have to adhere to the script verbatim, but was able to listen and respond to her daughter's fears naturally, giving the scene a frightening air of reality.

In some instances I have used this "voice command" technique to direct a scene I thought up on the spot. As I've watched a scene develop, and heard the improvisational dialogue spoken, I've been able to interject ideas and needed dialogue to keep the scene heading toward some sort of climax or resolve. This approach allows the filmmaker to complete his or her scenes with a reasonable shooting ratio while trolling the mysterious depths of story and characterizations. This is what "trusting in the flow" is all about. If you're lucky and inquisitive, you may suddenly find yourself shooting scenes that aren't simply what you envisioned, but artifacts of the age in which you live. You may perhaps be able to create a movie in which the overall intelligence and message transcends the script from which it was spawned.

Feeding Cast and Crew on a Budget

The reason for this section is to remind the filmmaker that he or she has an obligation to help keep alive the people who are aiding in the production of a feature. Regardless of what level of no-budget you operate on, it is important to at least pick up a few meals, lunches and dinners, during the length of time you are shooting. If you are producing on a minuscule budget where every dollar counts, then you will probably have to depend on the help of a friend to prepare a few home-cooked meals for your five- or six-person group. Just remember that you don't want to sink your ship by feeding cast and crew such a heavy meal that they can't do their jobs afterward. Keep the food light: heavy on the vegetarian, pasta, perhaps seafood and chicken, light on the roast beef. If you don't have a credit card to take everyone out for some Chinese or Thai food, you could always buy some hamburger and cook chili, or meatballs for spaghetti beforehand, then serve it for a dinner (inquire in advance if cast or crew members are vegetarians, or have special dietary needs). If the story you are filming is the kind that depends on a growing depth of emotions, you could heighten that intensity by serving everyone turkey day after day after day. I'm kidding of course, but the point is, buy your production personnel some meals, especially breakfast when the call to the set is super-early, dinner when you run late. And always have on hand an array of soft drinks and snacks (commonly referred to as "craft services"). Check out **<www.hollywood-911/directory>**, looking under "craft services" for state-by-state listings.

On my *American Orpheus* shoot I was fortunate to be able to afford a catering service for ten days, supplying my twelve-member cast and crew with three meals a day for around $4,000. This money was the best investment I've ever made in a production. The food was so good that it actually put smiles on people's faces, including my own. While I was pushing myself and everyone else to do the impossible of shooting a fully lit color feature in ten days, I got wonderful meals and well-ordered breaks in shooting three times a day. The good food gave me another burst of energy for the next five-hour segment of work. Contact your local caterers to see if there is a deal that you can afford. It will be the best money you'll ever spend.

Continuity

On the set the moviemaker will want to be absolutely certain that for shots that must cut together, the actors are wearing the same clothes and making the same movements for the camera on each consecutive take. If the actor is wearing a hat in the first shot, then he must have it on when you shoot from a different angle for a scene where those two shots are meant to cut together. If the hat has accidentally been removed before the second take is shot, then it will simply disappear at the cut as if by magic. Of course, if it is your intention to use the potential of movie magic in the shot, then this is one of the secrets. But for the "normal" movie, continuity must be observed. On big-budget productions, where scenes are always shot out of sequence and only selected takes are printed, the person in charge of continuity must keep a detailed record of each aspect of the filmed scenes ("continuity breakdown") so that a major mistake will not occur. On a low-budget set the director is responsible for noticing any discrepancy in continuity. He or she must have a sixth sense that "something" isn't right, if mistakes are to be caught in time. And the actors must also share responsibility by bringing the same clothes to the set for scenes that are continuous. Since scenes on a low-budget shoot are usually shot in order, its fairly easy to catch mistakes in mismatched clothing. The real challenge is noticing hand and facial movements and having actors repeat these movements for the next take so that each shot will successfully edit together in the completed scene. When the small crew of a low-budget feature is totally committed to the movie being made, everyone is constantly on the alert for mistakes in continuity.

Shooting Titles on Location

A very creative way of saving money on your feature is to shoot your titles while on location. Not only does the creation of titles during the location shoot save you the cost of shooting titles on an optical printer, but usually filming your "title sequence" at the location enhances some aspect of the movie's central concept.

One method of creating titles on location is by painting them on a wall and panning over to them, one at a time. The credits could be painted with a spray can in the style of New York City subway graffiti. Or the credits could be carefully set up in painted or stick-on letters, white or different colors. There are many interesting ways of creating original titles, and it is up to the filmmaker to choose the typeface and concept of filming titles that best supports the idea of the film.

Another method of shooting titles is setting stick-on letters on clear plastic sheets and filming these credits with the scene showing through behind the acetate as we did on *Morgan's Cake* and *The Last Roommate* shoots. By using a 9.5–57 wide-angle zoom lens, one can keep in focus both the letters on the acetate and the scene that shows through. The most difficult problem of shooting credits in this manner is avoiding light flares on the plastic and making sure that the words are level and centered. Our white titles for these movies would have had to have been optically printed by a lab at a cost of many hundreds of dollars. For *The Last Roommate* we spent $25 for the white Helvetica stick-on titles and acetate sheets, and $120 for the filmstock and processing/work print. And for my *American Orpheus* shoot, stick-on main titles were successfully incorporated into the first shot (see photo, page 112), solving the problem without extra lab costs.

Location Miracles

This is just a reminder not to overlook location miracles that stare you in the face while you shoot your tightly scripted and storyboarded story. Make use of the shadows that fall across a windowsill, real stories from your actors, special sounds, everything that crosses your path during the week or two that you are filming. During the shoot of *The Last Roommate*, we discovered our actress, Jean Mitchell, had actually lived through the experience of being terrorized by an insanely jealous boyfriend, which was what the story we had selected to film was about! So we took advantage of this irony by filming Jean in vignettes talking directly to the camera, telling her real stories and changing the name of her real boyfriend to our character's name, Greg. And because her fear of her real boyfriend was still very real, she had covered both front and rear doors of her house with one-inch plywood, adding a wooden plank across the back door for security. We were able to film scenes using these special situations to enhance the story we were telling. Filming at Jean's house also gave us a chance to observe her special touches to the surroundings. She had tied a bunch of dried roses to the end of a curtain string and this shriveled bouquet became a curious image when the curtain was lowered in a shot, the flowers dangling in front of the window with an ominous presence. Keep your eyes open and make use of the special miracles that exist around the creation of a movie.

Saving Film on Each Sync Take

Now that the big moment has arrived and you are ready to roll the camera and sound recorder to film your actors' performances on location, you should know the most efficient way to mark sync for your shots. A great deal of film and tape can be saved by marking and notating all information about the coming take on sound tape and clapboard *before* the shot is begun. First, the number of the scene and take is written in chalk on the slate. The production assistant then reads off the information on the slate, indicating scene number, take number, and some identification of the scene's location (for example: "Hallway . . . Morgan's house!"). This is recorded simultaneously on the sound tape by the soundperson. With the actors in place, the lights on, and the camera framed and wrapped with a "barney" to muffle it, the soundperson (who has carefully aimed his or her mikes and set sound levels with the actors' normal voices), awaits the command from the filmmaker to "Roll sound." When the filmmaker feels everyone is ready to begin, he first announces, "Quiet on the set." Then, after making sure that the slate is visible in his framing of the shot, he calls out, "Roll sound." The soundperson verifies he or she is recording sound by calling back, "Sound rolling." The filmmaker starts the camera (he or she has already run ten seconds of film at the beginning of the new roll, the required length of head leader the labs usually request), and, after a few seconds to get it up to speed, calls out, "Mark it." The assistant closes the slate, making a *clack* for the sound track and a visual sync for the picture, and steps out of the framed scene. Giving the actors a pause to settle down, the filmmaker calls out (softly), "Action," or some appropriate word ("OK, go"), and the scene begins. Instead of wasting valuable footage running the camera while the clapboard is read for scene and take numbers, this method of reading (and recording) the identification on the slate *before* running the camera, and then shooting film of the slate just for the few seconds it takes to "clack it" for sync mark, saves several feet of footage on each take and several hundred feet of footage by the end of a feature shoot.

Benefits of a Tight Shooting Schedule

Shooting your feature on a low or no budget most likely means that you'll have to complete the filming within a seven- to ten-day schedule. There just isn't any money to extend the process a moment longer. Since you're probably getting everyone to work for you at much reduced rates, you must release them back to their real lives (real salaries) as soon as possible. The main effect of a tight schedule on a production is that it keeps it moving at a very fast pace. If you can't trust your intuition, can't keep making decisions at breakneck speed, then you won't have a feature film. This is undoubtedly the main truth we demonstrate at our Feature Workshops (see chapter 9), where we shoot *and* edit a complete feature in just ten days. Your only choice is to jump in headfirst, submerge yourself, and keep striving for the best ideas and shots to back them up. You need to shoot at least twelve 400′ rolls to have *any* choices in the editing. That means you have to run through at least two rolls a day. Even if your budget expands to allow for shooting four rolls a day for ten days (it took Kevin Smith thirty-seven 400′ rolls to create his indie hit *Clerks*), there will be no time for second-guessing. In a sense you have to stop thinking and just *do*. So you have no choice but to believe in yourself. Have you ever done that before? Have you ever just jumped into a project with total faith in yourself? That's pretty hard to do. There are always those nagging doubts. But with a tight budget there is no time for doubt. Your only hope is to produce results. This speed of production also allows you an element of freshness and spontaneity, the lifeblood of the best and most successful indie features.

Movie Stills/Videos of "Work-in-Progress"

Even on a no-budget shoot it is vital that you take some stills of the production: well-lit, sharply focused photos of the lead actors on the set and shots of scenes from your movie. These stills will be invaluable to you later when it comes time to publicize your finished feature film. Perhaps you know someone who is a photographer with a good camera (Leica, Nikon) who would help you for a small fee, supplied filmstock, and a title in the credits. Remember that one great photo used as a graphic in ads and on posters can make the difference between getting an audience (or distributor!) and not. Have you seen the photo from the movie *Man Bites Dog*? It's memorable for the gun being shown so outstretched from the arm (shot in wide angle, deep focus, right next to the lens) that it's literally "in your face." That photo has become an icon for the film.

You may also find that the use of your carefully taken stills, whether photos or slides, is crucial to telling a part of your filmatic story. Several of my earlier features used montages of images from stills to reveal a side of the story that wasn't shown in scenes during the shoot. My first feature, *A Man, a Woman, and a Killer*, featured a three-minute sequence of behind-the-scenes narration backing up images shot as slides by one of the lead actors, Ed Nylund. These pictures showed emotional moments between the young leads, Dick Richardson and Carolyn Zaremba, and the development of their real love relationship on the set. So sometimes the stills you take on the set can be invaluable in editing, help you fill gaps in the story you are telling.

Once you have shot your film, give yourself a moment to relax and look over the stills, selecting a few of the best ones that you'll want to have reproduced. Producers & Quantity Photos (6660 Santa Monica Boulevard, Hollywood, CA 90038) gives one of the best deals to the filmmaker, charging approximately $35 per twenty-five glossy 8″-by-10″ copies of an image, with a small one-time fee of around $20 for negative work. Call them at (323) 462-1334.

In this video age you may also want to consider hiring a friend to document your shoot. With the combined high-quality images and portability of new digital video cameras, including every type of accessory from tripods to steadicams, you can record the making of your epic on video at "broadcast quality" for just a few hundred dollars worth of tape. And if your film turns out to be the hit of the year, all that video footage can be used for a behind-the-scenes look at the director at work. You may find that in a few years you can produce your own DVD (the prices keep dropping) and run it as streaming video on the Web. Or maybe some of the footage will find its way into your "electronic pressbook," a videotape used by publicists to promote your film and its ideas.

Developing and Work Printing at the Lab

After your first day of filming you should be anxious to drop off the exposed rolls of 400′ film that you ran through the camera to see if your images have been realized. Each can you will turn in to the lab has been carefully wrapped with tape around the edge to make sure that the film inside will not be exposed to the light. The black paper bag that each fresh roll of filmstock was initially wrapped in when you loaded the film into the camera magazine in the changing bag has also been placed around each roll, when the camera was unloaded. On each can you have already applied a label carefully listing the type of stock you have shot, the length of each roll (400′ or maybe shorter), your name, address, phone number, and number of roll (in the order that you shot). The length of the rolls is an important bit of information for the film handlers inside the developing room and must not be omitted.

Arriving at the lab you either turn over the rolls to a lab person over the desk, or if it is after work hours, insert the rolls in a slot called a "night drop" in the side of the building. If you deliver your rolls to the lab at night, make sure that each roll has been pushed into the slot far enough to hear it "clunk" down inside the building. Most labs offer a "daily" processing/work print service, which means that you will be able to pick up a work print of what you shot the following morning and be able to screen the footage. You can dream about seeing the results of your filmmaking labors as you drive home and get some sleep before the next full day of shooting.

At this point in the filmmaking process, you have already begun to build a relationship with the people at the lab. Someone there, probably the manager, has already helped you to budget your "feature film at used-car prices." And you probably have already met the people who work behind the counter where you picked up your stock for the shoot. All these relationships are important to you; once you have some friends inside the building, dealing with the lab will be much more pleasant. Also, it is important to feel that they are taking special care with your original and giving you the best quality possible in all services. When you call the lab to find out if your work print from your first day of filming is ready, you definitely know that you are involved with the people at the lab. They put you on hold while they check. At this point you can only pray that they have successfully run your film through the printing machines without any mishap (machines breaking down, original footage scratched, destroyed, or lost somewhere in the lab). Control over your project is now in the hands of the lab. Many labs, like Monaco (San Francisco), Du Art (New York), and Western Cine (Denver), have Websites, and you can gain some confidence (and familiarity) by logging on during this type of limbo (<www.monaco.com>, <www.duart.com>, <www.westerncine.com>, etc.).

When you hear that your work print is ready for pickup, you can heave a sigh of relief. There was something on the film to print, and the lab didn't lose or destroy your precious film. The lab will ask you if you wish for them to "vault your original," which means they will store the original film you ran through your camera (off which they made your work print), placing the film in a safe, cool location, with careful identification to locate it later. The worst catastrophe that can occur during a production is for the original film from your shoot, essential to making high-quality prints, to be lost. Entrusting this precious original to a lab for storage is a crucial decision. Probably the best solution would be, if you could afford it, an expensive fireproof safe, too heavy to steal, in which the original footage (film or video) would be stored. But since this solution is usually too costly, the filmmaker finds him- or herself trusting the lab with the irreplaceable original footage.

Processing Without a Work Print

The work printing of your footage is one of the largest expenditures on a low-budget feature, and you should give every consideration to determining exactly what your particular film requires. If your feature is simply shot, in sequence order with few cuts, it is possible to skip the expense of using a work print. This method of using the original for (light) editing and assembly is ideal for the "long take" style of filmmaking, since all the filmmaker needs to do is sync up each scene in order with the sound track and then hot-splice the picture together, keeping the sound track synced to the picture (see chapter 6). Extreme caution must be used when handling this original film (wear white cotton "editor's" gloves!), and each piece of editing equipment that comes in contact with the footage (Moviescope, synchronizer, flatbed editing machine, split reels) must be thoroughly checked to make sure it won't scratch or tear your original footage. To test the equipment, run a piece of clear or white leader through the machine several times and then examine both sides for scratches.

For movies with multiple cuts and lengthy editing needs, it will be best to spend the extra money on a work print. And, of course, if you have shot your feature on negative stock, it will be necessary to make a work print to see exactly what you have. But even with negative stock you can save some money by checking the original (very carefully) and omitting the work printing of scenes you know are worthless. And if your project is so expansive that you will need to raise additional money for the last stages of your production, you will definitely need a work print to show to prospective investors.

Another option is to get a "dirty dupe" work print from the lab: This is a low-quality, high-contrast black-and-white copy of your film for editing purposes that usually costs about half of the usual "one light" work print. While this "dupe" is certainly adequate for editing your feature, the lack of quality of the images may not give you the necessary pleasure and excitement needed to maintain the energy you need to edit during the months ahead. Even though you can remind yourself that the original is really of superior quality, it may become depressing to stare at second-rate images every day while you compile your film. And if there is any need to interest investors in your film, it will be almost impossible to convince them your film is any good if all they see on the screen is poor-quality images. I think it is much wiser to go through your original and make a good-quality "one light" work print of *only* usable shots, thus saving as much money as possible while still having a work print you will enjoy. Of course, if you are editing on computer, you will be able to screen all your footage on a monitor, with images recorded and timed directly from your original, with sound synced electronically. This will show you exactly what filmatic quality you have achieved.

Video Versus Film Work Print

More often than not these days the low-budget feature filmmaker finds him- or herself confronted by the question of whether to go to video for work printing and postproduction. If you can save thousands of dollars editing on video, the decision seems to be already made, since money must be saved at every turn. But video is cheaper only in certain cases, usually when you have a personal nonlinear computer editing system for free hourly editing. A film work print is cheaper if you have inexpensive access to flatbed editing machines (both FAF in San Francisco and 911 in Seattle offer half-day, single-day, and weekly rates) that you can pair with your home-built editing bench (see chapter 3 for detailed plans), and basic equipment, including Moviescope, sound reader, sync block, rewinds, and reels, for editing any hour of the day or night without overhead. (See chapter 3 to compare cost of a computer edit with that of 16-mm film.)

Money and the Lab

A word or two should also be said about your relationship to the lab with regard to money. When I think of my moviemaking over the last twenty-five-plus years, one of the main things that comes to mind is that I was often able to finish my projects because I could bargain with the lab. Without being able to charge expensive services such as sound mix, answer printing, occasional titling, and video work printing, I could not have produced my features without long delays. And without being able to get special reduced rates in processing and work printing, I would not, on some occasions, have even been able to begin a project. At a crucial point in each of my feature productions, the lab has let me charge the thousands of dollars needed to finish. Because of their patience, I have always paid them off at the earliest possible moment with money I received from grants, teaching salary, TV sales, or sheetrocking. Even the lowest-budget feature is relatively expensive, and you must be able to complete the project as soon as possible to avoid having an unfinished movie *and* unpaid bills (visit **<www.frugalliving.about.com>** to learn new creative methods for daily budgeting). It is vital to establish credit with the lab at the earliest opportunity, so that when the editing is completed you will hopefully be able to charge the sound mix and answer print if money has run out. The pressure on a moviemaker is too great to let his or her project drag on for years because of lack of finishing funds. But remember the obvious fact that your lab bill must be paid off, even if it means selling your other used car, your possessions, or your house.

note: Keep track of all your invoices from the lab (and other film and video work) to make sure that you haven't been charged twice for services or products.

Checking Your First Footage

It is a great feeling to hold that first roll of work print in your hands in anticipation of what you will soon see projected on the screen. It's a hundred times more exciting than Christmas. And probably you will do what most filmmakers do, which is roll some film out in your hand, just to make sure that there is actually something on the film. For all the multitude of ideas, decisions, accidents, last-minute changes, improvisation, and location miracles that went into the first roll . . . the question "Did it work?" now arises. In moments you will view part of your film, and you will see not only the projected images on the screen but also all the drama that came before and after each shot, including your hopes and dreams for the project. For these reasons you will want to screen this first roll several times, first to enjoy the shock of seeing your ideas turned into actual filmatic images, and then, as the excitement wears off a bit, to look at the footage with a more critical eye, checking for the following problems:

- ☐ If you see scratches on the film during projection of your work print, it is important to check your original to find out if the scratches are also present there. If they are, then you have either been using a faulty camera or a faulty magazine, which must be replaced before continuing the filming. And if the original is not scratched, then thank your lucky stars that only your work print was scratched, probably by the projector, and this will not affect the quality of your final print. Some scratches can be removed during printing by a process called "liquid gate" (see chapter 6 for a description), but deep scratches will probably remain forever on your film, so use great caution when screening original footage. Ask the lab technician if he or she has a special projector used only for original film. If so, you can almost be guaranteed that it doesn't cause scratches, since the lab uses the projector to check jobs that it can't afford to ruin. Even with every guarantee that a projector is "scratch free," the filmmaker must exercise his or her paranoia and still run a bit of leader through the projector to double-check for scratches. Remember that with a used-car-prices budget you can't really afford to waste film, time, or filmatic moments that will never come again.
- ☐ Check your lighting. How does the quality of the images you shot feel to you? Is the mood correct for your story? Are the shadows dramatic or clumsy? Now is the time to make a lighting change, so do your best to evaluate the success or failure of your lighting concepts.
- ☐ Watch for any foreign objects in the picture plane, such as microphones, extension cords, light stand legs, a hair in the gate of the camera, or anything that might destroy the believability of your movie.

- ☐ Is everything in focus? Are your actors' faces in focus when they are the center of attention? Soft focus can be effective for certain moods, but if this is not your desired result, it can greatly diminish the quality of your film.
- ☐ Are your actors giving honest performances?
- ☐ Is the camera steady, or do you detect shaking, jiggling, bad compositions, poor pans, or uncertain gestures that will detract from your story? If the camera work is sloppy, you may want to try again and reshoot your first roll of scenes.
- ☐ Check for cuts and transitions. Can you string your footage together as you've shot it? This can be further tested once you have synced the picture and the sound track (see chapter 6) and actually edited the scenes together.

note: One of the most difficult things to achieve in making movies is to clearly see footage that you shot yourself. If you worked the camera, almost any footage you screen will seduce you. So, when checking out this first roll of processed film (or video work print), bring along a friend who may be able to supply you with some critical observations.

Checking Your Recorded Sync Sound

After the first day's shooting, it is also very important to make sure you are recording on-location sound that has good quality and levels, and the essential sync pulse to run sync with your picture. Your first step is to transfer the ¼″ tapes recorded on your Nagra, or the cassettes recorded on a Sony Walkman Professional, onto mag track (if you ordered a video work print, you've already got picture and sound synced up by the lab).

There are two "schools" of sound transferring. One group says that it is best to equalize the location sound while transferring it to mag track, adjusting treble and bass for each take. The other group believes that the sound from location should be recorded with the widest range of highs and lows (no equalization) and then equalized during the mix. I personally favor the latter method, because I like to select the quality of sound of each scene during the mixing process to tie each edited scene together with appropriate sound values. Also, I believe equalizing during the mix adds up to higher-quality sound on the print. Only if your budget cannot afford a mix of any kind would I recommend equalizing and setting uniform levels during transfer, enabling you to "mix" your tracks by making a straight copy of the spliced-together sound track for your print.

After you have transferred the location sound onto mag track for your first 400′ of picture, you will want to listen to the track to make sure the quality is the best that can be achieved. If possible, try to play the mag track on an interlock projector that is in a booth separate from the theater where you will listen to it. Check for the following problems:

- ☐ Hissing or electric static
- ☐ Drastic changes in sound levels
- ☐ Muffled dialogue
- ☐ Street noises (airplanes, cars, buses, people shouting, etc.) that disturb sound quality
- ☐ Sound speeding up or slowing down due to faulty equipment

What you want to hear is "clean sound": distinctive dialogue without overbearing background noise. And by syncing up the mag track with the picture work print and projecting the sync footage, you will be able to determine if the sound track is doing its job of turning your film into a watchable movie. If the dialogue is sync with the picture, and the sound doesn't distract from the experience on the screen, then you have adequate sound. (This formula for evaluating the quality of your movie's sound track is equally appropriate when viewing a synced-up digital video work print on computer. Ask yourself, "Do the scenes work?!")

There is such a thing as "great on-location sound," but usually the low-budget filmmaker can't afford it, and hasn't ever experienced it. Before I shot *A Man, a Woman, and a Killer*, Wayne Wang and I were working on a short film starring painter Jim Albertson. We had needed a soundperson because our regular sound recordist friend was unavailable. On the wall at a local lab I spotted a card that read NEELON

CRAWFORD—SOUNDMAN and hired him by phone for the one-day shoot. After I transferred the ¼″ tapes recorded on his Nagra, I played the mag track synced with work print on an interlock projector at the lab. And while I watched the location sync takes, I experienced a strange sensation. I actually turned around at one point during the screening, thinking that someone else was in the room. The tracks were so clean and clear that none of the usual electronic imperfections I had grown to expect accompanied the experience. Even though it cost me one-quarter of my shooting budget for *A Man, a Woman, and a Killer*, I hired Neelon and his assistant, Lee Serie, for $1,500 (1973 dollars) for the two-week shoot (this price included his Nagra microphones, and miscellaneous sound gear).

If the recorded sound from your location shoot is poor, then halt the production and be prepared to shoot the first rolls over. Don't skimp on hiring a good soundperson. Poor-quality tracks will haunt and finally destroy your production.

Screening Footage for Cast and Crew

A very important decision during your shoot is when and how you screen the footage ("rushes") for your actors and collaborators. After you have privately screened the footage and checked it out for technical quality, you must decide if showing it to the cast and crew will inspire them—or simply confuse them. If you are working with nonactors, the screening of this first footage could destroy their natural performances. Maybe they have never seen themselves on film (or video) and the shock of the images will make them too self-conscious to continue. If the shoot runs for several weeks, there will be a lot of pressure on the director/filmmaker to show the developed footage. Look at the film and decide how a screening will best serve the production's needs. If the footage looks good, is in focus with good camera moves, then my advice is to show the first 400′ roll, silent, to the cast and crew if you believe the energy on the set is low, or if you believe that there are doubts regarding your abilities as director.

If you are editing on computer, this screening decision is slightly less critical. You probably won't mind various cast and crew members seeing synced and well-timed footage on the monitor during editing, since it tends to look incredibly beautiful as video.

On *The Last Roommate* production, the collaborators were skeptical about beginning to shoot (and spending their production money) without a completed script. I told them that if they didn't like the first footage we shot, then we would cancel the production. There was no way around a screening of the first roll of film, so this became a make-or-break situation. Luckily, the footage we shot looked great, and everybody was pumped up to continue spending their time, money, and energy to complete the movie.

Filmmaker George Csicsery (*Where the Heart Roams*, *"N" Is a Number*, **<www.maa.org/pubs/books/numb.html>**) told me that he thinks a person can only see his or her film the way the rest of the world sees it *once,* and that is when the work print and sound track are screened, sync, for the first time. This is probably true. The first screening of your sync footage is very special and important to your production, so it is the filmmaker's responsibility to be ultra-sensitive to all the details surrounding the screening. This show is the "premiere" of the results of all the effort that went into your film by dedicated and talented people, so ideally the viewing should take place in a good screening room with a few bottles of liquid refreshment. Usually, not only the participants of the shoot but also members of their immediate families and friends will want to see the results. If this expanded audience is too much for your jangled nerves, then restrict the first showing to just those members of the cast and crew who were on location making the movie. Save the families for the first rough-cut. Each screening plays an important role in the process of reducing the footage down to the final cut-and-polished gem that is your desired result.

Completing the Shoot

Whether or not you have decided to screen the first roll of footage for your cast and crew, you have a lot more shooting to do before you have enough film from which to cut your feature. And in the days or weeks ahead, you will enter a zone of creativity and energy that only someone who has experienced it will totally understand. At all moments of the day and night you will be striving to do your best to get your scenes recorded on film (or DV). As the days pass and you see one after another of the shot rolls accumulate, your confidence will grow stronger with the realization that you are actually able to make your feature. If there are strong emotions on the set, then you will make use of them during the shoot. Ideas are coming to you even in your dreams, and you pay attention to them and invent new scenes and camera moves. By the time you complete the filming, a very special emotional bond will have formed between you and your cast and crew members, and you will feel part of this film family for years to come.

Filming does not always go smoothly, and sometimes actors become so emotional that they quit mid-shoot. This and every other problem that occurs on the set will be up to you to solve, so that your hard work is not in vain. If you lose an actor or actress, you need to quickly find a replacement. If someone leaves two-thirds of the way through the filming, then change the story to accommodate his or her absence. If you run out of filmstock (videotape, DV cassettes, etc.), or money, sell something quickly to get you through. Come hell or high water, you must complete the job.

After all the scenes are shot, and you have screened the results for the cast and crew, the production people drift away, leaving you with strands of plastic (or electrons) to weave into gold.

6

Postproduction: Editing Your Feature

Congratulations! You've looked at all the film rolls that you shot for your feature and there are literally thousands of images permanently etched in emulsion. You have been surprised, delighted, and at times disappointed by the results, but nothing can dampen the great relief you feel in knowing that you've successfully completed your shoot. You are tired, but refreshed and excited, the way an athlete feels after running a hard race. The experiences of directing and shooting your movie have rejuvenated your spirit, and for these feelings alone you know that all the money and effort expended have been worth it. And as you become reacquainted with the normal routines of your life—work, girlfriend/boyfriend, regular meals and sleeping hours—you still seem protected from mundane activities because you know that you've got something "in the can." You also know that your sound recordings are usable because they had a sync pulse, and were clean and clear while being transferred to mag stock.

If you went the Betacam SP time-coded digital video work print route (see chapter 11), with your film lab helping to facilitate making a video copy off your film's original negative, then your relief and excitement for the project may track a slightly different emotional course than when editing on a film work print. Instead of being able to examine footage by hand and project it on a screen as a "1-light" low-quality silent work print, you will view your footage as electronic signals on a computer or video monitor. And, when you do, you'll be amazed to see perfectly timed images balanced for exposure, and hear sync sound adjusted for volume and clarity (the lab syncs up sound to picture electronically, using time code as a reference guide), presenting your footage at optimum quality. But sometimes there's a danger initially viewing your footage in such a high-quality state, since it may be discouraging to realize that what you've seen is the best it's ever going to get (and it doesn't feel good enough . . .). At least when you screen a film work print on a projector you can imagine that the final answer print will look superior to the low-resolution copy. And it usually takes a few weeks to sync up picture to mag sound track (see "Syncing It Up," page 156), giving you a chance to bond with your 16-mm footage as you cut. With a film work print it's easier to remain optimistic throughout the editing process, knowing that scenes will run smoother in the final print than they do with tape splices that jump during projection, and that sound will greatly improve with a good sound mix, etc. Having a video work print forces you to be much clearer and realistic about your footage from the very beginning of the editing process. Try to remember the youthful enthusiasm that got you into moviemaking in the first place. Remember that every step of production has taken tremendous courage and fortitude. Be aware that even pristine video-work-print footage can change in intrinsic value once scenes are assembled, and that sometimes a "marginal" shot can be transformed into an important one as you achieve the final cut. So this is certainly no time to collapse under the strain of momentary doubts.

Whether you decide to finish your movie as a film print, or as a digital video product with music, titles, fades and dissolves, even special effects, laid in by computer during editing, you must let your curiosity keep you fueled for the hard work ahead. I'm sure that after a couple of weeks of recovering from the shoot, you will probably grow restless, a sure sign that you're ready to dig in and edit your movie.

Making the First Splice

On the next pages you will find diagrams for operating a tape splicer. After spending a few minutes making practice cuts and splices, you are ready to begin syncing up picture and sound track.

MAKING THE FIRST SPLICE

Picture blade makes cut along frame line.

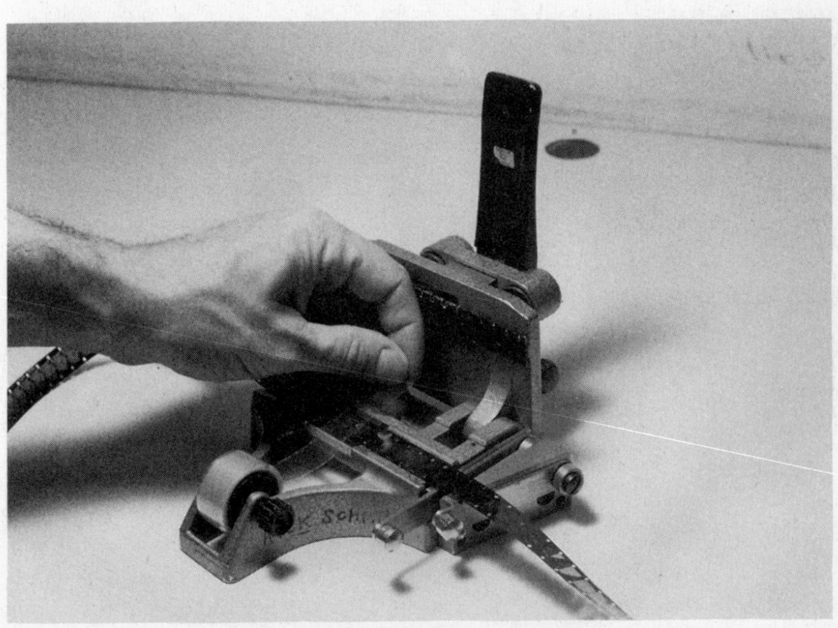

Clear tape pulled across ends of film to be spliced.

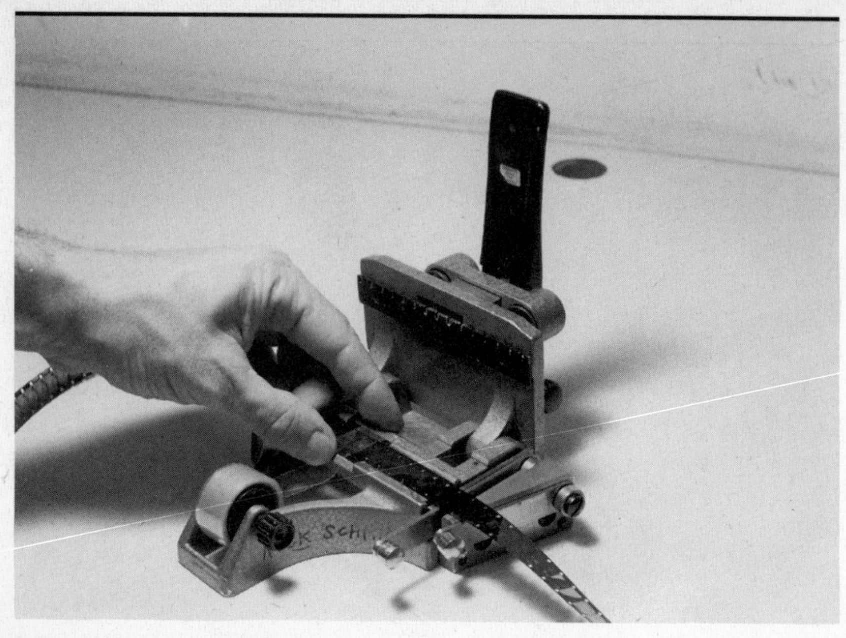

Tape pressed tightly across splicing area.

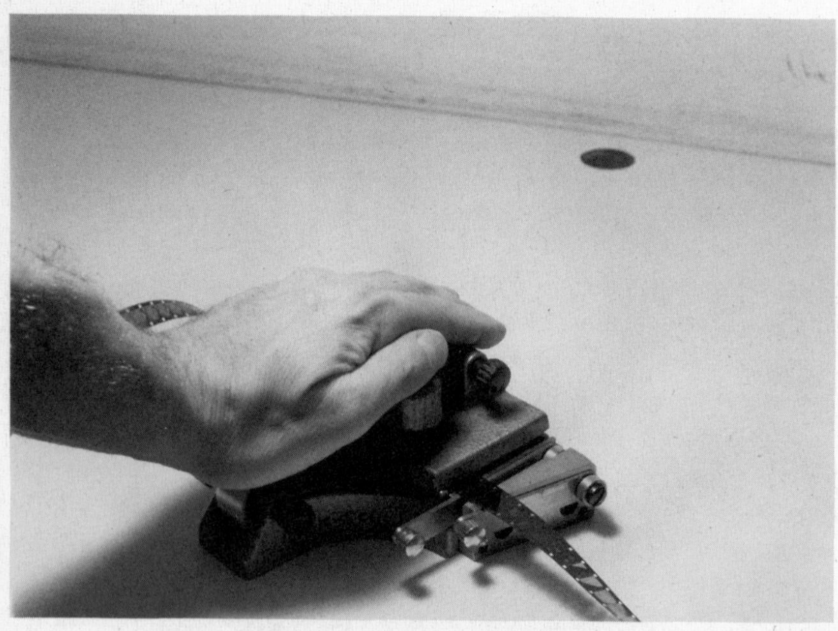

Splicer lowered, handle pressed to cut tape.

Tape splice checked for punched sprocket holes and cleanly cut edges.

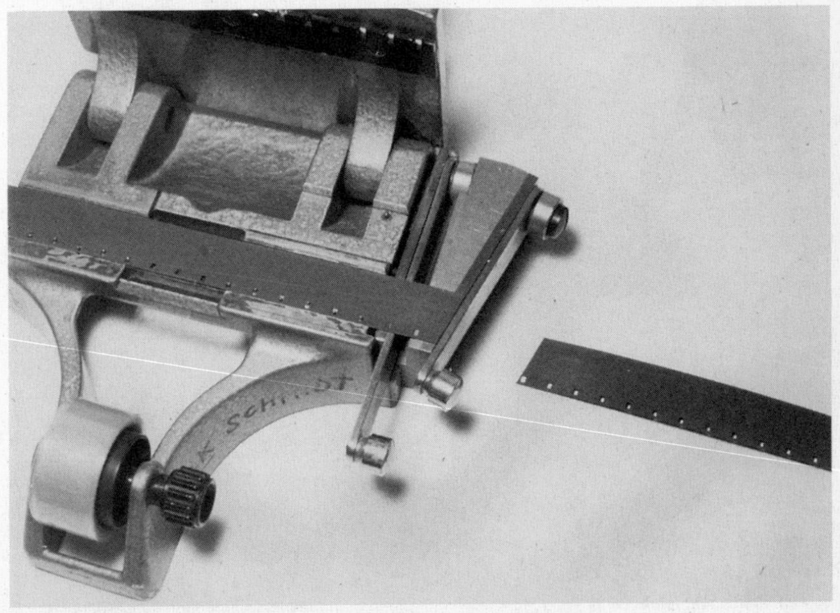

SOUND TRACK SPLICE

Mag track cut by angled (outside) blade.

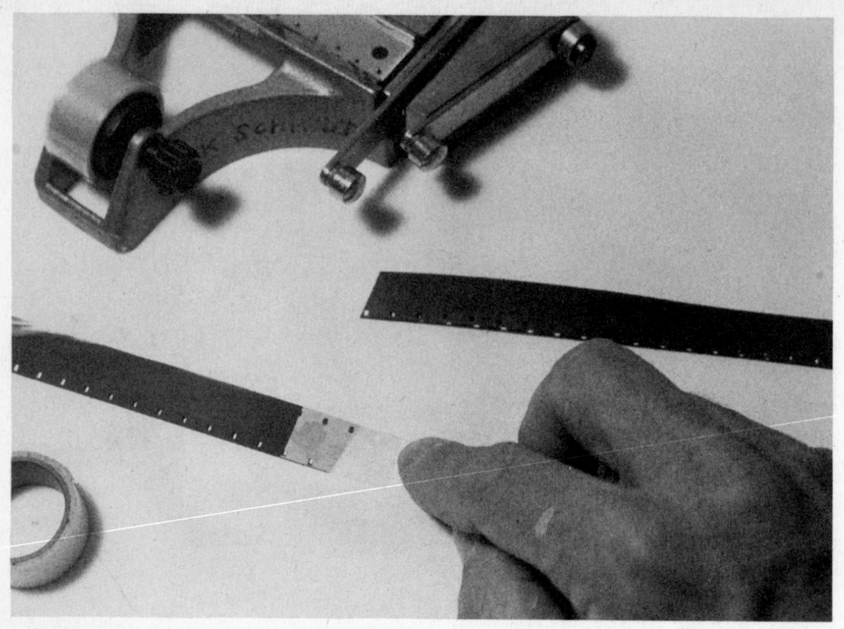

Sound tape placed on mag, lining up sprocket holes and edges.

Flip side of track readied for splicing.

Ends pushed together for splice.

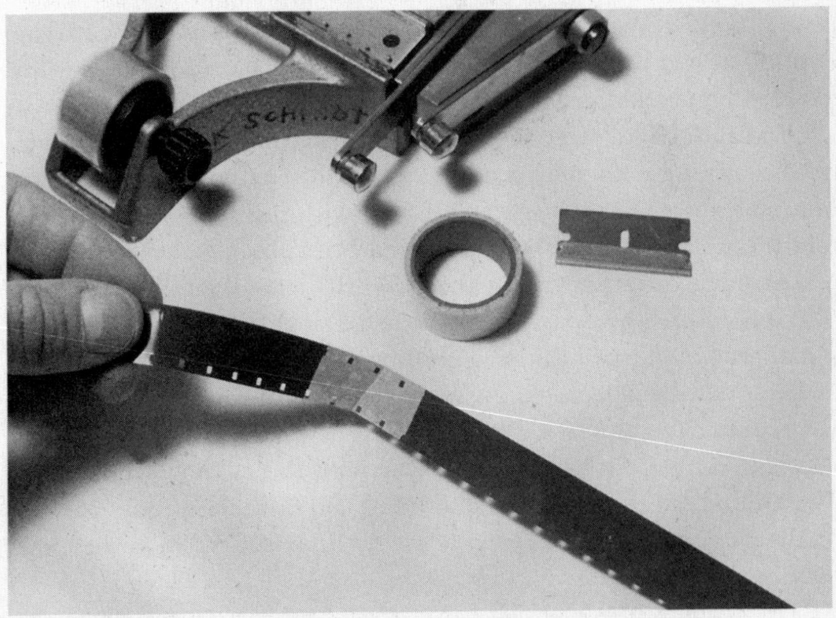

Completed sound tape splicing checked for alignment of holes and edges. You can trim tape hanging over the edges with a razor blade.

Syncing It Up

Whether you are editing on a flatbed machine or on an editing bench using a synchronizer, with Moviescope, rewinds, and sound reader, the procedure for syncing up your picture with your sound track is the same. In either case you want to adjust the length of the picture or sound track so that at the beginning of each scene the frame where the clapboard closed is in sync with the *clack* on the mag track.

Place your picture roll and sound roll either on the flatbed editing machine spindles or on split reels for your rewinds, sound reel closest to you. Thread the film and sound track through the flatbed machine, or through the synchronizer on your editing bench, taping the ends on the take-up reels. Reeling or rolling the film and sound track ahead, make the "sync mark"—a vertical line with a circle in the middle of it—on a frame about six feet in from the head ends. (See photo 1 on page 157.) (It may be necessary to splice some additional leader to the front of your picture roll to give you the needed length for your leader before the first images appear.) This mark will be used to line up the two rolls when projecting or editing them, and should be made with an indelible marking pen on your picture leader and mag track.

Roll ahead until you come to the first image on the picture roll, and make a vertical mark with a grease pencil on the frame line where the image begins. Directly across and in sync with the mark on the picture roll, mark the mag track with a vertical line using a sharp-tipped felt pen, making sure that you have marked the same frame line for both rolls (photo 2). If necessary, use blank mag track ("slug") to extend your sound sync *clack* past beginning picture sync (for splicing needs). Roll on ahead until you come to the frame on the film where the clapboard closes and mark an *X* with your grease pencil. Mark a similar *X* with your felt pen on the mag track in sync with the picture *X* (photo 3). Then roll ahead until you come to the sound of the clapboard closing on the mag track and mark a circle with your pen at the spot where the *clack* is heard.

Using the *X* mark on your mag track as a pattern for where the clapboard closes on the picture roll, place the *O* mark of the mag track *clack* directly on the *X* so that the two frames line up (photo 4 on page

SYNCING IT UP

1. Sync marks on picture and sound track leader, lined up on synchronizer.

2. *X* marks where clapboard closes; vertical line marks beginning of scene. Repeated on mag.

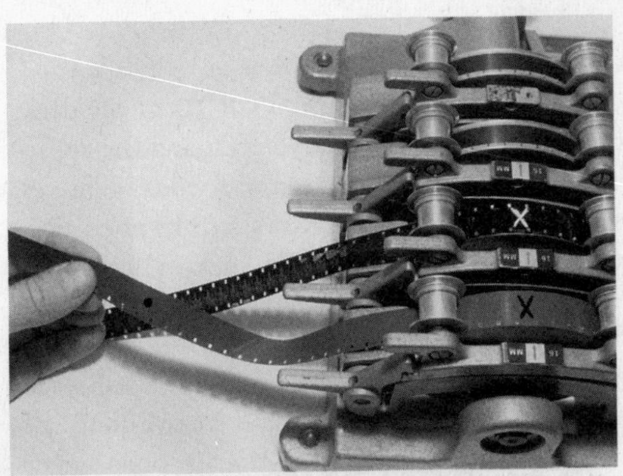

3. Circle marked at sound of clapboard.

159). Move the two pieces of mag track along in your hand, making sure that they stay together and don't slip. When you come to the mark on the mag track that shows where the scene begins, make a mark with your pen on the frame line of the sandwiched mag (photo 5). Cut the sound track at this new mark with your splicer (photo 6) and also at the mark where the scene begins, and roll up the excess cut-out piece on a core.

Tape splice your sound track together and roll up ahead to check your sync. The *X* of your picture should be in sync with the *0* of your sound track (photo 7 on page 160). As you roll your picture and mag track to the beginning of the next scene to sync up, you should notice that words and sounds correspond to the images you are watching.

syncing tips: When syncing up your film and sound track, it's necessary to have a small roll of blank mag track as well as black leader on hand to extend your rolls when either picture or sound takes are short because of a run-out while filming. You will also need several empty cores for collecting outtakes (see "Filing Your 'Outs,' " on page 161) while syncing up. And you will want to splice the picture work print on both sides to make sure it won't catch in the projector or on the edge-numbering machine.

Rick Schmidt's Secrets of Editing

Now that your rolls are synced up and you have repeatedly screened, flatbedded, rewound, or fast-forwarded on VCR (Beta SP deck, computer screen . . .) the resulting "rushes" for yourself and the appreciative (and at times critical) audiences of cast, crew, friends, relatives, experts, and idiots, it's time to get down to the brass tacks of editing. And although the process isn't such a secret as I'm making out in the title of this section, the information I've amassed during the year and a half of grueling editing on *A Man, a Woman, and a Killer*, the three years of torturous editing on *1988—The Remake*, two and a half years of bringing *Emerald Cities* to completion, and my month-long job helping Wayne Wang on the final cut of *Chan Is Missing*, plus the en-

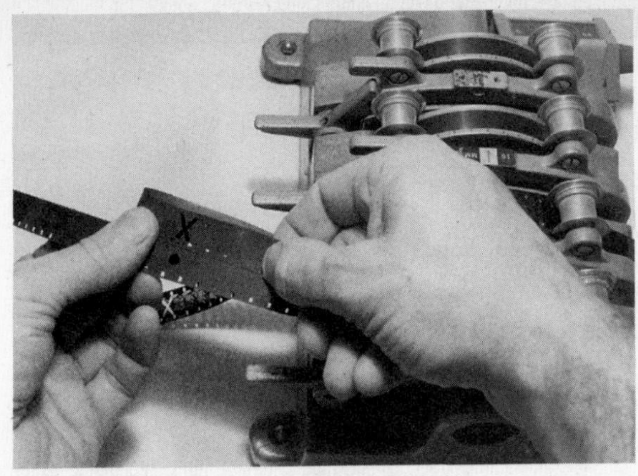

4. Circle and *X* on mag lined up.

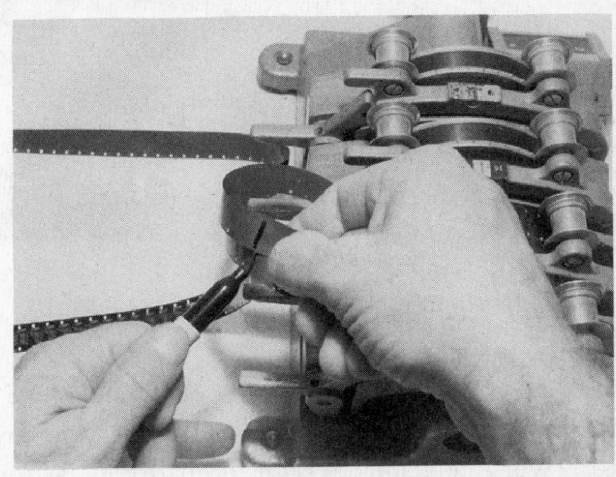

5. Correct beginning of scene marked on mag.

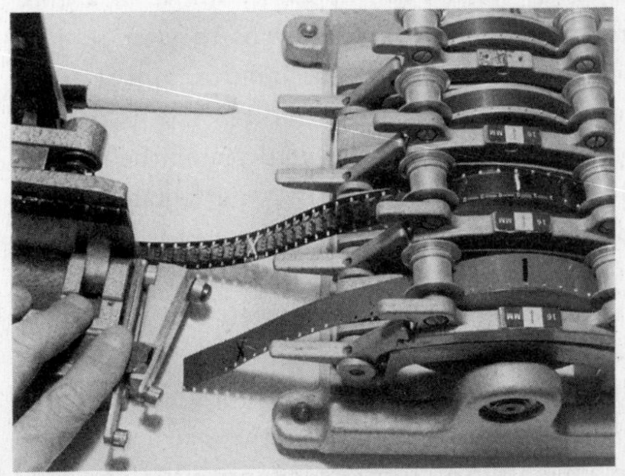

6. Mag cut at new mark and where scene begins.

7. Picture in sync with mag track.

joyable collaboration with Peter Boza and Mark Yellen while editing *The Last Roommate*, and other subsequent ten-day crash-edits on Feature Workshops movies tend to qualify me as something of a sage for surviving such difficult tasks. What I can hopefully impart is a good sense of the best approach to the editing solutions to your project, while keeping you spiritually afloat during the months, and at times years, that lie ahead as you complete your feature. The two main things to remember as you begin are (1) since you created the maze of scenes, you also hold the secret key that will give your footage the life of a cohesive movie; and (2) editing a feature is a long process, and to complete your movie you must somehow survive the financial and emotional pressures while still being able to delicately feel the essence of your film. It has been my long-standing belief that a person must continue to grow as a human being during the span of his or her editing process, so that hopefully at a certain point up the road a revelation can occur that transforms the overwatched footage into a fresh-spirited work of art. Only when the scenes you know by heart jump away from you as bright new moments you've never felt before should you believe that you have completed your task. It is to this end that I share my techniques of editing.

Edge Numbering

For complex editing of a feature film, edge numbering of your picture/work print and mag/sound track is a must. By having edge numbers in sync at every foot of your picture and sound track, you can use sound or picture separately without fear of losing sync. If you can't afford edge numbers, you will want to put small white paper tabs on picture and sound track, in sync, while editing your feature, or use a new Sharpie fine-point permanent marker pen to lay in a changing codelike pattern of marks in the margin of both picture and mag, between sprocket holes, a "poor man's edge code." Without edge numbers or marks it becomes much more difficult to file the edited "outs" of your picture and sound track so that you can retrieve them later.

Filing Your "Outs"

As you edit your feature, shifting scenes around, cutting different shots and sounds together, it is important to be able to locate these outs quickly so as not to disrupt the flow of ideas as you work. Of course, if you edit a video work print on computer, all outs are immediately accessible on hard drive, or from the video masters if files are mislabeled or accidentally deleted. Before editing begins, each scene on a picture roll should be listed by content and corresponding edge numbers in a logbook. As each piece of film is filed on the picture or sound roll, it is taped on the roll with a consecutive number written on the tape, and then listed by edge number in the logbook under each specific roll. As outs are moved back into your edit, a line is drawn through the number and edge number listing in the logbook. Since all filed pieces of picture and sound are taped together in numerical order, an editor can quickly find the needed footage by watching the num-

ROLL #7

Scene	Edgenumbers
Jean enters clinic (Int.)............	DD0001 - 0031
J. enters clinic (Int.) short take......	0032 - 0040
J. enters clinic (Int.) short take......	0041 - 0071
J. sits down (clinic)..................	0077 - 0103
J. sits down (wide shot)...............	0109 - 0127
View at window of clinic...............	0130 - 0172
Bruce and Jean outside.................	0173 - 0292
Jug shop, Bruce enters.................	0299 - 0306

PICTURE OUTS	SOUND OUTS
(1) 0045–50 (J. clinic)	(1) 0045–50 (J. chair)
(4) 0085–92 (J. sits)	(3) 0052–53 (J. asks question)
(9) ~~0093–94~~	(6) ~~0093–94~~ J. sits
(21) 0115–118 (J. looks at window)	(7) 0095–103 " "
(22) 0152–172 (cars)	(11) 0152–172 (loud cars)
(24) 0241–292 (end J.+B outside)	(17) 0241–292 (end J+B outside)
(32) ~~0301–302~~ (car reflection)	(24) ~~0301–302~~ (car reflection)
(33) 0304–305 (good take)	(27) 0304–305 (good sound)
(37) 0093–94	(28) 0093–94

Edge number logbook—sample page.

bers on the roll. Even with hundreds of entries and several filed rolls of picture and sound, this filing system is a quick and accurate way of "housekeeping" footage while sustaining creative inspiration.

Viewing Your Footage as a "Movie"

The first step you want to take to really get an idea of the value of your scenes is to cut out the clapboards and flashed frames at the beginning and ends of each take. By removing this footage (and carefully filing it on your picture and sound rollouts), you can begin to see your scenes in a movie context. Scenes still need to be edited "fat," with all beginning and end pauses left on until the order of a sequence is determined. These pauses will later be cut down to pace the film and make transitions.

The first screening of spliced-together scenes is often disappointing because without the lightheartedness of the "off-camera" moments that clapboards provide, the movie becomes much more serious and studied. But remember that the editing process has just now begun. Also, repeated takes and out-of-order cuts don't give your film a chance to look finished or complete. It is not wise to show this rough assemblage to anyone, especially your investors, unless they are very experienced in editing low-budget features. Although this screening may be disappointing, it is important to understand that each show is vital to you as an editor, so that when it comes time to make decisive editorial decisions, you will know your footage well enough to make the correct choices.

Placing Scenes in Order of Your Story

Usually, by this point at the beginning of the editing process, the moviemaker's postfilming depression has bottomed out with thoughts such as "It's all shit!" or some equally profane statement. The anger and frustration of seeing your headless mass of footage must now be rechanneled into the stubborn conviction that you will turn your footage into a feature if it's the last thing you ever do. To edit a low-budget movie successfully, it often means that you must somehow turn a sow's ear into a silk purse. And with determination and creativity it *can* be done.

Before shuffling the scenes of your movie into the order of your story, you must write a list of the scenes as they appear in your assemblage. This list will allow you to locate each desired scene out of the thousands of feet of sync film footage (or enclosed in videocassettes, on DVD disks, etc.). Instead of using a sentence to describe each scene, as you did for your filing logbook, you will want to devise a code word or two that identifies your scenes. Scenes from video work print should also be identified by time code for quick access later. This abbreviated list can easily and quickly be reshuffled on paper while you search for the correct scene order of your movie.

Once you have completed your lists of which scenes are in which film rolls, it's time to write down your scenes in order of the story. Though not all low-budget features are designed or meant to tell traditional "stories," it is still assumed that within each body of footage there is a best order of sequence, one that makes each movie as powerful as it can be. For the very abstract feature, an editor may have to test hundreds of different-ordered sequences before determining the best one. And even with a conventional low-budget feature, it may take many tries to get the order right, since it's often the case that scenes and transitions will be missing and will have to be created in postproduction.

After you have made a list of scenes in what you believe is the best order for your story, the assemblage is completed by locating each scene and splicing sync picture and mag track together (video time code, of course, gives you immediate retrieval capabilities for a digital assembly). If you were smart enough to shoot your titles on location, you will find that once these credits have been edited into the film, it will look a lot more like a "real" movie. And most software computer editing systems can access titling features, or have partnered up with Adobe Photoshop and Adobe After Effects for amazing titles coupled with special effects. For scenes that are made up of many short takes, your assemblage will continue to appear rough and unfinished until the pieces of film have been edited tightly together and paced correctly for their order in the sequence. It is best to wait as long as possible before making a "final cut" on multifaceted scenes, because each scene must be cut long or short, fast or slow, in context to the surrounding scenes and the order of the story.

Cutting for Structure

After you view the assemblage of your movie in the order that seems best suited for your story, it will quickly become apparent that scenes work best when they function properly as part of a filmatic "structure." No piece of film or scene can be correctly cut until the editor knows exactly what job that footage is trying to do within the context of the whole work. For a fairly straightforward feature, the structure may be as simple as identifying introductory scenes, middle scenes that sustain action and plot, and ending scenes that conclude the story.

On the other hand, for an exceedingly complicated film such as my *A Man, a Woman, and a Killer*, whose foundation of "reality" continually shifted, it was impossible to edit two scenes together until the structural "key" was discovered after a year of editing. Moving scenes around for months and getting nowhere, I returned to the clapboard footage in which some very precious and revealing moments had occurred. Discussions with co-director Wayne Wang led me to the idea of recording narrations of each character (the man, the woman, and the killer) telling who he or she was as a person in real life, and talking about the other characters and events of the filming. The final key to the structure came when I realized that the lead character, Dick, could be defined as someone "seeing reality as if it were a foreign film he was watching." I had used the creative device of subtitling English words with English titles in some of my previous short films, so it became obvious that subtitling Dick's words and the words of other characters (much of which he had actually scripted for the movie) added the necessary structural element of the film. In a scene of Dick writing in his journal, which we had filmed on location, subtitles would be edited in to silently tell the story. This film was very perplexing to edit during the year of failed screenings and dead-end assemblies. But when I discovered a structure that suddenly made every action and scene understandable, the final editing became exhilarating.

It must be obvious to the reader by now that editing a feature film is more than just sticking scenes together in some kind of order for the story. The highest level of editing requires that the filmmaker rethink his or her original idea in terms of the actual footage being edited. With luck it will be necessary for the filmmaker to put him- or herself through an intense mental exercise in which knowledge of life is expanded in order to complete the editing of his film. If you wrote and shot your feature in an original way, your way, then what really exists on film is a complex survey of your feelings, emotions, observations, prejudices, beliefs, and personal attitudes about your world. What the editing process then represents is an attempt to unify and make sense out of all these disparate parts of your life. Shuffling scenes around to find the best order for your film must be accompanied by an intense desire to seek out the truth of your own life.

Testing Your Edit

Whether you are editing on a homemade workbench with rewinds, Moviescope, sound reader, and synchronizer, on a rented flatbed machine, or digitally on computer, in order to fully understand the power of your cuts it will be important to occasionally screen your film before an audience. By seeing your images projected on a screen or monitor, and by hearing your sound track transmitted through different speakers, while a few friends watch with interest, you are able to view your edit within the context of a theatrical presentation. The presence of just one other person in the screening room can help to give you the objective viewpoint needed to see your film clearly. These informal screenings are not intended to present anything even remotely approaching a finished film and you must always inform your little audience that they are about to see a "work-in-progress," to avoid embarrassment for all concerned. And although there will most certainly be many disruptions and bad edits in the early stages of cutting, out of each screening you will gain some insight regarding various juxtapositions and orders of scenes. Sometimes it will be hard not to react defensively when talking to people after your screening, especially if you yourself are disappointed with what you have just seen. Sometimes footage can be so complicated to edit that each screening fails, resulting in uptight silences for audience and moviemaker alike. Nevertheless, because it is your responsibility to make the film the best it can be, it is necessary to withstand these showings.

Since interlock projectors are expensive to rent, and screening rooms (for film or video) cost even more, an editor must constantly search for free facilities at film schools, or labs, or contact friends who will help him or her screen the film without a fee. Some filmmaking organizations, like FAF (Film Arts Foundation) of San Francisco, offer screenings of "works-in-progress," but this type of public screening should be used only at the final stages of editing. A preview screening can be frightening, but not as frightening as being stuck with an expensive answer print of a poorly edited feature film.

Beginning a "Rough Cut"

If the structure of your movie continues to be evasive, mentally let go of your efforts in this direction and instead focus on improving the edit within particular scenes. If you shot several scenes using the "freeze" technique to create cuts in the action (see chapter 5), it will be enjoyable to edit these pieces together. Since this type of editing is straightforward and easy to accomplish, the process will give you the necessary rest from the mental workout of figuring out the whole feature. At other times in the editing it will be a good idea to send yourself on a few days' vacation, just to clear out your head. Making a feature has often been compared to running a marathon, and anyone who has existed in, and survived, the later stage of editing will attest to this comparison. So it is important to vary the type of editorial job you are performing, making sure that every decision is an intelligent one, not muddled by confusion and fatigue.

By repeated viewing of your assemblage on a flatbed machine or computer monitor, you should notice that some combinations of scenes seem to give off more energy than others. By having experienced many different juxtapositions of scenes, you can now begin to edit your favorite combinations tightly together, removing the pauses that have been left on the front and rear of your scenes since initial assembly. Be careful to accurately file the footage cut out of your scenes, since it is very likely you will need to retrieve these pieces when trying other combinations ("outs" of a computer cut are immediately accessible if digitized scenes are still on the hard drive). Once you've made several successful transitions between scenes, your film will seem to spring to life. This is the magic of editing. Because you gave yourself time to learn about your footage, you now have the ability to fuse scenes together in an exciting way. And with each new edit you come much closer to understanding the film's internal structure.

It is now time to return to the opening scenes of the story, to edit together a convincing first-five-minute sequence. I've learned with each of my features that once the first few minutes of a movie were established, once I could get it rolling, the rest would fall into place. These first minutes of editorial structure will teach the audience the "rules" of your storytelling. Your cuts will set the groundwork for the unfolding film. For each feature the beginning must reflect the heart of the story and introduce the material in a positive and interesting way.

While editing the beginning of *Chan Is Missing* for Wayne Wang, I was able to design a credit sequence that clearly defined its essence. In the cut that Wayne showed me, there was a scene in the middle of the film in which a young woman played a loud version of the song "Rock Around the Clock" on a phonograph in her upstairs room. What was interesting was that the song was sung in Chinese. And months earlier, when I had synced up some of the footage for Wayne, I had noticed a shot of the lead character driving a cab through Chinatown, with alternate reflections of white sky and dark buildings on the windshield. I suggested to Wayne that the Chinese "Rock Around the Clock" song be used in conjunction with the shot of the cabbie as the beginning of the movie. I also figured that superimposing the main titles over the windshield of the cab, titles in white letters when the reflections were dark, titles in black when the reflections were white, would give the sequence some snap. The final result set the Asian-American tone of the film, introduced the main character and his profession, and presented the credits in an elegant way. By following the lead of this beginning footage, the film seemed to tell us what to cut next, and soon the entire movie meshed into place.

Discarding Your Favorite Scene

There's a classic saying in editing that often the secret of your cut is hiding behind the seductive beauty of your favorite shot. At the beginning of the editing process, a writer/director/cameraperson often extols the beauty of one magnificent shot with which he or she is totally in love. In fact, if the moviemaker could not look upon the perfection of this wondrous shot at each screening, he or she would have quit editing long ago. This shot is so incredible that the rest of the footage almost looks shoddy in comparison. As the filmmaker/editor continues to cut, suffering through the normal range of disappointments and discoveries, just the knowledge that this great shot exists sustains his or her drive to complete the movie. But at every turn in the editing, the feature seems to run dry. Except, of course, for the splendor of this gorgeous shot, the story can't seem to keep its momentum. If only all the shots had been as perfect as the unparalleled and utter excellence of . . . THE GREAT SHOT. There is only one solution I know of to rescue you and your movie from this editorial Ferris wheel. With all the willpower you can summon . . . you must remove this exquisite shot from your footage . . . (steady now) . . . file it deeply in your outs, and enjoy the rebirth of your project.

Sound Effects and Music

As you continue to refine the cut of your scenes, you may want to add sound effects that enhance the original shots. As the camera zoomed out the window slowly in *A Man, a Woman, and a Killer,* I added an eerie, almost inaudible sound that cut off with the first sound of dialogue. In a scene where Ed Nylund was taking pictures of the two other characters outside in a field, I cut in the sound of a reflex camera shutter being cocked and released. And in another scene where Ed was giving a long monologue in the Mendocino Hotel dining room, I cut in the sound of low restaurant ambience to give the impression of other people milling about (removing the ambience near the end of Ed's monologue added a powerful yet subtle emotional punch to the scene). With these small touches the power of each scene increased, and in turn affected all the scenes around it.

The use of music can also boost the morale of a film, giving an injection of warmth, terror, joy—whatever emotion an edited sequence requires. Music was added to the beginning images, the title sequence, and the ending shot of *A Man, a Woman, and a Killer*, to give the film a "real film" feeling. It's my puritanical belief that music, as an ingredient in a film, should be used very sparingly and only when necessary.

To add either sound effects or music to your movie, you need to purchase a roll of mag track "slug" (usually about $20 per 1,200′) equal to the length of the roll of edited footage in which your effects occur. After syncing up the roll of slug with your edited roll and marking sync at the beginning (a vertical line drawn through a circle), you roll up to where the effect is needed and cut it in. Then splice the slug to the end of your effect and roll ahead, in sync with your edited roll, to the tail end, so that both rolls are exactly the same overall length. Many sound effects are available on records or CDs, and you can transfer each needed effect to mag stock for your editing needs or just record from CD for your computer cut. For specialized effects that aren't available, you will need to record the sounds yourself with a Nagra or Walkman Professional recorder and then transfer the results onto mag. To use original music in your feature, you will need to get a written agreement that grants you the use of the tracks (see appendix G for "Music Rights Agreement"), and probably also pay a fee that can range from around $80 (the cost of music for the main credits of *A Man, a Woman, and a Killer*) up to several thousands of dollars per song.

A better solution for obtaining music for your film would be to purchase an electronic keyboard and make your own (see "Digital Music for Movies," chapter 11). Prices range from $150 up to more than $2,000 for keyboards that include built-in speakers, twelve preset rhythms, twenty different instrument voices, four electronic drum pads, and other effects. Some models include digital synthesizers, with internal cassette/disk recording capabilities. If your electronic keyboard can record right onto its own cassettes, as soon as you have composed your musical score you can transfer the sound directly to mag stock and edit it into your movie, or transfer it by midi to a computer cut. And some keyboards now have the capability to store a certain length of music in their minicomputers, so that by projecting your film and playing your composition back with the push of a button, you can finalize the appropriateness and length of your score. Even if you don't consider yourself a musician, you'll find you can enjoy playing with one of these keyboards, and can, surprisingly, create effective sound tracks.

The "Breakthrough Cut"

If you continue to spend several hours every day for several months working at editing your rough cut, testing new orders of scenes, reworking the first five minutes, and perfecting the editing of each scene, you are bound to experience many small breakthroughs and maybe even the "breakthrough cut." The major breakthrough of editing a feature-length movie occurs only after the structure of your story has finally been revealed and you have edited your scenes together with the stability and intelligence gained from this discovery. How will you know when you have hit upon the "breakthrough cut"? If you have to ask, then it hasn't happened yet! The best way I can describe it is that when the breakthrough cut occurs it's as if the movie flies away from you, becomes whole, a living entity that you can't believe you had a role in creating. Everything works.

A breakthrough cut has not occurred unless every scene and sequence of picture and sound functions better in the cut than ever before. During the months of shifting scenes around to find the best order of your story, you have probably noticed that in each tested edit certain scenes seem more lively and function better than others in the context in which they are presented. And then later, in another cut, the same scenes seem to drag while other previously clumsy scenes look better. This is happening because without knowing the structure of your footage, it is impossible to edit in the correct pacing for each scene in your movie. The most difficult thing about editing is that if even one transition between scenes drags or falters in some way, every scene that follows will suffer and seem mistaken. When the structure of the feature tells you the purpose of each segment, then and only then can you make the perfect breakthrough cut.

The Missing Pieces

Sometimes footage will be unyielding and stiff, as it was for *A Man, a Woman, and a Killer*, and you can never reach a breakthrough cut without the addition of other elements into your movie. Whether you need a narration that ties together your structure, a series of still photographs backed by music that fills in the gap in your story, or titles explaining each segment, it is always hard to admit that you failed to supply yourself with all the needed images and sounds during the shoot. In Hollywood you probably would have been fired and sent back to the bush league for not supplying adequate "coverage." But in the world of independent, low-budget production, you have the opportunity to use this "failure" to invent original and distinctive solutions for your movie, solutions that may lead you to the "key" of your edit.

Adding Narrations

Chan Is Missing would still be sitting on a shelf gathering dust if Wayne Wang hadn't realized that his film needed a series of narrations to pull it together. At first he recorded narrations by three characters as I had done for *A Man, a Woman, and a Killer*, but after testing them in the edit he came to realize that only the voice of the older character should be used. By limiting the narration to one character, the cut achieved the desired unity, defined the older cabdriver as the main character, and revealed its structure. The addition of the narration allowed the main character, a sixty-year-old Asian-American, to comment on his journey through the heart of Chinatown, giving the movie the airiness and humor that made it such a success. Seeing the different aspects of the Asian-American culture through the cynical eyes of an older, "established" member of the community was exactly the right touch, the right concept that knocked the structure of the film into place.

Before recording the narrations for your movie, you must first define the concept of these "voice-overs." Will they talk about exterior things such as uncovering a mystery as in *The Maltese Falcon*? Or will they speak for the interior thoughts and dreams of your character (or characters), as in the film *Wild Strawberries*? What is the character's point of view? Will your characters speak in their own voices, making up their own words, or will you script what they say? As best you can, you should carefully design each narration in length and content, so you know where to edit it into your assembly. Since these narrations are meant to "save" your film and solve structural difficulties, they should be as tightly constructed as possible.

Once you have determined the text or improvisational outline of the narrations, you will need to find a suitable sound studio or situation for the recordings. For $250 an hour plus the cost of recording tape, you could record your narrator(s) in the finest-quality sound studio in your area. If this rate is affordable, nothing beats using a good facility where you are guaranteed crisp, clean recordings. But if you are on a limited budget and know you can only afford one hour to record your narrations, you must be extremely well rehearsed and organized. Another consideration may be that you wish to use the professional setting of a sound studio to intensify the recording session; to make sure your amateur actors perform under pressure similar to that of the shoot.

A cheaper way to record your narrations would be just to sit in a quiet place and speak directly into an audio recorder as I did for my feature *Emerald Cities.* For that recording I used my $100 Panasonic cassette deck, speaking into its built-in mike. Because the speed of the tape was not perfect, my recorded voice sounded a bit strange and distant, but this was fine for its use in the movie. Using a Sony Walkman Professional recorder with an expensive, high-quality mike, and recording in a super-quiet location, you could almost duplicate the recorded sound of a high-quality sound studio. But remember that you will need to pay the cost of the mag stock and a transfer fee for recording audio signals onto mag. And often it is much more difficult in informal situations to elicit satisfactory performances from your actors, because you waste time with repeated takes, and waste money with increased tape and transfer cost.

If you have a DV camera and FireWire (IEEE 1394) port on your computer, then your narrations could be recorded onto "CD"-quality audio (on videocassette) and "captured" to batch files for a computer cut. Whichever way you decide to record your narrations, always put the quality of your recording first on your list, charging the costs, if necessary, so that these sound tracks won't haunt the editing of your production with muddled voices and noisy background interference.

Photos as Transitions

In almost all of my features I have used a series of photos to tell part of my story. In *A Man, a Woman, and a Killer* I used footage shot from color slides taken by Ed Nylund during the shoot that told a visual story of the off-camera moments. Working with the art department of a film lab, I devised a concept of the pictures "sliding" in and out from the left side of the frame, in the tradition of the early slide projector. After setting up a rhythm of images entering and leaving the frame at different speeds, I varied the camera moves with pans and dissolves. The few hundred dollars this effect cost created an over-two-minute sequence in the final film (this same effect can now be easily accomplished in Adobe After Effects for free!).

For my film *1988—The Remake* I used images from a photo album of Ed Nylund's growing up, while he narrated his life story. I also used a long sequence of color slides picturing acts from the *Showboat 1988* audition in my ending titles, around fifty images, each of which showed the performer(s) and information about his or her current activities or status. The printing of the slides and titles cost many hundreds of dollars (again a job for Adobe After Effects!), but since I could charge the work at the lab, I was able to afford excellent camera work at a time when I was flat broke.

In *Emerald Cities* I once again used photos as part of my film. With the help of videomaker Liz Sher (**<www.ivstudios.com>**) I videotaped snapshots from my childhood using her ¾″-format JVC camera. I later transferred these shots to 16-mm as part of a video section that recurs throughout the film. Shooting these photos cost me about $20 for the ¾″ tape and another $150 for the transfer to 16-mm film.

Shooting Additional Footage

After you have edited in your narrations and maybe even added a sequence of photos to your movie, it may become necessary to shoot some extra footage that you now realize must be included in the cut. These "pickup shots" may be as simple as shooting toward the sidewalk from a moving car or filming a close-up of a hand reaching in to change a radio station. A full-scale production team should not be assembled unless it is painfully obvious that many additional sync scenes must be shot to complete the story. And no additional footage should be produced until you know *exactly* what is missing from your movie. Shooting more footage must not be an exercise in avoidance of editing, and should only be done after the maximum pressure has been applied in search of the best cut.

Final Tightening and Pacing

Hopefully, by this point in the editing of your feature, you understand completely what your footage is "trying to say." If you don't, and no firm structure can be put into words, it's not worth trying to tighten up the edits. This final editing process must be based on the firm foundation of the correct order by scenes, with a well-defined beginning, middle, and end. An early attempt to "fine edit" will only bring disappointing results and extra work for the editor. If you *have* been able to figure out the structure of your story or artistic statement, then you should be able to cut out all extraneous frames and footage from each shot.

If you look over your assembled rough cut with an eye toward awkward moments, overstated and elongated scenes, any interruption in the flow, this is the time to correct these problems so that every frame of your movie contributes to the story you are telling. Like Michelangelo, who believed that he was freeing the human figure trapped below the surface of the marble he was carving, you must help the real movie emerge, shedding the footage that clearly doesn't belong in your cut. Once you have successfully edited together the first five minutes, every scene and shot that follows will tell you how tightly it should be cut.

As each scene is tailor cut, your feature assumes a life you never thought it had. Check the beginning of each scene during your screening. After the tightly edited first five minutes, are there scenes that have an extra few seconds of pause before action or dialogue begins? By knowing the structure of your story, you are aware that certain series of scenes should move fast before cutting to a slow scene. If you cut the fast scenes to the bone, allowing for no extra frames to disrupt the action, when you make your cut to the slow scene the pause of action and sound will eat up the energy. As editor you can count the beats before the dialogue begins: . . . one . . . two . . . three . . . four . . . dialogue. It is your job to select the right amount of pause before the dialogue begins. Will it be four seconds long? Eight seconds? Sometimes the beginning few seconds of a scene have a loud sound that disrupts the feeling of the shot. Just that one sound will disrupt the flow of cuts in your movie, and must be cut out. Now your cut will seem smoother, cleaner, and healthier. And when the first words of dialogue are spoken you will seem to be hearing them for the first time, hearing the ideas and emotions behind the words. Cleaning up your edits can turn a dull scene into a clever one.

After experiencing the enormous difference made by your small corrections, you begin to take charge of every filmatic moment. In some places in your sound track you have listened for months as an actor stumbled over the beginning word in an important stretch of dialogue. Now it is time to locate that three-frame mistake, cut the frames out, and replace them with room tone that you recorded while filming on location. (Editing software systems, like Avid, make it extremely easy to patch over bad sound areas by electronically duplicating adjacent sound tones.)

As has happened throughout the editing process on your feature, correcting one cut or transition leads you to other work. Every scene and shot, movement and sound, is felt in the context of what exists around it in the movie. A scene that has been adversely affected by a clumsy cut several scenes back now springs to life after the earlier cut has been streamlined.

> **note:** If you have been editing your original picture instead of a work print, this final process of tightening up cuts must be avoided until your rough cut is completed and you cut your original into A and B rolls for printing, because each shot will lose a frame at beginning and end during "hot" splicing.

Finalizing the Structure

Now that your movie is close to completion, you will want to borrow some 2,200′ reels that will allow you to screen almost sixty minutes of assemblage at a time (or view your entire digital computer cut on an extra-large "movie screen" monitor). This gives you a chance to get a feeling for the overall movement, so that by designing in some resting places (fade-outs and dissolves), you can insure that the feature will continue to flow for its length of seventy to ninety minutes. After screening the first sixty minutes and then the remaining footage, repeat the screening using the 2,200′ reel for the last sixty minutes of the film. If you have some extra money, you can screen your results at a professional facility that switches projectors at reel changes to see the movie run continuously (cost: around $200). This is the *only* way to know for sure if the feature is correctly cut for theatrical presentation. What's important is that you get a feeling of where a few fade-outs should occur, and if some footage or scenes should be removed for the sake of the whole movie.

For sound mixing and printing, you won't want any one film roll to run over 1,100 feet in length (about thirty minutes). This is about the maximum amount of footage that can be supported by the sprocket plate on your flatbed editing machine. It is also the largest amount of mag track that can be loaded onto most mixing machines. Although many labs can print more than 1,100 feet of film at a time, handling rolls of original film over this size is dangerous in terms of footage slipping off the core. Since you will want to assemble your finished film into two large 2,000′ reels for ease of shipping to showcases and film festivals, it is necessary to design the best way for rolls 1 and 2 to splice together (reel 1) and the best way rolls 3 and 4 (reel 2) can be combined.

The technical needs of printing dictate that the best way to end reel 1 is with a fade-out, and the best way to begin reel 2 is with a fade-in. This allows for projectionists to splice together your film for showings in black leader where the connection will not be noticed. Also, if footage is lost because of faulty splicers, lost frames in the black leader after the fade-out or before the fade-in will not ruin the transition between the reels. Usually, if a film has only one fade-out and one fade-in during its entire running length, it occurs about halfway through the film in order to break up the time for the audience. If this is appropriate for your filmatic structure, then you have satisfied both the technical needs of printing and the aesthetic needs of your film work.

On page 179 are photos of the correct notations for fade-out and fade-in, and dissolve for printing. Although you may not be ready with your final cut for printing, now is a good time to start testing different lengths of fade-outs and dissolves to see which one is correct. If you have edited your film digitally, then you probably have already experimented extensively with these various lab effects, perhaps even utilizing some video moves (spins, page turns, etc.) for your film transitions. Most labs offer effects in lengths of eight frames, sixteen frames, twenty-four frames (one second), thirty-six frames, forty-eight frames (two seconds), seventy-two frames (three seconds), and ninety-six frames (four seconds). By drawing two lines in grease pencil on your work print, from a point at the edge of your frame line, converging twenty-four frames later to a point at the middle of the picture (see photo 1), you have indicated a one-second fade-out. When projecting your film, as these two converging lines wipe from the sides of the frame and meet at the middle in one second, you will be able actually to experience your fade-out and adjust it if it runs too short. Photo 2 shows how to indicate a dissolve by drawing a wavy line in grease pencil from a point where the dissolve begins, through the cut between the shots representing the middle of the effect, to a point on the second shot where the dissolve ends. When marking a dissolve, make sure that there is original footage of your shots equal to the length of overlap you've indicated. Once again, during a screening you can feel how the length of the effect functions for your cut, as you watch the wavy lines moving from side to side on the screen.

note: If you are editing original footage instead of a work print, *don't* mark your picture with grease pencil since this may scratch the emulsion (it will also be very difficult to remove for clean printing).

Preparing Sound Rolls for the Mix

Before you can properly mix your sound onto one unified sound track, you need to split your sound between two or more rolls. Perhaps by now you've noticed that some of your recorded scenes are too loud in volume for where they fit in your edit. And during your screenings you have sometimes kept your fingers on the volume control, turning down the sound when that scene is on the screen. By sep-

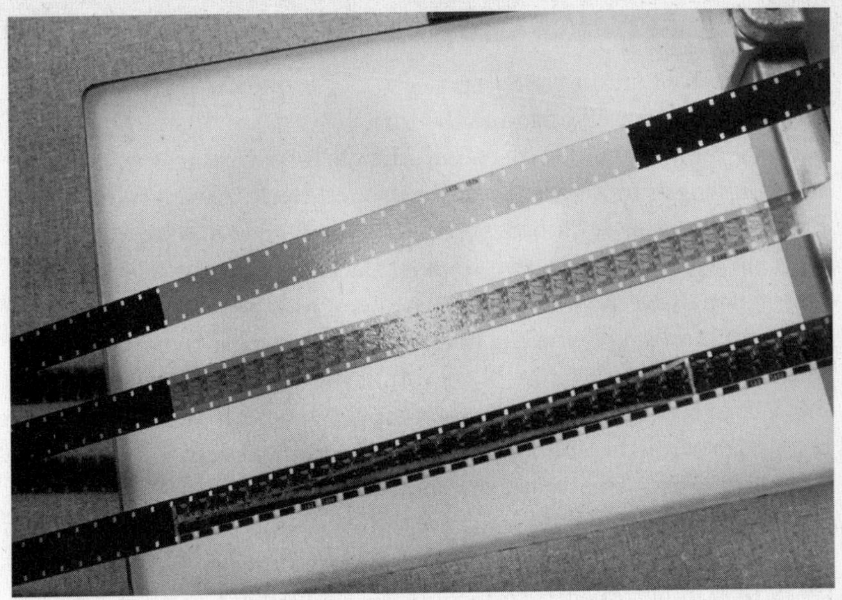

1. Original film and clear leader checked against fade-out, marked on work print.

2. Original A and B rolls checked for dissolve against marked work print. Wavy lines indicate to the lab that you want a dissolve.

arating each sound in your scenes, you can finally set the volume level for each scene as well as adjust the tone.

To split your tracks you need a blank roll of mag or sound slug, equal in length to the length of your sound track. As you roll through your synchronizer or flatbed, you place a mark on the blank roll in sync with the splice between two sounds. Back up the rolls and undo the tape splice between your sounds. Then cut your blank roll at the mark and switch rolls, splicing the blank roll to the sound track and the remaining sound track to the blank roll in the synchronizer. By alternating each particular sound in your movie, you empower the mixing technician with the ability to adjust volumes and equalize sounds, so that scenes mesh and transitions succeed in turning your pieces of film into a movie.

Before mixing your sound tracks, you will need to write out a cue sheet that indicates each correction and adjustment in sound, and at what footage count it occurs. This cue sheet is a vital guide, absolutely necessary to a technician who must mix a film he or she has never seen. Ask the sound mixer for a cue sheet form.

To make sure there are no imperfections in the splicing tape or dirt on your sound track, you will want to clean your mag tracks with special mag cleaner (available at full-service labs), wiping each side with a moist cotton swab. If the tracks are not thoroughly cleaned, "pops" may occur on your precious and expensive mix. When using toxic cleaning fluids, make sure that you are in a *very* ventilated room, even using a fan, as I do, to make sure that you aren't poisoned by the fumes.

In order for your printed rolls to maintain their sync sound track when spliced together in assembled reels for projection, adjustments must be made before the mix. The sound track on your print will run twenty-six frames ahead of picture, so that it will be broadcast in sync by projectors that read the sound twenty-six frames ahead of where the picture image is projected. If you plan to splice the last image of roll 1 (which has a sync sound track) to the first image on roll 2 (also with a sync sound track), picture-to-picture, when you assemble your print, then you have to account for the sound moving up twenty-six frames in printing or lose part of your sound track (generally the editing rolls you've called roll 1 and roll 2 become *reel 1,* and roll 3 and roll 4 become *reel 2* when their prints are spliced together for projection). This problem can be solved by removing the last twenty-six frames of sound from the end of roll 1, replacing it with twenty-six frames of blank leader, and resplicing that small segment of sync sound into the head of roll 2, cutting it in so (1) it's on the same numbered roll (either sound-A or sound-B) of the mix, and (2) the twenty-six frames from roll 1 butts against right where the first frame of sync sound on roll 2 begins.

Here's what happens during printing if you've done this maneuver correctly. When roll 1 is printed, the entire sound track moves up twenty-six frames, filling in the blank twenty-six-frame hole created at the end of the roll. That means that if you cut off the black tail leader at exactly the last image frame of your print at the end of roll 1, you'd still have your sound coming right up to that cut point (you can actually look at your print on a light table and see the sound track doing its spiky graphlike motion right up to where image ends and black leader begins). On roll 2 the sound track has also moved up twenty-six frames in its entirety during printing, so that the sync twenty-six-frame piece of r-1 sound you placed at the head has moved up, its last frame now even with the first frame of picture image. If you cut off the black head leader of roll 2 exactly at first frame of image, you'll again find that you have spiky sound waves on your print's sound track, right from that cut point on. Do you see how this works yet? When you show reel 1 of your movie, and the splice point connecting roll 1 to roll 2 passes through the projector, the first twenty-six frames of sound on roll 2 will supply the "twenty-six-frames-ahead" sound for the last twenty-six frames of images for roll 1.

note: It is important that the twenty-six frames of sound track be switched to the same A or B roll so that during the mix the setting of volume and tone (equalization) will be consistent for both the little twenty-six-frame piece at the head of roll 2 and the previous levels on roll 1, to insure no change in sound at the splice. Before the mix check each splice on the sound tracks to make sure they are tight and haven't stretched from repeated screenings or editing. Replace all faulty splices that threaten to cause mistakes during the mix.

The Sound Mix

One of the most important procedures of your editing process is the several hours you spend mixing your sound into one composite track for printing. Not only does the mix fine-tune every sound in your film, but it also immediately tells you if the filmatic structure of your edit is correct. As each sound is adjusted for equalization and volume level, the pace of your movie speeds up. If your structure is correct, the mix will feel as if it's tightening up your cuts and energizing your transitions. If you understand how your story "breathes," then in the mix you can properly control the internal movements by keeping some sections quiet, while other sections hit hard. As I've mentioned in an earlier chapter, since a good mix is vital to the quality of your feature, don't shortchange your effort by settling for a "bargain" mix just to save a few hundred dollars. At a high-quality mixing studio, you should be able to mix a feature with ABC sound rolls in under eight hours. I helped Wayne Wang mix *Chan Is Missing* in seven and a half hours. While it is very scary to sit in a mixing studio that costs $125 to $185 an hour (plus the cost of mag stock), the results of your expenditure will usually be well worth it (for computer software sound mix see "The Digital Sound Mix," chapter 11).

If you come to the end of your editing and have absolutely no possible way of raising another $1,000 for a high-quality mix, you may be able to locate a special "underground" high-quality mixing facility in your area. Begin by checking at your local film school to see if such a low-cost facility is known and available. In each mixing situation, regardless of cost, it is important to follow the advice of your technician, remain calm, and bring some food (sandwich, drink, snack) to keep up your energy.

Screening Your Sound Mix

Screening your work print, synced to your sound mix, with all your sound working together on a clean track, you should feel the footage moving twice as fast as ever before. Although there is a definite risk to screening original composite mixed sound, as editor you need to see your film in as close to a final form as possible. You also must know the exact quality of the mix so that if there is faulty printing or damage to your mixed track, you will be able to give the lab a convincing argument for redoing your print at no added cost.

This may be the time to have the courage for a semipublic showing of your feature, possibly at a screening room, or friend's apartment. It is very important to submit your film (and yourself) to a final test with an audience, because it is necessary to be completely satisfied with your edit before cutting apart your original footage for printing. Since you lose a frame at every splice when conforming your original A and B rolls, make sure that the movie you see being projected with your mix is the movie you can live with for years to come. If there are major mistakes—this may be hard to accept—return to the editing room and, with careful consideration, keep editing.

If you make careful splices, you can cut out a section of mixed sound track, in sync with a shot or scene you have removed, and not hear any sound disruption or *pop* on the sound track of the print. If you do cut your mixed track, be very careful to make sure that your picture and sound track are in sync when you mark your mixed mag track with ink pen before lowering the blade of your splicer. And after removing the sync footage, do a final check by syncing up the mixed sound track together with your picture work print to make sure each piece measures the exact same length in frames.

Conforming Original for Printing

Just as you have checkerboarded your sound into AB (and possibly C) rolls for your composite mix, you will now need to checkerboard your picture rolls of original footage into AB rolls, in preparation for making your print. If you have been editing your original rolls all along, you will want to place them in a final checkerboard position for printing, at the same time editing out the few frames you left at the front and rear of each scene during your rough cut, which you knew would be lost to splicing. While the process of conforming original footage to work print (in checkerboard rolls for printing), or splicing the original together in checkerboard rolls that you edited without work print is basically the same, in concept, for all different film-stocks, there is enough difference between conforming Reversal stock and Negative stock to require separate discussions. And AB rolling original that has been edited instead of work print also has unique problems that must be separately addressed.

AB Rolling from a Work Print

The first step for conforming Reversal or Negative stock is to obtain a clean, dust-free editing bench. Your home-built, Formica-topped editing bench would be perfect for AB rolling, although when AB rolling Negative stock you may want to rent a special editing table with a built-in fan that blows all dust out of the enclosed shell of the table. On rewinds you need three 1,200′ split reels (reels that split apart to hold film on cores), one for your original roll, one for an equal length of black leader, and another for your work print. And you need four take-up 1,200′ reels, two for your original checkerboarding rolls, one to take up your work print, and one to roll up the original outs as you cut. If you plan to conform your AB rolls at home, you will need to rent a hot splicer with which to glue the film together. If you rent an editing room in which to AB roll, this facility should come with the reels and splicer you need to complete your job. It is also wise to wear white cotton gloves while handling your original film, since sweat and oil from your fingers will help dust to collect on the film. Once you have gathered together all the implements necessary for conforming, you are ready for the next step of listing edge numbers and pulling out original in order of the film's scenes.

For AB rolling of Reversal stock, an editor would first begin listing shots of the edited work print by first and last "latent edge numbers." Along the edge of your work print you will notice small numbers that are printed into the film. These "latent" numbers, existing in duplicate on your original footage, are not to be confused with the edge numbers that you may have had printed onto your film at one-foot intervals for keeping sync. Once you have written down this list of latent edge numbers for each shot in your edited work print, your next step is to locate each segment of original film holding corresponding numbers. After rolling once through your original rolls (labeling the top of each can with the edge prefixes enclosed), your next job is to locate each piece of original in order of your edit and roll it up on a reel. When you find the correct shot in your original footage that corresponds to your work print, cut out the entire take, including the clap board and the flash frames at the end of the shot, and tape it onto your reel. Once you have pulled your original footage, carefully roll back to the beginning ("heads out"), so that the first scene of your movie is first on the roll.

> **note:** When reeling original footage, always keep a steady tension on the film to insure that you won't form creases in the emulsion ("glitch marks") because of uneven pressure. And when filing outs, use *only* special tape for original film that pulls off easily and leaves no gum residue.

The next step is to measure out ample black leaders for your A and B rolls and work print. Since you probably haven't used a long leader in editing, it will be necessary to add several feet of leader between sync mark and first image of the work print. Most labs require 12′ leaders, but since lab needs vary you should call the lab that will print your film and ask them what they prefer. All rolls are then placed in the synchronizer and rolled up to a sync mark on the work print. Place sync marks, drawn on white stick-on tabs for better visibility, on each of the black leader AB rolls, and roll up to your first work print image for matching.

AB rolling of original Negative or Reversal filmstock follows the same basic procedures, but in every instance greater caution must be used in order not to scratch the emulsion with rough handling. Since repeated reeling of Negative film is risky, each stage of handling the original must be completed as carefully as possible. For this reason "pulling the original" takes the most time to complete. After the latent edge numbers are listed in order of scenes off the work print, each roll of original is checked at the first scene for edge number identification and is appropriately tagged. Please note that instead of rolling through the rolls of original in search of edge numbers as we did with

Reversal stock, the original Negative rolls still haven't been reeled. Now, instead of "pulling" each scene and shot in order of the work print scenes and rolling them up on a reel, we slowly roll from one end of the Negative to the other end, as each shot is identified by edge number, cut off at the beginning and end of each take, and rolled up carefully on a separate core with identification label.

Splicing of Negative original also requires special care and handling of the film. The first thing to know is that Negative original must be glued with a splicer that has been specially adjusted for Negative film, to insure that no frame lines are seen on the print. When renting a splicer you must remember to specify that you will be AB rolling *Negative* film and need their *Negative hot splicer.* Before beginning to splice once again, clean your editing bench of dust and clear all unnecessary equipment and items from the tabletop. Aside from your rolls of black leader that match the length of your feature, you will need a few hundred feet of Negative "clear" leader. When your editing space and your head are organized, you are ready to begin the assembly of your original into AB rolls.

For both Reversal and Negative film, the basic AB rolling procedure is the same. To best illustrate the process, the following plates will show how each new scene is matched at each cut on the work print. Rolling to the end of your first matched scene, make a mark on both the original and black leader with your grease pencil, *one frame longer* than where your scene ends on your work print (photo 1 on page 188). That extra frame of black leader and original will be cut off during hot splicing. After you've cut off both rolls at the marks, match the latent edge number of the original for the next scene with the edge number of the work print, and cut off the original *one frame longer* than the beginning frame of the new scene (photo 2). You are now ready to splice your original and black leader together in a "checkerboard" of A and B rolls.

The first hot splice you will want to make will be the black leader of the preceding scene to the original of the next scene. Place the black leader on the splicer, *one frame past* the center line, holding the film tightly between the top pin and guide (photo 3). Lock down the splicer on the black leader and lift up that half of the splicing bar. On the other half of the splicer, repeat the procedure with the original for the next scene, holding the film tightly between the pin and upper guide while locking it down, making sure that it sticks out *one frame longer* than the center line edge (photo 4 on page 189). With your finger press down the excess frame of original (photo 5) and scrape off the emulsion with the retractable scraper, pulling it across your film end a few times. Brush on liquid film cement in one movement across the scraped end (photo 6) and immediately close down the top bar of the splicer, locking that side to the base, at the same time closing your cement bottle (photo 7 on page 190).

To hot-splice the original from your previous scene to black leader, the same procedure is followed, but this time the film and black leader must be looped around the splicer to make the splice (photo 8). Again, you must remember to set the black leader and original in the splicer *one frame longer* than the center line. After both splices have been completed, check your A and B roll to make sure the splices are in sync and that the latent edge numbers of your original line up with those of the work print (photo 9). Photos 1 and 2 back on page 179 show examples of Negative AB rolls set up for fade-out and dissolve. Notice that a length of clear leader must be added to the black leader equal and in sync with the fade-out effect.

Once again you can benefit from making test splices before actually beginning to AB roll your feature. To test the strength of your splices, gently make a slight twist at the cut and see if the two ends separate at the edges. Only test your splices on the AB rolls with the greatest sense of caution, making sure you don't rip your original. If splices you've made on test pieces of film, using outs from your original and some of the same black leader, hold up after being tested, you should have the same dependable splices throughout your AB rolls.

note: The utmost care must once again be taken to make sure that a Negative original doesn't get damaged by running it along the editing table or coming in contact with equipment. Fortunately, most labs now offer a service called "liquid gate" during printing, which fills in most imperfections and scratches and removes dust by printing your film through a liquid coating. Liquid gate is essential for printing a clean, high-quality image in Negative or Reversal film.

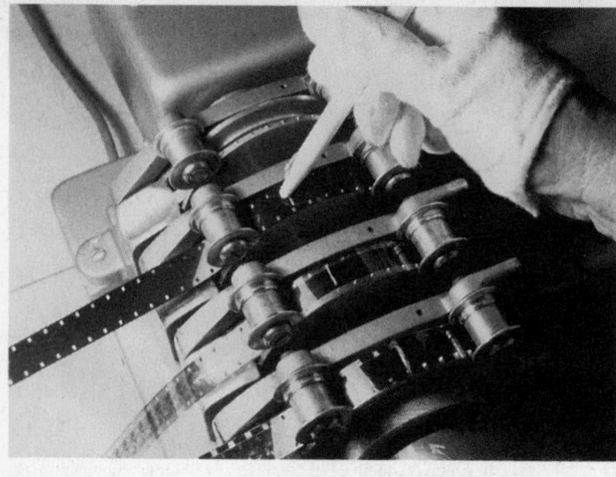

AB ROLLING

1. Original picture and black leader marked in sync, one frame past work print splice.

2. Original scene to be added, cut one frame longer for splice.

3. Black leader inserted in hot splicer, one frame longer than cutting edge.

4. Black leader and original clamped in splicer for cut.

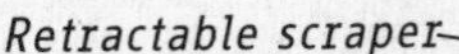

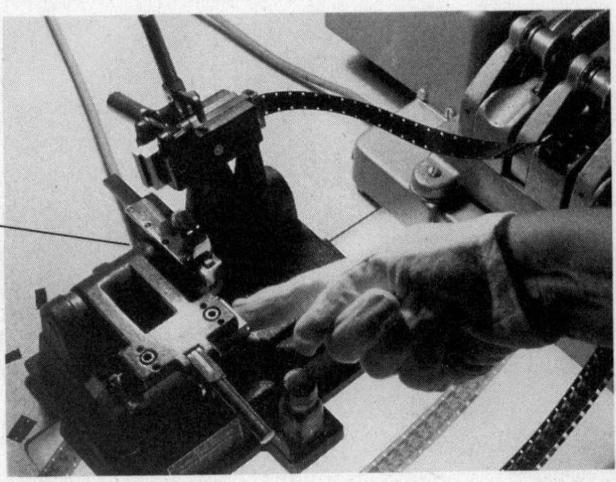

5. Extra frame of original bent down before removing emulsion with retractable scraper.

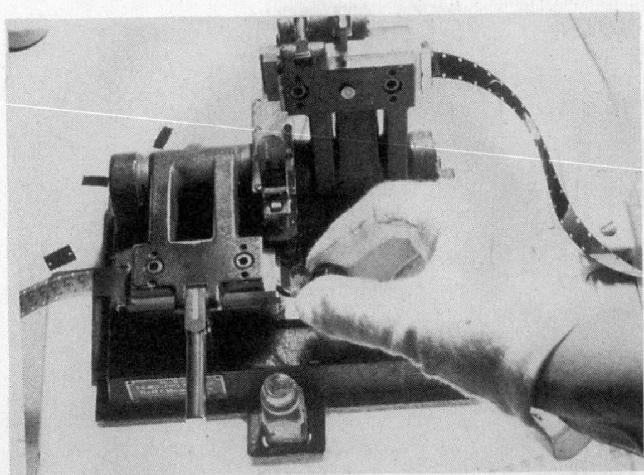

6. Applying fast-drying glue to emulsion-scraped edge of original film.

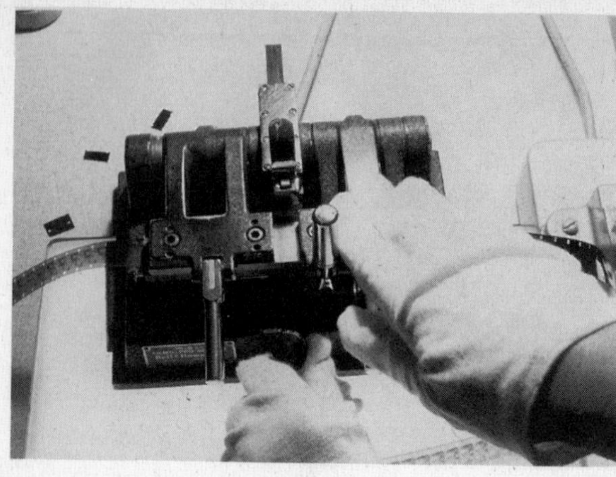

7. Clamping original film and black leader together in a hot splice.

8. Ready to hot-splice black leader onto original from previous scene.

9. Examining "checkerboard" AB rolls, checking splices and edge numbers against work print.

AB Rolling Without a Work Print

If you have not been able to afford a work print for editing, having instead edited your original into a final rough cut, and also mixed your sound in sync to your original picture, AB rolling your film is much less of an effort. Since your film is already in order of assemblage, it will obviously not be necessary to spend hours locating original film. After you have cut and synced up proper-length leaders for printing, also sync up your mixed sound track. If you haven't anticipated the loss of a frame at the beginning and end of each shot in your original, then you will have to cut out and resplice your sound track to keep sync. If this sounds incredibly messy, then either AB roll on a synchronizing block, correcting your sound track as you cut (mixing the tracks *after* AB rolling the original), or somehow dig up additional funds for a work print. Of course, if your film is made up of only seven or eight long takes, it won't be much of a problem to sync up your mix at these few cuts.

Cue Sheet for Printing

For each AB roll of your film, whether Reversal or Negative, you will need to supply the lab with a cue sheet for printing instructions. Since each lab has its own particular needs so far as the form of cue sheet they require, ask them for guidelines. After splicing your AB rolls together and carefully reeling them back to "head out," set the original rolls back in the synchronizer, at the sync marks, and set the counter at "0" feet. As you roll through your completed rolls, fill in your cue sheet, while at the same time checking that splices are in sync. This final checkout is vital to insuring that your printing will be correct. Also, check each dissolve and fade-out against your marked work print to make sure that it is correctly placed and spliced. Once you have reached the last frame of your images and marked down the final footage count on your cue sheet, carefully and firmly roll up each AB roll, one at a time. Finally, place each set of AB rolls in a can or protective box, including its cue sheet, and your film is ready to be given to the lab for printing.

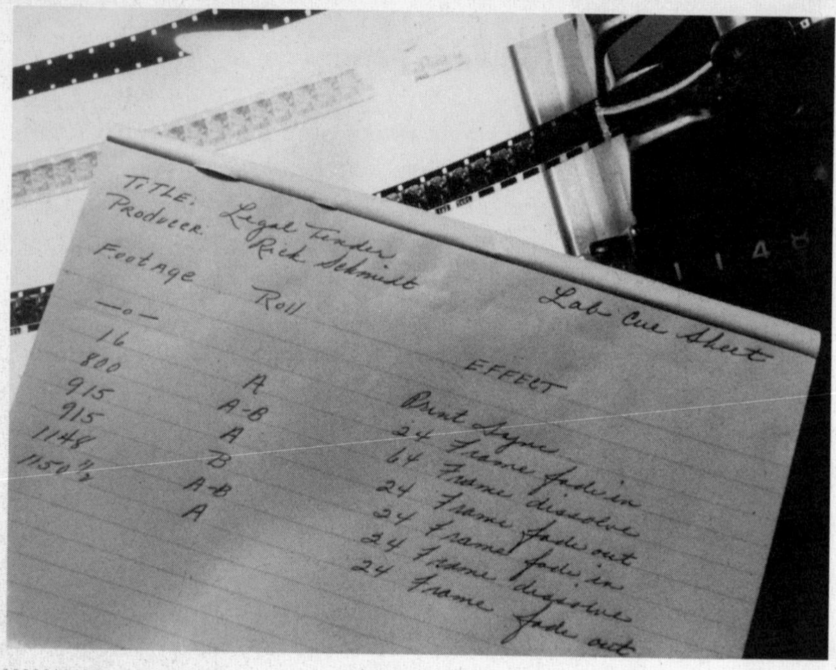

Lab cue sheet with footage count, roll, and effect identified for printing. Ask your lab technicians what they require.

If this process of conforming AB rolls for printing seems just too daunting, contact a professional editor who specializes in this procedure. Andy Pratt, at Negative Cutting and Conforming ([206] 521-9193), is Seattle-based and an expert at conforming indie productions (he cut our *Blues for the Avatar*). He'll help you meet your Sundance print deadline, but schedule as early as possible!

note: It's best to let the lab mark your sound mix mag track for the correct "print sync," twenty-six frames behind your "dead sync" (the sync mark of your AB rolls and mix). In this way you will be assured that this procedure is done correctly and that your sound track will be in sync with the picture on the finished answer print. And if the lab does this incorrectly, then they will be responsible for supplying you with another print, free of cost.

Lab Procedures for Printing

I've always spiritually approached the lab with the idea that if they make a mistake on my film because of some confused decision, it's *my* fault because I didn't make it absolutely clear what I wanted. By taking total responsibility for the outcome of your printing (short of obvious lab mistakes), you have a good chance of getting a perfect answer print on the first try. Since most labs consider the answer print a "trial" print, with the attitude that they will produce a good print after a few tries, the filmmaker with a budget for *one* print must be exceedingly precise at every stage of communication to get this first print correct on the first try.

Since a feature-length film is a major printing project for most labs, you should ideally be granted the opportunity to review the footage, roll by roll, with a "timer." The timer is a person who adjusts the exposure of your scenes (if necessary) and works with filters to balance the color of each shot. Although most labs now use a machine such as a Rank Cintel to electronically balance color and exposure, it's still important to communicate with the individual who will be responsible for the overall look of your finished print. Ask him or her to explain what changes he or she would recommend in the areas of exposure and color correction. If you've shot your film in black-and-white stock and purposely underexposed for richer blacks, you definitely don't want an uninformed timer to "correct" those exposures. If you don't speak up, you can be guaranteed that the timer at the lab will work feverishly to pump light into dark scenes, unless you communicate that the dark quality is what you desire. And if you don't want any changes of exposures on your film, write at the top of your cue sheets "NO LIGHT CHANGES" and underline the words. A rule of thumb when dealing with the lab is that if you have done anything at all "creative" or unusual, make sure you tell the lab how to handle that footage.

After you roll through your original AB rolls with a timer, checking fade-ins and fade-outs, dissolves, and cuts between scenes as logged on your cue sheet, your months, maybe years, of work . . . your film . . . is in the hands of the lab. As I've mentioned earlier in the book, if you reach the printing stage of your film and don't have enough cash to complete the film, most labs will extend you credit if you make some amount of "good faith" payment (usually half down) when ordering the answer print. By arranging to pay off the remainder of your lab bill at so much per month, you are then able to complete your project, using your feature to earn money with rentals and video sales, and to enter film festivals and grant contests.

note: The final control you should exert over your feature is in ordering that the lab *make your answer print on Estar-based 16-mm stock*, and that the print be sent out for *protective plastic coating by AFD Photogard* (953 North Cole Avenue, Hollywood, CA 90038, [323] 469-8141, <**cuinps@aol.com**>) to insure against projector damage. The Estar-base printing stock is so strong that almost no projector can break your print, and the AFD Photogard coating insures that the wonderfully clean and clear images that you've worked so hard to create won't become obliterated with new scratches from each additional screening. My prints are unbroken and still look as new as when they left the lab, even after numerous film festival and theatrical showings. Be very clear with the lab that you won't accept your print unless it has been protected as ordered, with Estar base and AFD Photogard.

All you can do then is wait, hoping that you have been specific enough about all aspects of your film to deserve a perfect trial answer print. If you have let the timer know that you have enough money for only this one print, maybe he or she will be sympathetic to your cause and work extra hard to get it right. At any rate, you now have a few weeks' vacation while the lab prints each roll with the changes and corrections you have detailed. While you try to remain calm, awaiting word that the first reel is "up" and ready for viewing, you can daydream about how all the pieces of picture and sound, fades and dissolves, effects, music, and credits are merging into a real movie.

Screening Your Answer Print

As soon as the rolls that make up your feature have been printed, you will want to screen them at the lab's best screening room, to check for mistakes in picture and sound. This screening should include only you and your major collaborators (co-director, cinematographer, producer), with whom you created the movie, and the lab technician. Because of the shock of seeing your print for the first time, it may take several viewings to actually see mistakes. Of course, major errors in color balance, missing fades or dissolves, loss of sync, garbled sound, or poor print quality will be easy to recognize. Although each lab has its own set of standards with which to gauge the necessity to reprint "lab errors," below is a list of mistakes that should warrant corrections at the lab's expense.

- ☐ *Improperly timed main titles.* If your titles are white on a black background, or superimposed over a scene, they should be a solid white and not look grayish or uneven.
- ☐ *Missed cues for fade-in, fade-out, dissolve.* If you have clearly stated on your cue sheet the footage count for beginning and end of your effects, plus the length in frames, the lab is responsible for delivering a print to these specifications.
- ☐ *Overall incorrect exposure.* If you've been a customer at a lab for several years (and several feature-length projects), they may be willing to completely reprint your feature because it was printed either too light and washed out, or too dark and muddy. Because an answer print is regarded as a trial print, you will have to forcefully (but calmly) argue your point. It will help a great deal if your timer is dedicated to helping you create a perfect print because he believes in your film.
- ☐ *Imperfect frame line registration.* Only after I received my second *Emerald Cities* print, mailed back to me from the Australian Film Institute seven-city tour, was I able to screen the film and catch the frame line registration mistake on the fourth reel. I had been under so much pressure to get the film printed and air-expressed to the tour that I hadn't been able to screen the results. Even though I

brought the mistake to the lab's attention five months after the printing, they stood behind their work and supplied me with a newly printed roll. On the screen this mistake was visually obvious because at every other cut between shots, a white line appeared at the bottom of the frame. Examining the print over a light table, it was easy to see that the frame line was not centered exactly at the middle of the sprocket hole.

- ☐ *Obviously poor color balance.* If the faces of your characters are reddish-purple instead of flesh-tone, you deserve a new print.
- ☐ *Excessive scratches.* If you are printing from Negative or Reversed AB rolls, and have ordered "liquid gate," the images of your film should not be covered with white dust marks and scratches. If this is what you see, first check your invoice to make sure the words *liquid gate* are written on your print order, then request a new print.
- ☐ *Picture and sound out of sync.* If you projected your film's work print with the mixed sound track and they were in sync, and you rolled through your AB rolls and they were in sync with your work print, then the lab is at fault for slipping sync during their printing process, and they owe you a new print.
- ☐ *One missed light change, or one lost fade-out or dissolve.* Usually, your lab will reprint just the part of your film where the mistake has occurred, and your print will now have a splice in the middle. Although this acceptable lab practice will anger the perfectionist filmmaker, the splice will be virtually unnoticeable during projection. If there is more than one mistake, calmly pressure the lab to print over the whole roll.
- ☐ *Bad sound.* How bad does your sound have to be to get the roll reprinted? If there is hissing that sounds like electronic disruption, and this sound definitely isn't on your mix, you must firmly make a stand with the lab, if necessary, to get a new print. Also, if there are noticeable sound-level differences between the rolls of your feature, ask the lab to please reprint whichever roll is in error. You must be firm in declaring to the lab that varying sound levels are unacceptable. If you hear *pops* or other imperfections on your sound track that were not heard when you screened your mix, insist (in a polite way) that these faulty rolls be reprinted at the lab's expense.

Assembling Your Print

After you are happily holding the several perfectly printed rolls that make up your feature, it is time to splice them together onto two large reels, to simplify projection and future mailing and handling.

All that's left to do on the production of your feature is to make a few splices connecting rolls 1 and 2 (reel 1), and rolls 3 and 4 (reel 2), and to roll them up on large 2,000′ reels. You will also want to splice on protective head and tail leaders on which you will identify the name of your film, your name as director/producer, and a return address and phone number. Most labs will give you an editing bench for an hour, with hot splicer, for this purpose.

If you printed your movie on Estar base from Negative, you will need to tape splice your print together, carefully taping both sides of the picture, since it is impossible to hot-splice on Estar-base stock. In any case assemble your film in order, first rolling your head leader for roll 1 onto a 2,000′ reel. Then splice roll 1 to the leader and reel up to the end. Splice roll 2 to the end of roll 1 and reel that roll to the end, filling up your first reel. Splice on your tail leader and then, taping the end of the leader to an empty 2,000′ reel, roll the assembled rolls 1 and 2 back until you are at the head end. Securely tape the end of the head leader to the roll after writing "reel 1" on it with a Sharpie pen. Then repeat the procedure with rolls 3 and 4 ("reel 2" inked on its head leader). For reduced expenses during mailing, I recommend assembling your film on plastic reels and packing it in a double 2,000′ plastic case. This reduced weight of your print is doubly important when you become a touring filmmaker and have to carry your heavy print(s) from airport to airport. Once your print is assembled and securely packed into its carrying case, take it and walk out into the sunshine . . . *you've done it!* Now it's time to show the finished results to your production team.

Screening Your Print for Cast and Crew

Showing a completed movie to cast and crew is a thrilling moment for any writer/director/producer. In a way, you have served their talents by laboring many months to edit your feature to completion. And, of course, without all their help and belief, there wouldn't even be a movie. Along with the thrill of showing the new work, there also comes the pressure of wondering how it will be received. So to give your feature the opportunity to look its best, try to obtain the highest quality screening room possible. Maybe your lab will let you use its screening room to show the film to a few of your friends. If your timer wants to see the results of his or her effort, he/she might help you to arrange an in-house screening at your lab (for free). Even if your screening costs you some money, make absolutely sure that the technical aspects of projected picture (sharp, bright image) and sound (clear, good acoustics) are at their best, since this showing represents such an important moment for everyone involved. For my first showing of *A Man, a Woman, and a Killer*, I rented the main theater at the Pacific Film Archive in Berkeley for the two-hour Sunday-afternoon show. For a small amount of money, I was able to screen my feature in one of the finest theaters on the West Coast.

After you have exposed your friends and colleagues to the special "underground" preview screening, packed up your print, and brought it home, you may feel a bit of the emotional letdown common at the completion of such an extensive project. You have survived a trial by fire, and now it's over. You've seen the wonders and the secrets of your movie (and life) revealed, and now you wonder "What next?" You're impatient to do something, but at the same time too tired to really do anything. And you may be scared because you owe several thousand dollars to the lab and are not sure how you can raise this amount of money to pay them back. But you do have a feature-length movie, and after a few days of rest it's time once again to get to work—work that can be done by writing letters, phoning, e-mailing, surfing the net and filling out forms—the work of *promotion.*

7 Promotion

After each part of the process of making a feature-length movie, it seems that the last round of difficulties to overcome has been the worst and taken the most amount of time out of your life. After shooting is completed—ten days of directing, lighting, designing sets, composing shots for your cuts, loading and unloading your camera (or popping in those mini-DV cassettes!), spending your money—it's easy to feel that the hardest part is over. Then comes editing, and as the months run by while you search for the structure of the story, you come to realize that the editing process is even more demanding. It may take years to complete this careful task in order to make every scene and transition work to build the cut into a unified whole. And when you project your first print of the film (screen the VHS, DVD, or stream it on the Web), you experience a real sense of exaltation. Against all odds, you have created a feature-length movie, almost by willing it into existence. Surely the most strenuous part is over now.

Well, the hardest part *is* over once the project is completed, but now it's time to enter the next phase of your movie and your life—promotion. In the world of high-budget, commercial film production, the director's responsibility ends when he or she turns over the feature to a distributor, who handles all the promotion and marketing from that point on. Since a feature produced at used-car prices is, to put it bluntly, quite unlikely to attract immediate attention from a commercial distributor, it's up to you to promote your own film.

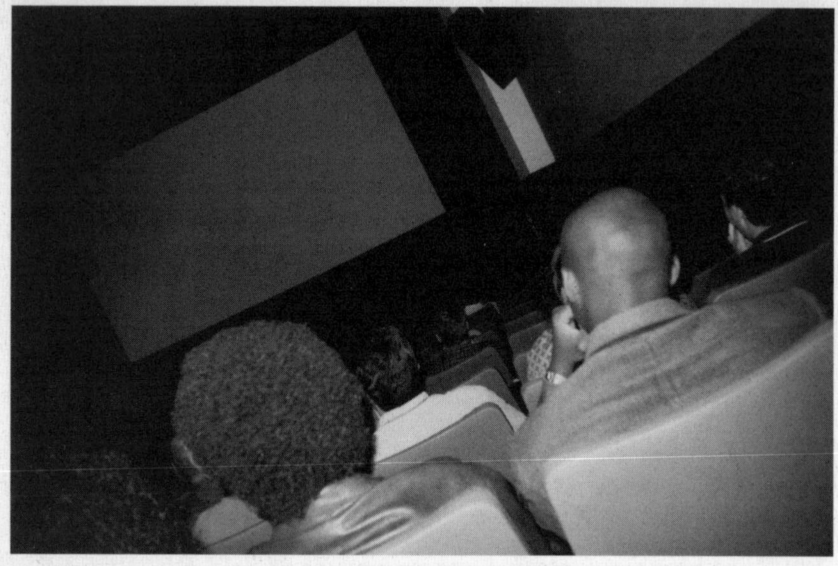

The blank screen at IFFM looms (Angelika Theatre, New York City), as moviemakers, distributors, actors, and agents await the next video projection of a "work-in-progress."

Fortunately, many avenues are open to the talented and persistent low-budget feature filmmaker—film festivals, New York and regional showcases, television and Web premieres. With each showing you can arrange, you will gain more exposure and, if you're lucky, a little more money as well. Once your movie has been seen—and admired—by the "right" people, you may be approached by a distributor who wants to handle your now-successful feature. By that point, ironically, you may even conclude that you're doing as good a job on your own as an agent could do for you.

Although each phase of the moviemaking process takes a good-size bite out of your life, it's promotion that actually lasts the longest. Promoting your low-budget film will require a relatively small amount of money and a great deal of time, energy, and determination. Here are the various steps you can—and should—take to insure that your production will receive the attention it deserves.

Preparing Your Promotional Package

Commercial distributors today still employ the same basic mechanisms they used during the silent era: press releases, posters, newspaper advertisements, and the occasional well-timed scandal. The no-budget feature filmmaker can also use any and all of these methods to make sure his or her movie is seen by as many people as possible. While a major distributor may spend as much as $10,000—almost our total used-car-prices production budget—just designing and printing a full-color poster, you can finance a successful promotional campaign with an expenditure of $500 to $1,000—and a lot of creative and practical ingenuity.

Video Copies for Promotion

Since the moviemaker who creates an ultra-low-budget feature out of economic necessity doesn't usually have the financial ability to just rent any commercial theater and advertise for a "world premiere" as a distributor would do, the first step is to try and secure some paid showings for the newly completed film. And because you only have one 16-mm print of your feature, and that print probably cost you every cent you could scrape together (including some charging at the lab), it is essential that you use that print *only* for actual showings—rentals, film festivals, and the like. For promotion, you should use inexpensive video copies. Prices vary quite a bit, but in 2000 you can make a high-quality copy of your film on ½″ Betacam SP for approximately $600, a master copy from which to make inexpensive VHS dubs. Many labs now have video departments with machines such as the Bosch and Rank Cintel that specialize in high-resolution, high-density color transfers from film to video.

You can easily pay more than $1,000 to transfer a film to video if you have to pay a technician $250 an hour to balance the color and exposure for each individual scene. But if your film print is correctly balanced for color and exposure, you should be able to have a high-quality video copy made more cheaply, by running that print through the video transfer machine only once, without stopping. This low-cost method of transferring your film to video falls into the category of "video dailies"—the video work prints that high-budget production companies use to review each day's shooting.

Since each major city will probably have several labs available for video transfers, it is important to shop around to locate the best deal. You could save hundreds of dollars with a few phone calls. Monaco Lab in San Francisco ([415] 864-5350, ask for "Video"/Anne O'Toole, **<anne@monacosf.com>**) offers a 10 percent discount for customers who pay cash up front for dubs (or any other lab services).

You can also save some money by supplying your own videotape stock for the transfer. For a feature-length movie running seventy-five minutes, you will need a ninety-minute cassette of Betacam SP videotape, which costs around $55 per cassette. The lab or video facility that transfers your film to video will charge you perhaps $95 for the tape, costing you an extra $40. If you buy your own tape, make sure that you have purchased the exact same type, number, and brand used at the transfer facility. But beware! There is a risk factor involved in trying to save on stock. If the tape you supply causes any problems, the lab will not be responsible for redoing the job.

Once you have your Betacam SP "master copy" of your feature, you can make inexpensive video copies of high quality at a "dubbing service." To insure that your master Betacam SP copy is not damaged by continued copying, I strongly recommend first dubbing a "submaster," also in Betacam SP, that can then be used to strike additional copies for promotion. (Be sure to store your master copy in a cool place, away from motors, magnets, or metal shelves.)

To begin your search for a film festival that will present your feature, you will need at least twenty-five VHS copies dubbed from your Betacam SP master. This should be enough to enter all the major film festivals that are interested in American independent features, assuming that as soon as each video copy is returned to you, you mail it out again.

For copies of 100 or more you should find prices for dubs in your area comparable to those of Film Craft Lab (23815 Industrial Park Drive, Farmington Hills, MI 48335, [248] 474-3900, **<lipner@filmcraft.com>**, ask for Dominic T. Troia), which offers the incredibly low price of $3.50 per tape, with an extra charge of 60 cents per box with full window album cover (you supply graphics).

Promotional Graphics

Even before your movie is completed, you can begin to create the graphics (poster, letterhead, pressbook, etc.) that will help publicize your product. It's the graphics of your feature that will make it seem *real* to others. Film festival organizers usually require a pressbook and poster (if one is available) when you enter the competition. And they usually request a couple of photographs from the production ("stills") for their catalog, and newspaper coverage. These materials are equally useful for submitting your film to showcases, television stations, Websites that screen video, and other venues.

The Pressbook

A pressbook is exactly what the name implies—a book for the press. Some production companies spend many thousands of dollars printing up a slick cover with high-tech graphics to better promote their movie to the critics (and thus to the public). Critics are handed these pressbooks as they enter the screening room, giving them a chance to be impressed before the curtain rises.

Usually the independent moviemaker doesn't have the money to print multiples of such an elaborate graphic presentation as a full-fledged pressbook. But by renting a computer at a nearby Kinko's, he or she can create a few pressbook covers on glossy stock (posters, postcards, fliers, etc.) that do the job. The pressbook should contain a page with a synopsis of your movie and a full list of credits, along with any current reviews. Some stills from the movie that have a strong graphic/image power should also be included.

For our synopsis of *The Last Roommate*, we created our graphics by using a still from the film that was given a "bullet screen" effect, available at many typesetters, in which concentric circles form the image we are seeing. If you shop around, you should be able to find a talented typesetter who can help you create similarly striking special effects for

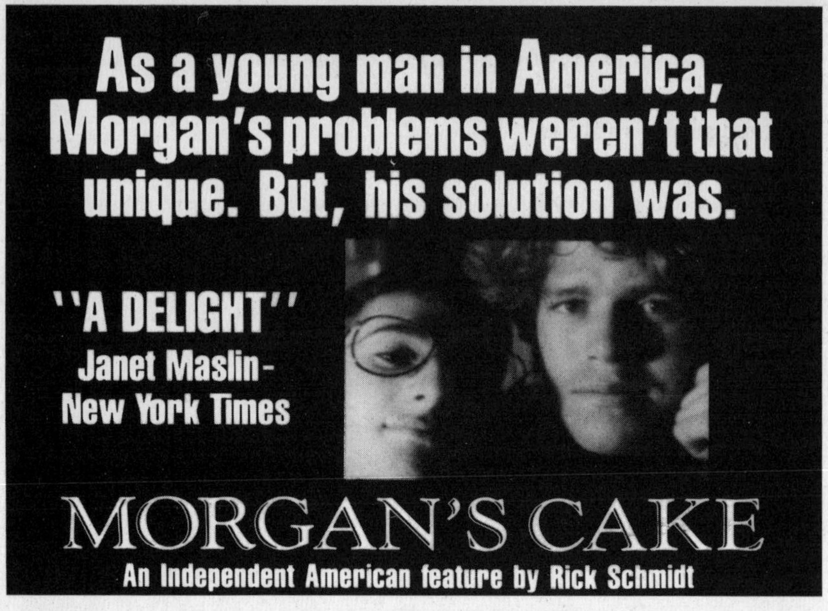

As a young man in America, Morgan's problems weren't that unique. But, his solution was.
"A DELIGHT"
Janet Maslin-
New York Times
MORGAN'S CAKE
An Independent American feature by Rick Schmidt

Still from *Morgan's Cake* used in newspaper ad for theatrical premiere.

very little money. Total typesetting costs for our synopsis of *The Last Roommate*, including the bullet screen effect, were only $30. If you have a powerful home computer (Pentium, Mac G-4) you can create this effect and many more, with Adobe Photoshop or some other appropriate graphics software program.

The Still

You can shoot stills directly from your 16-mm film print by using a special adapter lens that fits on most 35-mm cameras. The adapter has no f-stop control. If you aim the lens holding the 16-mm film at the sun and "bracket" the shots by adjusting the speed of the shutter (1/60, 1/100, 1/250, 1/500, etc.) you should be able to shoot a well-exposed still. You can rent this 16-mm adapter lens from some film equipment rental houses. An easier alternative will be simply to take 35-mm photographs on location during the shoot.

It is fairly expensive to print 8″-by-10″ prints in black-and-white if you order each print separately, but there are special photo services that will make you twenty-five prints for about $50 (see "Movie Stills/Videos of 'Work-in-Progress,' " chapter 5). To find this deal, call around to the photo services in your town.

If you were savvy enough to have someone document part or all of your shoot on digital video, then you can create pristine photographic stills digitally using Radius PhotoDV software with its included Adobe Photoshop and FireWire connection for capture and output. This same #1394 FireWire card gives your computer digital in-and-out capabilities for capturing your digital video movie footage into the computer for nonlinear editing on their Radius EditDV, Adobe Premiere, Apple's Final Cut Pro, other editing systems (see chapter 11, "Digital Video Workstations"). The cost of Radius PhotoDV software and FireWire card to Mac or PC is approximately $300 (add $600 more to acquire the full Radius EditDV/MotoDV editing software package).

The Poster

Posters are the most radical way to advertise your showings, by taking your graphics to the street. With posters you can spend a few hours pasting them up, stapling them on bulletin boards at a university, and create an audience for your movie. The several hundred posters put on the street to advertise the showing of rushes from *1988—The Remake* brought over a thousand people to the screening.

The expenses for this type of advertising are the initial cost of the typesetting, halftones from photos, and the printing costs for 500 to 1,000 sheets. By keeping the graphics black and white and using cheap paper, you can create inexpensive posters that you can use to advertise your feature as well as to fill out its pressbook. As long as you don't print the date of a particular show on the poster, you can always use it for future shows by adding a sticker with show times and locations. I have even reused part of the graphics of my posters as cassette covers, when selling my films in the home video market.

If just *one* poster will serve your promotional needs, then that can be accomplished fairly inexpensively. When our Feature Workshops movie *someone like me* showed as a "work in progress" at the IFFM in

Bullet screen effect.

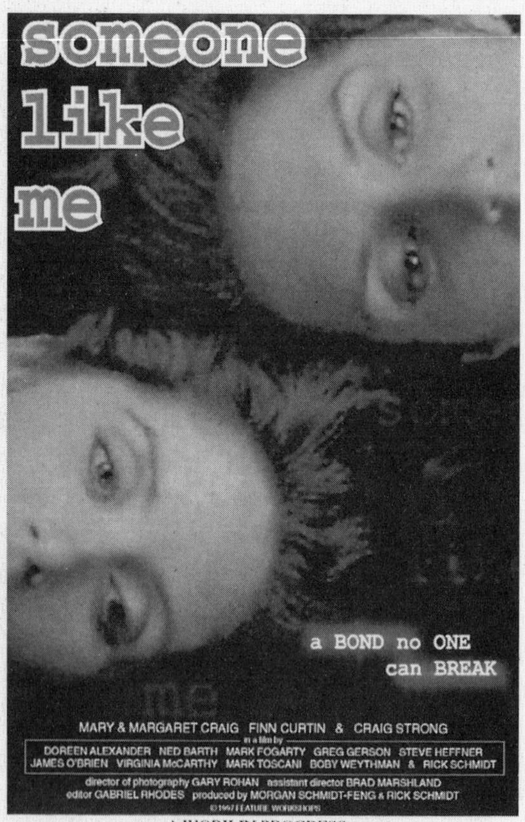

someone
like
me
a BOND no ONE
can BREAK
MARY & MARGARET CRAIG FINN CURTIN & CRAIG STRONG
in a film by
DOREEN ALEXANDER NED BARTH MARK FOGARTY GREG GERSON STEVE HEFFNER
JAMES O'BRIEN VIRGINIA McCARTHY MARK TOSCANI BOBY WEYTHMAN & RICK SCHMIDT
director of photography GARY ROHAN assistant director BRAD MARSHLAND
editor GABRIEL RHODES produced by MORGAN SCHMIDT-FENG & RICK SCHMIDT
A WORK IN PROGRESS
SCREENING: ANGELIKA FILM CENTER
WEDNESDAY, SEPTEMBER 23
THEATRE 5, 11:00am

Postcard designed and produced by co-writer/co-director Steve Heffner for IFFM '98 screening of collaborative Feature Workshops movie, *someone like me*.

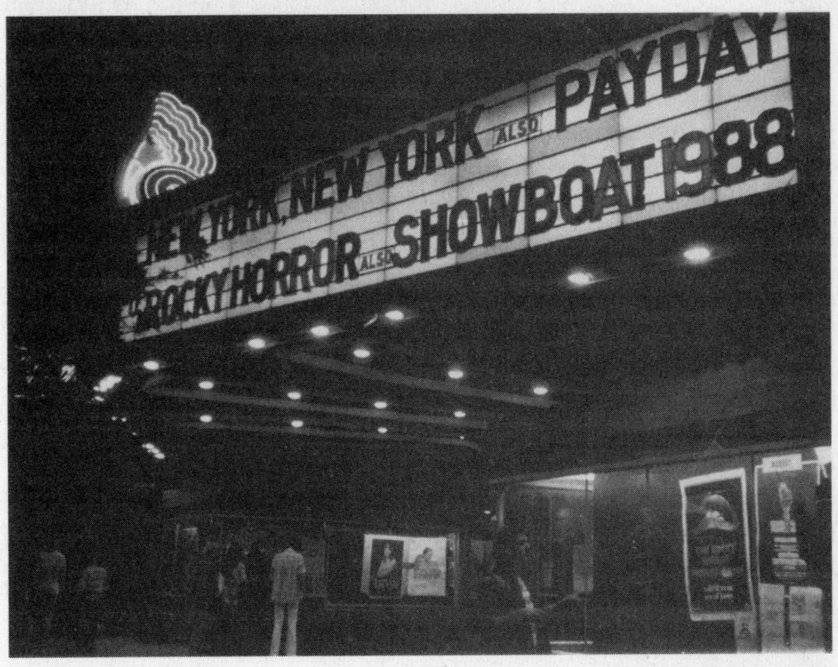

Los Angeles premiere of *1988—The Remake*. It can happen. Photo by Julie Schachter.

1998, one of the co-writer/co-directors, Steve Heffner, brought along a poster graphic he'd designed on Adobe Photoshop 4.0, saved on a 100 MB Zip drive disk. At Kinko's SoHo branch he rented a computer ($8/hr.), quickly added the time and date of our show, and ordered a printout of 100 glossy postcards, plus a 30″-by-40″ one-sheet movie poster for pickup by the next-day deadline (total cost around $200).

If you don't have the time or inclination to produce your own poster, get in contact with Tribune Showprint in Earl Park, Indiana ([219] 474-6061; fax: [219] 474-6062). They are the company that makes low-cost rainbow-colored posters for sporting events and rock concerts, and can help you meet your deadline in style.

Film Festivals

If a low-budget feature filmmaker is lucky, he or she may get a chance to see his or her film acclaimed a "work of genius" by a European film festival after being scorned by a local showcase. (It has often been proved that the farther away from home an artist travels the better chance he or she has of recognition, so don't get discouraged by negative reactions to your movie in your hometown.) A film festival offers the chance to see one's work in relation to other productions from around the world, and this is important to every artist.

The best place to start looking for appropriate festivals these days is on the Internet, where you can find Websites for virtually all the so-called "important" film festivals (the kind that basically lock out no-budgeters), as well as some good new alternatives. Along with scads of small indie start-up fests from coast to coast (and microfests invented by anyone with a personal Website), you'll find a new crop of digital film festivals that offer real hope for distribution of personal and innovative movies on the Web. Jump in by accessing a big list of current festival outlets at **<www.filmfestivals.com>** to get the overall picture of what's available (400+ festivals!). Or log onto **<www.media lawyer.com/festival.htm.>**, which also has extensive listings on festivals from around the world. Another great Website with festival lists and information (articles, trends, many other resources) is the grand Filmmaker Magazine, **<www.filmmag.com>**. Visit this terrific indie Website weekly. And don't forget **<www.filmthreat.com>**, filmmaker Chris Gore's cutting-edge "Film Threat" online magazine, which magically appears in your e-mail basket every Sunday night. It includes refreshing interviews with working indie filmmakers, crazed letters to the editor, beautifully biased movie reviews plus current festival posting and updates (and check out Gore's latest book on indie filmmaking, *The Ultimate Film Festival Survival Guide* [Lone Eagle Books, 1999], which covers the festival beat firsthand, with great interviews of filmmakers in the trenches).

If you are intent upon applying to *only* those festivals with *no entry fees* (and why wouldn't you be, considering that many festivals charge $35 to $50 per feature-length entry!), then click yourself right over to this well-organized site **<www.kilima.com/noentryfee.html>**, which offers contact information and some direct e-mail links to numerous "free" festivals (list includes everything from the New York Film Festival to Figueira da Foz International in Portugal). Mainly, it's your job to keep focused on just those festivals that will give your special product a *real* consideration.

Perhaps the first American film festival to approach for your "U.S. premiere" would be the Telluride Film Festival in Colorado, **<www.telluridefilmfestival.com>**. Although a tremendous long shot for the first-time writer/director, a premiere at Telluride guarantees the most intense media focus for your feature (a favorite "discovery" festival for Roger Ebert and other critics) in probably the most relaxed and humanized setting. But be cautioned that they will only accept movies that have had *no* screenings or festival exposure. Their small selection committee usually begins screening in June, for the early September festival. Contact the National Film Preserve at (603) 643-1255, Box B1156, 53 South Main Street, Hanover, NH 03755, for information and application. While it's certainly worth taking a shot at getting your film into Telluride, don't tie up your entire festival effort waiting for their response. You must enter several festivals to give your movie a chance for success.

Although more major film festivals than ever are now interested in low-budget American features, the list is still very small. Below are eight festivals that are interested in and supportive of this type of indie feature, and if your movie is presented at any one of them, it will probably be seen by representatives of other festivals. As soon as you have a good idea of when your feature will be completed, you should check Websites of these festivals to request applications.

London Film Festival
(November)
British Film Institute
127 Charing Cross Road
London WC1, England
www.ibmpcug.co.uk/lff.html

AFI/LA Fest
(October)
2021 North Western Avenue
Los Angeles, CA 90027
(213) 856-7774
www.afifest.com

ROTTERDAM INTERNATIONAL
(JANUARY–FEBRUARY)
P.O. BOX 21696
3001 AR ROTTERDAM
THE NETHERLANDS
www.iffrotterdam.nl

BERLIN FILM FESTIVAL/FORUM
(FEBRUARY–MARCH)
ATTN: LYNDA HANSEN/LAHA
115 EAST 92ND STREET
NEW YORK, NY 10128
www.fdk-berlin.de

FIGUEIRA DA FOZ INTERNATIONAL
(SEPTEMBER)
APARTADO DOS CORREIOS 5407
1709 LISBOA CODEX, PORTUGAL
FAX: 01135118126228

SUNDANCE FILM FESTIVAL
(JANUARY)
ATTN: INDI COMPETITION
225 SANTA MONICA BLVD.,
8TH FLOOR
SANTA MONICA, CA 90401
(310) 394-4662
WWW.SUNDANCE.ORG

TORONTO INTERNATIONAL
(SEPTEMBER)
2 CARLTON STREET, #1600, TORONTO,
ONTARIO M5B 1J3, CANADA
(415) 967-7371
www.bell.ca/filmfest/

SEATTLE INTERNATIONAL
(MAY)
801 EAST PINE STREET
SEATTLE, WA 98122
(206) 324-9996
www.seattlefilm.com

The New York Premiere

While you await word of which U.S. or foreign film festival will select your work for the "World Premiere," your next step is to promote your movie in New York City and try to get it a New York premiere. If you show your feature at a high-quality showcase or museum and get good press, then word of your fabulous movie will instantly spread to all other parts of the country because of the wide distribution of the *Village Voice*, *The New York Times*, and other publications. The best-quality premiere, the one that gives you the brightest spotlight and the most important press coverage—a review in *The New York Times*—is guaranteed if you have the good fortune to be selected by the New Directors/New Films showcase run by The Film Society of Lincoln Center.

New Directors/New Films
The Film Society of Lincoln Center
165 West 65th Street, 4th Floor
New York, NY 10023
(212) 875-5610
www.filmlinc.com

In December 1988 my son Morgan and I were thrilled when we heard by phone that *Morgan's Cake*, our no-budget $15,000 movie, had been selected for a forthcoming New York premiere (March 1989) at this prestigious showcase. Given that they only select two or three American features per year to round out their small twenty-movie international program, it was quite an honor. Keep in mind that when you submit your feature to New Directors, you are also exposing your fine work to their year-round programming for the Walter Reade Theatre, Independents Night (an IFP monthly screening series), and the New York Film Festival Selection Committee (several programmers serve double- and triple-duty). These knowledgeable film experts can make your career overnight, so make sure that you are sending them a top-notch VHS video copy or film print for review. And be cautioned. As with *any* important New York screening, you must guarantee their showing will be a New York or world premiere.

The Whitney Museum and the Film Forum also sponsor independent film and video programs that guarantee a *New York Times* review.

Whitney Museum
Attn: John Hanhardt
945 Madison Avenue
New York, NY 10021
(212) 570-3676
www.echonyc.com/~whitney

Film Forum
Attn: Karen Cooper
209 West Houston Street
New York, NY 10014
(212) 627-2035
www.filmforum.com

If all these showcases see your independent feature and turn you down, don't be discouraged. It usually takes a few tries to be selected. I was turned down by all these showcases in New York when I tried to get a show for my first feature, *A Man, a Woman, and a Killer*, before I was selected by the Bleecker Street Cinema. From that showing I received press coverage in both *The New York Times* and the New York *Daily News*. Here are two other showcases in New York City that are worth trying:

First Look
Tribeca Film Center
375 Greenwich Street
New York, NY 10013
(212) 941-4011
www.tribecafilm.com

Anthology Film Archives
Attn: Jonas Mekas
32 Second Street
New York, NY 10003
(212) 505-5181
www.arthouseinc.com/anthology

Promotion by Letters, E-Mail, and Phone

If you can't afford to travel to New York and promote your film in person, write (e-mail or fax) letters to the various showcases, telling them about yourself and your feature. After a few weeks call person-to-person and ask for the director of programming. This will cost you some money, but at least you will be able to talk to the person who can make decisions regarding your movie.

Yes, it is like gambling—spending money in hopes that you will get something in return. You are betting on yourself and your good work. My attitude is that you should try *all possibilities* to give yourself a chance to survive the first feature (and get rolling on the next). And if no one in New York City will touch your feature with a ten-foot pole, it is time to try some "alternative" festivals.

Indie Fests

As a backlash against the exclusivity of major film festivals, moviemakers from several large cities in the United States have taken it upon themselves to start up their own festivals, some of which have grown in prominence on the indie scene. One of the most notable is the Slamdance International Film Festival. It was begun by filmmakers Jon Fitzgerald, Shane Kuhn, and Dan Mirvish as a response to Sundance Film Festival's decline as a venue for "small" features (their features and those of their friends were rejected . . .). Slamdance was so effective at establishing itself as a viable option for real indies in the same small town (Park City, Utah), and getting strong media attention in its first year, that Sundance honchos actually barred Slamdancers from their parties. I feel honored that our Feature Workshop movie *Blues for the Avatar* was screened at Slamdance as part of their second-year program.

Another important indie underground festival that has sprung up in response to Sundance is the Los Angeles Independent Film Festival, founded to give struggling Southern California (and elsewhere) moviemakers a thread of hope that their honest feature-length efforts haven't been in vain. They've even introduced production grants to first- and second-time producers with projects budgeted under a million, so go for it!

SLAMDANCE FILM FESTIVAL
(JANUARY)
6381 HOLLYWOOD BOULEVARD, #520
LOS ANGELES, CA 90028
(323) 466-1786
www.slamdance.com

LAIFF
(APRIL)
5455 WILSHIRE BOULEVARD, #1500
LOS ANGELES, CA 90036
(213) 937-9155
www.laiff.com

In its eighth year as a champion of cutting-edge indie cinema, the New York Underground Film Festival continues its plan to "fearlessly defy the mainstream expectations." The *Village Voice* has called it "the king of do-it-yourself fests," so it's worth entering your no-budget feature before the month of March rolls around again. In the Midwest, the Chicago Underground Film Festival gives indie moviemakers an alternative to being rejected by the exclusive Chicago International Film Festival. Roger Ebert says of the underground festival, "What you get for your money isn't just admission to the films, but admission to a subculture." And Adam Langer of *The Film Festival Guide* calls it, "The most refreshing offbeat film event in Chicago." Maybe your offbeat feature will be part of their next program.

NYUFF
(March)
225 Lafayette Street, #401
New York, NY 10012
(212) 925-3440
www.nyuff.com

Chicago Underground
(August)
501 North Lincoln Avenue, #278
Chicago, IL 60614
(773) 866-8660
www.cuff.org

And don't forget the alternative to the alternative film festivals, like the Chicago Alt. Film Festival, which calls itself, "Chicago's premier film festival of American Independent filmmakers . . . celebrates the best in independent films by emerging and established filmmakers, and provides a forum for exhibition, recognition, and education." So if you live in or near Chicago, you have several options to show your work. Some alternative festivals are strictly for the inhabitants of their particular city, like the San Francisco Indiefest, which seeks feature-length works produced just in the Bay Area, and includes not only 16-mm and 35-mm, but also video works on VHS and ¾″.

Chicago Alt. Film Festival
(June)
3430 North Lake Shore Drive, #19N
Chicago, IL 60657
(773) 525-4559
members.aol.com/chialtfilm/fest

San Francisco Indiefest
(January)
1803 Ninth Avenue
San Francisco, CA 94122
(415) 929-5038
www.i.am/indie

If you've made a gay or lesbian film and only feel comfortable entering your work in film festivals that understand and appreciate your particular worldview, there are several excellent alternative U.S. and foreign festivals available. Beginning with foreign showcases, the Melbourne Queer Film and Video Festival seeks work of any genre or length and advertises that "works will be considered for screenings at seven other queer fests around Australia" (accepted formats: 16-mm, 35-mm, VHS tape, SVHS, ¾″ video). The London Lesbian and Gay Film Festival is an international noncompetitive event that accepts features, shorts, and documentaries dealing with lesbian and gay identity and experience (70-mm, 16-mm, 35-mm, VHS [PAL, SECAM, or

NTSC], or ¾″ video). If you have a no-budget feature in 70-mm, this is the one for you!

MELBOURNE QUEER FILM FESTIVAL
(MARCH)
1/35 CATO STREET
PRAHRAN, VIC 3181, AUSTRALIA
qfa@rucc.net.au

LONDON LESBIAN AND GAY FESTIVAL
(APRIL)
NFT, SOUTH BANK
LONDON SE1 8XT, UNITED KINGDOM
www.bfi.org.uk

After sending a few tapes abroad, you'll want to enter your gay or lesbian movie in the San Francisco International Lesbian and Gay Film and Video Festival as well, the world's oldest alternative festival for this kind of work (they show more than 150 films and tapes from over a dozen countries). Maybe you'll be fortunate to be chosen to premiere your work in one of the grandest cinema showcases in the U.S., the huge Castro Theatre. Because of overflow attendance, works are also shown at the Roxie Cinema (where my *Morgan's Cake* had its San Francisco premiere) and the Pacific Film Archive in Berkeley.

The Outfest: Los Angeles Gay and Lesbian Film Festival is another great chance for your work to be seen by important distributers and TV buyers, who can hopefully help you earn money back from your personally financed indie feature. They show more than 250 films and videos in eight venues, including several U.S. and world premieres, and sponsor special panel discussions, seminars, and major retrospectives.

S.F. INTERNATIONAL LESBIAN AND GAY FILM AND VIDEO FESTIVAL
(JUNE)
P.O. BOX 14792
SAN FRANCISCO, CA 94114
(415) 703-8650
www.frameline.org

OUTFEST: LOS ANGELES GAY AND LESBIAN FILM FESTIVAL
(JULY)
1125 NORTH MCCADDEN PLACE, #235
LOS ANGELES, CA 90038
(323) 960-9200
www.outfest.org

If you're a woman who believes that it's a man's world (an old boy network) when it comes to filmmaking, then you might want to enter one that excludes them. New York Women's Film Festival in April, and Women in the Director's Chair Film and Video Festival have given well-earned recognition to women who persevere in this tough line of work. When I taught a film production class at University of Santa Cruz in the late 1980s, I wondered how the three female filmmaking students felt surrounded by fifteen young men. I hoped that they could hang in and graduate as moviemakers since, though outnumbered, they were obviously talented. Maybe they did, and got to show their works at Sundance, as well as at one of these two excellent showcases.

New York Women's Film Festival
(April)
341 Lafayette Street, #302
New York, NY 10012
(212) 465-3435
www.nywfilmfest.com

WIDC
(March)
3435 North Sheffield Avenue, #3
Chicago, IL 60657
(312) 281-4988
www.widc.org

If you're a film or video artist, man or woman, who also happens to be black, there's a festival specifically for you. If your movie has a black person in a key creative position of producer, writer, or director, give this one a try.

Black Independent Film and Video Competition
(October)
405 14th Street, Suite 515
Oakland, CA 94612
(510) 465-0804
<www.blackfilmmakershall.org>

If you'd like to win five acres of land near Taos, New Mexico, and settle there in this new millennium, then the Taos Talking Picture Festival in April is a good bet for you. The "Taos Land Grant Award" is given to the director of a new feature-length film or video that tells an innovative story. The Taos Land and Film Company that awards the grant says that they hope to plant media artists in the fertile soil of northern New Mexico to create a filmmaking community. To be eligible, the feature must be seventy minutes or longer. The only other overall requirements for entry are that your films and videos be completed within the last eighteen months preceding the festival, and that the showing (if selected) be a New Mexico premiere.

Another small festival of note is South by Southwest Film Festival and Conference in Austin, Texas, home of Richard Linklater (*Slacker*, *The Newton Boys*). They pride themselves on showing the best of the independent films and lure the hottest directors (Kevin Smith, Jonathan Demme, Atom Egoyan, etc.) south to participate. There are panels, four days of conferences, a three-day trade show, and a nine-day film festival with numerous premieres. It's certainly worth a try if you have any budget left for festival applications and mailing.

TAOS TALKING PICTURE FESTIVAL
(APRIL)
1337 GUSDORF ROAD, STE. F
TAOS, NM 87571
(505) 751-0637
www.taosnet.com/ttpix/

SXSW
(MARCH)
P.O. BOX 4999
AUSTIN, TX 78765
(512) 467-7979
www.sxsw.com

WWW Digital Fests

Perhaps your final salvation for getting your important cutting-edge feature-length work shown is on the Internet's World Wide Web. Check out D.FILM digital festival, **<www.dfilm.com>**, which I have to admire because where they list "Fees" on their online application is the comment "None. Entry fees suck." They are "looking for works that demonstrate some innovative new use of technology, strongly convey ideas or tell stories, entertain and inspire audiences to create films themselves."

To run a full feature on the Web, see **<www.sightsound.com>**, another one of the new cutting-edge sites that offer feature-length downloads of indie movies (the film *Pi* got its Internet Pay-per-View release here, a month-long exposure of video streaming in April 1999, cost $2.95 per viewing). Or check out **<www.ifilm.com>**, a full-service indie Website where you can submit work for streaming, access tools for scheduling, find cast and crew, music, classifieds, etc. They've recently partnered with Bolt.com (**<www.bolt.com>**) to present the "first teens-only national film festival," called Bolt Indies. And **<www.alwaysif.com>** (Audience Awards On-Line Film Festival) shows close to 100 features, with each film entered receiving its own Website page to list bio, cast, and synopsis (free advertising!). Apply online and mail them a VHS. Or try **<www.reeluniverse.com>**, where they may select your movie for promotion, and set up a link back to your Website (you receive 100 percent of all sales!).

RESFEST, **<www.resfest.com>**, is also a good means of exposure on the Web (and check out the great RES magazine). These sites have how-to information, offer links to other festivals and happenings, and lead the way for self-distribution on the Web.

Next, to protect yourself so that the end-of-the-rainbow Sundance dream doesn't haunt you beyond one day, please log on to **<www.filmmag.com>** and click on the Non-Ink Section link which offers the "Low-Budgeter's Guide to Sundance," a six-part series about attending the festival in Park City, Utah, written with refreshing humor by Jim Taylor, co-producer of Brad Anderson's *The Darien Gap*. My filmmaker friend Jerry Barrish questions the entire film festival concept at this point, asking, "Why do we, the filmmakers, bust our gut to produce a low-budget movie with our own money, then gratefully hand over our precious print, no rental fee, so a festival can charge $7 per person?" He continues, "Without us, our years of struggling without salary to write, shoot, edit, and print our features, these festivals wouldn't exist!" (Do you feel the edifice crumbling . . . ?) "Why do they get paid high salaries while all we get is 'the honor' of showing our work for free?" I think Jerry's got a point here, don't you?

Numerous microfests have also popped up on the Web, and whether or not they will actually help your cause (get some money back to you from sales), it's just plain inspiring to see new venues that are suddenly available. No Dance Film and Multimedia Festival (**<www.nodance.com>**), also based in Park City, Utah (guess where their name derived from), is a good place to start. Their screenings formats include VHS, DVD, and streaming video. Festival director and founder James Boyd says, "The DVD projection quality is far superior to VHS tape, and much cheaper than creating a film print. The film print is dead." Thanks, James. We needed that nudge over to making digital video features (see chapter 11)! If you're an 8-mm or Super 8 filmmaker, check out the Small Movies site, **<www.citynet.com/~fodder>**, for encouragement (you're not alone), numerous links, and vital information about labs that can still process your footage.

American Showcases

While you are waiting for responses from various festivals and New York showcases (or after you have actually been turned down by these venues), it's time to begin working on an "in-person" tour of the United States. Although it works best when you have some New York press to show the directors of other showcases, it is possible to build your tour from scratch.

Your first immediate step should be to access an incredible indie Website, **<www.tramline.com/tours/filmmaking>**, and click on Filmmaking Tours. Then, after reviewing their massive offering of over 1,000 film links under twenty-three categories, click on Stop 6—Flicker (**<www.sirius.com/~sstark/>**), a site that celebrates the avant garde. Listed under its numerous great links you'll see Venues: Alternative Film and Video Exhibition Spaces. That's where you'll find Websites of various showcases in both the United States and Europe, many with direct e-mail links for making contact with programmers. They include everything from New York's Millennium, which presents in-person filmmakers and their work (also conducts classes and workshops, rents editing and filming equipment, and takes submissions for articles, reviews, manifestos, schemas, and proposals for their Millennium Film Journal, **<www.sva.edu/mfj/>**), to Total Mobile Home Micro Cinema, a thirty-seat San Francisco theater that takes place in a basement ([415] 431-4007), Exploding Cinema in London, England, **<www.backspace.org/exponet/>**, and the 100-plus-seat Blinding Light Cinema in Vancouver, British Columbia, **<www.blinding light.com>**. If you're thorough, and spend some time Web surfing and e-mailing letters of inquiry, you should be able to book yourself into several theaters and launch your movie.

Lists of other showcases may be available at such foundations as AIVF in New York, **<www.aivf.org>**, FAF in San Francisco,

<www.filmarts.org>, or at local filmmakers' co-ops such as Canyon Cinema in San Francisco, <www.canyoncinema.com>, which will sell you their mailing list of 250 showcases that most often rent independent films. But since many showcases operate on such a low budget that they can't afford the higher price for feature-film rentals ($150 to $200), think twice before spending your postage reaching all the listings. Remember that the showcases nearest your hometown will probably be the most difficult shows for you to get . . . so don't get discouraged. Once you are booked for a show on the other side of the country, contact your local showcase and give them another chance to be part of your national tour.

After you and your movie are selected to appear at your first in-person show, the next step is to try to book more shows in that region of the country. A moviemaker needs several bookings in each area to make a profit. Ask the programmer who selected your feature to help you find other screenings.

Schedule your shows tightly together so that they occur every other day, if possible, with time to visit with the programmer and see his or her city and then make your flight connections to the next screening.

The most important tip I can give you before your initiation into the world of the touring moviemaker is this: Try to get an airline credit card. For many years I scrambled to raise the necessary $500 plane fare to get to the shows to earn the money to pay for the flights. The most I've ever earned on one tour was $3,300 for eight shows. Subtracting the $700 for airfares, my actual earnings were around $2,600, and I was on tour for three weeks. By now you must realize that this is a hard way to make a living.

Still, the benefits of showing your feature at in-person shows greatly outweigh the difficulties. First, you are able to screen your work for an interested audience and then hear their feedback during the in-person discussion following the show. There's no better way of finding out if you have touched your audience, reached them with your ideas and images. Audio-record each in-person show, creating a taped record of a touring moviemaker (you) doing his or her best in the year 200___, showing a feature entitled _______________. If your movie is very provocative, it may infuriate your audience, as my film *Emerald*

Cities did when I showed it at Cinema Arts Centre in Huntington, New York. The programmer, Vic Skolnick, had told me on the phone that he thought it was "a hard film," but that he wanted to show it in his theater. During the in-person portion of the screening, the audience response seemed to be divided. One half seemed to love the movie and thanked me for bringing up important issues, while the other half seemed annoyed that the movie had put them on such a big "bummer." One guy, a professional-looking man of about forty, seemed to be approaching the stage with the intent of harming me in some way. Quite a show! In St. Louis I had another hot response from a member of the audience at Webster University, where programmer David Kinder screened *Emerald Cities*. At this show I was pushed hard enough by the hecklers to actually become more articulate about my film and its relationship to the world.

Another benefit of these in-person shows is that the reviews you receive may help convince other showcases and film festivals that your work is valuable and should be seen. So make sure to keep copies of all press your movie receives.

Although the money from the shows will not make you rich, it does help to get an extra $1,000 to $2,000, visit strange and exciting cities, and occasionally be treated like a celebrity. And who knows—maybe one of your reviews will catch the eye of a distributor.

Television Premiere

Since the video revolution has opened up many doors to sales in television, you should try to show your feature to some cable, PBS, even network people. Page 222 gives the most accessible national television outlets for low-budget indie feature-length movies.

The surge of indie product and the prominence of the Sundance Film Festival have led to the formation of the Independent Film Channel and Sundance's very own Sundance Channel, both of which have given hope to some moviemakers that their features may actually see the light of day. Unfortunately, the Sundance Channel tends to go with the bigger, glossier indie flicks (the kind with recognizable stars), or

THE INDEPENDENT FILM CHANNEL
1111 STEWART AVENUE
BETHPAGE, NY 11714
(516) 803-3000
FAX: (516) 803-4506
www.ifctv.com

INDEPENDENT TELEVISION SERVICE (ITVS)
51 FEDERAL STREET, #401
SAN FRANCISCO, CA 94107
(415) 356-8383
FAX: (415) 356-8391
www.itvs.org

HBO
1100 AVENUE OF THE AMERICAS
NEW YORK, NY 10036
(212) 512-1000
FAX: (212) 512-7452
www.hbo.com

SUNDANCE CHANNEL
1633 BROADWAY, 16TH FLOOR
NEW YORK, NY 10019
(212) 654-1500
FAX: (212) 654-4738
www.sundancechannel.com

WNET/THIRTEEN
450 WEST 33RD STREET, 6TH FLOOR
NEW YORK, NY 10001
(212) 560-2000
FAX: (212) 560-1314
www.wnet.org

NATIONAL ASIAN AMERICAN TV
346 NINTH STREET, 2ND FLOOR
SAN FRANCISCO, CA 94103
(415) 863-0814
FAX: (415) 863-7428
www.naatanet.org

previous Sundance festival winners. But the Independent Film Channel still seems adventurous, often showing an unknown movie by an unknown director.

WNET/Thirteen offers arts and cultural programming on public television, and handles both acquisitions and original productions. P.O.V./The American Documentary, a showcase for feature-length documentaries (220 West 19th St., 11th Floor, New York, NY 10011, [212] 989-8121; Fax: [212] 989-8230, **<www.pbs.org/pov>**), is part of their programming. I've also included ITVS in this list because it represents a creative force in the world of television programming, even though its main charter is to fund indie projects from conception. But if you're still at the planning stage of producing a low-budget feature (up to $300,000), it's worth the couple of days you'll need to compile a funding application.

HBO has been instrumental in bringing several important movies to the screen through its documentary programming and adventurous feature acquisitions. Don't rule them out for either buying your scrappy indie feature or helping to fund an original concept. And if you're Asian-American, you might have a shot at getting your Asian-American indie feature shown on National Asian American TV (they not only support and distribute Asian Pacific/American media productions, but also organize the annual San Francisco International Asian American Film Festival).

It is still a long shot that one of these outlets will purchase your movie, since your low-budget feature probably has a number of qualities that make it "unbroadcastable." Your movie probably has no recognizable stars, unconventional editing and structure, and perhaps even some profanity. But occasionally the door cracks open and a "weird" film or video will be purchased. I was lucky to get such a "bail out" when the Learning Channel purchased my *Morgan's Cake* feature for over $16,000 ($1,000 beyond its total cost) because it fit well into their current series entitled *Growing Up*. To get a financial break like this, you first have to hear about programming needs, and then apply with VHS copy and written materials. So watch your moviemaking magazines and film-related Website links for these timely announcements. Many cities also have a local independent PBS channel and arts-oriented cable channel that might be more open to including your independent feature in their programming.

Although you might get paid as little as $300 for a TV showing on PBS in your hometown, you would have the satisfaction of reaching many thousands of people with your movie. And this television exposure won't really wreck your chances for future showings at film and video showcases, which play to very specialized audiences. You should bear in mind, however, that New York showcases, such as the Whitney Museum and Film Forum, insist on "premiering" movies they present. If you decide to accept an offer to show your work on PBS in New York, you would most likely be forfeiting the chance for an important New York premiere and the reviews in *The New York Times* and the *Village Voice* that would follow. So make sure the amount of money you will be paid is enough to make it a wise decision. If Film Forum will pay you a $2,500 guarantee, plus a percent of the box office receipts for a two-week run of your feature, and PBS offers you $4,000 for one showing at 10:00 P.M., which "premiere" would you select?

In Europe, several countries have well-funded television stations that produce and purchase low-budget features. For a small fee you can purchase the most up-to-date listing of European buyers from the Independent Feature Project (see "The Film Market," below, for more information). In Germany alone there are three channels that pay from around $10,000 to $50,000 for each feature they show. And in England Channel Four has purchased many independent movies (including my second feature, *1988—The Remake*, for which I was paid around $13,000). Write a personal letter (e-mail) with a short synopsis of your movie's contents. With luck, you may receive a request to send a VHS videotape for preview.

ZDF/ARTE GERMAN TELEVISION
ZDF-STRASSE 1
D-55100 MAINZ 1, GERMANY
ek15@zdf-host.de

ARD
AM STEINERNEN STOCK 1
FRANKFURT, GERMANY 60320
info@ard.de

WDR
APPELHOFPLATZ 1
50600 KOLN, GERMANY
georg.berg@wdr.de

CHANNEL FOUR
60 CHARLOTTE STREET
LONDON W1P 2AX, ENGLAND
www.channel4.com

The Film Market

While feature-length movies are sold every day at various film markets around the world, the average independent producer doesn't have enough financial resources to afford the travel, hotel rooms, and PR materials necessary to participate. The one event I can recommend is the Independent Feature Film Market (IFFM), held each year in New York City, run by the Independent Feature Project (IFP). Begun in 1979 as a support group to aid the independent feature filmmaker, IFP provides the format of its film market at reasonable rates while maintaining a low-key and congenial atmosphere for both film buyers and moviemakers alike. If your feature has failed to attract attention at either film festivals or showcases, the Independent Feature Film Market offers you one more crack at selling your work to buyers from American and European TV, including representatives from Germany, England, and other progressive countries that buy original work. You may even be surprised to find your feature invited to several European and American festivals by week's end.

INDEPENDENT FEATURE FILM MARKET (IFFM)
104 WEST 29TH STREET, 12TH FLOOR
NEW YORK, NY 10001
(212) 465-8200
www.ifp.org

Once your completed 16-mm or 35-mm feature is accepted for presentation at the market (a limited amount of DV features are also chosen), you will be required to pay a fee of $450 ($400 for early registration), which covers the costs of your screening at a high-quality theater and the printing of a catalog containing a photo, short synopsis, and contact address and phone number for your movie. For $400 ($350 if early submission) you may submit your rough cut as a "work-in-progress," screening 25 minutes by video projection to raise finishing funds. If you don't have friends to stay with in New York City, the film market will help you find affordable housing. Like any good festival, the IFFM offers many opportunities for socializing, chances to meet buyers as well as other filmmakers who may become lifelong friends. To take advantage of the Independent Feature Project's continuing programs, screenings of features, seminars, and monthly newsletters, you may want to join as a member. Yearly dues cost $100 for individuals, $65 for students. For information on the East Coast, call the Independent Feature Project in New York; to inquire about IFP/West, call (310) 475-4379. For IFP/Midwest call (773) 281-5177. They've lately added branches North ([612] 338-0871) and South ([305] 461-3544).

Distributors

I have the urge to make this section of the book the shortest one of all. Just two words—STEER CLEAR! Does this mean, don't distribute? But how can a film be seen by the general public if it doesn't get distribution?

One of the dreams of most independent directors is that a distributor will pick up his or her feature film, blow it up to 35-mm from 16-mm, and present it at the best theater in New York to rave reviews. And, for some, such as Wayne Wang (*Chan Is Missing*), Jim Jarmusch (*Stranger Than Paradise*), Spike Lee (*She's Gotta Have It*), and Kevin Smith (*Clerks*), this dream has become a reality. But no distributor will pick up a low-budget feature unless that film first proves it has the potential for pulling in an audience. This proof must be first in the form of a BUZZ that is somehow generated out of the movie as it slowly begins the birthing process. Since a truly original and innovative "breakthrough" feature is a movie that hasn't been witnessed by anyone before, often coming with the baggage of no known stars and an odd structure (see *Clerks*), it usually surprises everyone (especially the makers!) when it starts to garner interest, festival showings, and finally attention from distributors. The people who will inevitably get it into theaters (Miramax, Fine Line, October Films, Fox Searchlight, Strand, Roxie Releasing, Sony Classics, etc.) will have to be convinced that what they see on the screen is *good.* A couple of great screenings can kick this off. And if you are fortunate to have a consultant like Bob Hawk (ICI) in your audience when the movie *works* (as Kevin Smith did for *Clerks* at the IFFM), or Lynda Hansen (LAHA), who seems to be able to spot winners (see "Agents" on page 231), you'll quickly find your little backyard project sprouts wings and begins to run *your* life. Hawk (recently co-producer of the Sundance hit *Trick*) and Hansen are constantly cornered in hall-ways and theater lobbies, asked informally by Sundance selectors and New York festival friends if they've seen "anything good." When they do, they sing it from the rooftops. Suddenly, you have a flood of festival invitations. You'll travel to Park City, then Berlin, and back to New York after Denver. Your credit cards will take

Hunter Mann pursues his alternative method of 16-mm film distribution, bicycling around the country with his "Highway Cinema" trailer filled with film prints (Harrod Blank's *Wild Wheels* documentary among others), EIKI projector, even plug-in audiocassette and mike for background "theater music" and announcements. Photo by Rick Aubert.

a hit for charged airline tickets and food (not all festivals cover flights and/or per diem), and maybe a second "release" print, but you don't care. Your message machine and e-mail are jammed with requests from distributors for preview tapes or DVD. And inevitably it will all come down to a few vital shows and resultant newspaper or magazine coverage, when you and your movie get catapulted over the pack, into the stratosphere of BUZZ = $ + FAME/VISIBILITY. Hopefully, you and your compatriots are emotionally prepared for this rocket sled, and all your contracts (actors' releases, profit-sharing papers—see appendix) are in order.

If you manage to beat the odds and your feature is suddenly hot, you must be *very* savvy in selecting the right distributor. Only a few distributors are skilled at making money with an "offbeat" independent feature. New Yorker Films in New York has been regarded as a top distributor for several years. It specializes in award-winning foreign films, "art" films such as Godard's, and occasionally American films that review well, such as *Chan Is Missing* and *Atomic Cafe*. New Line Cinema of New York has successfully distributed the low-budget features of John Waters (*Pink Flamingos*) and for a while handled my feature *1988—The Remake*. Several large distributors, including New Line, Miramax, Sony, 20th Century Fox, and Samuel Goldwyn, are now distributing smaller films through new spin-off companies, in an attempt to handle less-mainstream (but equally profitable) "theatrical" features.

New Line's Fine Line Features (**<www.FLF.com>**) has successfully released a number of indie (albeit well-funded) films, including Atom Egoyan's *The Sweet Hereafter* and John Waters's *Pecker*. Sony Pictures Classics (**<www.spe.sony.com/classics>**) seeks rights in all media for indie and foreign features from script stage to completed films (*Crumb*, *Henry Fool*, *In the Company of Men*, etc.). Fox Searchlight (**<www.foxsearchlight.com>**) has been fairly bold in its indie acquisitions (*The Brothers McMullen*, *Star Maps*, etc.). And at the top of the indie food chain sits Miramax (**<www.miramax.com>**), deserving some credit for distributing *Clerks*, and *Chasing Amy* (also *Good Will Hunting*, *Velvet Goldmine*, *Life Is Beautiful*, etc.). Fortunately, the definition of what's "commercial" keeps changing, to include even feature films shot on digital video. October Films (**<www.octoberfilms.com>**) deserves considerable credit for distributing the amazing Dogme 95 digital video movie *The Celebration* by Thomas Vinterberg (mini-DVCAM transferred to 35-mm for exhibition). Zeitgeist Films (**<www.zeitgeistfilm.com>**) (*Irma Vep*, *Fire*, *Poison*, etc.) is also an adventurous distributor worth approaching. Good Machine (**<hpaarte@goodmachine.com>**) had the guts to distribute *Happiness*, *Ride with the Devil*, *Luminous Motion*, others. And Next Wave Films in Santa Monica, California (**<www.nextwavefilms.com>**), even offers $100,000 completion funds to those no-budget digital video features they believe are commercial.

And if that wasn't enough distribution possibilities, a new company in Chicago called Art in Motion ([312] 726-0110) has set up a

Website for holding the world's first film auction in Los Angeles (see <www.films4auction.com>). By the time you read this updated and revised edition of my book they should have already put their first 20 feature-length selections on the block (they say the real success of their venture depends on finding "20 terrific films"). Maybe YOUR FILM will be just what they're looking for when the next auction is conducted. Check out their Website and see how you can apply.

Am I softening on my attitude toward distributors? Not completely. But the key to happy distribution is signing the right contract with an honest company.

The one thing all these distributors have in common is their expectation that, since they are taking such a big risk in handling an independent feature, they should be well paid if the venture succeeds. If you sign the wrong contract, you can be giving one of these distributors over 90 percent of the earnings of your film.

If you want to earn any money under a distribution agreement, you must first understand the difference between "gross" and "net." If you sign a contract that promises you 50 percent of the net earnings of your feature, you will receive half of the money left over from the ticket sales after the distributor pays off all the office help, his or her salary, advertising costs, printing and promotion, travel expenses for the distribution rep to foreign film festivals, cab fares, business lunches, and expensive dinners. In other words you will receive about 10 percent of the money your feature earns, if you're lucky, after doing 100 percent of the writing, producing, directing, shooting, editing, casting, and financing. Does this seem fair? Does it seem right that the person who sells your movie should get almost the total financial benefit from your good work? Perhaps, if the distributor (Miramax, Sony) has the clout to distribute widely enough that your 10 percent equals several hundred thousand dollars.

A far better deal would be a contract offering you 50 percent of the gross, stipulating that of every dollar returned to the distributor from the theater you receive 50 cents, period. This is the deal that you want, but it is almost impossible to get. Another way to alter the contract in your favor is to agree to a net deal but limit and detail (in the contract) exactly which expenses may be paid for out of the net proceeds. In my contract with New Line Cinema for *1988—The Remake*, I limited their

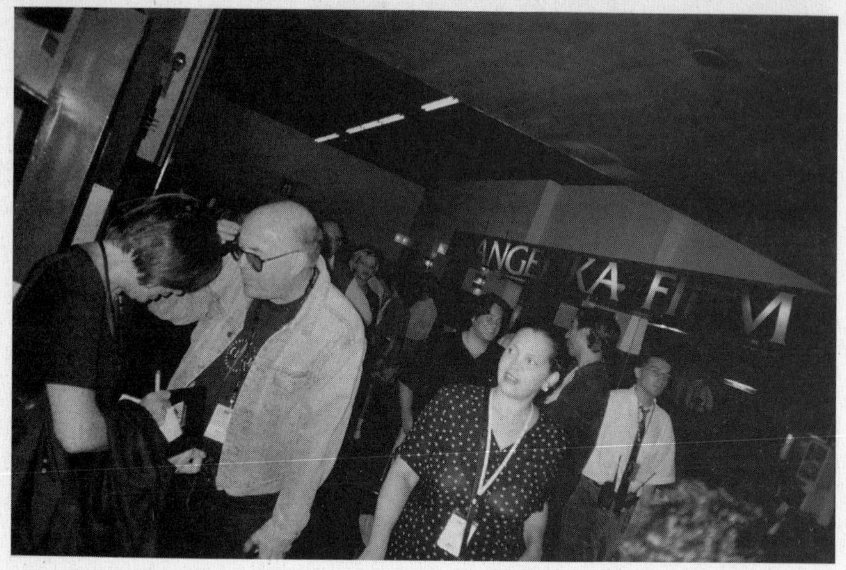

Robert Hawk of ICI (Independent Consultation for Independents) gives valued advice at IFFM, near theater where he discovered the indie no-budget hit *Clerks*.

net expenses to $3,000, so that I would receive a true 50 percent of the earnings from our 50–50 deal after these initial expenses.

In practical terms very few independent moviemakers receive any money from their distributors beyond the "advance," the initial payment for purchase of distribution rights. And usually the distributor offers *no* money up front for a "risky" independent feature. If you want to make any money on your distribution deal, you should be prepared for a tough negotiating session. Ask for an advance, insist on either a gross deal or a detailed limited net deal, and be sure to add a clause stipulating that the distributor does *not* have any legal rights to edit your film under any conditions. *And don't sign any contract with a distributor until you first review its contents with the best entertainment lawyer in your area.* Even if it costs you $1,000 (which you may be able to arrange to pay from rentals or out of the advance), hire a good lawyer who will check every word in the contract and change the particularly offensive clauses so that you will have at least a glimmer of hope of receiving some money. Don't be so overcome by the dream of distribution that you give away all the earnings of your "breakthrough" feature.

Agents

For the most part no quirky, no-budget independent feature can make it in the marketplace and get major distribution without a certain groundswell of success. That success might begin with being selected for Sundance Film Festival's Dramatic or Documentary Competition or New Directors/New Films in New York. These extremely prestigious festivals guarantee that your work will be solidly in the spotlight and have the potential for substantial success. Usually by this point the movie will have attracted enough attention for film agents, who position themselves to have preexisting deals with certain features that they believe will emerge as the success stories of the year. Certain agents, like John Pierson (Grainy Pictures, 44 Market Street, Cold Spring, NY 10516, [914] 265-2241, **<www.grainypictures.com>**), who have strong track records for launching small films, can actually add to the fire of interest in a feature by signing it on for representation. Pierson's involvement was one of the crucial steps that led to the success of Kevin Smith's *Clerks* being sold to Miramax in 1994 out of the Sundance Dramatic Competition. Look for Pierson to have an even stronger influence on the sales of indie features now that he and his Grainy Pictures have been given their own distribution pipeline through Disney-owned Miramax. And on his weekly Independent Film Channel show, *Split Screen,* he's become a star himself, now searching the country for the next wave of hot moviemakers to interview.

An earlier contributor to the *Clerks* success story was Bob Hawk, a consultant with ICI (Independent Consultation for Independents, 1870 North Vermont Avenue, Suite 507, Los Angeles, CA 90027, [323] 856-6205 or [212] 946-1048) who "discovered" the no-budget feature at a sparsely attended screening at the IFFM in New York. ICI can help some features find a home with festivals and honest agents, as well as assist the filmmaker in earlier stages of production, scripting, and final cut. When Hawk is unavailable to consult on movies he confidently leaves Lynda Hansen's name and contact numbers on his answering machine, knowing that she and her company LAHA (115 East 92nd Street, New York, NY 10128, [212] 534-6497; fax: [212] 534-7897, **LAHAAA@aol.com**) can offer advice on proposals, screenplays, rough cuts, marketing and festival promotion at the highest level (her credentials as U.S. rep to the Berlin Film Festival's Independent Forum for New Cinema, one of the most important venues in the world, should leave no doubt as to her expertise and international connections).

Those many filmmakers whose "undiscovered" low-budget features won't be the hit of the year must decide between self-agenting their features or turning the movies over to lesser-known agents and distributors, gambling that the expenses incurred by the agents won't outrun any actual funds earned in the marketplace. For some filmmakers, like Jerry Barrish, whose career began by having his first feature, *Dan's Motel* (80 minutes, 1981), selected by New Directors/New Films in New York, with strong interest generated by New Yorker Films for distribution, it has been an uphill battle to get the financial return his films deserve. Although Barrish has amassed an impressive record of festival screenings (including Berlin Film Festival's Forum, Edinburgh, Rotterdam, etc.) and sold repeatedly to German TV, it has often been the agents who have received the money from TV sales, as they have recouped their unchecked expenses for hotel room, food, and air travel fees to festivals and film markets. For example, Barrish's third feature, *Shuttlecock* (87 minutes, color, 1989), earned $14,000 at the Roxie Cinema in San Francisco, all of which was owed his agent for costs already incurred from sales trips to Cannes and the IFFM. Even though the film, which won a top prize at Rotterdam, is now distributed in Europe, Barrish has not, as yet, seen either statements or earnings beyond his advance. His one consolation is that the European distributor fronted the money to blow his film up from 16-mm to 35-mm (saving him more than $20,000). Because there are so few real possibilities for sales and distribution of low-budget features, the moviemaker may be better off acting as his or her own agent, sending out well-targeted VHS cassette copies with personally written cover letters, and using an experienced entertainment attorney (instead of an agent) to negotiate sales, review contracts, finalize payment. Perhaps then it will be you and your significant other who will enjoy a well-earned working vacation in Cannes, meeting those few distributors who have expressed genuine interest in your unique product.

Indie Cinemas

If you've gone the route of searching for festival and New York premieres, U.S. and European TV buyers, and shown your new feature at IFFM but come away empty-handed, you can still hold out some slim hope of seeing your movie on a commercial theater's screen. There remain just a handful of indie theaters in the United States that give a part of their schedule over to personal "handmade" feature films and videos. These obstinate programmer/owners shuffle indie premieres in with solid repertory fare (*Jules and Jim*, *Citizen Kane*, *The Man Who Would Be King*, *Eraserhead*, *Pink Flamingos*, etc.). If you ever wanted to visit San Francisco, maybe you'll be fortunate enough to have your unusual cutting-edge movie appreciated and booked into the Roxie Cinema for a week. Or if you crave some cool, rainy weather mixed in with the aroma of fresh-brewed coffee, try Seattle's Grand Illusion Cinema and Little Theatre (part of The Northwest Film Forum collective, parent to Wiggly World Studios, in whose facilities indie films get produced and edited).

Once your movie is chosen for presentation, be prepared to pay for some of the cost of advertising, and possibly cover half of a publicist's fee (especially in San Francisco, where you can't expect to fill a theater playing an unknown indie movie without a skilled publicist. Karen Larsen of Larsen Associates, [415] 957-1205, a Roxie regular, builds your pressbook, uses her media contacts to get print and radio interviews, and runs your press screenings in a professional way so as to elicit needed reviews and Pink Section coverage in the *San Francisco Examiner*, etc.). Most theaters will pay you a guarantee fee ($200 to $300) against a split of the box office gate (maybe 35 percent to you, 65 percent to the theater after expenses). If the publicity breaks wide and in your favor, you should walk away from a week-long run with at least $1,000 over your costs. Give these theaters a try.

Roxie Cinema
Attn: Bill Banning
San Francisco, CA 94103
(415) 431-3611
<www.roxie.com>

Grand Illusion Cinema/Little Theatre
1403 NE 50th Street
Seattle, WA 98112
(206) 329-2629
<www.wigglyworld.org>

Other Forms of Distribution

Whether or not your movie receives the kind of reviews and attention that will attract distributors, you will want to consider some alternatives. Instead of signing away most of your future earnings to a commercial distributor, why couldn't you rent a theater, do modest advertising, hire ticket takers, and earn the most possible money from your successful run? One major obstacle to this simple alternative is that the best theaters in New York are locked up, "owned" by certain distributors who make payments to insure that the theaters are available only to their companies. But in other areas of the country, an indie producer can rent his or her own local theater (this is called "four walling") and earn a much higher percentage from a film's showings. The largest drawback to four walling your feature is that it takes a great deal of time away from what you probably should be doing—making movies.

Aside from running your own shows at various locations, there are many other opportunities for showings that you can pursue on your own—at regional showcases, on college campuses, and in independent theaters. For some feature filmmakers, like Joe Berlinger and Bruce Sinofsky (*Brother's Keeper*, *Paradise Lost*, etc.), who have turned self-distribution into an art form, the rewards are high, their earnings now topping the million-dollar mark. The essence of self-distribution is simple: People who want to rent or buy your movie get in touch with you by phone or letter. You tell them your price and then, if they agree, you arrange to send them your print after receiving their down payment. If you trust them, you might allow them to pay you after their use of your print. All the details of this process vary with each situation. Usually, you will pay for the shipping to the showcase and they pay for return postage when they mail it back. For my first few rentals, I was incredibly excited that *anyone* wanted to show my film and would actually pay me for its use. But after the initiation of renting a movie and having it returned damaged or waiting in vain for the "check in the mail" to arrive, I began wondering if there wasn't a better way to handle distribution. Fortunately, there are some practical low-cost alternatives to doing it entirely on your own.

For a small annual membership fee of around $40, a co-op distributor, such as Filmmaker's Co-op in New York or Canyon Cinema in San Francisco, will handle all rentals, mailing, and invoicing for you. In return, they receive a reasonable percentage of the rental charge—usually 35 to 40 percent. Most co-ops are very honest, considerate of the filmmakers, and careful with stored prints and rentals. And although this type of service will generate few rentals unless the moviemaker commits to spending some money advertising his films, occasionally you will be surprised with an extra $50 when you really need it.

Advertising for Alternative Distribution

Because of the ads I've run for my features in *Film Comment* magazine, which reaches between 30,000 and 50,000 interested filmphiles (<**www.filmlinc.com/fcm/fcm.htm**>), my films have been selected for showings at several commercial theaters in the United States. In 1983 the St. Marks Theater (now defunct) in the East Village section of New York City ran *Emerald Cities* for two Friday/Saturday midnight shows for which I had been given a $150 advance guarantee (check sent to me before the show) versus a 35 percent cut of the gross receipts. I earned about $650 for the four shows. The ads also helped me get three in-person shows, each of which paid me $600 to appear with *Emerald Cities*. Subtracting my $510 travel expenses ($1,800 − $510 = $1,290), and subtracting the cost of my ads in *Film Comment* ($1,290 − $600 = $690), then adding in my earnings from the St. Marks show ($690 + $650 = $1,340), the total shows made a small overall profit that I wouldn't have made if I hadn't advertised.

Advertising can pay off in other ways as well. When I went around to the video stores to sell my features on cassette, one store buyer in San Francisco immediately ordered all my tapes, saying that he had heard of my films. This sale was due to my constant advertising in *Film Comment* (contact advertising manager Tony Impavido, [212] 875-5622, <**webmaster@filmlinc.com**>, who's been known to give indie filmmakers special discounted rates).

For a very targeted audience of indie film lovers, another magazine I'd recommend advertising in is *MovieMaker*, actually run by a fellow indie moviemaker named Tim Rhys (his feature *Men in Scoring Position* can be found at festivals and in video stores). As publisher/editor he has taken this dream of a magazine from being a small Seattle-based "zine," to a full-fledged far-reaching voice of the independent (contact their advertising manager, [360] 579-1292, or send e-mail to <**staff@moviemaker.com**>). If you have a budget of around $5,000 and want to wage a full-scale advertising campaign, then you should be able to afford a quarter-page ad in several popular filmmaking magazines, including *Film Comment*, *MovieMaker*, *Filmmaker Magazine* (western region advertising sales at [213] 932-5606, eastern sales at [212] 581-1825), *RES* magazine ([213] 932-5606, <**advert @resmag.com**>), the *Independent Film & Video Monthly* ([212] 807-1400, <**displayads@aivf.org**>, and San Francisco's *Release Print* ([415] 826-5173, <**info@filmarts.org**>).

Perhaps these days, if you have a Website for your indie movie(s) as I do (<**www.lightvideo.com/films.htm**>), the wisest use of your advertising budget might be to promote your Website online, with services like Trafficboost ([800] 271-1601, <**www.trafficboost.com**>), which resubmits your site to hundreds of search engines for a revitalized presence on the WWW. Or you can buy space on a "banner," those nicely prominent rectangular boxes that load onto the top half of your computer screen whenever you access a search engine. For approximately $1,000 you can reach hundreds of thousands of Web surfers during the time that it will be displayed.

And don't overlook the possibility of getting your features reviewed in magazines, which could be free advertising worth hundreds of dollars. Mail your VHS copy and pressbook to the current critics you admire, offering them the chance to discover you and your work.

Setting Prices

When you set your prices for rentals of your feature, print purchases, or videotapes in VHS, make sure that you don't price yourself right out of the market. I've tried to keep my prices reasonable: $175 for seventy-minute features, $200 for ninety-minute features for rentals in 16-mm to small theaters and showcases. And for the purchase of a print, I charge an extra $500 over cost. I have sold several hundred videotapes of my features to stores in the San Francisco Bay Area by charging the reasonable price of $35 wholesale. Since it costs me under $10 to produce each tape, I'm basically tripling my money with each sale. Some of the buyers in the stores have told me that other independent filmmakers want $49.95 for their tapes, and the stores refuse to pay that much for something that isn't mainstream.

For your in-person shows, the prices vary quite a bit, but you should try to keep your minimum price around $200 to $250. On your first time out as an unknown writer/director, it might help to be looser with this minimum and take what you can get, since many showcases have disappeared in the last few years and many others have been forced to cut their budgets. Don't price yourself out of the market, but don't sell yourself too cheap, either. Overcome your shyness and ask if any travel allowance can be made available. Perhaps several showcases can share the expense of your round-trip airfare. If a showcase wants you and your movie, it will certainly try to meet your financial needs.

The Long Haul

It is not unusual for a foreign film festival or showcase to call you up two years after you began promoting your feature to tell you they want to show your fine work. If you've made an entertaining, thoughtful, and original feature, you will continue to get a sprinkling of rentals for years to come. Be patient. My feature *1988—The Remake* was chosen for showing at the London Film Festival in 1980, two years after it premiered at the Whitney Museum in New York.

And the video and Internet market will continue to demand new feature-length works, so while you begin to conceive and script your next movie, some time each month should be spent promoting your completed feature. You may even want to purchase a mailing list of video stores to do a major mailing and/or set up a Website specially devoted to this first feature.

While you continue to search for feedback and shows for your recently completed feature, using the video copies (DVD, etc.) to apply for grants, film festivals, and purchases by video stores, you must also pause for reflection. Of course, it's important not to fool yourself into thinking that you are making a living with your feature if in fact you are not. Be realistic about your expenses, keep a running account of the money you spend for typesetting, postage, travel fares, so that you can honestly evaluate your "business of moviemaking."

But no matter how much or how little money you make with your first feature, you should enjoy the recognition that you have succeeded, that you have actually fulfilled your goal of creating a feature-length movie. Regardless of what anyone thinks of your work, the completion of it is a great accomplishment, and you should celebrate this achievement. Remember that some artists, such as Van Gogh, were never appreciated in their lifetimes, hardly sold a painting . . . so try to enjoy any rentals and savor every sign of success. And while you wait for responses from festivals and showcases, use the glow of your accomplishment to begin thinking of your next project. If you are thorough in your promotion, you should have a chance to try again—with Feature Film at Used-Car Prices #2.

8 Reality Check

Let's say that you somehow, against all odds, pulled off the no-budget production of a feature-length movie. And when you finished the cut and showed it to all interested parties (friends, parents, investors, cast and crew) everyone raved about your accomplishment. You were flying high. You had done it. Look out Kevin Smith, Spike Lee, and Jim Jarmusch! A star was born. The sky was the limit. Easy street was around the corner. You were made to feel extremely confident in your feature by everyone concerned, and with that optimistic feeling you began the process of promotion. You made VHS dubs of your movie and started submitting them to the most obvious film festivals: Sundance, New Directors, Seattle, Berlin, Rotterdam, London, New York, Chicago, Denver, AFI/LA, even Cannes. You checked your calendar, wondered if you'd be in France in May, perhaps Park City for Sundance in January, New York in September. You had fantasies that you expected to be realized, and you awaited the call. But when the letters showed up, each one a differently phrased rejection, a sense of defeat, maybe even betrayal, began to emerge. How could a work as good as yours continue to be overlooked at the (dumb) festivals? What the hell was happening?

You soon learned that one major mistake you had made was trumpeting to all your friends and associates which festivals you had entered. Now all they did was drive you crazy asking you about Sundance. You had been so sure. . . . And at the IFFM (Independent Feature Film Market) in New York City you had shown to a full and enthusiastic house and received compliments, but the festivals in Europe hadn't bitten. Berlin had sent you a curt letter, erasing the promise of German TV sales in two sentences (I got much too used to those form letters before I finally got in with *Morgan's Cake*). Somehow you'd been set up to expect a lot more positive response from the festivals. You had at least expected to get in one. But no go. A total bust.

If your low-budget feature was so good, then why didn't any festival (art museum, showcase, theater) want to show it? Let's say for now that the fault lies entirely with *them.* It is possible that the movie you created was so artistic that no one was prepared to understand it, much less accept it (see Ray Carney's foreword). If your movie is cutting edge, it might take a few more years for your "ahead-of-its-time" feature to find a home. Or maybe you hit upon such strong issues, dug so deep into the psyche of America, that no one can stand the results of your filmatic vision. Your movie may have pushed too many buttons within the panel of experts at Sundance and built up a distaste for it that resulted in its dismissal (I like to think that is why my *American Orpheus* failed to make the final cut in 1992 when it was among the final sixteen dramatic features under consideration). So your feature *is* good, it's just that no one wants to show it or have anything to do with it. Can you really believe that? Is your ego sufficient to handle all that rejection, downcast looks from friends, a bit too much sympathy from family members? If your feature is that good, then don't give up. Try some of the smaller festivals that can offer you a great show, good attendance, even press coverage (Cinequest/San Jose, Olympia Film Festival in Washington, Ann Arbor Film Festival, Wine Country Film Festival/Napa, Aspen, etc.), while continuing occasionally to tempt the majors (San Francisco, Boston, Venice, Locarno). Have you tried Telluride? How about Stockholm International (**<www.filmfestivalen.se>**)? How can you be sure that you haven't been lax in your job, sunk your movie because you couldn't maintain a positive mood. You need to get the proof from *all* festivals (that nice big pile of rejection letters) before you can say for certain that no one wanted your work.

On the other hand, what if your movie is as unworthy as your (well-hidden) doubts might say? How can you deal with such an artistic failure? The only way I know to make use of an artistic disaster is to give it another shot—try again. If you honestly made your own brand of mistakes, entered into the making of a feature with your own ideas about content and form, then the true nature of your accomplishment can only be realized up the road, a couple of features later, when the new ground you are intuitively carving out for yourself will finally coalesce. Until then you must not get discouraged. Your work is too valuable. And the temptations to forget your individual path will be immense. Pressures from all sides will seem to be forcing you toward making a more mainstream second feature, one that will try to more closely resemble Hollywood's product. You may find yourself actually writing a script that runs exactly 118 pages, has strong story lines, plot points, even characters with known actors in mind. You want to do it "right" this time, never having to feel like a failure again. Right? Is that how it is?

What happened to your personal vision? How ornery and crazy does a moviemaker have to be to try it his or her way for a second time in a row? How about for a tenth time in a row? Most great art that you've seen didn't just materialize from the artist's hand on the first try. It took years of hard work, often decades, for that artist to finally swoop in on the nugget of perception that was his or her gift to the world. And it took an equally long time for that artist to master the particular technical expertise of his or her craft to make such a convincing statement, whether it was in oil paint, carved marble, video or film.

Do you think it gets easier to make your original film (or digital video feature) as success and fame roll in? Matthew Harrison, an indie filmmaker who has enjoyed the triumph of Sundance (his feature *Rhythm Thief*, <www.reel.com/movie.asp?MID=9279>, shot on a paltry $11,000 and completed for a total budget of $36,000, won the Sundance Jury Prize), and has received those multi-million-dollar production windfalls (his $4 million *Kicked in the Head* was produced by Martin Scorsese, and another release, *My Little Hollywood*, is now available), has this to add: "You can have an indie hit or even two or three, and it can be just as tough to get a film financed, or even tougher. There is no easy ticket. You have to be making movies because you truly love them, and that will show in your film. If you're in it for the fame or to make a fast buck, nothing will crucify you faster than making a feature film."

Great art takes a lifetime of hard, relentless work. Are you up for that? Did you forget that a first feature is just the bare beginning of your career? You hardly got your toes wet and you're ready to quit? That's ridiculous. Won't it be enjoyable to tell your friends that you're making another movie? Won't it be worth it just to see the look on their faces? When they ask you "Why?" you can tell them that you're an artist, and all artists are crazy. They'll probably nod knowingly and end up helping you again.

9

Feature Workshops

For many readers who have reviewed the first eight chapters of this book, the idea of directing and producing a feature may seem as distant a dream as when they first picked up the book, since raising even $12,000 is quite difficult to do in an age when often half of all earnings goes just to rent. Other practical-minded individuals who shun credit cards and believe in the axiom "A penny saved is a penny earned" (but can't save nearly enough to make a feature-length movie) may be stuck in their self-imposed rut of deciding that the sacrifice of economic stability is too high a price to pay for even such a major aspiration as moviemaking. And then there are those veterans of filmmaking wars who have somehow scraped up the necessary funds to grind out a first feature, often at a cost of $20,000 to $30,000, and then had difficulty recouping their investment. Psychically weakened from their failure to get invited to major film festivals, and worn out from explaining to relatives and other investors that no money has, as yet, been earned, they may think that the idea of making a second feature seems ridiculously far-fetched. Yet for both the first-time dreamer and the veteran with one or more features under his or her belt, there may still exist a flicker of hope that lack of money won't put an end to their promising careers. In the following pages I describe a method of making features by collaboration in which filmmakers can band together and produce a super no-budget feature by sharing costs and workload.

Rick's Feature Workshops

Since 1993 I've advertised in both print media and on the Internet that I'm conducting something called Feature Workshops (**<www.lightvideo.com/workshop.htm>**). The ads stated that for the price of $2,500 participants collaborate with me on writing, directing, shooting, editing, and completing a feature-length Pro-DVCAM digital video movie in ten days (a higher price of $3,000 is charged when we shoot on 16-mm film). In 1997 I was joined by a full ten collaborators for a 16-mm shoot, men and women from different parts of the country whose backgrounds formed a rather spectacular array of disciplines. We had a cartoonist from Washington State, a psychologist from Southern California, a security guard from upstate New York, an arts administrator from Philadelphia, an Eagle Scout/film student from a top university on the East Coast, an editor for a corporate newsletter, an opera singer booked two years in advance in Europe, a female script supervisor looking to break away from the tedium of commercials, a graphic designer/filmmaker who worked at a TV station in New York, and a couple of film students from the Midwest. It was exciting to imagine just what kind of movie could be extrapolated from this interesting bunch of people.

Before the ten collaborators joined me in Berkeley, California, my son and co-producer, Morgan Schmidt-Feng, worked feverishly to pull talent and crew together for the August 17–20 shoot dates, and arrange affordable Avid editing between August 21–26 (at eighteen, Morgan starred in and associate-produced *Morgan's Cake*, and now had his own production company, **<filmsight@aol.com>**). He somehow found a pair of attractive twin women for our lead actors (needed for the premise I envisioned—twins switching identities on their boyfriends), while pulling together a top-notch crew consisting of cinematographer Gary Rohan (**<gary_rohan@yahoo.com>**), soundman Greg von Buchau (**<gvonbuchau@aol.com>**), and assistant director Brad Marshland (**<marshlands@mindspring.com>**) (a writer/director with his own feature, *Liar's Dice*). To this great central core Morgan added skilled gaffers (Jason Prudoch, Lana Beinberg), cut a great deal

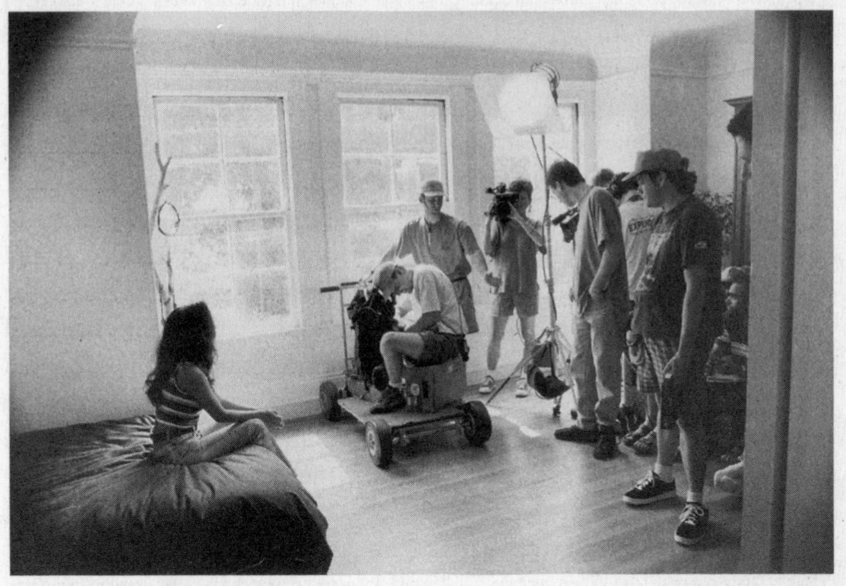

Cinematographer Gary Rohan prepares a dolly shot for Feature Workshops movie, *someone like me*, while Kate Taylor, center, videotapes the writing/directing process with Alan Richter for their documentary, *Cinovation*. Photo by Chandra Clarke.

on a lighting package (at indie-friendly Arthur Freyer Lighting of Berkeley), secured the twins' agreement to shoot in their house, found a great spacious and airy apartment for a secondary location, hired an affordable caterer, basically took care of all those pesky details so crucial to a *normal* feature shoot. And at the last minute we were unexpectedly joined by some very talented actors, including San Francisco's Finn Curtin, plus Craig Strong and Brandie Smith, who drove up from Los Angeles to be a part of our movie.

It was an exciting moment for me when I met all the participants for the first time at a Berkeley restaurant the evening of August 16. I handed out "Feature Workshops" hats and our profit-sharing contract (see "Collaborative Feature Agreement," appendix J), while a photographer snapped our portraits from all angles (this moment and the intensity of the four-day shoot is thoroughly covered in a documentary entitled *Cinovation*, produced by West-Pac Video and Mission Features (<**mesafilms@aol.com**>). I was as impressed with the friendly and earnest personalities of the participants as I had been with their astute e-mails received over the previous six months while we worked up concepts and scenes for the film. Now I could actually meet everyone face-to-face!

The next morning we all hooked up at their hotel and rolled in caravan-style over to the twins' house a couple of miles away. And I guess the oddest problem of the shoot came up almost immediately, as we all stood in the surrounding sidewalk and driveway areas outside of the twins' house. Can you guess what it was? Morgan and I looked around and suddenly wondered just how the hell we would be able to squeeze the group of twenty-plus people and all the gear (camera, lights, video tap monitor, cables, etc.) into the twins' modest bungalow-style house for our first shot! At any rate, as with any unforeseen problem that arises on the set, we just jumped in and went to work. And thirty minutes later we were all happily ensconced inside, participants and actors watching the video monitor from the cable-laden living room as I framed up the kick-off shot of the twins at the kitchen table. Before the four-day shoot was over, all ten participants were able to write and direct scenes (most for the first time), block out their shots with help from the cinematographer, rehearse with actors and nonactors, adjust lighting to best effect, overcome trepidation and obstacles to create the footage from which we culled a feature-length eighty-minute Avid cut by day-ten (thanks to our sleep-deprived genius editor Gabriel Rhodes). The resulting feature, *someone like me*, can be previewed on the Web at: <**www.lightvideo.com/cineplex.htm**>. I'm proud of the fact that Miramax asked to see our full 80-minute cut on VHS of *someone like me*, after we screened as a "work-in-progress" at IFFM 1998. While they didn't purchase it (you would have known the title if they had!), their interest in our little movie has to be taken as a tremendous compliment, further proof that the workshop method is a viable means of producing no-budget features for the marketplace.

Here's a look at our budget for this top-quality 16-mm production.

10-Day Feature Workshops Budget (16-mm with Avid Cut)

Cinematographer (Eclair NPR/4-day shoot)	$ 1,200.00
On-location soundperson (time-code Nagra)	$ 1,200.00
Sound assistant (boom man)	$ 200.00
¼″ audiotape (for Nagra)	$ 200.00
Filmstock (16 rolls @ $101 ea./Kodak "Vision" #7277)	$ 1,616.00
Producer/production manager (3 months' prep.)	$ 2,000.00
Gaffer ($50 day/4 days)	$ 200.00
Lighting package (lights, stands, floor dolly/4 days)	$ 305.00
Equipment insurance (4 days)	$ 500.00
Assistant director (vital on an 11-director set!)	$ 500.00
Lead actors' fees (2 actors @ $400 ea.)	$ 800.00
Supporting actors (2 actors @ $200 ea.)	$ 400.00
Rental car (1 week)	$ 418.16
Location rental (3-room flat)	$ 200.00
Catering (food for cast and crew members/4 days)	$ 1,000.00
Misc. supplies (copies, batteries, snacks/water)	$ 200.00
Travel/lodging/gas (actor's travel expenses, etc.)	$ 250.00
Lab processing (6,400′ 16-mm @ .12/ft.)	$ 768.00
Prep film for Betacam SP video work print	$ 166.76
Transfer film to video (8.5 hours silent @ $185/hr.)	$ 1,572.50
Sync ¼″ sound to video (9.75 hours @ $90/hr.)	$ 877.50
Videotape stock (Betacam SP/6 90-min. @ $70 ea.)	$ 420.00
Avid editing suite (6 days/100+ hours)	$ 2,175.00
Avid editor's fee (covering his costs . . .)	$ 550.00
Original music score (9 songs)/DAT for edit	$ 500.00
VHS video dubs (20 w/rush order, 80 min. ea.)	$ 323.87
	$18,542.79*

**Sales tax on some items (filmstock, audio tape, video cassettes) brought this total closer to $19,000.*

While we're busy running lists, here's what our lighting package looked like for this August 1997 Feature Workshops shoot:

Lighting Package (16-mm/4-day shoot)*

Qty	Item	Cost
1	2K 8″ Junior @ $45/day	$ 45.00
2	1K Baby @ $35/day	$ 35.00
2	⅔ 50′ Stinger @ $3.50/day	$ 7.00
1	Doorway dolly @ $30/day	$ 30.00
3	Junior combo stand @ $6/day	$ 18.00
8	C-stand w/ gobo head and arm @ $5/day	$ 35.00
8	Assorted flags @ $3/day	$ 21.00
1	Assorted grip clips	$ 10.00
2	Cardellini clamps @ $3.50/day	$ 7.00
5	Apple boxes @ $2/day	$ 12.00
12	Sandbags @ $2.50/day	$ 30.00
1	Pidgeon plate (included)	$ 0
8	Furniture pads @ $2.50/day	$ 20.00
		$270.00

Because of our incredibly tight schedule of ten days for shooting *and* editing, most of the production and postproduction costs are higher than you'd normally encounter when working your own no-budget 16-mm feature through the system. Hopefully, in your own hometown you can barter with cast and crew members to reduce shooting costs below these figures (you help them later on *their* features!). And surely you can edit at reduced rates during off-times at your local facility or build your own editing bench or digital workstation as described in chapter 11, assembling your cut leisurely on a home computer with nonlinear editing software like Adobe Premiere, EditDV, Final Cut Pro, or . . . Eat at home instead of being catered (we needed every second on our set to shoot our feature in four days so catering was crucial!). However you pull it off, what's important is that you move forward with your dream to make movies.

**Some totals for individual rented items may represent price breaks given by the equipment facility, where they generously gave us a "one-day" price for 4 days of usage!*

Collaborating in 35-mm

If you're a person who likes to think BIG, then there's no reason why you should rule out shooting in 35-mm with a group of collaborators (or perhaps even fronting the entire budget yourself to write and direct your own feature). Here's a 35-mm shooting and editing budget made up by cinematographer/producer Alan Richter of Mission Features (*Wands of Sound*) in Santa Barbara ([805] 966-0516, **<mesafilms@aol.com>**) for our future 35-mm Feature Workshops that should be affordable to most serious filmmakers who have some sort of steady income. If you can round up eight people, each with $4,500, and pull together a good cast and crew, here's the budget for you:

35-mm Collaborative Budget (5-Day Shoot/2-Week Edit)*

Director of photography ($350/day)	$ 1,750
Soundperson ($350/day, on location)	$ 1,500
Gaffer (2½-ton grip truck/lights, $400/day)	$ 2,000
Total	$ 5,250

Panavision Camera Package	
Panaflex-X, w/follow focus, 2 batteries, cables, iris rods, sliding base plate, long & short brackets	$ 690
1,000′ magazine	$ 144
500′ magazine	$ 100
Lenses/ultra-speed (f/1.3–1.9—14-mm, 24, 35, 50, 75, 125—$48/each/wk.)	$ 228
Lenses/normal speed (f/2–2.8 $33/3 each/wk.)	$ 198
Zoom-Lens (f/3, 20-mm–120-mm)	$ 270
(Lens package will depend on filmstock chosen and locations. F/3 necessitates using more lighting.)	
Zoom control	$ 69
Follow focus cable	$ 39

**Again, some totals represent price breaks, and will be less than the sum of per-diem cost multiplied by days on the job.*

Quick release plate	$ 15
4 X 5 matte box and sunshade	$ 150
Sachtler head tripod w/spreader, hi-hat	$ 210
Filters ($30 each)	$ 120
Total (pending lens selection and filters)	$ 2,233

Filmstock

35-mm filmstock (110 min. @ 2:1 shooting ratio, 19,800′, 320T stock)	
15 rolls 1,000′ ($585/1,000′)	$ 8,775
12 rolls 400′ ($230/400′)	$ 2,760
Total	$11,535

Lab Costs

Develop normal/$.117/ft. (19,800′)	$ 2,400
One-lite daily/$.208/ft. (10,000′)	$ 2,080
Video prep	$ 90
Transfer to Betacam SP ($200/hr., 1 hr./1,080′) keycode reader encode film edge numbers, interlock ¼ audio w/time code and smart slate during transfer (keycode data system included)	$ 1,850
Total	$ 6,420

Editing/Print Costs

Avid editing (edit suite, 2 wks @ $2,000/week)	$ 4,000
Editor (2 wks @ $750/wk.)	$ 1,500
Conforming original for printing	$
Answer print (80 min., A&B roll, wetgate, 10,000′ @ $.996/ft.)	$
Sync optical track Neg ($380/10,000′)	$
Subtotal	$30,938

Contingency	$ 2,500
Travel to Panavision (from Santa Barbara, California)	$ 150
Catering (5 days)	$ 1,000
Grand Total	$34,588

Please note that the costs of conforming original, making answer print, and optical sound Neg have been left blank. This budget above will only get you to a finished cut on Betacam SP video master, laid off from your Avid computer cut.

DVCAM Movies by Collaboration

Another way to go with cost-saving collaborative film work is shooting on DVCAM digital video. Editing by home computer (recording on to DVD when it becomes economically feasible, etc.), you can turn out finished work for distribution to the video stores, the Internet, or even to theaters, if a high-quality video-to-film transfer is within your, or an interested distributor's, budget. At Feature Workshops we have had very good luck "going digital," with our April 1998 Pro-DVCAM feature, *Loneliness Is Soul* (94 min., color, copyright 1998), winning a top prize in the Main Feature Competition at Figueira da Foz International Film Festival in Portugal, against more than thirty other mostly 35-mm movies from around the world (see budget for DVCAM features in chapter 11, "Digital Video Workstations"). It was inspiring to watch our "little" movie fill the huge screen in the main theater with just VHS video projection, its sound track clean and clear, channeled through the theater's powerful sound system. I'm sure others felt the way I did—that digital moviemaking had truly "arrived."

So the collaborative process works, sometimes quite splendidly. And, of course, you don't need to go through Feature Workshops, but can arrange your own "workshop-styled" collaborative production, to save money by sharing costs and workload. Following are some chapter sections that deal with forming and maintaining your moviemaking team, keeping good cheer alive throughout the intensity of conceiving, shooting, and editing a collaborative feature.

Ten-Way Collaborative Features

If you could round up ten people like yourself, men and women who share your dream, who could afford to pay in a total of $2,500 each over the period of a year, then with that total budget of $25,000 you could become a producer/director. And it is possible that not everyone would want to be a director like yourself. They may not want to write and direct scenes, but will enjoy recording sound or shooting camera for an equal share of revenues earned up the road. Perhaps you'll find that you end up with an ideal collaborative group. From among the people you approach about making a collaborative feature, you might find a (1) cinematographer, (2) soundperson, (3) lead actor, (4) lead actress, (5) writer, (6) expert at lighting/dolly/electrical, (7) camera assistant approved of by the cinematographer, (8) set designer/costumer, (9) line producer/production manager, with yourself (10) as co-writer/director/co-producer. Each of your ten experts would pay their $2,500 share to work with you on your premise, and each would receive in return an equal percentage of ownership in the movie. If you could successfully and accurately budget your feature in 16-mm (or DVCAM) so that all costs could be covered within the $25,000 total budget, then each person working with you for the common goal would receive (like you) 10 percent ownership. This would all be spelled out in a contract similar to the one I used for my Feature Workshops (see appendix J).

This (ideal) arrangement in which you are the only person who wants to attain the status of a *movie director* may exist only as a pie in the sky, but it's worth spending a bit of time seeing if it is feasible. What you must be most cautious of is the cinematographer who actually wants to direct and other unsatisfied people who will eventually get into an ego war with you on the set. You have to be sure that each person (actor, technician, writer) is well grounded in his or her expertise and has no hidden agenda that will rock your boat. Can you be sure that nine intelligent people working *with* you, not *for* you (remember they are equal shareholders), will blindly follow your each and every command as you direct the feature? A strange thing happens when friends suddenly watch their best buddy play God, talk in an authoritative tone, order people about. After a few days, resentment starts to build up. Maybe it's subconscious, but it's still there. A simple request by you might blow the lid off. They've watched you be totally "full of yourself" for three days and they just can't take it anymore. In the normal professional world of big-budget moviemaking, you would be expected to be such a firm leader. But with your friends you will be held accountable for being something more than an equal buddy. Maybe the solution is to work entirely with strangers, so there's no baggage that can drag down the production.

What if the only people you know who are interested in making movies are your filmmaking friends or fellow film students? Can you all rise above petty concerns to pull off a collaborative feature? Is there enough glory for everyone? What if each person is a graduate student in film or video production, fully capable of doing any job, from shooting and recording sound to writing scenes and directing actors? Could this highly skilled group get together to make a collaborative feature? I would like to think so. But the overall concept of collaboration would have to be designed to accommodate the situation. Since each person in this case probably wants to direct his or her own movies, there is no way you can relegate them to other jobs (even for an equal share of the pie). Each person must be able to direct or they certainly won't join the project. What if the feature is made up of ten segments of equal length, seven and a half minutes each, for a total of seventy-five minutes? Given the fact that each 400′ roll of filmstock equals about eleven minutes of screen time, if each person directs two 400′ rolls, shoots their part of the story with a 2:1 accuracy, and edits their portion down to a prescribed length (270′ of 16-mm), then each will be a proud owner/creator of a collaborative 2,700′ (75-minute) feature-length film. As each filmmaker (film student, knowledgeable professional) directs his or her particular portion of the film, all the other directors-in-waiting fill in with the needed technical duties. Most filmmakers will want to shoot the film themselves, but I suggest sticking with *one* cinematographer, to at least keep the look of your movie consistent.

How is a ten-way collaborative feature written? If each participant wants to direct (ten directors!), then an agreement has to be reached among the interested parties regarding the basic premise. Everyone

Videographer/co-producer Morgan Schmidt-Feng frames shot on his DSR 200 Sony camera for production of *Loneliness Is Soul*. Copyright 1998 Feature Workshops.

must search for, and finally vote on, one overall concept for the film. Whoever comes up with the best idea gets an additional title in the credits ("Story by ______________"). From there each writer/director either picks a part of the story or draws straws to see what his or her contribution to the project will be. The entire group must agree on not only the basic premise but also the ideas behind each of the ten segments, so that a kind of overarching confidence can be infused into the moviemaking process. Each person has to be turned on to the entire concept in order for it to be allowed to move forward.

At every stage in the project, there must be checks and balances, ways of determining that the movie is getting done to professional standards. After the premises are discussed and one unanimously selected for production, then an outline must be written. Each of ten story sections would then be derived from the outline, with each section written as a separate treatment by each director. Again the group would read all treatments, suggest improvements in some, approve others, until everyone is solidly behind the script. In these meetings it helps if one person is elected as spokesperson, but the final authority remains equally divided among the members (fellow investors all!).

Collaborative Budget

A vital first step of your ten-way collaboration is to assure yourself and all other participants that the money for the completed feature is actually secured and available for production. Without this power to get the film done, none of the meetings will have the necessary edge. The money must be in place, deposited in a bank account. Probably the most practical thing to do is to open a business account either in the title of the motion picture you are about to make, or in a company name. If you want to make sure no one can back out after committing to the project, select a parent or accounting firm to write checks. Or pick two members of the group who must co-sign checks. Whatever you decide, make absolutely sure that the budget for the feature is available *before* you even start conceptualizing your film.

If you and your compatriots have access to film equipment (cameras, Nagras, editing gear) and can each fulfill the changing roles of technicians (soundperson, gaffer, etc.) then a small budget can accommodate either a decision to shoot color, or more black-and-white filmstock, additional locations, more actors, better all-around services. If your fellow filmmakers are skilled enough to cover (with you) the jobs of cinematographer, soundperson, and conforming of original footage into AB rolls for printing, then you can drastically reduce the budget of a "used-car" shoot, thus requiring much less than $2,500 per person for the production of a 16-mm collaborative feature. Your budget for a black-and-white feature, listed backward from hard costs of lab work, would look something like this:

Film School Budget (16-mm)*

1 80-minute liquid gate Answer print (2,880′) . .	$3,744.00
Final sound mix (film school) mag stock only . .	$ 150.00
Sound transfer (¼″ to mag) mag stock only . . .	$ 250.00
Negative cutting (done by collaborator)	$ 0
Black leader (3,000′) for conforming	$ 300.00
Work print ($.215/ft.) 5,600′ 16-mm B&W . . .	$1,204.00
Processing original footage ($.15/ft.) 5,600′ . . .	$ 840.00
14 400′ rolls Kodak 7222 B&W neg	$1,082.20
Soundperson (only need 14 rolls of ¼″ tape) . . .	$ 98.00
Salaries, 2 lead actors (fellow students)	$ 0
Titles (by computer)	$ 0
Flatbed editing (free school equipment) + tape . .	$ 22.00
Edge number 5,600′, picture and mag	$ 168.00
	$7,858.20

Dividing this budget up among the ten collaborators, it's apparent that for considerably less than $1,000 per person, a group of earnest filmmakers can produce a feature film at used-car prices if free equipment can be obtained. The project can either be divided up into a ten-way collaboration at $785.82 each, or reduced in size to a five-way collaboration at $1,571.64 per person to limit the possibilities of personality clash. And if this five-way production consisted of a committed cinematographer, producer, soundperson, writer, and director, then the people responsible for production of the film would finally follow a normal configuration. The bottom line is knowing that you can make a feature film with very little money if you have friends who share your dream.

Keep in mind that with the advent of the digital age, a budget of almost $8,000 can buy you a top DV camera ($3,000–$4,000), a computer, and nonlinear editing software. If you and your friends are prepared to forgo film and shoot on high-resolution digital video instead, your collaborative budget could buy you a production company's

**These low lab prices reflect potential "student discounts."*

Actor/writer/director Michael Bolgatz tells his real-life story against barn backdrop, for Feature Workshops '98 movie, *Maisy's Garden*. Photo by Allison Farquhar.

worth of moviemaking equipment, making subsequent features produced by the group as affordable as just the cost of Mini-DVCAM videocassettes (a couple hundred dollars at most for each movie!). Think about it.

Ten Short Stories Versus Ten Segments

To create a ten-way collaborative feature that allows everyone a chance to direct, there are basically two different ways to approach the scripting. In one case each of the ten writer/directors is responsible for producing a separate part of a central story. Either through choice or luck of the draw, each collaborator is given a particular part of the script to work on, writing approximately twelve pages that will ultimately be part of a 120-page script. This might become a difficult proposition given the multitude of writing styles and differences in attitudes toward directing, but remember that this actually happens in Hollywood! Numerous writers are hired by big-budget productions to fix an important script for which directors are hired and fired seemingly at will. I personally favor a second approach, in which each writer/director is responsible for coming up with an original short story, that will either play off of the other nine stories by virtue of using the same actors or theme, or be completely different. Even if different actors are used for entirely different stories, a certain continuity will, in fact, be conveyed in the viewing experience (see *New York Stories* by Coppola, Scorsese, and Woody Allen). And the more quirky each person's writing and directing, the more refreshing the overall result.

No matter what direction is chosen for the story or stories that make up the collaborative feature, what's important is that each participant feels a certain freedom of expression and is able to write and direct his or her segment without excessive scrutiny and criticism from others. It is important to the project as a whole that the potential for spontaneous fun and creation is maintained. And why even bother, if it won't be an enjoyable experience? The production can't be allowed to turn into an argumentative free-for-all. Each collaborator must have the ability to make a contribution without the experience becoming too much of an ordeal.

Of course, the group may find that one or two segments out of the total ten are just not up to par, and this is something that must be dealt with by the group as a whole. Will there be an allowance for some reshooting? In a worst-case scenario, when the writer/director of a particular segment thinks his or her work is great while everyone else thinks it stinks, does the group impose their value systems on the individual? Before the money starts getting spent, there must be some sort of document, signed by all participants, that states the parameters for freedom of expression versus acceptable quality.

Quality Control Agreement

If ten different people are going to try to collaborate on producing one feature-length movie, then there must be some control over the finished product in order to protect everyone's investment of time and money. But this control must still give leeway for unhindered creative work and expression. While the following provisos may not cover any and all collaborative circumstances, I hope that they will offer a direction for agreement.

(1) If an entire segment, or substantial part of one, is out of focus by mistake (as opposed to "soft-focus" for conceptual creative reasons), then those faulty areas must be reshot.

(2) If sound recorded on location is poor quality (garbled, fuzzy, out of sync, etc.), then the scenes that depend on those recordings must be reshot.

Have we stepped on any creative toes yet? Has this agreement reasonably "encouraged" the collaborator to reshoot his or her precious work? Have we in any way ignited an ego, offended one of our fellow writer/directors? Is there a way for each collaborator to take responsibility for his or her own quality control, so others don't have to shove rules down his or her throat? The minefield of hurt feelings and bruised egos must be avoided at all costs. Somehow the collaboration must keep all of its members empowered with high expectations and the ability to deliver good works.

Look again at the first two items of our agreement. Try to imagine the absolute craziest problem that could arise in the areas of either out-of-focus images or bad sound. Maybe one of the collaborators favors a type of pinhole imagery, where every shot in the segment is slightly blurry, all straight lines a bit curved with distortion. Let's also say that the collaborator has purposely recorded the dialogue in and out of sync, so that sometimes the words are in the mouths of the actors, sometimes not. The end result of this dynamic filmmaking is an eight-minute film that looks to be of poor quality, but actually delivers a strange point of view. Will all the other participants see the brilliance? The answer is yes, *if* in the early stages of writing and preproduction the filmmaker lets the other collaborators in on the filmatic goals he or she aims to achieve.

What if the poor-quality images and sound are real mistakes? What if the low quality of a particular eight-minute segment stands to pull the entire feature-length experience down with it? How will the filmmaker be informed of his or her failure? And what will be the procedure for the reshoot? Where will the extra money come from for purchasing additional filmstock, rehiring the sound recordist and cinematographer if necessary, and processing the footage? If each film school collaborator pitched in $78.58 that would equal the $785 needed to budget a redo of one segment. Each collaborator must be made aware in the contract that he or she will be responsible for doing a reshoot if his or her work does not attain professional standards as outlined. It should be a privilege, not a punishment, to be able to have a second chance at producing a segment of the feature.

Of course, if a professional soundperson and cinematographer are hired to work on all the segments, along with each of ten writer/directors, it should be obvious from the images and sound on the first eight-minute segment whether the level of quality is suitable. All collaborators must see the first dailies, screen the synced-up footage, and then vote unanimously either to continue with the technicians or to hire new ones.

The key to quality control is *communication.* While the contract will state in plain language the agreed-upon rules for the group ordering up a reshoot, the best protection against future problems is if at every stage of production every member of the group is familiarized with everyone else's work. These "checkpoints" should occur at the obvious intervals of (1) story concept, (2) treatment, (3) script, (4) shooting schedule. If each of the ten collaborators reads all the other existing story lines—treatments running a couple of pages of description—and, later, eight-to-ten pages of scripting, then not only will they all have confidence in the abilities of their fellow collaborators, but each collaborator's own contribution will be positively affected by all the other segments. Some small kernel of consciousness from each person's contribution will have a way of influencing the total work, somehow making it speak with a more unified voice.

Writing/Directing en Masse

If your particular Feature Workshop uses the simplest structure for creating a ten-way collaborative film, that probably means that the same actors will be used in each eight-minute segment. It also means that the same technicians will shoot and record sound for all the separate parts of the film. And if the technicians are recruited from the group of ten collaborators, that means that not only will the cinematographer and soundperson help shoot and record sound on everyone else's segment, but he or she will also shoot and record sound on his or her own part. The stabilizing influence of using the same people for these jobs throughout the production is probably the most desirable control of quality.

The shoot should also be organized in the simplest and most direct fashion. If the ten stories have been designed to build into an overarching structure with a beginning, middle, and end, then it will probably be to the advantage of the project to shoot the segments in order, giving the actors a chance to develop their characters naturally. Shooting in order will also help to protect the performances from the intervention of ten different directors. The actors will be better able to have a hand in navigating themselves along, instead of depending solely on the input of each director.

If the shoot is scheduled to take place over a ten-day period, then each writer/director is expected to accomplish his or her work in just one day. A list should be drawn up showing which director is responsible for which day. Once the shoot begins, the process of group effort will in a way resemble the handing off of the baton in a marathon relay race. Goodwill and best wishes will accompany each new director as he or she takes up the cause and leaps into the fray. It will be all for one and one for all. Because everyone depends on the good work of each of the other participants, petty jealousy and envy will be put aside. Any competitiveness, usually harmful in such situations, can only help in this case as each person tries to outdo the other collaborators in creating the best segment that he or she possibly can. Think of the wonderful energy when Carreras, Domingo, and Pavarotti, the three greatest tenors in the world, appeared together on TV for the first time at the Baths of Caracalla in Rome. After each singer completed a song, he would retreat to the dressing room at the rear of the huge stage, giving a hearty "high-five" hand slap to the next fellow tenor. These three tenors put aside their normal competitive feelings and worked hard to give one of the greatest single operatic concerts of our time. That's how you want it to be for your collaborative project.

Morgan Schmidt-Feng watches video monitor of lightweight Fly-Cam mini-crane, framing shot transmitted by its tiny 3-chip video camera (available at <**video@odonata.com**>).

Auteur Theory Debris

There are people who will say that to make a good or great work of cinema with such a ten-way collaboration (ten voices!) is impossible. They will throw the "auteur theory" in your face, stating precepts and postulates about how only one singular vision can enact a work of high art. Of course, they are right to a certain extent. A movie will certainly be much better if the ideas of the writer/director are not diluted by factors of annoyance and interference, the kind of power plays that occur on almost every Hollywood set. An artist must be able to express himself or herself in an intuitive way, with the freedom to make creative choices without compromising. These decisions must be made with joy, introspection, and acute observations. To be an "author" of an artwork is an honor and a privilege, something almost sacred. Aren't you just a bit curious about what a feature made by ten committed artists with a common story thread or theme to hold it together would be like? Does this in any way dilute the "auteur theory"? In a grand way this kind of true collaboration, where each person delivers a personal vision to the screen, only reinforces what the auteur concept is all about. Ideally, a collaboration of several personal visions can deliver an experience of earthshaking proportions (see *Hoop Dreams*, by Steve James, Peter Gilbert, and Fred Marx). It can certainly be a celebration of the power of art. How could that much humanity be denied?

Editing by Segments/Cinematic Jazz

Probably the biggest threat to a cohesive, unified movie made by a Feature Workshop group would be having ten different cuts from ten different directors. Of course, if the collaborative feature is made up of short stories, each different in concept and execution, different editing styles won't distract the viewer. In fact, the audience for that film would relish the various cinematic approaches to the segments. The main threat to the quality of a feature-length movie constructed of different short stories would be a lack of precision in some cuts. If one of the ten directors failed to come up with the tightest cut for the material, allowed extra beats in the pacing, and killed the performances with clumsy intercutting (basically was inept as an editor), then the entire project would suffer. So perhaps the solution here is to again assign *one* person as editor, as we have been fortunate to do at Feature Workshops.

A movie is nothing until it's cut. Only editing can infuse magic into a loose collection of shots. Even the worst flick you've ever seen probably contained at least some of this editorial magic. On a basic level, most motion pictures can convince the viewer that when the two main characters are talking together, and one is seen on the screen at a time, they are in the same room. This, of course, is rarely the case, since often each actor's lines are delivered to a point off-camera, without the second actor present. But the magic of cutting, first to one speaker, then another, allows the audience to put the conversation together in their minds. And in that most simple task of editing a two-way conversation, there is almost an endless number of variables for the cut. The director may decide to have each speaker complete his or her statement each time before cutting over to the other person (as in *My Dinner with Andre*, where monologues were long takes, giving the audience ample time to absorb each actor's personality). Or maybe the director will enact a more "modern" cut, hardly ever letting a character finish a complete sentence without clipping the last few words with a cut to the listener. This type of "distractive" editing tries to convince the viewer that what is being said is, in some way, important, even though usually it just isn't. In fact many movies depend totally on convincing the audience that what they happen to be watching is entertaining, a sleight of hand accomplished by the frenetic pace of the cuts. Hopefully, none of the ten directors in your collaboration will have to resort to such contrived editorial manipulations, as they work with the editor to tighten their segment.

If a moviemaker gets in touch with his or her creative powers, then something called "cinematic jazz" can occur. In that state of creative grace, every intuitive decision is correct, all the elements of the movie are somehow able to manifest a unity of images and sounds, ideas and emotions, that results in a profound experience for an audience. It is as if the "hand of God" has intervened; some supernatural, omnipresent force has guided the artist to accomplish a feat of creation beyond the powers of mere mortal human beings. How could a person conceive, write, shoot, and edit such a diverse body of ideas and emotions into a perfect whole? How could he or she achieve the perfect cut?

Consensus (or Not)/Final Cut

Each person is born with tastes and attitudes. Somehow we just know when something is right and when it's not. In editing, you may have a hunch that more energy and clarity can be derived from "the cut," while your best friend thinks it's great as is. When someone else would have stopped editing and gotten the movie printed or transferred to DVD), you continue on in the editing room, spending perhaps another year in search of the cut that helps transform the material. How can an eager group of collaborators tolerate your additional editing time? How can they wait the extra year your sensibilities require? And how difficult will it be to try and ferret out the best cut possible when your fellow collaborators insist upon completing the film by an arbitrarily imposed deadline?

A "Completion Agreement" can be drawn up that includes a deadline date by which the film must be completed. If that date is reasonable, giving the writer/directors six months after the shoot to complete editing on each segment of the feature, with leeway for a six-month extension if absolutely necessary, then major fisticuffs can be avoided. And since many participants of a Feature Workshop are probably trying to make a first feature, it is imperative to the success of the venture that everyone understands that the creative process can't be kept neatly in a bottle. There needs to be ample time to work out the problems associated with attempting a ten-way collaboration. Certainly, each participant must possess a good degree of patience and kindness toward the creative antics of others. If all goes well, one and a half years from the inaugural meeting with your collaborators you will be sitting in a theater watching all your and their good work hit the screen.

Promotion Power/Pulling Strings

As soon as your collaborative feature is completed and all your partners are delighted with the results, thoughts will quickly turn to promotion. Which festivals must be entered before what upcoming deadlines? Will you submit your completed movie to the Independent Feature Film Market in New York (September)? Of course, a good-quality video copy will be essential to get your movie seen; the cost is usually around $700 for transfer from 16-mm film to Beta SP and ten dubs to VHS. Even if your group is broke, having spent every dime on the production, it will still be necessary to come up with this transfer cost. And following that will be the costs of packaging and mailing VHS cassettes to festivals (application fees!), TV buyers, and showcases for future shows and sales. Most likely, members of your collaborative team will be able to pull a couple of hundred more dollars from someplace (piggy bank, MasterCard, etc.) to back up a feature they are proud to have created.

Also, it's possible that a few of your moviemaking partners will have connections you only hear about now that the movie is looking good and being praised by others. Maybe someone in your group has an uncle who owns a cineplex. Another person's father works in TV, film distribution, or designs Websites. Maybe someone's dad is in advertising. From ten collaborators may come some very surprising leads. Hopefully, the cooperative power of the group will get your masterpiece out into the world, maybe even earning back all the investments!

Whatever money does come back from shows, film festival prizes, TV sales, etc., must be divided up equally among all the members as soon as the check(s) clear. You will not want to conduct business the way it's done in the real world of distribution, where payments are made to the producers on a quarterly basis, after large deductions have been taken for "operating expenses." All members of the collaborative team (along with any actors and technicians promised profit points in the production) must be paid fairly out of the gross profits, quickly and efficiently.

If you want to know the complete score on your feature (film or video), you will enter it in every festival in which you may have a chance of acceptance. Only when you have in your hand a fistful of rejection letters, along with some acceptance notices, can you be absolutely sure that you haven't sunk your own chances for success by faulty promotional thinking. Dub 100 VHS tapes at a time, considerably lowering your per unit cost (see "Video Copies for Promotion," chapter 7). Get those tapes into the mail (UPS, FedEx when appropriate), along with film festival fees (certain festivals will require fees to help with their operating costs, so just pay the small amounts with a minimum of grumbling—try to remain positive!), and wait for the results. Don't let the first few rejections throw you and your collaborators into a funk. Keep trying. Your movie will only be a current feature for the first year after it comes out. Most festivals *only* want current, cutting-edge features completed in the last twelve months, so make sure you don't let yourself down. Don't become your own worst enemy. Be thorough. Follow through. Explain to your fellow collaborators that it can sometimes take as long as four years after a film is released before it sells to TV (U.S. or Europe), even when there is initial interest.

As you navigate the unpredictable waters of promotion and distribution, keep in mind that you and your fellow collaborators have done the impossible: turned the mysterious, expensive process of writing and directing a feature-length movie into an affordable experience. No rejection letter from a narrow-minded film festival can take that accomplishment away. If you are as persistent as you needed to be just to complete your collaborative feature, you will surely enjoy the benefits of your promotional efforts.

10

Shooting in Analog Video

Although for a while I considered removing this chapter completely from this new edition, figuring I'd just upgrade it into the following chapter on DV (digital video), it has occurred to me from e-mail correspondence with beginning filmmakers that not everyone can afford the latest cutting-edge DVCAM products. The few times that I've recommended that someone shoot in DVCAM (over film) to kick-start their feature filmmaking career, I've been surprised to hear back that "all I've got is Dad's camcorder." My immediate response has been, "Grab that [whatever video camera is currently available—especially for free], and go out and MAKE A MOVIE!" Filmmaker/actor Evan Jacobs did just that recently, using a Hi-8 to make a movie entitled *Curse of Instinct—108's Final Tour* (<**www.b-movie.com/jacobs/jacobs.html**>). His documentary covers the final days of the New York–based Hare Krishna band "108," their alternative lifestyle, unusual philosophy, and spiritualism, and gives the viewer the experience of being inside a subculture (plus it entertains us with great live performances of their songs "Deathbed," "Opposition," "Killer of the Soul," "Thirst," etc.). Jacobs didn't sit around waiting for funding or DV equipment, and he was happily rewarded when his movie became one of only seventeen selected by the Park City Sundance-alternate NO DANCE festival (<**www.nodance.com**>) in 1999, and won a Golden Orbs award.

The point is that no one ever became an accomplished feature moviemaker without practice, and video (with cheap videotape or cassettes) offers an excellent way to put your ideas about storytelling with images and sound into action. Videotape is affordable and reusable, though I recommend that tape be shot only *once,* each cassette carefully labeled and archived, to remind yourself that you're shooting carefully and for keeps, and that every shot *could be* important to the edit of your movie. Give yourself enough professional respect to believe that what you're doing is just as important as anything done by Hollywood or the indie film community.

Since the DV revolution will surely render other nondigital video formats less desirable, that translates to lower prices for rentals, great bargains for used equipment, and more opportunities in general for new filmmakers getting their hands on older top-of-the-line video cameras, decks, and editing facilities. Here's a look at what video equipment might be available in your community (or in Mom's closet!).

Selecting the Right Video Format

Surely by now most people have heard of VHS, Hi-8, and even ¾" video formats. At one time or another all these formats were considered viable means of recording video for playback. In millions of homes sit these old VHS camcorders and Hi-8s, bought to record that trip to Europe or Little League games. The batteries are dead, the lenses dusty, but these cameras can be brought back to life to serve the beginning filmmaker who has a vision. And while most of these older home-video formats are not "broadcast quality," nowhere near as sharp in resolution as the mini-DV or DVCAM digital cameras, they can still be used to make a movie with good, clear images and clean sound. If there is a Radio Shack near your house, you can order new batteries for that Hi-8 and perhaps even get a deal on a box of cassettes.

Some future feature filmmakers will find themselves becoming overly concerned by the technical end of moviemaking with video, worried about the "graininess of transfer to film" from these "inferior" formats, thinking negatively before they even attempt to shoot a scene. Well, fair enough. You want to be professional from the start and have "the best" equipment, best editing facility, and best result. But sometimes a little grain brings some expected drama to your movie. A movie called *The Celebration* was shot by Thomas Vinterberg following his Dogme 95 doctrine of moviemaking (see chapter 11), and regardless of it being one of the grainiest movies I've ever seen on the silver screen, it's one of the best! *The Celebration* has won numerous honors (Cannes gave it a top award), shown everywhere (New York Film Festival, etc.), earned a ton of money in its theatrical run, and is now in your video store. And it was shot with a "consumer" grade (not "professional") Sony PC-7E Mini-DV camera! Rent it. When that movie is finished with you, you'll know without a doubt that "content" rules.

If you have to rent equipment because no video camera sits in your closet, the prices for rental of these "amateur" formats is much less than for broadcast outfits. A camera in VHS rents for approximately $50 a day ($150 a week) and Hi-8 rents for around $65 a day ($200 a week). Shooting in either of these older formats saves you hundreds of dollars on the initial camera rental, money which you might consider using to transfer your video to film or DVD as a final result (see chapter 11 for various companies and rates of current video-to-film transfers).

I began my feature *Morgan's Cake* by borrowing a Hi-8 video camera and shooting some on-the-street interviews and scripted scenes with my son Morgan (age seventeen at the time). Because I was still in debt to the lab for *Emerald Cities* print costs, the only way that I could at least get my mind on a new project was by scraping up $12 for a Hi-8 cassette and just beginning. For my first shot I convinced three high school guys to sit in a Chinese restaurant and talk to the camera lens as if it were Morgan, giving him their advice about registering for the draft. Even though I shot in a very-low-light situation (neon lights on the restaurant's ceiling), a one-minute test showed that Hi-8 transferred to 16-mm film with excellent picture and sound quality. I also shot several interviews with street people (a stoned hippie, a hustler) talking to Morgan (the camera's eye) about the draft, and I was very impressed by the fine-grain resolution and clean sound track. By then I had purchased a mike and a microphone extension arm (cost $90) that held it off the camera body, insuring that I wouldn't pick up extra camera noise from a squeaky cassette.

At most high-quality video-to-film transfer facilities, you can choose between either transferring your video directly to a finished 16-mm print with optical sound, or transferring it to a "double system" that provides you with an original picture roll, work print, and sync mag track for editing. The most economical transfer you could make would be going directly to the 16-mm answer print from your final cut on video, but this process would not supply you with an original needed to make additional prints from your AB rolls. At this point you would have to ask yourself why you didn't just shoot it in film in the first place.

Lighting for Video

Whether you are producing a feature-length video as an end product, or shooting "amateur format" video that will be transferred to 16-mm film, it is important that you use enough lights to insure that your video camera will record the strongest image possible. Video cameras "like" light, and even with broadcast cameras, which can successfully record in very-low-light situations, lights are a production necessity for giving your images commercial "snap." Since what you see on your video monitor during taping is "what you get," examine your image for a well-defined sharpness and bright quality. Ask the people at your rental agency which lights they would recommend, and ask any other questions that will help to insure a successful videotaping.

I must add that when I shot my first few video movies, I used only available lighting sources, taping with only the natural light flooding into a room, or the illumination of a single lightbulb. And although the videotape-to-16-mm transfer appeared grainy and dark at times on the final black-and-white film product, for the most part the mood created by the low-light situations actually enhanced the concept of my work. The important thing is to decide what "look" you are trying to achieve and then use all means necessary, within the used-car budget, to achieve this end.

Actually, one of the hottest software plug-ins for Adobe After Effects (see chapter 11) is something called Cinelook from DigiEffects (818 Monterey Boulevard, San Francisco, CA 94127, [415] 841-9901, <www.digieffects.com>), that allows the filmmaker editing on computer to *add* grain, dirt, scratches, hair and dust to video, so it reads like damaged film. Cinelook offers fifty different preprogrammed stock settings for attaining an authentic "film look." And their companion product, Cinemotion, is a digital video plug-in for manipulating moving sequences, so that you can use footage from Beta SP, DV, SVHS, or Hi-8 with Adobe After Effects to simulate a true telecine video-to-film transfer sensation (this software also includes a plug-in to "letterbox" your movie for creating that wide-screen 16:9 viewing ratio!). You may be ahead of the game shooting with older video cameras that already deliver a desirable grainy image texture.

Shooting and Directing in Video

One of the most tragic mistakes made in shooting video is that with the knowledge that shots can be forever retaped, all the intense focus that accompanied the limitation of one-to-one film shooting on no-budget movies is forgotten. Shots that should have been recorded in one minute are taped in ten. Everything seems worth taping, piling up a maze of loosely constructed video that will be exceedingly difficult to edit when the time comes. My major recommendation in this section is to shoot your video one-to-one, only repeating a take when a major problem has been identified. The pressure of this frugal approach will hopefully force you to tighten your grip on the concept of your production.

Directing actors for your video feature is basically no different than for a film production. And once you have impressed upon the actors that you don't plan to tape constant retakes just because video is reusable, you should be able to encourage the same dynamic performances as you would have for any film shoot. One advantage of using video is that you can tape a performance continuously for an hour or longer instead of the eleven minutes offered by a 400′ roll of 16-mm film. To direct a quality video feature, it's really necessary to apply the same sharpness of purpose, the same intensity, as would be needed for a similar film production.

Saving Costs on Video Editing

If you have shot a complex video feature that requires hundreds of hours of editing to complete, it is obvious that you must find an alternative to paying the $20 or $30 per hour fee that many facilities charge for their postproduction suites. Fortunately, in most large cities there are now numerous nonprofit video facilities offering discounted rates that will help you finish your project. In the San Francisco/Oakland area the Film Arts Foundation ([415] 552-6350) offers VHS editing at $45 for a five-hour shift (nine hours for the same price, if you can work graveyard shift of midnight to 9:00 A.M.). If you look hard in your area you may find even cheaper facilities. In New York City, The Media Loft ([212] 924-4893) offers VHS editing at $20 an hour ($40 an hour with technician). If you know you will be editing for over fifty hours, video facilities such as Video Free America in San Francisco ([415] 648-9040) may offer a special package rate that should save considerable editing cost.

Another good solution for editing may be to make dubs off your original video masters and assemble the scenes at home on a two-VCR system. You should be able to buy two used VHS VCRs for around $100 at garage sales. By hooking into your TV as a monitor (if proper connections exist) you could watch your footage, assembling and reassembling the scenes until the rough cut was complete. If you had originally shot your video feature with Betacam SP, then your videotapes would have time code numbers that would allow a technician to match your original taped scenes to the order of your edited "window" dubs, just as we matched our original 16-mm footage to the edited work print using latent edge numbers. Of course with powerful computer prices dropping, and editing software such as Avid Cinema easily affordable (around $150), there's no excuse not to link your filmmaking dreams up to the digital revolution (see chapter 11).

Promoting and Selling Your Video Feature

Once you have completed your video feature, and have made high-quality dubs in several video formats, you will want to enter video festivals and contests in the United States and Europe. In the last few years there has been a great increase of interest in independent video, with many major film festivals offering special programs celebrating video art and sometimes even streaming their video selections on the Web. And many major museums, such as the Whitney Museum in New York City, now present ongoing video programs featuring in-person shows. With the recent improvement of video projectors, there are now many more avenues for video presentations, including many video clubs in Europe and the United States. Videomaker Joe Rees, of Target Video in San Francisco, was one of the first video artists to take his show on the road, traveling with his punk-music tapes and high-quality video projection system to numerous video clubs in Europe for sold-out performances. While many major film festivals accept video works for consideration as part of their programming, the best way for a videomaker to secure a current listing of appropriate festivals and contests for his or her work is to jump on the WWW and type "video festivals" into a search engine slot.

The main point is that you've broken the ice with video, actually made a feature-length movie with actors, locations, dialogue, music, cuts, and titles. You have a chance to analyze just how well you did by seeing the results shown on your home TV screen, or perhaps even projected at a film festival. Now your moviemaking career (which you may never have imagined happening) has begun, and you can soon apply your experience to movie #2. Maybe your next video production will have the advantage of using some of the powerful DV tools that are now available.

11 Digital Video Workstations

Certainly one of the main reasons for revising my book was to write this additional chapter on the use of new DV formats for shooting feature-length movies and to introduce various computer-editing software systems. DV, in case you haven't heard, is the digital video format now used in cameras, recording decks, and playback units produced by a variety of more than 100 companies. In short, DV has revolutionized the recording of images and sound electronically, so that you and I, with much greater ease and lower cost, can simply go out and shoot a broadcast-quality movie. And since the images and sound recorded on DV exist as "digital information," they can be edited by computer and output without *any* loss of resolution or fidelity. For someone like me, who began his filmmaking career by using an early Sony portapack ½″ video camera and backpack deck for shooting black-and-white images of low-res density, shooting DVCAM features of jewel-like resolution, with color and "grain" that resembles the fidelity of 16-mm film, is a real shocker. Yes . . . video that looks like top-end film! That's why the DV format deserves attention beyond the previous "video" chapter.

In 1998 I entered one of my favorite Feature Workshop "ten-day" movies, *Loneliness Is Soul*, at the Figueira da Foz International Film Festival in Portugal, and was delighted when I heard by fax that it was accepted. It was exciting to learn that in September I would be returning to that coastal resort town, a couple of hundred miles north of Lisbon, for an all-expenses-paid week. To make sure that I would be presenting the best-quality digital video feature possible, I carried along the ninety-four-minute Betacam SP "submaster" copy made off the master Betacam SP original tape, the direct output from our Avid computer edit. But upon arriving at the festival after about seven hours of train rides, and reading the program notes for our movie in the main theater lobby, it quickly became apparent that they had somehow come to believe that our top-quality VHS represented a *film*, not a DV movie. Our feature was listed to screen in the "Main Feature Competition," with thirty or so other mostly 35-mm features from around the world! In my submission letter I had clearly written that the enclosed VHS represented "a digital video Pro-DVCAM movie," but because of the superior image quality, well-lit scenes, and clean, clear sound track, it had easily been mistaken for a movie shot on film.

While privately delighted that our little video movie had registered such a high level of technical (and artistic) respect, I panicked a bit, obviously worried that there was no way our electronic feature could be shown properly in the large main theater. So I offered $500 (more credit card abuse) to the festival if they could come up with a Betacam SP deck and video projection system. They couldn't. On a Monday night, at the perfect screening time of around 9:00 P.M., they wheeled their little VHS video projection cart into the middle aisle, about ten rows back, hooked up sound through the main speakers, and projected *Loneliness Is Soul* on their huge screen. I was amazed by the quality of picture and sound. With the 1:85 aspect ratio we had designed into our shots and letterboxed while editing on Avid, the image actually fit their large Cinerama-sized screen. Our luck at having such a great image was due primarily to the fact that before our movie was projected they had run another video, a fascinating documentary entitled *The Unholy Tarahumara*, by Kathryn Ferguson of Tucson, Arizona, who was bound and determined to adjust the video projector so that her movie (about a tribe of Mexican Indians losing their ancient ways of living) would be at its best. So I had been the lucky recipient of a well-tweaked system. As a result, our no-budget collaborative movie with seven writer/directors responsible for its creation (*A "Film" By*: James J. Coakley, Hal Croasmun, Morgan Schmidt-Feng, Alexander Marchand, Michael Rogers, yahn soon, and Rick Schmidt) was awarded a top prize by the international jury, convincing me and others that DV had certainly come of age.

In the chapter ahead I look forward to explaining what DV cameras are available at affordable prices, along with some low-cost nonlinear digital editing options for home computers, using your DV camera as a playback unit for digital capture via a FireWire. I'll also examine affordable computer platforms best suited for editing DVCAM, and help you build a fully configured digital workstation right in your home, with camera, sound mixer and mikes, small lighting kit, computer and editing software. Most importantly, I hope to convince you that shooting on DV is not a poor second to shooting on (expensive) film. For the filmmaker who wants to shoot more than one feature-length movie in his or her lifetime, I offer hope that you can actually forge a career as an "e-feature filmmaker" and continue making creative and original electronic feature-length works for just the cost of DV tapestock (nine hours for $150) once you attain access to the basic digital equipment.

DV Websites

Perhaps your first foray into the realm of DV should include browsing a few of the main Websites, where you can get an up-to-the-minute sense of what new products are available, and learn where the movement is going. Everything is changing so fast that you need to get a current read on the choices for computer platforms (Mac, PC), editing software, cameras, and distribution outlets. One of the best Websites I've found to get an overall picture of the emerging DV scene is Maxie Collier's DV Filmmaker Report, **<www.dvfilmmaker.com>**, a real labor of love that he created with no money by teaching himself Web design. He generously points out that he used Netscape Composer, **<www.netscape.com>**, to design his site, and created banners with **<www.bannermaker.com>**. And he also used **<www.animationonline.com>** for design elements, and linked to **<www.hotmail.com>** for free e-mail.

His site also offers numerous DV links, reviews and articles on recent movies, plus a free listing for your DV movie (with a built-in link, sending Web traffic directly back to your movie's site), and a message board for DV moviemakers to discuss problems and network. You'll also find information on the latest DV hardware and software, ads for discounted equipment, everything you need to get started in this new medium.

Collier will e-mail you a free weekly report on everything happening on the DV scene, as well as offering *The DV Filmmaker's Handbook* for sale at a reasonable cost of $29.95. Just leave your e-mail address at his sign-in subscription slot (he also plugs **<www.greenspun.com>**, a company that manages his 100+ flood of daily e-mails).

<www.dvcentral.org> is another great Website for familiarizing yourself with DV and researching precisely which hardware and software to buy or lease. This site offers lots of information about cutting-edge DV companies, reviews of various software editing systems, and has numerous links to keep you informed. You'll soon discover that some companies offer you the complete package—DV camera, editing software, and computer platform, everything already configured for maximum compatibility at relatively low cost. Promax, **<www.promax.com>**, has good deals on bundled Adobe Premiere (or Apple's Final Cut Pro) editing software and G-4 Macintosh computer packages for around $4,000. Their top package includes a Sony or Canon DV camera, recording and playback deck, small playback TV, plus computer with editing software, if you have around $12,000 to spend (click on their site for the latest upgrades and discounted prices).

If you favor using a Windows NT computer platform, then Truevision, **<www.truevision.com>**, from Pinacle Systems offers a ready-to-edit turnkey system for Avid's Xpress editing program, on an IBM Intellistation workstation, including their Truevision Pro-Targa board for video capture and playback at Betacam SP broadcast resolution, for around $9,000 (check their Website for current prices and upgrades).

When you buy a compatible turnkey system, you save yourself a lot of headaches (frozen memory, computer bugs . . .), and I recommend that route if you're basically computer-illiterate as I am! (Check in current magazines, like DV, **<www.dv.com>**, and on the Web for the most recent configured systems containing camera, computers, and software, and their slashed prices for 2000!)

Before I begin to examine the array of DV cameras and editing systems discussed ahead, I'd first like to talk about a group of very committed DV filmmakers, operating as "Dogme 95," who have recently had a tremendous artistic and commercial impact on world cinema. Their amazing DV features, for which they have received rave reviews and prizes from all over the world (their movies are transferred to 35-mm film for presentation at the top film festivals like Cannes, New York, etc.), derive from a well-formulated artistic manifesto, which helps keep their creative priorities straight and uncorrupted in a world of rampant commerciality.

Dogme 95

Every so often a movement comes along that catches the imagination, and for those DV minimalists and purists who are disturbed by current trends of overproduction, Dogme 95 might just be the ticket for you. Keep in mind while reading the following "Vow of Chastity" that such high-profile video movies as *The Idiot* by Lars von Trier (*Breaking the Waves*), and Thomas Vinterberg's *The Celebration* (shot on mini-DVCAM), sprang to life from these strict filmmaking rules (Soren Kragh Jacobsen and Kristian Levring are the other founding members of Dogme 95).

The Vow of Chastity

I swear to submit to the following set of rules drawn up and confirmed by DOGME 95:

1. Shooting must be done on location. Props and sets must not be brought in. (If a particular prop is necessary for the story, a location must be chosen where this prop is to be found.)

2. The sound must never be produced apart from the images or vice versa. (Music must not be used unless it occurs where the scene is being shot.)

3. The camera must be hand-held. Any movement or immobility attainable in the hand is permitted. (The

film must not take place where the camera is standing; shooting must take place where the film takes place.)

4. The film must be in color. Special lighting is not acceptable. (If there is too little light for exposure, the scene must be cut or a single lamp be attached to the camera.)

5. Optical work and filters are forbidden.

6. The film must not contain superficial action. (Murders, weapons, etc. must not occur.)

7. Temporal and geographical alienation are forbidden. (That is to say that the film takes place here and now.)

8. Genre movies are not acceptable.

9. The film format must be Academy 35-mm.

10. The director must not be credited.

Furthermore, I swear as a director to refrain from personal taste! I am no longer an artist. I swear to refrain from creating a "work," as I regard the instant as more important than the whole. My supreme goal is to force the truth out of my characters and settings. I swear to do so by all the means available and at the cost of any good taste and any aesthetic considerations.

Thus, I make my VOW OF CHASTITY:

NAME

DATE

While I still relish the freedom to shoot film in B&W (or decolorized video), and occasionally like to import a prop to a set, there's a refreshing "housecleaning" element of this list of dos and don'ts. As a proponent of "Reality Filmmaking"—putting the real before the artifice of script, plot, or story—I can certainly embrace the essence of Dogme 95.

Do we really need to see another movie about murder, showing people killing each other? Thank God, they've forbidden that tired subject matter. And low-budget filmmakers have for decades been recording sync-sound on location, using those tracks as the *only* source of sound for their movies (I've never done it any other way!). So why use dubbing unless you're making an animated movie like *A Bug's Life*? I also find it very positive to consider leaving the director's name off the movie, since it prompts the filmmaker to reexamine his or her basic intent of purpose. If you're doing movies just to become "famous," the absence of your name in the credits will certainly rectify that aberration. Also, by making "genre movies" unacceptable, the founders of Dogme 95 protect themselves from falling into the trap of blatant commercialism, insisting instead that the focus be placed on meaningful content and personal discovery. Because these Danish moviemakers have used cheap consumer-grade digital video to make their personal features, *and* have been successful at the box office, they have almost single-handedly transformed the definition of what's "commercial" or "distributable" within the ranks of the theatrical motion picture industry. Thank you! (Type "Dogme 95" into any search engine slot on your computer to pull up several Internet sites for updates on their latest DV movies.)

At any rate, if you have some real-life drama taking place around your life and are willing to shoot in color video, going right for the truth within the strict guidelines of Dogme 95, then sign and date your Vow of Chastity right here in the book, and START MAKING MOVIES!

Canon's XL1 with interchangeable lenses and a super-lightweight body (just six pounds)—the "progressive scan" camera of choice for filmmakers. Photo courtesy Canon Inc.

JVC Professional GY-DV500U 3-CCD camera (**<www.jvc.com/pro>**), fully loaded with interchangeable lenses, XRL microphone inputs, FireWire, SMPTE timecode generation, and 750 lines of resolution to Mini-DV (under $5000!).

DVCAM Cameras

Canon

Perhaps one of the most earthshaking developments of recent years within the DV community has been the creation of the Canon XL1 3CCD Mini-DV Digital Video camcorder with 16X changeable lens and optical stabilization (<**www.canondv.com**>). Not only does this camera look great from a filmmaker's point of view (something super-appealing about this design . . .), but it also records images superbly. Like many other DV cameras, the Canon XL1 delivers a fabulous image even in low-light situations (Canon advertises that their pixel size of 72 square microns is 150 percent larger than the pixel size on comparable models, which they say accounts for an overall improvement of 4db in sensitivity (go measure pixels on other cameras if you're a comparison shopper). For most filmmakers the attraction to the Canon SL1 begins with the familiar option to replace lenses for varied situations, as they would have done with film cameras. This gives the user the ability to shift between a potential focal range of 24 to 2,160 mm. But the camera is much lighter than most film cameras, weighing in at around six and a half pounds. Another great advantage is that the camera offers simultaneous audio recording on four channels (that can be set on different levels of quality, from 16 bit to 12 bit), and output separately as well (most cameras only have two-channel availability).

Another impressive feature of the Canon XL1 is that it offers a "drop-frame" system that is extremely accurate for editing. Since it actually records images in frames like a film camera (in "progressive scan," at thirty frames per second), an editor can have confidence that he or she is selecting an accurate in or out point when making a cut. Other cameras use an interlacing frame pattern, which certainly works for production, but doesn't feel as film-accurate. For those with less money to spend, most any Mini-DVCAM camera will deliver the superior image, but if you are planning to edit by computer with any sophisticated precision, you'll need a camera like the Canon XL1 that can (1) deliver dependable time code that precisely identifies each recorded frame, (2) has the proper chip technology to be operated by

Sony's DCR-VX1000 Mini-DV, the lightweight, high-resolution video camera that started the e-film revolution. Photo courtesy Sony Corporation.

the keyboard of a computer so camera can be used as a playback machine for sending images to the computer for "capture," and (3) offers changeable shutter speeds for recording at 1/60 and up (1/60 is said to be the best setting for potential 35-mm film transfers). At any rate this camera really delivers, and for an affordable price of around $4,000.

Sony

In the last year there have been several upgrades in Pro-DVCAM cameras, with Sony dropping prices while raising quality. Since we shot *Loneliness Is Soul* (1998) using my son Morgan's Sony DSR 200 "3 chip" Pro-DVCAM camera, Sony has come out with the Professional DSR 300 at similar cost (around $7,500). Sony literature explains that it offers "superior picture quality by adopting 10-bit Digital Signal Processing, three Power HAD CCDs (sensors which result in high sensitivity, low smear level, high signal-to-noise ratio of 62 db and a high horizontal resolution of 800 TV lines), and high quality DVCAM recording." With its new TruEYE feature (virtually eliminating hue distortion), DynaLatitude (managing the contrast of each pixel), and Skin Detail (giving the subject a more pleasing facial complexion so

Sony's new, cutting-edge DSR-PD100A Mini-DV camera, with two scanning modes, progressive scan (for still), and interlaced (video), PCMCIA "stick" digital still storage, directional microphone, and a fold-out viewing screen. Photo courtesy Sony Corporation.

that his or her face remains brighter and holds better contrast levels when shot in a car or in shady settings, etc.), a better-quality image can be obtained under more difficult shooting situations.

Of course for those filmmakers who want a cheaper deal, Sony's broadcast-quality VX1000 DVCAM camera offers the moviemaking dream for a price of around $3,500. It's small, lightweight, affordable, and delivers a fantastic image. And their new DSR-PD100A Mini-DV camera, in the price range of $3,000, offers an enormous range of professional DV capabilities in a compact frame. Visit their Website for their latest breakthroughs in DV technology, **<www.sony.com/professional>**, or a Sony dealer near you.

Panasonic's AG-EZ30U Mini-DV, 7 7/16″ long and weighing only .39 pounds (world's smallest 3-CCD camera). Photo courtesy Panasonic Corporation.

Panasonic

Panasonic also offers an array of new DV cameras, including the ultra-compact AG-EZ30U mini-DV, weighing only about a half pound, the lightest and smallest 3-CCD camcorder on the market. This small camera offers a built-in SMPTE time code generator, and a 4-pin IEEE 1394 "FireWire" interface for transmission to either another DV camcorder or 1394-equipped personal computer. It can record up to sixty minutes, produces 460 lines of horizontal resolution viewable on an onboard color LCD monitor, and features four channels of 16-bit digital PCM sound. The AG-EZ30U also offers a zebra-level indicator (usually only found in high-end cameras) that allows the operator to determine the optimum image exposure for top-quality visuals. And, most importantly, it is equipped with an external mike input and IR remote control for key functions (price around $4,000). If you're making a movie in tight quarters where it's important to have an unobtrusive camera and keep a low profile while you tape, then this is the one for you! Check out their Website, <**www.panasonic.com**>, for new products and updates.

For the best deals in *any* DV camera purchase, check out the B&H company in New York (<**www.bhphotovideo.com**>). They seem to be able to turn most retail prices into near wholesale ones.

DV On-Location Sound

Once you've selected which DV camera to buy, it's vital that you gang it up with high-quality, dependable on-location sound recording equipment, to insure that your excellent images are accompanied by equally excellent audio. My son Morgan enhanced his DSR200 camera package with a Shure FP32 3-audio channel portable DAT mixer with shoulder strap ($1,000), Technica 473A shotgun directional microphone ($400) powered by phantom 48 volt from mixer, a couple of Letrosonic wireless microphones with Countryman lavalieres (said to be among the most water-resistant at cost of $500), boom pole ($200), and top-quality cables ($150). The mixer is highly portable, much lighter to wear over the shoulder than the more expensive (but excellent) Nagras of our filmmaking days, but equally effective. When operated by a skilled soundperson, who sets correct levels so as not to distort or underrecord (which will bring "room tone" up in volume with any dialogue during playback), and aims and repositions the mike correctly between the actors speaking dialogue, this DAT mixer delivers great recordings. And since the audio signal is recorded directly onto the DVCAM tape in the camera, there are no separate "sound rolls" to be synced up as when shooting film, just a clean, clear, sync stereo recording to accompany the video images. Check out <**www.locationsound.com**> in Burbank, California, which supplies top-quality sound equipment to productions worldwide.

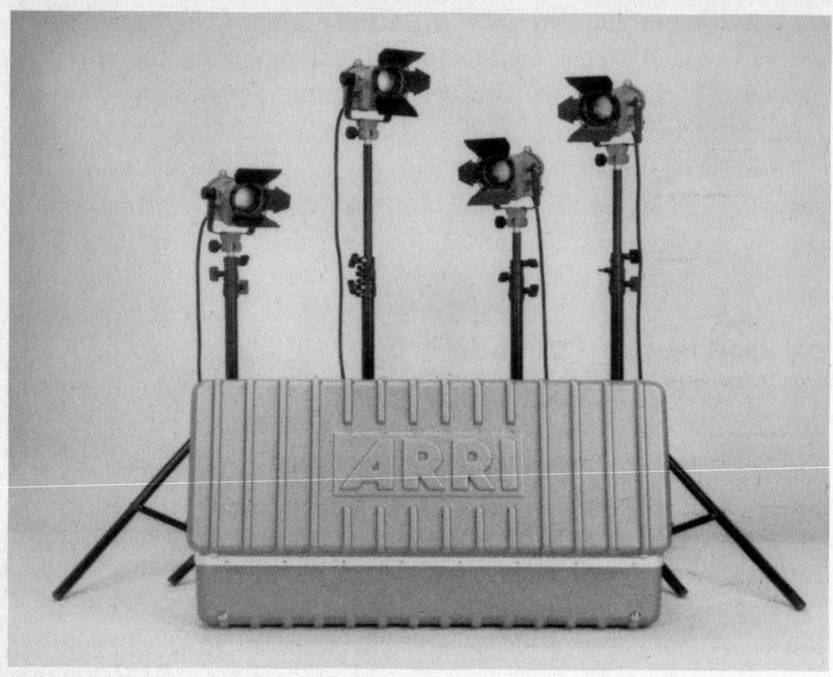

Arri 150/4 Fresnel lighting kit, with handy shipping case for travel. Photo courtesy Arriflex Corporation.

Portable Lights for DV

When my son Morgan formed his FilmSight production company (<**www.filmsight.com**>), he treated himself to an excellent Arri light kit (<**www.arri.com**>), for around $1,000, consisting of three lights (one 650, two 300 Arri Fresnels) and stands, all fitting tightly into one large suitcase for checking in as luggage at the airport. These lights have been essential for our Feature Workshops shoots at exotic locations, such as when we ventured to Death Valley Junction in January 1998 for our production of the DV feature *Welcome to Serendipity*. They are powerful enough to solve most basic lighting needs, especially effective when the subject(s) of the video shoot is/are in a small space, sitting or standing, or moving in a well-defined area around a room, so that the range of illumination doesn't become ineffectual.

For larger shoots Morgan and I rent full lighting packages. These generally come with more powerful lights, an array of c-stands, flags, gels, extension cords, along with a dolly (with skateboard wheels) and track for beautifully magical effects. Here's a list of what we rented for our August 1998 production of *Maisy's Garden*, all for around $400 for a six-day shoot:

C-stands (5)
Flags (4 solids, 24″ x 24″ x 36″)
Doorway dolly (with skateboard wheels)
Dolly track (3 8′ sections, 1 4″ section, and curved 6′)
2 K (Mole Rochardson) Fresnel
Shiny boards (2), 4′ x 4′ gold and silver sides, plus two stands
Junior stands (2)
Nets (assortment of stop reducers)
Assortment of gels

Editing by Computer

While we use the powerful (and expensive—$50,000) Avid Media Composer editing system exclusively for our Feature Workshops DVCAM shoots (our main editor, Mike Rogers, is a wizard on Avid, so we happily pay the $1,000 to $1,500 for a week of computer time plus his salary to insure we have a shot at finishing our movies within ten days), there are many other computer editing software systems that are less than $10,000. After reviewing cost and system requirements of various nonlinear editing (NLE) systems that appeal to you (because of alluring ads or good word-of-mouth), you should sit in front of a few computers and, with the help of a technician/salesman, actually try to edit. Or check at NLE Websites for free downloadable demos. Ask yourself the question, "Does this particular method of thinking {editing} really appeal to *me?*" Maybe you're a visually oriented person and you need to see the logic in the symbols or edit commands, which vary greatly from one system to another. Some systems, though effective, require weeks of training before an operator can fluently make editorial decisions and execute them on the computer. Other programs have simplified the editing process giving the first-timer the opportunity to learn and begin editing in a matter of hours. So each e-filmmaker must do enough research to discover the edit system that best fits his or her emotional, physical, mental, and financial needs.

While you are researching editing software systems and taking some for a test drive, you'll probably notice that some operate on a IBM PC while others are exclusive to Apple's Power Macintosh. If you are used to either of these platforms at home, then you may want to stick with that type of computer for this big next step—leasing or purchasing the most powerful computer you can afford for editing movies.

Workstation Platform and Setup

While some people feel strongly that Macs are more "media friendly" with their 500+ MHz, G-4, "drag and drop" technology for moving files around and running video, others think that something like the IBM Intellistation Workstation sporting Windows NT, 500+ MHz processors is the ticket. At this point, part of your early "platform" decision-making will be affected by which DV editing software you've chosen to use, since some editing systems are only Mac compatible, while others are specifically designed for a Windows NT. Obviously, these are all big decisions, since you'll be committing thousands of dollars. I took the leap toward Apple's Power Macintosh G-3, with a hot-rodded 300MHz sporting 8 gigabytes of storage (with plans to add an additional 18 gigs soon). I doubled the factory RAM, up to 128MB from 64MB, and had a FireWire #1394 card installed before I left the store. This computer was purchased before the new "blue and white" G-3's hit the market, with their included FireWire (now Mac G-4s offer three FireWire ports!) Am I smarter than the people who choose IBM (or know something they don't)? No. I just felt comfortable sitting in front of Mac-based Avid editing systems several times a year for 100-plus-hour seven-day crash-edits at my Feature Workshops, watching the ease with which our genius Avid editors, Gabe Rhodes (**<gaber@leland.stanford.edu>**) and Mike Rogers

(**<ahmana@earthlink.net>**) moved files around, and finally felt the urge to commit in that direction. Check out this Apple Website in Australia, **<www.apple.com.au/documents/whymac/whymac.html>**, for a more in-depth discussion of platforms.

Since consumer Mac technology is able to deliver such a strong and fast (and easy to learn) machine that's easy to upgrade to much higher RAM and more gigabytes for capture of hours of digital video, I expect to enjoy all the elements of this particular computer as I head into the learning curve of mastering editing software. And it takes some time to learn about such systems as Digital Origin's EditDV/MotoDV, Media 100, Apple's Final Cut Pro, or Adobe Premiere, and the new FilmLogic. For those who haven't heard, FilmLogic is a software application with plug-ins for Adobe Premiere and Media 100 that *insures* your EDL (edit decision list) remains nailed at twenty-four frames per second when going from 16-mm or 35-mm film to nonlinear computer editing and back to film again for cutting original to make an answer print. The software maintains a relationship between original camera negatives, sound rolls, videotape transfers; captured clips within its online database; and serves up a traditional film "codebook" to keep all the numbers straight so your final film won't be out of sync. And it gives you the choice of editing in 24 fps, 25 fps PAL, or 29.97 fps NTSC video rate, while still being able to return your digitized clips from NTSC video to 24 fps. This is the final piece of the no-budget feature filmmaking puzzle, since before now only expensive top-end editing systems like Avid offered video editing at film speed of 24 frames per second. You'll find their great product at **<www.filmlogic.com>**. This puts the means of production into the hands of *the people!*

Becoming Computer Literate

Once you've selected and purchased your basic computer platform and paid that $2,500 to $4,000 for a top-of-the-line Mac or PC, you will need to spend a little time setting up your hardware in a comfortable place in your home or office, plugging cables into a surge protector, installing software, reading manuals, in general bonding with your new acquisition. In some ways it is an almost sacred process, or it may feel that way if you've never had a powerful computer system in your life before. They actually do have a kind of personality. Sometimes they seem to act accommodating, happy to accept the new software bestowed upon them. At other times they react with defiance, alerting the user with pop-up warnings that something is wrong. Everyone gets to experience this bumpy interaction with a new system (along with a few "crashes" when the machine must be shut down or restarted). If the computer acts too finicky at this early stage, performs "stuttery" or remains frozen most of the time, you'll want to enforce your warranty and return it for a replacement. But it's pretty hard to do permanent damage if you're careful. Turn on your Mac G-4 in the proper order (#1—turn on monitor, then, #2—activate the mini-tower memory center by pressing down the top-right keyboard button, the one with a little triangle symbol!). New Mac owners will be happy to learn that with the OS system the computer always checks itself after a quick shutdown, using its internal "Disk First Aid" to test and repair its hard drive at time of restart. (I do recommend installing Norton Utilities software for further protection against crashes, and damaged disks, **<www.symantec.com>**.)

The main thing to remember here is that although you're anxious to jump right into editing, you need to be realistic about the break-in period. Plan on spending a few weeks just playing with your computer, enjoying its many diverse features. Experience the speed of receiving and sending e-mail (with a 56K or faster modem), and enjoy the super-realistic graphics and high-quality audio of computer games like Myst and Riven, etc. (I never really gave computer games much credit for being an "art form" until I played one called Obsidian, a fantastic, futuristic twenty-first-century game from Rocket Science & Sagasoft!) Try importing pictures to Adobe Photoshop from either your video camera or scanned images (if you don't have a scanner, you can order your photos developed directly to floppy disk or CD-ROM by Kodak) and altering pictorial reality with your cursor. You'll start wondering what would happen if you used Adobe Photoshop or After Effects software, paired with your Adobe Premiere editing software, to create an entirely new filmatic reality. At this point it will hit you that you could actually reshape the entire vision of your movie with your computer. With enough goofing around you'll start to get radical (and profound) new ideas that will eventually enable you to move this fairly young art form of cinema to an entirely new level.

In the meantime, though, relax and enjoy your new toys, giving yourself breaks between computer times to avoid premature burnout. Try instigating a rule of working only four hours at a stretch for starters (not a bad pace for editing). Soon enough it will be time to take the second plunge and spend a thousand dollars or more on editing software and its add-ons.

$10,000 Digital Movie Studio

For some people, like Gainesville, Florida–based producer Steve Kahler, it took a tremendous leap of faith (and some timely financial maneuvers) to join the digital revolution. To circumvent the problems he'd heard regarding "one-shot" indie features that left filmmakers burdened for years by credit card debt, he decided to "go DV" instead, refinancing his house to supply the $10,000 seed money he figured would cover the cost of a digital camera and computer editing workstation. He believed that once he had acquired the basic equipment, he could then shoot movies inexpensively (for just a couple of hundred dollars' worth of tapestock), and blow up DV to a 35-mm film print for festivals (Sundance!) and theatrical release if needed. Here's how he spent the ten grand to set up his home movie studio for *Click*, his debut Vietnam war picture:

Canon XL-1 digital video camera (w/ Pelican case)	$4,000.00
Bogen tripod	$ 550.00
DV-REX video-capture card (<www.justedit.com>)	$2,000.00
Computer capable of editing DV	$1,500.00
19-inch monitor	$ 600.00
18 gig Quantum Atlas 3, Ultra-Wide SCSI hard drive for editing DV	$1,065.00
	$9,715.00

Steve says the advantages to bankrolling his own movie are as follows:

1. **I now own my equipment.**
2. **I have my own video production company.**
3. **I can use that equipment to secure an income while I move forward on my next picture.**
4. **I own 100 percent of my movie. If I'm lucky and make a huge amount of money from distribution, then *I* pocket the profits, not the investors. (Okay, so I'm greedy!)**
5. **I'm the boss.**
6. **I get to make a lot more movies this way.**

If you need moral support (and most of us do), drop in at Steve's Website where he offers how-to assistance for Adobe Premiere nonlinear editing software, valuable filmmaking links, updates on his productions, DV production packages, and consulting: **<www.ccgnv.net/admitone>**. Or just e-mail him directly, **<admitone@ccgnv.net>**, or reach him by phone at (352) 378-0500. He says that if he can do it (and he didn't attend film school *or* college . . .), so can you!

DV Editing Software

It will be exciting, though a bit scary, to commit to buying a certain DV editing software and then actually get the box home. You've done your research and taken your best shot at choosing an editing system that you can afford, and that can take input from and export to your DV camera via an installed FireWire. And you have faith that you can master the routine without expensive consultation or classes. But it's at the moment that you open the box and thumb through the inch-thick manual that it really dawns on you: You've got some new things to learn. You may wonder if you're up to the task. Even a well-written manual, like the one for Adobe Premiere or Final Cut Pro, is a bit daunting. But if you stop worrying, start at the front of the book, and follow the clear instructions for installation, you'll be on your way. Have faith that after a few weeks of careful reading and experimentation, you will become a master of this new editing domain. If you haven't yet purchased your editing software, here are a few of the main choices currently on the market.

The Avid Xpress DV editing system for IBM IntelliStation Windows NT (priced under $10,000) contains distribution options for streaming video on the Web (Real media G-2, Windows Media, and QuickTime/Sorrenson). Photo courtesy Avid Technology, Inc.

Avid

There's no getting around the fact that if you can afford the $25,000 to $80,000 price tag, Avid is the best, most dependable editing system currently available, **<www.avid.com>**. For nonlinear assembly of footage, quick changes in the order of scenes, razor-sharp cuts in picture and sound, total sound mixing capabilities, accurate effects (fades, dissolves, more than 100 different wipes), real-time rendering of letterbox 1:85 cutoff as you edit, no real glitches in either memory saving or smoothness of editing operation, plus dependable output to broadcast quality Betacam SP (or Digital Betacam, DVCAM, DVD, etc.), it just can't be beat! Yes, it does take some time to learn to use it properly, and more time (like anything) to master, but once you do, you can perhaps perform editing miracles like Avid expert Mike Rogers does for our Feature Workshops, when he edits a feature down from twelve hours of footage to a ninety-minute cut in less than a week.

Mind you, these are twenty-plus-hour editing days. When you consider that Mike (who fortunately doesn't sleep much) has to (1) capture all the footage in the computer, labeling each shot for quick selection, (2) edit, while, at the same time, constantly being in search of the overall dramatic structure, (3) hone down scenes so that they cut smoothly, internally to themselves, (4) insert music and readjust placement until songs work perfectly with the story being formed, (5) type out all the credits of the movie, select special typeface for main title, and fit title sequences to length of musical score, (6) take time to redigitize all the scenes online, adding fades and dissolves and other effects for best-quality final cut, (7) do a complete sound mix (adjust volume levels and EQ, "sweeten" sections that need special attention), and (8) transfer final cut from computer memory to Betacam SP cassette after laying off a "black" to tape so the recording will hold its signal (another precious hour and a half of editing time). How he does all this in less than a week (and even finds time to receive input from fellow collaborators) is anybody's guess. No one knows. But it *is* possible to cut a feature this fast on Avid, with an experienced editor who is willing to go to the wall for you and your project (on each movie he edits, Mike owns an equal share of the gross points with my son Morgan, me, and the other co-writer/co-director collaborators, and receives a base salary, so at least there's a fair incentive connected to all his hard work).

For a feature-length project that is languishing over time (not "writer's block," but something similar . . .), I'd recommend giving yourself a couple of weeks on a rented Avid to see what you and an experienced editor can achieve (just make sure that you bring along a handful of original songs on DAT to insure the editor has some options for creating moods and transitions).

One note of caution regarding an Avid impulse purchase. Just as you should expect higher registration fees and insurance on a luxury car, there are some higher maintenance costs attached to owning this system. The company offers software maintenance at a cost of somewhere between $3,000 to $6,000 per year (a good thing if you can afford it) so that you'll receive the latest upgrades. And Avid expects their owners to upgrade the hardware components during the three-year life span of the system, at around 25 percent of the full purchase price. If you open any filmmaking magazine, you can be assured to find these older, "obsolete," Avids for sale or rent, by owners who have kept their editing systems alive with third-party add-ons, and you can probably get some good deals by shopping around. Avid has supposedly eased up on restrictions for such low-budget maintenance of their machines. And to remain competitive, Avid now offers its turnkey Showbiz Producer, an IBM Intellistation-based system for around $10,000 (includes computer, monitor, and software).

Avid Cinema

So as not to be lost in the no-budget moviemaking shuffle, Avid has teamed up with Apple Computers to offer a new editing system for beginning moviemakers called Avid Cinema (**<www.avidcinema.com>**), which is superaffordable (around $100 for software) and easy to use. The software is part of an integrated system that runs on Macintosh Performa and Power Macintosh Systems (cost with software and G-4 Power Mac computer included is around $3,000; Avid Cinema is also available for Windows/IBM platforms, and can also be paired to an i-mac, including a USB (Universal Serial Box) with FireWire adapter and ports for your video camera ($219). Using a combination of storyboard templates and a tab-driven interface, the Avid Cinema software guides the user through the process of creating a movie, from planning shots to final output. The accompanying literature states that they questioned customers about making movies and discovered that many people "weren't sure how to tell a story in

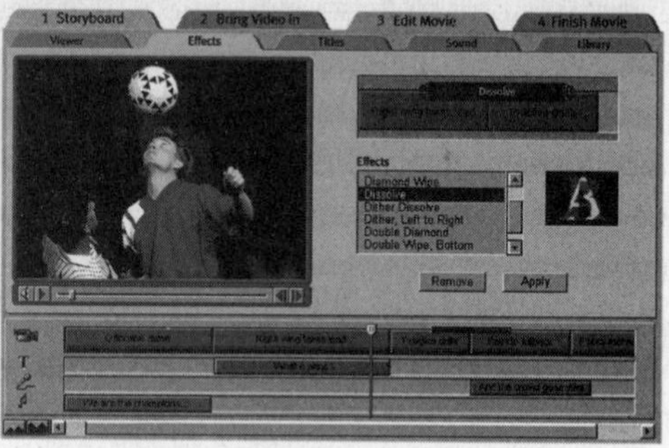

Avid Cinema editing software screen shot, showing time line with easy-to-read symbols for movie image and accompanying sync sound (video camera), narrations (microphone), Titles (T), and music track. Photo courtesy Avid Technology, Inc.

video." So Avid designed their software to walk the user through a series of educational steps in that direction. There are twenty different templates that represent common activities around the home, school, and office. In the software program are suggestions for shots and sequences, hints regarding length of shots, and advice on how to film and cut the results. After you lay out your entire movie on the storyboard templates, the software also makes adding sophisticated visual effects possible. Be advised, this storyboard template approach to planning (and cutting) the movie tends to make the user think in a particular way about making movies—"the Avid way." Fortunately, these templates can be customized (or completely changed), so that moviemakers can create their own movie structure (be original!). With a little effort, the user with a personal vision can probably corrupt this detailed moviemaking grid to serve his or her beginning moviemaking needs.

There are other ease-of-operating advantages to this introductory editing system that should bring some peace of mind to the user. With one click on the record button the video source footage can be "captured" by the computer and held in the memory for editing. Then, by opening the "edit movie" tab, the editor can see all the video shots represented by small slidelike pictures, displayed in a predetermined order by the template. From there, shots can be dragged and dropped into a new sequence. With Avid Cinema's multiple audio tracks, you can add original songs or live narration. For a finished look, the system offers twenty-five various transitional effects (wipes, peels, barn doors, as well as the normal fades and dissolves) and the ability to add titles that scroll. Once the final cut is set, you can output directly to VHS or save the work in several different QuickTime formats (for viewing over the Internet, etc.). This is a great introductory system that will help the user begin to see the possibilities of computer editing. From here, the next step is to experience more control over fine cutting, more options for effects, and inputting from a DV digital source for a broadcast-quality output. For all this, expect to pay $500 to $1,000 for the next level of professional editing software, and spend several weeks mastering the more complex systems.

Adobe Premiere

Look out, Avid! Here comes a scrappy company that wants to topple the giant! Abobe Premiere, which can run on either the Power Mac G-4 or Windows NT, offers a lot of editing wallop at a price you can afford (priced $579 at Website <**www.adobe.com**>). And they are smart enough to offer their software *free* for download on the Web, so you can give it a test drive for thirty days and see if it's appropriate for your artistic skills and pocketbook. At the end of thirty days, you'll know if it feels right. The 5.1 edition (and beyond) is specially designed for editing "feature-length movies" from a long-format base of three hours of footage.

So, in a sense, all you need to edit at home is to commit to one of the platform hardware providers. Windows NT (cost around $7,000) also supports other available editing software—Avid's Xpress 1.5 ($2,500) and Discreet's 3.5 ($14,995)—while the Power Mac G-4 (around $3,000) supports editing software from Final Cut Pro ($1,000), to Media 100 lx ($9,995), Media 100qx ($1,995), Scitex

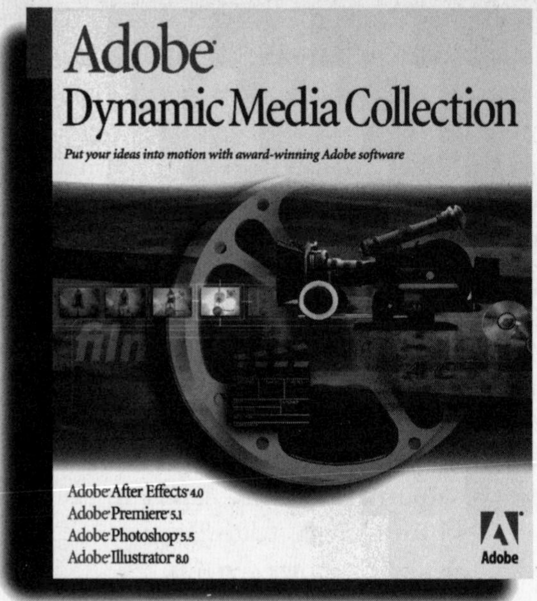

Adobe's Dynamic Media Collection includes four great software programs—Adobe PhotoShop, Adobe Illustrator, Adobe After Effects (Professional Bundle), and Adobe Premiere editing software—a tour-de-force of moving image and sound manipulation. Photo courtesy Adobe Systems Incorporated.

Digital Video Microsphere ($4,500), Radius Video Vision ML ($2,499), and the low-cost Strata Videoshop 4.0 ($495), a QuickTime-based editing package with audio mixing and 3-D features. Of course, the trick is tointegrate the software and hardware into a useful package that offers hassle-free editing (no computer freeze-up or crashing, missed cues, low-quality output, etc.). At any rate good luck on deciding to go either the Mac or PC route. With either platform you should be able to build an affordable nonlinear editing system that gives you a film lab right inside your own home.

EditDV by Digital Origin (formerly Radius, Inc.) is another effective NLE (nonlinear editing) system for Macintosh and PC computers. Photo courtesy Digital Origin Incorporated.

EditDV, MotoDV, PhotoDV, and RotoDV

EditDV from Digital Origin (formerly Radius), **<www.digitalorigin.com>**, (800) 572-3487, is another great nonlinear digital editing system for the Mac G-4 or Windows platform that is affordable to the no-budget indie moviemaker (cost under $900). Paired with the new "FireWire-equipped" blue Mac G-3 or G-4 (around $1,000 with FireWire IEEE 1394 card for installation in older Mac G-3s), this system seems to be very user-friendly. I was able to make immediate headway editing with just a quick read of the manual's first few chapters. Digital Origin offers a free download trial version of EditDV Unplugged (the entry-level $149 version of this professional product), at **<www.digitalorigin.com/unplugged/register.html>**, so you can see if this works for your DV editing mind-set. MotoDV software for Mac OS or Windows 95/98 is their excellent capture software

Canon's XL 1 DV camera is hooked up by IEEE 1394 FireWire (cord to right of nameplate), to Mac G-3 computer and Digital Origin's EditDV "capture" screen (note corresponding edit symbols on keyboard).

that keeps digitized files at top quality and expedites input and output (priced at $299). MotoDV Studio 2.0 with #1394 FireWire card for Windows 95/98/NT4.0 costs a bit more, $899, but also includes Adobe Premiere 5.1 full version (which usually sells separately for $899!), PhotoDV software, and Adobe Photoshop 5.0LE (watch for all these software packages to be updated).

Another new product offered by Digital Origin is RotoDV, a Mac OS software package that lets the moviemaker actually paint on his or her movie, change colors, add layers of effects and immediately review his or her work (cost $699, but watch their Website for some introductory price specials). They say you can "paint at the speed of video" and play back on QuickTime. And replicator brushes can clone areas of the image and reproduce them in other locations on the picture plane, giving you the abilities of an effects wizard.

Digital Origin is confident enough in their products to offer a thirty-day money-back guarantee (read restrictions at their home page). This company has been developing DV software from the very beginning, and I expect they will continue to offer new and exciting products for the digital moviemaker.

Media 100

Another good, time-tested nonlinear editing system is the Media 100, **<www.media100.com>**, which offers pleasurable editing, especially at the top range "100xr" level, which costs around $20,000 (read how the *Blair Witch* creators, Haxan Films, used the "xr" to make their hit movie, **<www.media100.com/press/releases/99 Blairwitch.htm>**). Several of my friends and associates are also using this system to edit their upcoming features. Mark Toscani, a writer/director participant of the August 1997 Feature Workshops movie, *someone like me*, purchased his own Media 100 soon after that production. Also, the documentary *Full Blossom*, about Roberts Blossom, the character actor (and poet), now widely known as the old man in the church with Macaulay Culkin in *Home Alone*, was edited on Media 100 by Brih Abee, in co-production with my son Morgan Schmidt-Feng. What's nice about this system is that you can get started at an affordable level, in the $10,000 to $18,000 range, and then build up your gigs of memory for longer projects. Or you might like the Media 100 RFE Remote Field Editor, a portable editing system that gives a moviemaker the option of editing on location on a Mac G-3 Power Book. You can edit as you shoot (!), create a new style of making DV movies.

If you are getting worn out by all the options and still wondering which nonlinear editing system to buy, you might enjoy this refreshing perspective on the Media 100 (and NLE in general . . .) from Laura Sherman, a young, first-time e-feature filmmaker from Clearwater, Florida:

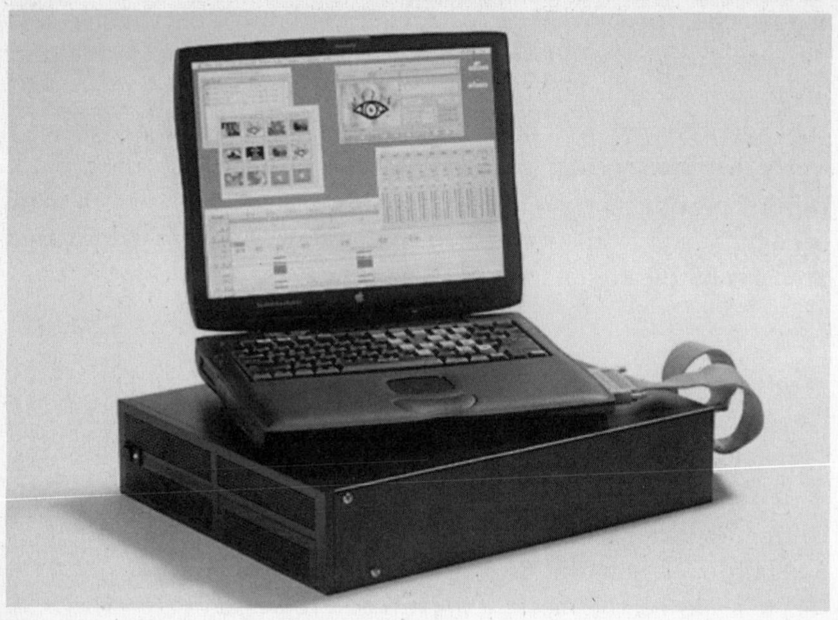

Media 100 RFE portable field editor for Power Macintosh G-3 laptop. Photo courtesy Media 100 Inc.

"I am editing my first feature film, *In the Open*, which I shot on Hi-8 video. I purchased a Media 100, which is a bit out of the range of a used-car budget, but I only spent $3,000 shooting the movie, so I could afford to spend a little more on the editing equipment! I bought the LE with 36 gigs for $18,000.

"I am truly thrilled with this experience! I simply import the media onto the hard drives and it stores each clip in a 'bin', with a picture representing the piece. After I have pulled in all my media for a scene, I simply drag the pictures to a time line program and I can cut them up there and put them together! It is so easy! Plus with a click of the mouse, I can insert a beautiful dissolve. The nice thing is that I can change things around quickly and effortlessly. If I don't like something, I can undo it or simply redrag the original clip from the bin over to the program again and start over! I have 4 sound tracks on this system as well and it is quite easy to separate the sound from the video,

Sony DSR V10, a compact (just 5 13/16″ x 5 5/16″ !) portable DVCAM player/recorder. Photo courtesy Sony Corporation.

so I can use the best sound take. Importing music is really easy as well! I find that I cannot sleep at night, as editing is too exciting and fun. I love watching my movie unfold before my eyes!"

I hope everyone who buys expensive editing equipment will share Laura's high enthusiasm for the process of rendering a movie with electronic magic (give her an e-mail at **<laurasherman@earthlink.net>** if you've got further questions about working with the Media 100).

Sony ES-7 EditStation

Another prohibitively expensive nonlinear editing system, Sony's ES-7 (available for Windows NT platform [cost $30,000] is a complementary editing system designed particularly for use with the DVCAM digital video format (of course, all the other high-end systems, Avid, Adobe Premiere Media 100, Final Cut Pro, can take a perfect signal from DVCAM if you have a DVCAM source deck or camera for playback). Once again, if you have the pocketbook for this level of system, by all means go to your nearest Sony dealer and take a test drive. If you're a fanatic for compatible systems (and cost is no object), it might appeal to you to have all your electronic equipment (Pro-DVCAM camera, recording and playback deck, monitors, your Walkman, etc.) be Sony products, <www.sony.com>.

Discreet

Another heavy hitter, Discreet, <www.discreet.com>, is very expensive (over $50,000), but a great system for online editing, digital image creation and manipulation, using an uncompressed system for real-time editing and creation of a movie. Check out the demo software at their extensive Website. Unfortunately, most of us don't own our house outright to trade in for the system. I'm still hoping that Discreet, which has designed a lovely, clear visual method of nonlinear editing, can come down to our level (used-car prices . . .) and supply no-budget moviemakers with a nonlinear editing system in the affordable range of $3,000 to $4,000.

Play's Trinity

The young, savvy designers and technicians at Play, Inc. (<www.play.com>) have created a movie-studio-in-a-box that they call Trinity, and ever since I've watched their free VHS demo I've wondered how I might incorporate their fine product into my life as an independent moviemaker. To begin with, for around $7,000 they empower the user with an amazing assortment of Trinity production tools: Live Production Switcher, 3-D Digital Video Effects, Non-Linear/Linear Editor, Character Generator, Paint, Animation and Compositing, Virtual Sets, Dual Channel D1 Still Store, and Chroma Keyer (input and output modules extra). What this amounts to is a setup comparable to a quarter-million-dollar TV studio! One of the most astonishing things I witnessed on their demo tape is how their 3-D program can supply a reflection in a teapot and off the surface of a shiny kitchen table from a video-generated TV image set at the end of the table. By compounding one effect upon another, the unreality of what you are viewing somehow takes on a real-life presence. We all know the peels, warps, and ripple effects, but Trinity seems to take it a step further, all the while maintaining a real-time rendering and broadcast quality. And their nonlinear editing system is easy to learn, incredibly fast, and operates without any delays for rendering. Your effects, transitions, titles, still stores, and animated graphics can be instantly positioned and "scrubbed" on the time line at broadcast resolution. I know I'm beginning to sound like their publicist, but I think the indie movie producer who is leaning toward DV as his or her medium of choice should consider talking to a salesperson at Play to see just what it would cost beyond the initial seven grand to gear up for DV production.

One more amazing Play product worth mentioning is their Pocket Producer, a hot-rodded Palm Pilot that can be used to log shots on location (or anywhere it can be connected to a VCR or camcorder). You can download the data storage to any Mac or Windows program, and even use it as a mini-edit system (cost is $395, and it still maintains the functions of a consumer Palm Pilot!). They plan to come out with more "handheld tools" for the electronic age, so keep a bookmark on their Website!

Apple's Final Cut Pro

At the National Association of Broadcasters (NAB) convention in 1999, Apple introduced its new nonlinear editing software product, Final Cut Pro (<**www.apple.com/finalcutpro**>). For competing software editing systems it had to be a shock to see Apple design and sell software specifically for its own new blue-and-white Mac G-3 (and G-4) that improved on almost all other current software systems. Suddenly, you could have a superaffordable nonlinear editing software that had an "After Effects" type composite tool right in its menu (all for

Apple's amazing Final Cut Pro software, with editing, compositing, and effects capabilities combined in an affordable and easy-to-learn program. Photo courtesy Apple Computer, Inc.

around $1,000!). They advertise that it costs a tenth of the price of competing systems, and they may be right. You get three-point editing (the in-out points of the source clip and either the in or out location of where the clip is inserted into your running cut), along with fit-to-fill, which uses all four points to insert a selected clip into a hole in the cut (it speeds up or slows down the images to fill in the gap). If you need to find an exact frame for an insert of a new clip, then the "match frame" command will get you there. And with "multitrack trimming" you can hone in on the precise cut you want, frame by frame, as easily and elastically as you can imagine.

As far as effects go, page 238 in the operating manual shows how you can adjust the motion path of a car while still in the editing mode! They also mention "alpha channels" (8 bits of information per pixel), which allows the editor to work with transparent images. It advertises

Scene from Final Cut Pro bin (left) being moved with drag-and-drop cursor to "overwrite" for addition to editing time line. Photo courtesy Apple Computer, Inc.

that you can "create and animate up to 99 layers of video using text, graphics, Adobe Photoshop files (with layers maintained) and additional video elements," which means that you can introduce animated elements into your movie as soon as you purchase the Final Cut Pro and Adobe Photoshop software (an amazingly powerful one-two punch of creative image manipulation). There are definitely a lot of bells and whistles on this software package, but what's best about it is the ease of actual editing, the beautifully designed source and assembly windows (large screens!) with easy central playback controls, and effects available right inside the system itself. Keep in mind that the more complex the effects, the more rendering time (and computer power) you'll need to see the composite. You may want to look into additional hardware options for boosting rendering time (like Ice, **<www.iced.com>**, which offers what they call "100+ killer effects,"

Paired with Final Cut Pro software, this new Power Mac G-4, with a monster 27 GB hard drive, rewritable DVD-RAM drive, 500MHz processor, three FireWire ports, and optional Apple Cinema display, completes your DV editing workstation. Photo courtesy Apple Computer, Inc.

PCI hardware, 3-D transition effects, title and graphic effects, color correction, boosting your rendering time to a rate of ten times faster, at a cost of around $4,000).

The final blessing of this incredible Final Cut Pro software (also available at **<www.promax.com>**, bundled with computer, mini-DV camera, DV deck and monitor) is that you get to see exactly how your video will look as a completed production with its proxy-free compositing (QuickTime is used to deliver the highest-quality stutter-free playback of images and sounds while editing, and for finalizing for distribution to formats like M-JPEG for DVD or the Web). It's obvious that Apple got some top editors into their R&D lab and asked them to specify (and design in) *everything* they'd ever need or want in a computer editing system, because this system seems to have it all. And get your hands on "Power Start CD-ROM," the tutorial from Straight Scoop Enterprises, (800) 965-3976, **<www.straight-scoop.com>**, the perfect companion software tool for learning how to use Final Cut Pro in an afternoon (cost $59.95).

So there are some of the choices for editing your movie on computer. In the coming years you can decide whether to be anchored to a large home computer, or to take your editing on the road with a laptop and software to edit on location, on an airplane, or in some cozy cottage at the beach. However it plays out, computer editing is helping to get the basic moviemaking tools out to the people, who can now turn their e-feature filmmaking dream into a reality.

The Casablanca (Nonlinear Editing *Without* Computer)

For some moviemakers who want to edit their DV on a nonlinear system but wish that they could forgo the headaches of having a computer, the Casablanca system from DraCo Systems ([303] 440-5311, **<www.draco.com>**) might be just what they're looking for. Priced not much higher than the average computer and NLE software (from $3,995 to $7,095, with an additional $1,695 for IEEE 1394 FireWire and cable), it allows the user to edit full screen on a video monitor and make cuts with frame-precise accuracy, using an easy-to-operate trackball for controlling your editing commands, with just a monitor or home TV needed for viewing. The system supports three audio tracks (many more can be added as you save tracks, turning the system into a multitrack-type configuration), and gives you the possibility of creating your own effects by combining an AB roll capability with image-processing options and adding titling and slow motion, backwards motion, stutter effects and freeze-frames, while providing the data rate and picture quality required for mini-DV and Beta SP.

The Motorola MC 68060 processor takes approximately twenty-five seconds to render one second of 2-D effects (a dissolve or fade), probably not too different a time frame than what you'll be used to with regular computer-based software systems at low-end cost (an eighty-minute program would take approximately eight hours to render). It can come with a changeable compression rate (fifteen settings from 40:1 to 3:1), and a removable 4 to 36 gigabyte hard drive for saving your work on multiple projects (they figure it will take 18GB to store ninety-two minutes of mini-DV at a quality setting). If you want to go another step up in price, you can also purchase the Heimdall DVD archive software and hardware (cost $1,499), bringing the entire "Casablanca & Heimdall DVD archiving" package up to about $10,000. This gives you the option of saving the complete configuration of the Casablanca's hard drive, plus all audio and video saves, onto a DVD-RAM cartridge (the DVD disk is inside a cartridge, not the kind that can be played back on a normal DVD player).

After all the built-in difficulties of learning computers and unlocking the mysteries of PC and Mac, a simple-to-learn editing system like this one is certainly appealing. It harkens back to the "flatbed" editing days, when you built your movie one roll at a time, added or removed scenes, and repositioned the assembly in search of the "center" of your story. You ran a couple of sound tracks (one sync and one effects or music track) and concentrated on the basics of making a movie before marking the work print for "effects" of fades and dissolves, added during final printing. For those old-time filmmakers who aren't quite ready to give themselves over to the computer gods for editing purposes, or can't quite accept the role computer editing will play in their future moviemaking lives, maybe a system like the Casablanca can help make the transition a little less painful. The Casablanca won a "Best Products of the Year" award several years running from *Videomaker* magazine (check out the multitude of good reviews at their Website), so it's worth considering this editing system for your upcoming productions. They occasionally offer "test drives," letting prospective buyers take an editing system home after they swipe your credit card (no charge is run), so do yourself a favor and give it a free home trial.

After completing your assembly to fine cut on the Casablanca, you may use a powerful home computer (the one where you get your e-mails) to capture the full cut digitally, then play around, add special

Adobe's After Effects software is used to matte out a portion of the picture plane for exposure adjustment (change to be applied throughout clip).

effects using Adobe's After Effects (or even Final Cut Pro), enhance your movie by adding all those layers of image and sound manipulation—motion graphics, titles, image blurs, fire and brimstone and multilayered sound/noise/music, all the tools you've seen advertised in magazines like *DV*.

For the true scavenging no-budgeter, the best part of the future may be finding good bargains on outdated editing software at discount stores or at garage sales, early editions of Adobe Premiere or EditDV that can still get good editing results on some early computer system. We don't need the most powerful computer to make movies. If you read the classifieds and hit a few garage sales each weekend, you'll eventually find some sort of used Pentium or Mac OS computer, maybe even a discarded DV video camera. Or check out **<www.ebay.com>**, where millions of people are selling their used items, from DV cameras to computers and software. Because of this future shock of new technology, you're really just a wish away from becoming an e-filmmaker, if you don't mind using the digital discards of your society.

note: Because of the youth of nonlinear computer editing systems, and the ever-changing M-peg formats on different platforms, the process of inputting and outputting to different compressions, editing a movie on a computer, and recording back to the format of choice can sometimes be taxing. And watch for other problems; it's easy to miss flaws in the image because of screening on a small monitor. The pacing on TV for a movie can be deceptive, and severe problems can arise with the negative cut list if you originate on film. Until you, as moviemaker, break the ice and get *one* movie completed on your home-grown digital workstation, you're going to have to be patient with computer freeze-ups, occasional lost saves, faulty digitization, and the hours spent learning these new skills.

One way to safeguard your time and effort *from the beginning* is to purchase learning tapes that give you a step-by-step lesson in using your editing software. If you've purchased Adobe Premiere, then you are fortunate that a company called Total Training (<**www.totaltraining.com**>, [888] Do-TOTAL) has put out a five-tape set (cost $249) on mastering this complicated editing software. The on-tape master of ceremonies, technician/wizard Brian Maffitt, does a great job of keeping the process understandable and clear, so that you can actually learn how to use this software system and get the most from your nonlinear editing efforts. Watch the tapes more than once, check out the included CD-ROM, and give yourself a chance to keep up with this new learning curve. (Total Training also offers a nine-tape set for learning Adobe After Effects, cost $599—highly recommended if you want to learn how to animate part or all of your movie.)

Website-Based Online Editing

For those moviemakers who have a computer and Web browser but don't want to invest large sums of money in new editing software or gigabytes of data storage, it might be very appealing to just rent a membership at an Internet Website that offers online editing. One company called VideoFarm.com (<**www.videofarm.com**>) supplies the user-member with a "timeline" editing system (similar to professional editing software products covered in this chapter), free transfer your digitized video at their Website, storage of DV data, high-resolution output for your final product after editing is completed, and video streaming of the results, all for under $100 per month. Whether their stripped-down editing system will meet your professional moviemaking needs is something each individual DV filmmaker must figure out for his or herself, but since the Website offers a free one-month trial after membership sign-up, there is ample opportunity to test their system for yourself and make that determination.

And you'll see Pop.com (<**www.pop.com**>) getting a lot of attention in the coming months. Steven Spielberg of DreamWorks SKG and Ron Howard of Imagine Entertainment are parenting this site, to present a mix of live action and animation, video on demand, live Web events, nonlinear interactive features and games. Through community-based links they will help people to script, direct, edit content, presenting Web "features" of one- to six-minute episodic streaming video segments ("pops"). And they will accept outside submissions as well as site-created Web movies for their multimedia contests, the winners granted contracts for development deals at DreamWorks and Imagine Entertainment. That probably means that if you win you'll be swallowed up by Hollywood! But hopefully someone like *you* can help change the system from the inside, show the studios that a *Blair Witch*–type bonanza can be earned with a movie even more original and personal than that high-concept masterwork. At these early stages of "online multimedia creation" it's hard to tell what impact Website-based editing and manipulation will have on the indie scene. Perhaps it will, more than anything else, inspire visually-oriented young men and women to jump into the world of original feature-length moviemaking. Someone with a borrowed DV camera and a "free one-month trial" membership at an editing Website, could change the future of moviemaking, show us our world from an entirely new and fresh point of view. Maybe that person will be YOU.

Digital Postproduction

Once you've shot your DV movie and edited it into some acceptable rough-to-fine-cut form, you'll need to begin thinking about using the new digital technology to enhance your audio tracks, and compose music for your sound track. It will be possible to mix sound either on your home computer, using the new digital tools to produce a top-quality audio track, or with the help of an experienced technician (and his or her cutting-edge computer system designed *strictly* for sound manipulation). Perhaps you'll need to transfer your digital video feature to film for theatrical premieres and important film festivals, or to DVD for distribution by satellite. In some instances the advances of the digital revolution will actually *save* your feature. Here are a few examples of how the digital age has helped my productions in the past, which should make you realize that virtually *anything* is possible in the twenty-first century.

The Digital Sound Mix

An example of my film work being helped by new technology was the sound mix I did for my 1995 Feature Workshop film *Blues for the Avatar* with Scot Charles at Alpha Cine Lab in Seattle (Scot has since left Alpha Cine, and mixes sound at his own facility, Blue Charles, [206] 783-6797). I scheduled a $135/hr. "cleanup" mix to prepare for a work-in-progress screening at the IFFM (Independent Feature Film Market), but dreaded one long stretch of sound track that was, I thought, permanently ruined by camera noise. This flaw in the recording was all too evident since the accompanying close-up visual was a ten-minute static shot of actor J. Cheyenne Wilbur's face as he delivered a monologue about falling in love while on a trip through London. And the poor sound quality was even more obvious when the picture cut to actress Tasha Roth McCormick as she listened intently to how Cheyenne and her mother (in the film) first got together. As an audience we listened with her not only to his words, but to the constant camera noise as well. It wasn't until Scot and I got to the monologue portion of the mix that I had any idea that a computer could cleanly erase the disturbance while leaving the quality of the spoken voice intact. Although it did take a couple of extra hours to remove camera noise, at the slightly higher rate of $185/hr., it was a very small price to pay for the resurrection of a crucial ten-minute chunk of a feature film.

The digital workstation Scot built at Alpha Cine Lab was powered in 1995 by the Mac II FX computer paired with Hewlett Packard hard drive, and used a modular plug-in system incorporating software called Digital Intelligent Noise System by DigiDesign to remove camera noise and other sound manipulations (imagine what's possible now with all the advances in computer and software design!). The client's mag track rolls were first transferred to ¼″ tape, then sync-locked to a ¾″ video copy of the film to be mixed, thus supplying an image and sound track that could be controlled by computer. After the sound was mixed to the satisfaction of the filmmaker, it could either be off-loaded to mag or recorded directly to video for cassette duplication or broadcast.

For filmmakers who wish to mix their sound tracks the old-fashioned way, recording directly from edited mag track onto a master mixed mag track, Will Harvey of Music Annex in San Francisco ([415] 421-6622) is able to make use of digital technology for noise reduction and patching while helping the filmmaker to avoid the added costs of transferring sound to ¼″ multitrack and work print to video. Because the sound is patched through a computer, he can control every aspect of sound quality as he did when mixing my *American Orpheus* feature (cost is around $300/hr. with a good discount down to $1,750 for an eight-hour day rate).

Digital Music for Movies

With his Korg M-1 8-track sequencer and tone generator keyboard, musician Paul Baker was able to compose and record the musical score for my feature *American Orpheus* (1992) with only $1,000 worth of equipment. The keyboard gave him 100 different sounds with which to create his compositions, layering eight different recordings over one another and electronically storing the results for mixing and mastering. The digital revolution has made it possible for musicians like Baker to professionalize their dream and create an inexpensive recording studio to produce their works.

Since 1992 Baker has composed and performed sound tracks for five Feature Workshop movies, as well as collaborating with numerous musicians, writing new songs for his solo projects, and putting all his work together at a Website (**<www.paulbaker.com>**) where interested parties can sample his latest compositions with RealPlayer (a free download he has available). Operating with a Mac G-3 (soon G-4) platform, he has now upgraded his mini–music studio with the latest software programs and hardware devices for top-quality recording, mixing, digital input and output to CDs, DAT cassettes, whatever format he needs for distribution. His software of choice is Digital Performer (**<www.motu.com>**), which costs around $600 (he mentions also looking into programs called Studiovision [**<synthony.com/Products/software/studioVisPro.html>**] and VST Cubase [**<www.us.steinberg.net/products.html>**], with prices ranging from $300 to $700). With this he pairs a $900 multitracking interface device, 2408 Mark of the Unicorn 8-in, 8-out (**<www.markoftheunicorn.com>**), so he can record more than two different instruments simultaneously, as well as multi output from Digital Performer (cheaper 4-in, 4-out interface PCI cards can be bought for $300 to $600). Along with the Performer, Baker has an additional $900 Mackie 1604 VLZ pro mixer (**<www.mackie.com>**), so he can bring in source material from an array of peripherals (CD player, tape deck, keyboards, samplers, etc.). A low-cost mixer with capabilities of eight to sixteen channels costs between $600 and $1,000. Pro Tools (**<www.digidesign.com>**), with its state-of-the-art audio mixing and enhancing software/hardware, is a great high-end choice if you have the budget.

For sampling he has a rackmount ESI 4000 Ensoniq (**<www.ensoniq.com>**) with a zip drive (about $1,200), and an Akai S2000 ($800), **<www.akai.com>**. To trigger samples and other tone generators he says any $500 to $1,000 keyboard controller will work fine. In a higher price range ($3,000 to $4,500), he says you'll find all-in-one keyboard workstations like Kurzweil K2000 series (**<www.young**

chang.com/kurzweil>) that include samplers and let you sequence without a computer. For a low-end workstation expect to pay $1,200 to $1,500 for keyboards like Roland XP60 (**<www.rolandus.com>**) or Korg KN364 (**<www.korg.com>**). Rackmount sound modules (**<www.rackmount.com>**) work with a keyboard controller and can give you a selection of tones for less money. The Kurzwell micro-piano (cost about $300) gives you piano, organs, and strings. Baker says the Digital Performer can be used as a sampler as well (and to check out several other inexpensive software plug-in programs from Waves [**<www.waves.com>**], DUY [**<www.duy.com>**], Antares [**<www.antares.com>**], and the VST Cubase system). For storing the digital data created on computer, a CD burner ($300 to $500) is vital, saving him the difference between storing 650MB at $2 per disk, or 1GB on an $80 Jaz cartridge.

What's interesting about Paul Baker's and my relationship is that I've never asked him to subjugate his music to my moviemaking needs. Out of almost eighty of his songs that I've used in my movies, few were actually composed and performed to fit a particular length of scene. Instead, I've selected preexisting, cutting-edge songs he produced for himself and tried them out in the rough cut (with the help of Feature Workshops editor Mike Rogers). I'll admit that it is surprising that this process has worked time and time again, but it has. And neither his time nor my postproduction budget has been overtaxed. I pay him a reasonable "one-usage" fee for the package of songs appearing in a particular movie (he signs a "Music Rights Agreement" [see appendix G] to establish his ownership of the songs beyond this musical score), and he doesn't have to spend days bending and stretching his songs to fit another person's work. It's a thrill for both of us when the final cut is shown and those original songs are heard and felt as part of a large-screen movie event. So don't be afraid to try and fit music from your best friend's band into your movie.

When Baker uses his digital equipment to compose for more traditional movies (where his music must fit preexisting scenes), he says he solves the timing problem in one of two ways: (1) He connects his stereo hi-fi VCR deck to a MIDI interface with SYMPTE, which is then connected to a computer port. After the editor copies the movie to a VHS tape on one side (L) of the stereo track, and records (or stripes) the other side (R) with LTC SYMPTE time code, the SYMPTE sonic pulse can lock to the internal SYMPTE channel in the music software, making the VHS deck the controller of the sequences' start and stop time. Or (2) he imports a movie file at low resolution (from CD, DVD, or Jazz file) into the sequencer program's QuickTime movie window. This way the playback results are immediately apparent for the marriage of music and images. Baker says this is the best route for someone who wants to compose for himself using only a Mac G-3 (or newer Mac G-4).

In case you don't have access to musicians with digital music studios, you might click on a new Website that represents over 100 music companies from around the world and provides pre-cleared songs and instrumentals specifically for use in TV, film, and multimedia (<www.licensemusic.com>). There are thousands of original tracks available for preview online, or as MP3s for free temporary usage.

Digital Printing at the Lab

Another way my films have been aided by the digital revolution is through access to the computer-controlled printing machines now used in some high-quality film laboratories to produce answer and release prints. I realized my good fortune at selecting Forde Lab of Seattle ([206] 682-2510) for printing work on my *American Orpheus* film during the question-and-answer session after its world premiere screening at the Rotterdam International Film Festival. Film producer Will Watkins, of the award-winning short *The Room*, asked me where, how, and at what cost I had produced the beautiful matte effects of the "little Indian girl" character magically materializing into existing scenes. When I told him the effect was accomplished simply by the standard "lab dissolve," he couldn't believe it. What had thrown off his perception was the fact that there was no obvious shift in the level of density of the surrounding frame, none of the obvious darkening and then lightening that usually accompanies a dissolve of two matching images. While the image was printed over itself (both shots that dissolved were exactly the same except for the inclusion of actress Katrina Eggert, who was placed into the shot while the camera kept its precise framing), the registration was so accurate in the printing machines that the two shots didn't set up the usual double-image blurriness that would have betrayed the source of the effect.

Speaking with Forde Lab manager Rich Vedvick upon my return, I learned that he had recently outfitted the lab with state-of-the-art electronically controlled 16-mm and 35-mm printing machines, whose on-board computers were responsible for adjusting the density by invisible increments during dissolves. For the best in 16-mm printing results (magical dissolves and dead-on registration), search out a lab that uses the BHP Modular Printer or its equivalent. With the BHP Modular Printer a technician at Forde Lab can choose from eight different fade curves, each setting offering a different quality of light exchange. The printer also has an option for selecting "liquid gate," which insures that your original is perfectly free of dust while being duplicated. Liquid-gate printing is essential for top-quality printing from negative original (see note on page 187). Since every function of the printer, from the mechanical drive to the programmable fader, is controlled by computer, the lab should be able to supply the filmmaker with a usable first print (answer print) more easily than older machines allowed. And your precious original footage used for printing is handled more delicately by the printing machine, since the computer dictates that the main drive more slowly begins and ends the movement of your film through its printing cycle, avoiding harsh stops and starts. In this way, less stress is placed on the thin plastic strips of 16-mm and 35-mm film that carry your images.

So when it's time to select a film lab, make sure that you inquire into exactly what kind of machines they use for printing, insuring that you can get the best possible results currently offered in this digital age.

Filmlook: Video That Looks Like Film

Some video producers who are trying to shoot high-quality video with feature-film techniques, with an eye toward distribution on videocassette, DVD, or the Web, will want to consider using a recent digital process called Filmlook (<www.filmlook.com>) that gives video the appearance of motion picture film. By offering a choice of either twenty-four or thirty simulated film frames per second, and rendering film texture, film gray scale, and color, the technicians at Filmlook give the video producer the choice of adding the element of filmlike sophistication to the feel of the images, elevating the appeal of the project. Certainly, the biggest benefit offered by this product is the immense savings of eliminating film stock, lab developing, and printing costs. But be cautioned that Filmlook acknowledges that only the top broadcast-quality video can be expected to get top results with their system.

Filmlook advises that video destined for their award-winning process (they received an award for Outstanding Achievement in Engineering from the Academy of Television Arts and Sciences) be produced on broadcast cameras (3 CCD DV video cameras get great results), and recorded on a broadcast tape format such as Digital Betacam SP, 1″, D2, or D3. The video camera's high-speed electronic shutter must *not* be used, and detail enhancement should be minimal. Any optical filters that would be used for a film shoot should be retained for the video camera. "Film-style" lighting with normal video levels and the obvious correct exposure control should be exercised during the shoot. Modification in gamma and overexposures/white clipping should be avoided. Filmlook asks the producer of videos to consult with them first before planning on using any D.V.E.-type moves, flips, spins, manipulations, computer animation, moving C.G.'s, fast or slow motion.

When you figure in their price for a seventy-five-minute video feature (around $6,450), minus either a 10 percent discount for airing a title "Processed by Filmlook" or a 20 percent student discount, this cost in the mid-$5,000 range appears almost affordable even to the low-budget moviemaker. They charge $95 per minute for the first thirty minutes, $80 per minute thereafter, with a ten-minute minimum charge of $950. For $300 you can make a test of your video footage up to three minutes in length. And given that this twelve-year-old company conscientiously color-corrects your movie scene-by-scene as well (included in the FilmLook price), and can turn out top-notch work in one day to meet your festival deadline (rendering on home-grown software can take literally a month for a feature-length video work), you may want to budget their fine service into your next production. Perhaps an investor can help out with this final, high-quality redigitizing cost. If you've spent your life examining the difference between video and film as I have, you're definitely in for a surprise. Filmlook really works! If you are a skeptic and can't believe that any digital process can change your video magically into film, then get in touch with Filmlook at 3500 West Olive Avenue, Burbank, CA 91505 ([818] 955-7082), to request supportive literature and an example of their effect on VHS cassette.

Video-to-Film Transfers

For those fortunate video producers who have managed to clear the hurdles of scripting, casting, shooting, editing on computer, and final off-lay to a master tapestock of some kind (Digital Betacam SP, DVCAM, DVD, D1, D2, etc.), their final decision, the last major cost of their production, might be to transfer their video to 35-mm film for theatrical distribution. Keep in mind that as digital video approaches the fidelity and resolution of film, and as Internet broadcasts of indie features increases (there are many great sites for video streaming, including the awesome **<www.ifilm.com>**, **<www.broadcast.com>**, and **<www.undergroundfilm.com>** with its elegant graphics and come-one-come-all attitude), the perception that a movie *must* be remade in a theatrical gauge to be a *real movie* will probably diminish. Once movies are broadcast by satellite to theaters and projected electronically to a large movie screen with all the impact of a 35-mm print, this last stage of video-to-film transfer will be unnecessary.

Companies like Digital Vision (**<www.digitalvision.com>**) are now working diligently to reduce grain and noise of video, color-correct and compress it to manageable files so that it can be cheaply and efficiently beamed to theaters by satellite. The costs of the process are determined mostly by the storage. For an average-length movie (two hours running time), equaling 50 gigabytes of storage, they are building encoders to create the necessary compressed files, and decoders at the other end of the pipeline for projection of data to the silver screen. Also needed are high-speed Internet-type file servers, and good, sharp projectors. (Judging from the great video projection I witnessed at NAB, these seem to be already in place.)

Swiss Effects

Some video-to-film services, like Swiss Effects (Jerome Poynton, [212] 727-3695 in New York, and 33 [0] 141 15 05 78 in France), **<swisseffects@access.ch>**, get their great results from transferring "interlacing video" to film, where all the video lines run together. The key to high-quality end results of either video-to-film or video programs encoded for satellite feed to theaters and Internet seems currently to rest with the differentiation between Progressive Scan video cameras (cameras that shoot an actual thirty individual frames per second) and Interlacing Scan (where the video lines intertwine). The inventors of the Swiss Effects transfer process say that there is no real "progressive scan/30 frame" process, just a scan that *appears* to offer separate frames. With progressive scan some of the old lines are calculated out to create the presence of what appear to be "frames." For the best transfer it seems logical that the sharpest signal would have all the scan lines delivering the sum total of information at the same time. With this reasoning, they say the Canon XL1 is not as good as the Sony VX1000 for video transfer to film. This is a critical topic for me, since I'm personally attracted to the Canon for its changeable lenses, cool look, and excellent-quality image and sound capabilities (for further discussion on these different scanning processes, see "SDTV," chapter 12).

Swiss Effects recommends PAL and 16:9 for the best results of their transfers (and *you* get to keep the final negative, to make prints at the lab of your choice). They say their transfers to film from video are the best in the world, so I'd definitely check them out.

Film Craft Lab

A good low-cost option for video-to-film transferring is the Film Craft Lab in Michigan (Dominic T. Troia, technical service representative, [248] 474-3900, 23815 Industrial Park Drive, Farmington Hills, MI 48335), which can knock out a seventy-five-minute 16-mm feature for

$105/minute = $7,875 plus tax (around $18,000 for a 35-mm print at $240/minute). If you want to own the negative or sound track you need to pay an additional $.40/ft./each for 16-mm ($.70/ft./each for 35-mm). Dominic at Film Craft is knowledgeable and friendly, and will be happy to discuss their CTR-3 Tri-Optical Telefilm Recorder system, how it works, and what the lab recommends for insuring that you provide the best video possible for transfer.

Film Craft Lab has a flier with tips for video setting on your camera before you shoot for a final film transfer. Here are the main ones: (1) **Maximize your video resolution.** Set back focus for maximum resolution, do not overenhance it. Look at your video on a high-resolution monitor to check out the actual image you are getting. (2) **Good lighting.** Use lighting to give separation from subject and background. Use enough light to give yourself noise-free resolution. (3) **Registering your camera.** Misregistration of your video camera will be more obvious when transferring images, since their Teledyne CTR-3 offers perfect beam registration. (4) **Use higher resolution video formats.** Keep in mind that ¾″ video footage gives only about half of the resolution of Betacam SP. Digital video (DV, Mini-DVCAM, Pro-DVCAM), recommended to achieve superior resolution. (5) **Maintain constant levels.** Don't change setting for every shot. Don't crush blacks, and watch white levels. Video levels should be kept below 105, the ideal being 100. Keep audio levels constant. "Hot" scenes can cause electronic noise. (6) **Be aware of entire frame.** Look for problems near raster edges (watch for those sound recording boom poles, etc.). (7) **Avoid serif type in credits.** Serif titles have tendency to bleed, so don't use them. (8) **Watch low-intensity reds.** Reds may take on a maroon or brown tone, so be supercareful to light this color properly if you use it at all. (9) **Reduce number of fast pans and titles.** The film will strobe slightly more because of the pull-down process (the reduction of the video's 30 frames/second to film's 24 frames/second causes a certain "steppiness" to motion in the film image), so page titles are preferable. And keep fast pans to a minimum. To these helpful hints Troia adds, "A theater screen is about four hundred times larger than your TV screen or computer monitor, so pay *very* close attention to your production as you shoot and edit."

Four Media Company

At the high end for video-to-film transfers, you'll find the Four Media Company ([800] 423-2277, 2813 West Alameda Avenue, Burbank, CA 91505, <www.4MC.com>), who are responsible for transferring almost one Academy Award–winning film per year for the last decade. Their video-to-film transfers use electron beam technology (which they invented, and are constantly improving and updating, to enhance further the compatibility of new formats). They are a very large "visual entertainment services" company with expertise in every aspect of video and film lab services (35-mm color production, 35-mm black-and-white production, 16-mm color production, on-line editing, off-line editing, tape sound, film sound, telecine/conversion, tape-to-tape color correction, transform to film from video, broadcast services [satellite broadcast], and duplication). They are a fully outfitted lab that prides itself on having top color timers and high photographic standards. Keep them in mind for all such lab services, including a blowup from 16-mm to 35-mm, or the reverse (reduction from 35-mm to 16-mm for restoration of old nitrate movies, going directly to an interpositive with answer print quality).

The costs are high for their transfer services, but worth it. They have a four-minute minimum at $434.50/minute for 35-mm = $1,738* (to transfer your video feature's trailer to film). Ten minutes of transfer will cost you $4,345*, and a 75-minute feature transferred to 35-mm will run about $32,587*. 16-mm is a bit cheaper, costing about $15,000* for the transfer of a 75-minute video. They do not include their negative (your movie's negative for printing that they've created with their electron beam technology) in the items you get to take home, but they're happy to strike additional prints for you at their lab. In a sense they believe they are protecting a client from creating a less-than-top-quality print (at a competing lab), by insuring that they retain possession of the negative.

Four Media highly recommends that a moviemaker get in touch *before* the shoot to insure that the final 16-mm or 35-mm film result will

* *Plus tax.*

look terrific. They have a comprehensive list of recommendations, dos and don'ts for shooting your video feature, that they will discuss by phone (ask for their brochure of lab prices and procedures). If you've seen anything from *Wayne's World* to *The Lion King* or *Hoop Dreams*, you've undoubtedly seen their fine work on the screen at your local theater.

note: Each moviemaker must thoroughly research this issue of "progressive scan" versus "interlacing scan" before he or she (1) purchases an expensive DV camera, and (2) selects a transfer house/process that will create their (expensive) final film print. Some DV cameras offer both progressive and interlacing scan, thus giving the buyer confidence that they'll be covered either way. You may want to also consider the purchase of a European Pal camera with higher resolution, that top transfer houses like Swiss Effects recommends (keep in mind that you'll need a Pal playback/record deck as well). And look for "hidden" lab costs on transfers, and other fees for owning the reproducible negative of your movie. Make sure that you have the full financial and artistic overview before handing your precious video masters over to any transfer company, and make sure you have a Digital Betacam submaster second copy before entrusting the final computer cut to anyone.

Considering all your choices of cameras and editing systems can be daunting, but in life we all have to make choices every day. Where will we work? Where will we live? Which apartment will we choose? Who will be our friend, lover, wife, or husband? What TV program will we watch (soon to become a more difficult problem with the coming of WebTV, streaming video, tapeless video decks with built-in computers that will locate and record your menu of shows each day from hundreds of new digital channels!).

One important choice will be how much to spend. To avoid high monthly credit card payments, try to keep to a real budget. Maybe a good choice is to buy a turnkey system from companies like Promax (**<www.promax.com>**) which includes camera, editing deck, computer, and monitor, so you're positive you have *everything* you need for moviemaking at around $12,000. But be aware that whichever DV camera or editing software you select, it will be outdated in a few years (and computers just keep getting more powerful). It makes no sense to go through life regretting every past decision and second-guessing each choice. Look upon the decisions you make as part of a learning curve. It may be that your growing interest in digital feature-length moviemaking is the start of positive thinking, of finding some real purpose to your life. It's time now to move forward, to put thoughts into action.

Once you have your digital moviemaking workstation securely located in your office or home, you can shoot your movies for just the cost of the tape cassettes, DVD disk, or completely free (record right onto the hard drive of your computer with "video capture" software). You won't have to answer to investors or anyone. Just let your intuition take over, let the decisions you make (hundreds more decisions) about story, casting, locations, shooting, and editing be based on your personal worldview. Make something adventurous—enlighten us (please!). Help your audience experience your own unique view of life instead of some trumped-up, Hollywood-style, rip-off, pseudo-action-thriller escapade. Aim your camera inward, and show us your real life and that of your friends (look what happened when Kevin Smith did that in *Clerks*!). That's the gift we'll be looking forward to receiving from you (streaming on the Web . . . or by satellite), as you become one of the electronic moviemakers of the new millennium.

12 HDTV and the Future

Well, the future is here! It's hard to believe that since I wrote the first revision of my book in 1994, we've seen the Internet, Websites, and e-mail taking over part of our lives, not to mention HDTV. There's hardly any way to write about the trends of digital filmmaking technology these days and beat the curve, because as soon as you hear about something new and exciting, it's already been unveiled on someone's Website, ready for purchase or downloading! At the NAB '99 (the National Association of Broadcasters) convention that I attended in Las Vegas, there was a great deal of new technology dedicated to the coming launch of HDTV broadcasting. Everywhere you looked, you saw those 2:1 ratio TV screens, large (at least a yard across), flat, ready to put up on your wall for the price of a VW station wagon. It seemed everyone would soon have a luxury screening room right in their own living room. I hope the future for filmmakers will include the thrill of seeing their own indie movies running full-length on these home-theater screens, hooked up from their computer by Web TV. It's already beginning to happen at **<www.broadcasting.com>** (owned by Yahoo), **<www.alwaysindependentfilms.com>**, **<www.reelplay.com>**, **<www.ifilm.com>**, **<www.reeluniverse.com>**, **<www.undergroundfilm.com>**, and others, where indies can submit their home-grown features for presentation on the Web, returning precious dollars to those moviemakers who risked time and resources to scratch together a production. We all now have wide-screen capabilities, by shooting digital video at 16:9 ratio (just like Hollywood), even with the cheapest consumer-priced DV video cameras, and with the proper editing and special-effects software packages (Adobe's After Effects, Effetto Pronto, Ice, Final Cut Pro, etc.), we can match Hollywood again in animation by creating entirely new worlds (Titanic-size!) right at home on our computer screen (as long as there are a few extra gigabytes of handy storage).

The guy I sat next to on the plane ride to NAB '99 explained how in the future people will have "bytes of Internet money," a kind of credit card that can be used on the Web, so that supercheap items costing under a dollar can be obtained without credit card fees or overhead. If I ran a 1920s-style Saturday matinee screening of my latest indie movie, and charged just a nickel of "Web-cash" per person, 10,000 people streaming the movie would mean a payday of $500 (or charging 50 cents per person would bring in $5,000—not a bad way to recoup production monies).

My fellow traveler further explained that when I move my cursor around on my computer screen with the mouse, there is a program in the computer that is redrawing the cursor at whatever new position I move it to, while at the same time filling in the area where the cursor used to be. That arrow isn't just sliding around on the screen. His point was that computers are much more complicated than the average person thinks. We home consumers like to push a button to wash our clothes, start up a car and drive, and edit movies on computer, hassle-free. Forget trying to understand these technological marvels. It's time to just jump in and use the advances to make your high-tech/low-budget movies.

HDTV

So far, what HDTV represents is that by 2006 we'll all have to purchase new TVs to receive a broadcast signal, thanks to a mandate of the FCC that will put part of the NTSC frequency out of business (this frequency is slated to be used for other purposes). The FCC mandate says, "High Density TV" must employ MPEG-2 compression, should accommodate six channels of AC-3 audio (Dolby) for broadcast in a 5:1 compression ratio, and should be able to send out

Sony HDW-500 videocassette recorder, designed for HDTV. Photo courtesy Sony Corporation.

4:3 SDTV pictures as well as 16:9 digital images. Its goal is to give us double the resolution we currently enjoy on our old TV sets.

It's a little strange to be confronted once again by the realization that there are haves and have-nots in America, that some of us will likely have to huddle around the only HDTV on the block (I watched Hopalong Cassidy on our landlord's four-inch TV set before my family finally bought a B&W console in 1951!). While the first HDTV models will supposedly be selling in the price range of $3,000 to $11,000, there may actually be "converter sets" available for purchase for around $150, which allow HDTV signals to play on your old TV. Still in question is how the old TVs will handle the 16:9 ratio (automatic "letterbox"?), AC-3 Dolby sound, or the expanded channel capacity (running out of numbers on the TV dial!). Yes, HDTV will be sharper, and it will arrive on your set in wide-screen format, but the problem remains the same—what will we be watching? Surely, the advertising of modern products will be enhanced, sharper bottles of shampoo (and sharper, more in-your-face gorgeous models to hawk the products), but what does all this have to do with the low/no-budget moviemaker? For one thing, any feature not shot with the 16:9 "letterbox" wide-screen ratio will seem passé. It's as if the broadcasters will be forcing everyone to shoot as creatively as the famous French writer-director Jean-Luc Godard did in his famous Cinemascope movie *Contempt*, which isn't a bad thing since that movie is a great example of the use of space on the canvas of the motion picture screen. Godard is the one who said, "You don't make a movie, the movie makes you." And if you go the DV route for producing your movies of the future, most video cameras already offer the 16:9 shooting ratio, so newcomers to the art of videography have a good run at becoming attuned to the new wide-screen ratio before confronting the excessive expenses of actually converting to HDTV.

Some companies, like HDVision of Irving, Texas (**<www.hdvision.com>**), have been shooting HDTV since the early 1990s, and may be able to shed some light on the problems (check out their Website). They say they can match a Super 16-mm film budget with HDTV as long as shooting is every day, not the documentary style of a couple of shooting days and then several days of travel.

SDTV

Standard definition television (recently just called DTV—digital TV) is similar to HDTV in that it's digital as well, but different because it runs as "progressive" scan. What's apparent is that within the range of megabits the FCC has allocated for HDTV (19.34 mbs/second), SDTV could broadcast three times the information (three separate SDTV channels), which, to some, represents three times the advertising potential. So there is a battle between TV broadcasters and computer companies (read Microsoft) over just how the DTV images will be drawn to the screen. Companies fighting to push their Web TV products want "progressive" scan, which is used on computer screens, while broadcasters are pushing for the "interlacing" scanning, like the kind we have on our old TV sets. For more information on the difference between progressive and interlacing scans, check out this Website from DemoGraFX high-technology research and consulting firm (**<http://home.earthlink.net/~demografx/intrice.html>**), which attempts to explain the difference. Will our television become like a huge computer that takes over a wall with its flat-screen format and Internet browsing, or will it be like having our own private screening room, turning into a motion picture theater screen (or both)? This decision and many others will be made for us. The indie moviemaker has to hope that the final result will enable more ease of distribution for his or her low/no-budget product. It will be time for filmmakers with features in the closet to take advantage of these new outlets for past feature-length works and begin the submitting process all over again. Old 16-mm movies with good, clean sound tracks and clear images (that can hold up to reframing at 16:9) may suddenly become highly desirable for this new HDTV marketplace. And more channels should equal more chances for sale of oddball movies made with a fresh and original style.

3-D Video and "Camera's Perspective" Software

At NAB '99 there were two products (other than the breakthrough editing software of Final Cut Pro) that surprised me the most as a moviemaker.

When I saw the sign for the Z-CAM, a 3-D video studio camera, I had to go over and check it out. What it can do is map the space before its lens, making a real-time separation between an object and its background. Against a blue screen it can do "depth-keying" instead of chroma-keying. It can shoot screenless blue-screen type imaging for TV studios, where foreground items can be recorded against any background and later displayed against other selected backgrounds. Since Z-CAM "captures and maps the third dimension," the videomaker can place various objects anywhere in a scene, in front of or behind something else (a person, or . . .), in real time.

Not only can the cinematographer/moviemaker rearrange reality, but he or she can add special 3-D effects in real time as well, including illumination, "augmentation of a 3-D scene," and interaction between real objects and those created by the imagination. The brochure says that this core technology of 3DV might be used for desktop scanning, geographic information systems (GIS), quality assurance, robotics vision, civil engineering, and medical devices. I like to imagine this unbelievable tool falling into the hands of a few crazy moviemakers/media artists who can incorporate this awesome technology to tell their story, use it to reshuffle reality in a way never seen before. Does this start giving you ideas for a movie? Dial them up on your modem (3DV System Ltd., Building 7, Yokneam Industrial Park, P.O. Box 249, Yokneam 20692, Israel, 972-4-959-9599, info@3dvsys tems.com, <**www.3dvsystems.com**>).

In another area of the NAB convention, an amazing effects software and hardware system called Effetto Pronto (Videonics, 1370 Dell Avenue, Campbell, CA 95008, [408] 866-8300, <**www.videonics.com**>) was being demonstrated. It operates in "a true perspective 3-D environment." The most stunning of its mind-boggling effects was the ability to add motion and perspective to the camera's path. They call it "camera view animatable in 3-D space." That means that the user can select the POV of the camera at any point in the picture plane (just like a modeling program) and then design the camera's motion (lift it high, as if on a crane, or bring it in low . . .) and program how Effetto Pronto will eventually approach its subject. Think about what this means. You can create a series of amazing shots and perspectives in postproduction, *after* you've shot your movie.

The user can also create the world into which the camera moves. Effetto Pronto gives you the option of building "unlimited layers" of graphic and motion effects, perhaps integrating a background imported from Adobe's Photoshop, adding uncompressed video (actual taped footage from your shoot) through a system such as Gallea, using DigiEffects, Boris, Ice, etc., to add fantastic effects filters (register at the Videonics Website for a free one-month test drive of this great product!). You can then paint and rotoscope scenes in detail (using built-in Puffin Designs Commotion software for motion tracking, etc.), rotate or warp any object on its X, Y, or Z axis, with Effetto Pronto supplying real-time playback capabilities and ultimate layoff of the finished work to any QuickTime-based nonlinear editing system like Final Cut Pro, EditDV, Adobe Premiere, Media 100, or Avid. And it does all this at speeds ten times faster than with software-only products (Effetto Pronto's hardware accelerator, with Dynamic Effects Caching, renders on-the-fly). It's fine products like Effetto Pronto (priced under $5,500, but capable of producing a million-dollar look) that will put the magic of DV into the hands of the artists.

Sony HDVW 700A HDTV digital video camera (the twenty-four frames/sec *Star Wars* camera will look similar, except for Panavision lenses). Photo courtesy Sony Corporation.

Twenty-four-Frames-per-Second Video

Thanks to George Lucas and his Industrial Light and Magic in Northern California, Sony R&D has created a video camera for the twenty-first century that can shoot at twenty-four frames per second and deliver forty minutes per tape of 1,920 pixels by 1,080 vertical lines of resolution for the new *Star Wars* movies. Since this camera shoots twenty-four progressive scan lines in the HDTV format, the motion of the recording will seem virtually identical to film, at the same time offering all the elasticity that video has enjoyed as a creative tool at ILM. The Sony technician I spoke with about this new breakthrough technology said that the camera closely resembles the HDTV 700A Sony camera, and its cost will be comparable to other HDTV cameras in the top professional range (approaching $100,000).

If you are in the market for a DV camera, you'll notice that the Canon XL1 and several other low-end Canon DV cameras also offer "progressive scan," but at the more typical video speed of thirty frames per second, while some Sony cameras allow the user to switch between "interlacing" and "progressive" scan. Keep in mind that if your DV production is aiming at a film blowup to a 35-mm film print for theatrical presentation, there are some facilities that believe an interlacing scan is superior to progressive for getting the best quality on the screen (see "Swiss Effects," chapter 11). Do some research before you make a new camera purchase, so you won't be stuck with a piece of equipment that fails to meet your future needs. What's certain is that filmmakers of the future will be shooting video at twenty-four frames per second, editing the results on their computers without generation loss, while enjoying complete control over their electronic images.

PCMCIA Card Technology

If you want a preview of where digital moviemaking equipment is heading, all you have to do is look at a photo of the new Nagra Ares-C field recorder, a sound recorder with no moving parts. That's right. Nothing moves except the numbers on the digital readout screen. Sound is recorded directly to Type I/II PCMCIA cards, thin credit-card-wide electronic storage "sticks" that can hold either eighty minutes of mono or forty minutes of stereo recording time. Sound is recorded without tape transports, disk drives, or magnetic components of any kind. And each stick can be recorded over and over, up to 100,000 (no more ¼" sound recording stock!). If two PCMCIA cards are placed into the holder when recording on location, then the Nagra will automatically switch seamlessly to recording on the second stick when the first runs out of digital space. Files can also be copied at high speed from card to card.

The Nagra Ares-C has other amazing attributes as well. It runs completely silently, has low power consumption (runs continuously for up to fifteen hours on just eight D-cell batteries), and can withstand hostile environments ranging from –5 degrees Fahrenheit (–20C) to +140 degrees Fahrenheit (60C). Plus it has an on-board non-destructive EDL-based virtual editing capability, which allows quick cut-and-paste to exact edit points with a scrub wheel locator. This all sounds preposterous, but it's true! Cost for this amazing Nagra Ares-C begins

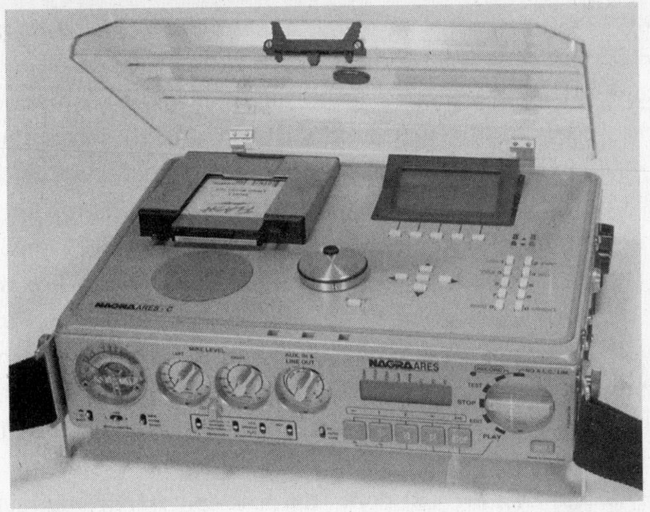

Nagra Ares-C records to PCMCIA "stick," with no moving parts. Photo courtesy of Nagra, Inc.

at around $7,900 (Nagra USA, 240 Great Circle Road, Suite 326, Nashville, TN 37228, [615] 726-5191, <www.nagra.com>).

The Sony DSR-PD100A DVCAM camera and other high-end digital video models now use this same PCMCIA card technology as a reusable still-image receptor for removable media, turning DV cameras into crossover digital still cameras as well. How long will it take before we record our indie digital features on memory cards the size and shape of credit cards?

Univisium

As many of us experiment with the new DV ratio of 16:9 to shoot our no/low-budget video movies, the discussion continues regarding which screen format ratio best serves both theatrical and TV presentation. Epic cinematographer Vittorio Storaro (*Last Tango in Paris*, *Apocalypse Now*, *The Last Emperor*, *Bulworth*, *Tango*, etc.) has well presented his concerns about his careful work being chopped and altered for different media in a treatise called *Univisium* (see

<www.univisium.com>, a Website dedicated to discussing the issues and history of movie formats). He asks that the various movie and technological companies get together and reduce the 65-mm film ratio by .21, as well as adding that same .21 to the HDTV format of 1:1.79, to reach a consensus on a 1:2 "one standard" format, suitable for both TV and theatrical presentation. It has to be discouraging for him to shoot movies for the large screen and then see his images force-fit into at least three different formats (4:3, 1:1.79, 1:85). Storaro says he recognizes the need for moviegoers to get together in a large "amniotic sac," to sit as part of an audience in theaters, and that's perhaps the best argument why "going to the movies" will continue as a pastime even when we all have our own HDTV cinemas at home. The huge theatrical screen will beckon us with its large-scale event movies (like *Star Wars II* and *III*). He just hopes that the epic movie you see on that theater screen is 2:1, a rectangle twice as long as it is high, and that the rebroadcast of that movie is in exactly the same shape (has the same visual content) as when it was first completed.

How does this controversy affect the low/no-budget e-feature filmmaker? It at least helps us pay attention to the ratio in which we shoot, since the shape of our movie image may make the difference between getting distribution or not. If you shoot a movie in traditional boxy 16-mm (4:3), are you willing to have the top and bottom of your image lopped off for a showing on HDTV? Did you plan for the widescreen "letterbox" when you shot on location (framing high, giving ample space over the top of your actors' faces?). Hopefully so. Univisium also begs the moviemaker to think in "epic" scale. Use all the corners of the frame. Let the location become another "character" in your movie. Shoot wide-open spaces. Stretch your vision. Put in your vote of confidence for 2:1 (register your approval with an e-mail at their Website).

Wrap Up

For those diehard filmmakers who refuse to accept video as a legitimate medium of expression, it's going to be a difficult period of transition. Once digital video becomes equal in every way to film, has

The new shape of desktop moviemaking—Apple's iMac DV "Special Edition" with built-in iMovie editing software and FireWire ports. Photo courtesy Apple Computer, Inc.

the same precise high resolution and is shot at exactly the same frame rate of twenty-four frames per second (and is more affordable), then what's there to argue about? And won't it be nice to know that after you've shot your scenes, you don't have to wait and worry while a film laboratory threads your exposed strip of celluloid onto a machine where it's run through a chemical bath for developing (at the high cost for processing and work printing)? The video (whether on "stick," disk, or tape) is ready for editing immediately. And your postproduction is totally within your control! From rough to fine cut, effects (and animated special effects!), sound mix and music, titles, and final tightening of resolution, it's all right at your fingertips, in your powerful home computer. You can have a good-paying job in the daytime and spend your evenings creating a movie (using the same time you used to watch TV—you can make your own shows!). Those "feature filmmakers" who've held on to the lofty concept of "directors" being some sort of elite class must now understand that it's a new game, and *anyone* with talent and creative gifts can play. And if you're the kind of negative person who fears competition and works to keep it down, you're in for a big shock, because there are some young kids out there, in America and Europe and elsewhere, who are going to make special movies that dazzle the eyes and mind, genuine works of art the likes of which the world has never seen before (all thanks to this e-film revolution). No need to panic, though. There are at least a few good years of watchful learning ahead, time to prepare for the radical shift in viewing habits, computer interaction, and producing skills needed for new formats of creativity. One thing for certain is that the moviemaker of the twenty-first century will have the opportunity to produce his or her masterworks, using these new tools of the digital age.

APPENDIX A

Collaboration Agreement

I, Michael Church, on this ______________ day of ______________, 1984, do agree to sell to Richard R. Schmidt the option to my writing THE MONOPOLE VERIFICATION EXPERIMENTS for production into a motion picture film. Schmidt agrees to pay $100 per year for this option and $1,000 after principal photography is completed as a salary for the scripting. After the $1,000 payment the option payments of $100 per year will terminate. If the final budget for the film is above $25,000 then Schmidt agrees to pay Michael Church one twenty-fifth ($\frac{1}{25}$) of the total budget up to a total of $10,000 for his writing and scripting.

Michael Church agrees that the final script for the film will be a collaboration between himself and Richard R. Schmidt and that the title appearing in the film will read SCRIPT BY MICHAEL CHURCH AND RICHARD R. SCHMIDT. It is also agreed that a separate title in the film will read ORIGINAL STORY BY MICHAEL CHURCH.

Schmidt with his signature below also agrees to pay Michael Church 10% of the profits above expenses for his writing and scripting of the film (if Schmidt is Producer) and $100 for the option in four $25 payments due the ninth of each month, January, February, March, April 1984. It is understood that with the signatures below Schmidt has purchased the right to Direct, Film, Edit, and Produce without restriction the film tentatively entitled THE MONOPOLE VERIFICATION EXPERIMENT.

______________________	______________________
Michael Church	Richard R. Schmidt
______________________	______________________
Date/Location	Date/Location

APPENDIX B

Sample Contract for Deferred Payment and Profit Sharing

Description of and Assignments of Interest of Profits in "Emerald Cities," A Feature-Length Motion Picture Film

Description

RICHARD R. SCHMIDT ("Schmidt"), doing business as LIVING LEGEND PRODUCTIONS (L. L. Productions/"LLP") for the production and distribution of a feature length 16-millimeter color motion picture tentatively entitled "EMERALD CITIES" ("the film"), shall be its producer, director, cameraman, and editor. The leading actors in the film will be Carolyn Zaremba ("Z"), Ed Nylund ("Ed"), Willie-Boy Walker ("Willie"), Lowell Darling ("Lowell"), Lawrence Falconi ("Ted"), Dick Richardson ("Dick"), and Kelly Brock Boen ("Kelly"). The crew will consist of Nick Bertoni (sound), Neelon Crawford (sound), Bill Kimberlin (assistant camera), with Julie Schachter (stills, continuity).

The tentative budget for the production of the film, exclusive of distribution costs, is $27,500.00, and Schmidt agrees to contribute $5,000.00 of that amount. Schmidt, as Producer of the film, anticipates that at least $22,500.00 as capital will be required to complete the production of the film, and an additional amount as capital will be required to arrange for and/or distribute the film. These amounts and Schmidt's $5,000.00 contribution will be the investment of the investors for the production and distribution of the film.

The shooting schedule for the film is for a five (5) day uninterrupted period beginning on or about December 15, 1979, in and about the Upper Mojave Desert region/Death Valley, California. This five-day shooting period will be one third (⅓) of the total on-location filming necessary to complete the film. The other two thirds (⅔) of the shooting is expected to take place in the San Francisco/Oakland area during a ten-day period on or before March 1, 1980, and the editing period thereafter is expected to be approximately five (5) months (August 1980).

Interests

All amounts specified below as salaries for work completed on the film tentatively entitled "EMERALD CITIES" will refer to only the first one third (⅓) of the total film production unless so indicated.

Bill Kimberlin (assistant camera) has received $300.00 out of a total of $750.00, the remaining $450.00 will be paid on or before February 15, 1980, for rental of Eclair NPR camera, Nagra and accessories, and salary.

Nick Bertoni (sound) will receive a total of $300.00 for sound recording on location salary.

Carolyn Zaremba (actress) has received $100.00 out of a total of $200.00 for salary on five-day shoot, with a guarantee of $50.00 per day for remaining acting on the film, up to but not exceeding a guarantee of $1,000.00 total salary for completing her lead role in the film.

Ed Nylund and *Willie-Boy Walker* will each receive $500.00 total for acting in the film, including the second period of the filming.

Lowell Darling, Lawrence Falconi, and *Kelly Brock Boen* will each receive $200.00 total for acting in the film, including the second period of filming.

Julie Schachter will receive $200.00 for stills and continuity for the film, including the second period of the filming.

Kathleen Beeler, William Farley, and *George Manupelli* will each receive $200 for second period of filming, as will Elizabeth Sher. *Flipper* and *The Mutants* will each receive $500 for music/performance.

Dick Richardson, and *Richard R. Schmidt* (writers), will each receive $500.00 total for their scripting of the film, including the second period of filming.

The first moneys received by LLP for the film will be first applied to payment of all outstanding accounts payable for the production and distribution of the film until paid in full; next to the repayment to the investors of the entire amounts of their contributions actually expended for the production and distribution of the film; and thereafter, all moneys received by LLP for the film will be paid by LLP as follows:

1. Director, producer, cameraman, editor of the film (Schmidt)	20%
2. Investor	7%
3. Leading actor for the film (Carolyn Zaremba)	10%

4. Supporting actor for the film (Ed Nylund) 8%
5. Supporting actor for the film (Willie-Boy Walker) 8%
6. Writer for the film, actor (Dick Richardson) 10%
7. Writer for the film (Schmidt) 5%
8. Video production (Joe Rees-Target) 5%
9. Additional cast for the film (Lowell Darling) 2%
10. Writer for the film, actor (Ted Falconi) 5%
11. Music/performance (FLIPPER) 2%
12. Additional cast for the film (Kelly Boen) 2%
13. Camera assistant for the film (Bill Kimberlin) 2%
14. Sound recording for the film (Nick Bertoni) 2%
15. Stills, continuity for the film (Julie Schachter) 2%
16. Music/performance (THE MUTANTS) 2%
17. Camera assistant for the film (Kathleen Beeler) 2%
18. Conceptual adviser for the film (William Farley) 2%
19. Additional video (Liz Sher) 2%
20. Additional filming (Jon Jost) 2%

The listed percentages (page 3) will be payable to each of the persons set forth in parentheses after each of the positions only in the event each of these persons actually performs the customary services for his/her position through the completion of the production of the film. Any person not providing such services will receive no percentage, unless otherwise agreed to by the producer. Any person, after earning his percentage, may assign all or any part of the same by written notification thereof to LLP.

By signing this agreement the parties hereto agreed to all terms and conditions set forth herein on this ______________ day of December, 1979.

Date and Place of Execution	Signatures
1. ______________________	______________________ Richard R. Schmidt
2. ______________________	______________________ Investor
3. ______________________	______________________ Carolyn Zaremba
4. ______________________	______________________ Ed Nylund

5. ______________________ ______________________
Willie-Boy Walker

6. ______________________ ______________________
Richard A. Richardson

7. ______________________ ______________________
Richard R. Schmidt

8. ______________________ ______________________
Joe Rees

9. ______________________ ______________________
Lowell Darling

10. ______________________ ______________________
Ted Falconi

11. ______________________ ______________________
FLIPPER

12. ______________________ ______________________
Kelly Brock Boen

13. ______________________ ______________________
Bill Kimberlin

14. ______________________ ______________________
Nick Bertoni

15. ______________________ ______________________
Julie Schachter

16. ______________________ ______________________
THE MUTANTS

17. ______________________ ______________________
Kathleen Beeler

18. ______________________ ______________________
William Farley

19. ______________________ ______________________
Liz Sher

20. ______________________ ______________________
Jon Jost

APPENDIX C

Deal Memorandum

Please keep one copy and sign and return the other to us.

From: Richard R. Schmidt

To: ______________

Re: Motion Picture currently entitled "MORGAN'S CAKE"

This Deal Memorandum describes how deferred payments, if any, resulting from the exploitation of the motion picture currently entitled "MORGAN'S CAKE" (hereinafter referred to as the "Film") will be paid. "Deferred compensation" will be payable from all gross receipts received by Morgan's Cake, a California Limited Partnership (the "Partnership"), from the exploitation of the Film after repayment of all production costs, including financing costs, and payment of all distribution costs. Richard R. Schmidt (hereinafter referred to as the "Producer") is the General Partner of the Partnership and the Producer of the Film. The Producer reserves the right to distribute the Film himself, in which event his distribution fee will be at market rates. Deferred compensation will be paid among all persons who provide services in the production of the Film who have not been paid in full. Payments will be made *pari passu,* with each person's share determined by the amount of money agreed to be paid to that person minus any money already paid to that person. The Producer will be in this equation in the same manner as all other persons. The amount set forth opposite your name below is the total amount of compensation for services to be rendered by you, as indicated above, on the Film. In the event you do not provide your full services during the production of the Film, you will receive either reduced compensation, based upon the ratio of the total amount of time provided by you in the production of the Film to the total amount of time agreed to be provided by you for the production of the Film; or, if you provide no such services, you will receive no compensation.

The Producer retains full copyright to the Film and reserves the right to make all marketing, financial and artistic decisions for the Film regardless of payment of any compensation to you.

If you approve of this arrangement, please sign on the line provided below for your signature and return one copy to us in the enclosed envelope.

MORGAN'S CAKE, a California Limited Partnership

By ____________________	____________________	$____________________
Richard R. Schmidt, General Partner	Your Signature	Amount

APPENDIX D

Sample Investment Agreement

Agreement

RICHARD R. SCHMIDT ("Schmidt"), doing business as L.L. PRODUCTIONS, intends to produce and exploit a 16-millimeter motion picture film tentatively entitled *THE ROOMMATE* ("the picture").

The following persons named below will participate in the writing, directing, filming, and editing of the motion picture, and upon completion of such services therein will each receive ten percent (10%) interest in the gross profits derived by Schmidt from the picture and its ancillary rights. All monies invested in the making of the feature length film (including tuition) will be paid back to each investor with 10% per year interest, this payment made before percentage interests will be paid. CCAC film department will receive 5% of the net profits as a fund for feature filmmaking.

This agreement may be executed in several counterparts, each of which shall be deemed an original and such counterparts shall together constitute one and the same agreement, binding all the parties hereto notwithstanding all of the parties are not signatory to the original on the same counterpart. Signers below will equally share all profits not assigned on page 2.

Date and Place of Execution	Signatures
______________________	______________________
______________________	______________________
______________________	______________________
______________________	______________________
______________________	______________________
______________________	______________________
______________________	______________________
______________________	______________________

APPENDIX E

Release

Release

FOR VALUABLE CONSIDERATION, including the agreement to produce the motion picture currently entitled "MORGAN'S CAKE," I hereby irrevocably grant to Morgan's Cake, a California Limited Partnership (the "Partnership"), its licensees, agents, successors and assigns, the right (but not the obligation), in perpetuity throughout the world, in all media, now or hereafter known, to use (in any manner it deems appropriate, and without limitation) in and in connection with the motion picture, by whatever means exhibited, advertised or exploited: my appearance in the motion picture, still photographs of me, recordings of my voice taken or made of me by it, any music sung or played by me, and my actual or fictitious name.

On my own behalf, and on behalf of my heirs, next of kin, executors, administrators, successors and assigns, I hereby release the Partnership, its agents, licensees, successors and assigns, from any and all claims, liabilities and damages arising out of the rights granted hereunder, or the exercise thereof.

______________________	______________________
Date	Signature
______________________	______________________
Street Address	City, State, Zip Code
______________________	______________________
Telephone Number	Social Security Number

I am the parent or legal guardian of ________________________. I hereby irrevocably consent to the foregoing grant and agreement. I agree to indemnify the Partnership, its licensees, agents, successors and assigns, and hold each of the foregoing harmless from any and all damages, losses and expenses resulting from any actual or purported disaffirmance or rescission of the above agreement by the signatory thereto.

______________________	______________________
Date	Signature of Parent or Guardian

APPENDIX F

Location Agreement

Location Agreement

Gentlemen:

I (we) hereby grant to you, your successors, assigns and licensees, the right to photograph, reproduce and use (either accurately or with such liberties as they may deem necessary) the exteriors and interiors of the premises located at ______________________________, and to bring personnel and equipment onto the premises and remove same.

You may have possession of the premises on or about ___________, 20__, and may continue in possession thereof until the completion of your proposed scenes and work, estimated to require about ____ days of occupancy over a period of ____ days.

However, in the event of illness of actors, director, or other essential artists and crew, or weather conditions, or any other occurrence beyond your control, preventing you from starting work on the date designated above, or in the event of damaged or imperfect film or equipment, you shall have the right to use the premises at a later date to be mutually agreed upon.

This is in connection with the motion picture photoplay tentatively entitled ____________________, and includes the right to re-use the photography in connection with other motion picture photoplays as you, your successors, assigns and licensees shall elect, and, in connection with the exhibition, advertising and exploitation thereof, in any manner whatsoever and at any time in any part of the world.

You agree to hold me (us) free from any claims for damage or injury arising during your occupancy of the premises and arising out of your negligence thereon, and to leave the premises in as good order and condition as when received by you, reasonable wear, tear, force majeure, and use herein permitted excepted.

I (we) acknowledge that, in photographing the premises, you are not in any way depicting or portraying me (us) in the motion picture photoplay, either directly or indirectly. I (we) will not assert or maintain against you any claim of any kind or nature whatsoever, including, without limitation, those based upon invasion of privacy or other civil rights, defamation, libel or slander, in connection with the exercise of the permission herein granted.

I (we) represent that I (we) are the owner(s) and/or authorized representative of the premises, and that I (we) have the authority to grant you the permission and rights herein granted, and that no one else's permission is required.

Dated: ______________ ______________________________

Signature of Owner or Authorized Agent

____

Signature of Owner or Authorized Agent

____

Print Name(s)

APPENDIX G

Music Rights Agreement

Licensor: ____

Address: ____

____

City/State: ____

This Synchronization License Agreement ("License") is made and entered into this ____ day of __________, 1993, by and between __________________ ("Licensor") and ____Rick Schmidt____.

1. In full and final consideration of the sum of __________________, receipt of which is hereby acknowledged, Licensor grants to Rick Schmidt the non-exclusive, irrevocable right, license, privilege and authority to record on film or videotape and use the musical compositions and recordings entitled ______________________ in synchronization or timed relation with the film production currently entitled ___________________________.

2. Licensor authorizes Rick Schmidt to use or cause to be used the aforesaid musical compositions and recordings in conjunction with the aforesaid film production in any manner he deems fit including, but not limited to, the purpose of advertising and exploiting said film production and the right to license and distribute the aforesaid musical compositions in conjunction with said film production throughout the world on any medium or forum, whether now known or hereinafter created.

3. The musical compositions and recordings licensed pursuant to this agreement shall not be distributed or exploited separately or independently of said film production.

4. Licensor hereby represents and warrants that he/she has the full legal right, power and authority to grant this license and that the performance rights to the aforesaid musical compositions and recordings are available for license through ASCAP, BMI, or SESAC.

5. Licensor warrants, represents and agrees that Licensor will obtain in writing all requisite consents and permissions of labor organizations, the copyright owners, and the Artist (if applicable) whose performances are embodied in the compositions and recordings and that Licensor will pay all re-use payments, fees, royalties and other sums required to be paid for such consents and permission, in connection with Schmidt's use of the compositions and recordings. If Schmidt so requires, Licensor will obtain such persons and deliver to him any documents that he requires to confirm that they will not look to Schmidt for any payments in connection with the compositions and recordings in the film production. Licensor will indemnify and hold FEATURE WORKSHOPS and its officers and directors harmless from any and all claims, liabilities, losses, damages and expenses including, without limitation, attorneys' fees and legal expenses arising from any breach of Licensor's warranties, representations or covenants under this license, or in any way resulting from or connected with Schmidt's use of the compositions and recordings.

6. The term of this license is for the worldwide period of all copyrights in and to the musical compositions and recordings and any and all renewals or extensions thereof that Licensor may now or hereafter own or control.

7. The rights granted herein shall inure to the benefit of FEATURE WORKSHOPS, its licensees, successors and assigns.

____

Date

By ______________________________ By ______________________________

APPENDIX H

California Limited Partnership Agreement

Private Placement Memorandum

DATED AS OF ___________.

$1,000,000 in 100 Units of $10,000 each
of limited liability company interests in
(Movie Title), LLC
A California Limited Liability Company (the "LLC"),
to be formed for the purpose of facilitating financing for the
production and exploitation of a motion picture tentatively titled:
____

THESE SECURITIES ARE OFFERED UNDER AN EXEMPTION FROM REGISTRATION UNDER RULE 506 PROMULGATED BY THE UNITED STATES SECURITIES AND EXCHANGE COMMISSION, AND UNDER CALIFORNIA CORPORATIONS CODE SECTION 25102(f). WHETHER THESE SECURITIES ARE EXEMPT FROM REGISTRATION PURSUANT TO SAID REGULATIONS OR OTHERWISE HAS NOT BEEN PASSED UPON BY THE SECURITIES AND EXCHANGE COMMISSION, THE COMMISSIONER OF CORPORATIONS OF THE STATE OF CALIFORNIA OR ANY OTHER REGULATORY AGENCY, NOR HAS ANY SUCH AGENCY PASSED UPON THE MERITS OF THIS OFFERING. ANY REPRESENTATION TO THE CONTRARY OR ANY REPRESENTATION THAT ANY REGULATORY AGENCY HAS PASSED UPON THE ACCURACY OR COMPLETENESS OF THIS MEMORANDUM OR THE OPERATING AGREEMENT ACCOMPANYING IT IS A CRIMINAL OFFENSE.

THERE IS NO PRESENT MARKET FOR THE UNITS AND IT IS NOT EXPECTED THAT A TRADING MARKET WILL DEVELOP. INVESTORS SHOULD NOTE THAT THERE ARE STRICT LIMITATIONS ON THE TRANSFER OF ANY UNITS OF A MEMBER.

THIS DOCUMENT MAY NOT BE USED LATER THAN ______, 2002.

This Memorandum is for the confidential use of the party identified on this page and may not be reproduced in whole or in part. If the offeree identified on this page decides not to invest, this memorandum must be returned to:

Name of Production Company
Street Address
City and State, Zip Code
Phone
Fax

For the exclusive use of: Copy No.

NOTICE: THIS OFFERING SUPERSEDES ALL PREVIOUS INFORMATION AND DOCUMENTATION REGARDING THE SUBJECT MATTER. NO OFFER MAY BE MADE EXCEPT THROUGH THIS PRIVATE PLACEMENT MEMORANDUM.

	PURCHASER PRICE[1]	UNDERWRITING DISCOUNTS, COMMISSIONS[2]	PROCEEDS TO LIMITED LIABILITY CO.[3]
PER UNIT	$10,000	$1,000	$9,000
TOTAL	$1,000,000	$100,000	$900,000

THIS OFFERING INVOLVES A HIGH DEGREE OF RISK. SEE "RISK FACTORS."

---

(1) Assumes that all of the Units are sold. The Manager may elect to begin operations when ten Units are sold. The minimum investment required is one Unit unless otherwise agreed to by the Manager. A total of 100 Units of $10,000 each will be offered. The Manager reserves the right to reject any subscription in whole or in part, to waive the minimum investment require-

ment for any potential investor or to allot to any potential investor less than the number of Units applied for by such investor.

(2) The LLC may pay a sales commission of ten percent on the sale of certain Units.

(3) Proceeds to the LLC are shown before deduction of organizational, legal and accounting expenses and other costs in connection with this offering (which costs and expenses are not expected to exceed $10,000).

This Private Placement Memorandum is intended to assist the Manager in making a private placement of Limited Liability Company units having an aggregate purchase price of one million dollars ($1,000,000). The Manager has not made application with the California Corporations Commissioner, with the Commissioner of Corporations of any state or with the Securities and Exchange Commission of the United States of America for registration of this Private Placement Memorandum and no state or federal regulatory agency has passed upon or endorsed the merits of this Private Placement Memorandum or the accuracy or adequacy of this Memorandum nor is it intended that they will. The Manager is relying on certain state and federal laws, regulations, policies, and judicial precedents which exempt this Private Placement Memorandum from the necessity of registration; specifically, Section 3(a)(ii) and 4(2) of the Securities Action of 1933, and Regulation D promulgated thereunder, and Section 25102(f) of the California Corporations Code. Accordingly, solicitation or sale shall not be made to any person unless the Manager has reasonable grounds to believe, and does believe, immediately prior to making such offer, solicitation or sale, that such person, either alone or together with one or more of his purchaser representatives (if any), has such knowledge and experience in the merits and risks of an investment in the units described in this Memorandum and that such person is able to bear the economic risks of such an investment. Further, in the event these units are sold in a state other than California, they will be sold only pursuant to an exemption in the various respective states and may be subject to additional restrictions on sale or transfer in such jurisdictions.

There is no public market for these units and, because there are expected to be only a limited number of investors and significant restrictions on the transferability of units, in all probability none will develop. The units may not be resold without registration or qualification unless an exemption is available with the appropriate governmen-

tal securities agencies. In addition, they are not transferable except under certain limited conditions set forth in the OPERATING AGREEMENT. Consequently, units should only be considered for purchase as long-term investments.

This LLC is a venture in a risky business, and investors who cannot afford a risk investment should not participate in the LLC.

The obligations and representations of the parties to this transaction will be and are set forth only in this Private Placement Memorandum, the Operating Agreement attached hereto, and the subscription agreement required to be signed by each Member. The information contained in this memorandum has been obtained from sources deemed reliable by the Manager but no representation or warranty is made as to the accuracy or completeness of such information.

Investors will be required to represent that they are able to bear the economic risk of their investment and that they (or their purchaser representatives) are familiar with and understand the terms and risks of this placement memorandum. The contents of this Private Placement Memorandum are not to be construed as legal or tax advice. Each investor should consult his or her own attorney, accountant or business advisor as to legal, tax, and related matters concerning this investment. All final decisions in respect to sales of Limited Liability Company units will be made by the Manager who reserves the right to revoke any offer and to refuse to sell to any prospective investor, if, inter alia, the prospective investor does not meet the suitability standards hereinafter set forth.

No offering, literature or advertising in any form should be relied on in connection with the private placement of these units except for this Private Placement Memorandum and the statements contained in it. No broker-dealer, salesman or other person has been authorized to give any information or to make any representation not contained in this memorandum and supplemental literature referred to herein, and, if given or made, such information or representation must not be relied upon as having been authorized by the LLC or the Manager. Accordingly, the recipient hereof agrees to notify the Manager in writing if he relies on documentation and/or information other than as provided herein. Agents, as the Manager may elect to utilize in connection with this Private Placement Memorandum, have not been authorized to make representations, or to give any information with respect to the private placement of the units proposed operations of this LLC, except the information contained in this memorandum. Neither the delivery of this memorandum nor any sale hereunder shall under any circumstances create the implication that there has been no change in the information contained herein subsequent to the date hereof.

Any distribution or reproduction of this Private Placement Memorandum, in whole or in part, or the divulging of any of its contents other than as specifically set forth herein, is unauthorized.

This Private Placement Memorandum does not constitute an offer to sell or a solicitation of an offer to sell in any state or to any person in which or to whom an offer or solicitation would not be permitted by law.

Summary of the Offering

The following summary is qualified in its entirety by the detailed information appearing elsewhere in this Memorandum. Each prospective investor and his offeree representatives should carefully read this Memorandum in its entirety and should not rely solely on this summary.

Manager:	(Your Name)
LLC:	Production Company, LLC Street Address City and State, Zip Code Phone Fax
State and Date of Organization:	A California Limited Liability Company to be formed in mid (Date).
LLC Term:	The LLC will continue until ten years from the date of its inception, the sale of all its assets, or the occurrence of certain other events. (See Operating Agreement attached hereto as Exhibit D.)
Tax Ruling:	The Manager has not applied for a tax ruling from the Internal Revenue Service (the "Ser-

vice") that the LLC will be taxed as a partnership and not as an association taxable as a corporation for federal income tax purposes. The Manager has not requested an opinion of counsel regarding such matters. (See "RISK FACTORS" and "FEDERAL INCOME TAX CONSEQUENCES.")

LLC's Objective:	To arrange for completion of preproduction and financing for a color motion picture tentatively entitled "_____________________________________" (the "Motion Picture"), a feature film written by <u>(Your Name)</u>. (See "DESCRIPTION OF THE MOTION PICTURE.")
	These objectives have the potential of providing cash distributions to the Members in excess of their Capital Contributions. There is no assurance that any or all of these objectives will be obtained. It is not expected that the LLC will generate federal income tax losses of any substantial amount in the initial years of the LLC or thereafter.
The Project:	Any and all rights of the LLC and any and all other agreements related to the Motion Picture are referred to herein as the "Project."
	On the Closing Date, the LLC will enter into an agreement with the Manager pursuant to which: (i) the Manager will agree to use his best efforts to produce the Motion Picture in accordance with the budget and plan outlined in this memorandum; and (ii) the Manager will assign to the LLC the right to produce the Motion Picture.
	The anticipated date of completion of the Motion Picture is __________, with an anticipated release in late ____. The Motion

	Picture will be shot largely on location in (City, State, Country).
Compensation and Fees to the Manager:	The Manager and his affiliate will receive substantial fees from this offering. (See "MANAGEMENT—COMPENSATION AND FEES PAYABLE TO THE MANAGER.")
Management of LLC:	The Manager will manage and control the affairs of the LLC. (See "MANAGEMENT.")
Finance, Production, and Exploitation:	In the event that the minimum funding level for the LLC is achieved, the Capital should be sufficient to complete preproduction and principal photography of the Motion Picture. In such event, the Manager will defer receipt of funds and reimbursements due them until the LLC has sufficient funds to complete the Motion Picture. No guarantee of exploitation or distribution can be made. However, the Manager believes that distribution of the Motion Picture will occur. (See "PROPOSED LLC OPERATIONS.")
Capitalization:	An aggregate amount of $1,000,000. (See "ESTIMATED APPLICATION OF THE CAPITAL CONTRIBUTIONS.") The Manager may elect to proceed when $100,000 in Capital Contributions have been received. (See "ESTIMATED PRODUCTION BUDGET SUMMARY.")
Participation in Costs and Revenues of the LLC:	All items of income, gains, losses and deductions, if any, of the LLC will be allocated ninety percent (90%) to the Members and ten percent (10%) to the Manager prior to receipt by the Members of Distributions equal to one hundred percent (100%) of their Capital Contributions and thereafter two thirds of one percent (0.667%) to the

	Members for each Unit owned. (See "Allocations of Profits, Losses, and Distributions.")
Subscriptions:	Seventy-five Units are offered for $10,000 each with a minimum investment of one Unit ($10,000); however, the Manager may accept subscriptions for less than one Unit. Each Unit may be purchased in cash. All subscription funds will be deposited in an escrow account at an institution chosen by the Manager. If on such date, on or before ___________, unless extended by the election of the Manager to a date on or before ___________ (the "Closing Date"), as offers to purchase ten (10) Units have not been received and accepted by the Manager and certain other condition precedent have not been satisfied, all subscription funds will be promptly returned to the investors without interest.
Operating Agreement:	The Operating Agreement of the LLC is set forth in its entirety in Exhibit D. Various references to the Operating Agreement in this memorandum do not purport to be complete and are qualified in their entirety by reference to the text of the Operating Agreement.
Glossary:	See "DEFINITIONS" section of the Operating Agreement (Exhibit D) for definitions of key terms used in this memorandum.

Suitability Requirements for Investors

Units may be sold to an unlimited number of "Accredited Investors" who meet the suitability standards described below. In addition, Units may be sold to a maximum of 35 Investors who are not "Accredited Investors" but who meet the suitability standards described below.

Accredited Investors

The federal securities laws and the securities laws of certain states provide that purchasers of Units must meet certain suitability standards in order to qualify as Accredited Investors. Each individual Accredited Investor will be required to represent in writing that:

(i) He is capable of making an illiquid investment and is an Accredited Investor as such term is defined in Regulation D ("Regulation D") promulgated under the Securities Act of 1933, as amended. A person is an Accredited Investor if: (a) his net worth exceeds $1,000,000 or (b) he has had income in excess of $200,000 in each of the last two years, or joint income with his or her spouse in excess of $300,000, and has reasonable expectations of reaching the same level this year.

(ii) He has, or he and his Purchaser Representative, if any, together have, such knowledge and experience in financial and business matters that he is, or they together are, capable of evaluating the merits and risks of investment in the Units.

(iii) He has carefully read the Operating Agreement and this Memorandum in making the decision to purchase the Units. He is acquiring the Units purchased by him without being furnished any sales literature or prospectus other than this Memorandum and the Exhibits hereto.

(iv) His Purchaser Representative, if any, has completed an Offeree Representative Information Schedule in the form annexed hereto as Exhibit B. Prior to the purchase of any Unit, the Manager afforded him and his offeree representatives, if any, full and complete access to all information with respect to the LLC, the Manager, and the LLC's proposed operations that he and his offeree representatives deemed necessary to evaluate the merits and risks of an investment in the LLC, to the extent that Manager possessed such information or could acquire it without unreasonable effort or expense.

(v) He is purchasing the Unit(s) for his own account for investment and not with a view to resale or distribution. He is aware that there are legal and practical limits on his ability to sell or dispose of the Units, and, therefore, that he must bear the economic risk of the investment for an indefinite period of time.

(vi) He recognizes that the purchase of the Unit(s) involves certain risks and he has taken full cognizance of and understands all of the risk factors related to the purchase of the Units, including those set forth under the captions "RISK FACTORS" and "FEDERAL INCOME TAX CONSEQUENCES" in this Memorandum.

(vii) Except as otherwise disclosed to the LLC in writing, he does not own, directly or indirectly (within the meaning of the attribution rules set forth in Section 318 of the Internal Revenue Code of 1986, as amended), any stock or other interests in any of the affiliates of the Manager.

Non-Accredited Investors

Units may be sold to a Non-Accredited Investor who makes a minimum investment of one Unit ($10,000) and represents in writing in his Purchase Offer and Offeree Information Schedule attached as Exhibits A and B that:

(i) He has a net worth (exclusive of home, furnishings and automobile) of no less than (a) $250,000, or that he is purchasing in a fiduciary capacity for a person who meets such conditions.

(ii) He is able to bear the economic risk of an investment in the LLC, which he understands is a speculative venture.

(iii) He has such knowledge and experience in financial and business matters that he is capable, either alone or together with his offeree representatives, of evaluating the merits and risks of an investment in the LLC as a Member.

(iv) He has relied on the advice of his own tax and legal counsel in evaluating the merits and risks of an investment in the LLC.

(v) His Purchaser Representative, if any, has completed an Offeree Representative Information Schedule in the form annexed hereto as Exhibit B. Prior to the purchase of any Unit, the Manager afforded him and his offeree representatives, if any, full and complete access to all information with respect to the LLC, the Manager, and the LLC's proposed operations that he and his offeree representatives deemed necessary to evaluate the merits and risks of an investment in the LLC, to the extent that Manager possessed such information or could acquire it without unreasonable effort or expense.

(vi) The Units he is offering to purchase will be purchased solely for his account, for investment purposes only, and not with a view to, or for resale in connection with, any distribution thereof.

(vii) He is an adult under the laws of the jurisdiction of his residence.

If Units are purchased in a fiduciary capacity, the person or persons for whose benefit the purchase is made will be required to meet the same requirements as other purchasers.

Certain states may impose higher or different suitability standards for Accredited and/or Non-Accredited Investors.

If an Investor is a LLC the net worth standard will be applicable to the LLC and the adjusted gross income standard will be applicable to each of its Members. If an investor is a revocable trust, each grantor of the trust must meet the net worth and adjusted gross income standards. If an investor is purchasing as a custodian for a minor, said standards will be applicable to the minor rather than the custodian.

The LLC will rely upon the accuracy of the representations of each investor to the LLC contained in his Offeree Information Schedule attached as Exhibit B. Any misrepresentation by an investor could have a material adverse effect on the LLC and subject him to liability for damage caused to the LLC.

In accordance with California law, the Manager will undertake all inquiries reasonably necessary to satisfy the Manager that the prerequisites for the exemption have been met, including requiring that each prospective investor fill out and return to the Manager the Offeree Information Schedule and his Offeree Representatives, if any, fill out and return to the Manager the Offeree Representative Information Schedule attached as Exhibit C.

Neither the Manager, nor any of his officers, attorneys or agents, will act as the Offeree Representative of any prospective Investor.

This offer can be withdrawn at any time before consummation and is specifically made subject to the conditions described in this memorandum. In connection with the offering and sale of the Units, the Manager reserves the right in his sole discretion, to reject any subscription, in whole or in part, to waive the minimum investment requirement or to allot to any potential Investor less than the Units applied for by such Investor.

Since there are substantial restrictions on the transferability of the Units, each potential Investor should proceed on the assumption that he must bear the economic risk of the investment for an indefinite period. Since the Units are not registered for sale to the public under the Securities Act of 1933 or the securities laws of any state, the Units may only be sold, transferred or otherwise disposed of by any Investor if, among other things, registration is accomplished or, in the opinion of counsel to the LLC, registration is not required under such laws. There is no public market for the LLC's securities and there can be no assurance any market will ever exist.

Risk Factors

Investment in the LLC involves a high degree of risk and is suitable only for investors who can afford to bear those risks and have no need for liquidity from such investment. Each prospective investor should consider carefully the risk factors attendant upon such investment, including, without limitation, those discussed below, and should consult his own legal, tax and financial advisors with respect thereto.

The Speculative Nature of the Business

The business of the production and licensing of motion pictures is highly speculative and has historically involved substantial risks beyond the control of its producers. Accordingly, there can be no assurance that the Manager will be able to raise funds sufficient to produce and/or license the Motion Picture so as to enable the Members to recoup all or any portion of their Capital Contributions or to yield a profit to them.

Production of the Motion Picture

If the Manager is successful in his fundraising efforts, and production of the Motion Picture is begun, the LLC will be subject to the risks inherent in producing the Motion Picture, including delays in photographing and editing acceptable footage for the Motion Picture, *force majeure,* or the possibility that the costs to complete the Motion Picture will exceed budgeted amounts, causing increases in development costs and possibly the failure to complete the Motion Picture.

Further, there is no assurance that all of the Units will be sold prior to the Termination Date. When $100,000 in subscriptions for Units has been raised, the Manager will undertake to complete the principal photography of the Motion Picture. The Manager believes that this sum will be sufficient for him to complete principal photography.

There is no guarantee that he will be successful in making the arrangements necessary to provide for the production of the Motion Picture.

The gross revenues derived from a motion picture are dependent, among other things, upon the production of the Motion Picture. Until the sale or other disposition of its rights in the Motion Picture, the sale of sponsorships, or the commencement of Distribution of the Motion Picture, the LLC will derive no LLC Revenues. The Manager is unable to predict the timing or amount of receipts, if any, to be derived by the LLC from licensing the Motion Picture.

No Prior Operations

To date, there have been no motion picture production and exploitation activities by the LLC or the Manager except as specifically set forth in this Memorandum. Until the commencement of distribution of the Motion Picture, the LLC will derive no LLC Revenues, unless sales of sponsorships generate LLC revenue. The Manager is unable to predict the timing or amount of receipts, if any, to be derived by the LLC.

While the Manager does have some substantial experience in filmmaking, and has written, produced and directed several films, no assurance can be given that the management team will make the Motion Picture succeed although, on the other hand, there is no reason to expect that they will be unable to do so.

Loss on Dissolution and Termination

In the event of a dissolution of the LLC, the proceeds realized from the liquidation of its assets, if any, will be distributed to the Members only after satisfaction of claims of its creditors. Accordingly, the ability of a Member to recover all or any portion of his investment in the LLC in that circumstance will depend on the amount of funds so realized and the claims to be satisfied therefrom.

Indemnification of the Manager

The Operating Agreement provides that the LLC will hold the Manager harmless against certain claims or lawsuits arising out of their activities and the operations of the LLC: If the LLC is required to perform under its indemnification agreement, any of its assets expended for such purpose will reduce the amounts otherwise available for its operations.

Principal Tax Risks

The LLC will not, and probably could not, obtain a ruling from the Internal Revenue Service as to its status as a LLC for federal income tax purposes or as to any other issue.

No tax opinion is expressed herein. There are material tax risks associated with an investment in the LLC. These risks include, without limitation, the possibilities that the LLC will be classified as an association taxable as a corporation, rather than as a partnership; or that the Internal Revenue Service (the "Service") may contest the characterization, amounts attributable to or the deductibility, or the tax period in which deductible, of certain items expected to be claimed as deductions by the LLC, including, without limitation, the payment of costs and expenses of the operations of the LLC and a portion of the management fees payable to the Manager. Because ownership of the Units is not expected to generate tax deductions in excess of LLC income, the LLC is not a "tax shelter" in the conventional sense. Accordingly, the Manager will not register the LLC as a "tax shelter" with the IRS. In order for the Members to be entitled to any federal income tax losses from the development of the Motion Picture, the transaction must be "engaged in for profit" apart from the federal income tax consequences. The resolution of this issue depends upon the facts and circumstances of each case, which cannot be ascertained in advance. **ACCORDINGLY, EACH PROSPECTIVE INVESTOR SHOULD CAREFULLY REVIEW THIS OFFERING WITH HIS OWN TAX ADVISOR IN ORDER TO EVALUATE THE INCOME TAX CONSEQUENCES OF AN INVESTMENT IN THE LLC.**

Limited Transferability of Units

Each Investor must represent to the LLC in his Purchase Offer that the Units he is offering to purchase will be purchased solely for his own account, for investment purposes only, and not with a view to, or for resale in connection with, any distribution thereof. The Units will not be registered under the Securities Act in reliance upon the exemption provided by Sections 3(b) and 4(2) of the Securities Act and Rule 506 promulgated thereunder. The Investors will have no right to require registration of the Units nor, in view of the nature of the Offering, is it likely or contemplated that such registration will take place. The transfer of Units by a Member to a new Member may be made only with the consent of the Manager, and in some situations only to Persons who meet certain suitability standards and with the consent of certain state regulatory authorities. The Manager has no obligation or commitment to repurchase Units from the Members and it is not likely that there will be a market for the Units.

Limited Liability of Members

The Operating Agreement provides that the Members are granted the rights, on withdrawal of the last remaining Manager, to elect any successor Manager(s) and to continue the LLC, to terminate the LLC, to amend the Operating Agreement, and to consent to the sale, assignment, transfer, exchange, license, or other disposition of all or substantially all of the assets of the LLC. While the existence of these powers will not adversely affect the limited liability of the Members in the State of California, the law is subject to modification at any time by legislative or judicial action and the effect of the existence of these powers on the limited liability of the Members has not been clearly established in other jurisdictions.

The Manager will take such reasonable actions as he deems appropriate to preserve the limited liability of the Members in all jurisdictions where the LLC operates.

Furthermore, in some jurisdictions, a Member may be personally liable for LLC expenses, liabilities and/or obligations in the event such Member participates in the management and control of the LLC.

Reliance on Management

The Members will not have a right to participate in the management of the business of the LLC or in the decisions of the Manager. Accordingly, no prospective Investor should purchase Units unless he is willing to entrust all aspects of management of the LLC to the Manager.

Distributions

If the Manager is unsuccessful in his efforts to develop the Motion Picture or if the LLC costs exceed its revenues, the Members may never receive any distributions from the LLC. Furthermore, the use of cash of the LLC to pay the costs of any borrowings of the LLC will defer LLC distributions to the Members and the Members may have to report income and incur federal and state income taxes in amounts in excess of the amounts of cash and other property, if any, actually distributed to them.

Lack of Arms-Length Negotiations

Agreements and arrangements, including those relating to compensation among the LLC and the Manager, the screenwriter, director and producer will not be the result of arms-length negotiations. The compensation plan may create conflicts between the interests of such persons and those of the LLC.

Effect of Reviews

The financial success of a film production is dependent, in large measure, upon the reaction of the public, which reaction is often substantially influenced by professional reviewers or critics for newspapers, television and other media. It is impossible for the Manager to judge in advance what the reaction of these reviewers and critics will be to the Motion Picture. To the extent that the Motion Picture receives unfavorable reviews from these reviewers and critics, its chances of success may be substantially diminished.

Distribution Arrangements

As of the date of this Memorandum, the Manager has made no arrangements for the distribution of the Motion Picture. It is anticipated that either prior to or after completion of the Motion Picture, the Manager will enter into a distribution agreement for the distribution thereof. However, there is no assurance that such distribution agreement will be entered into.

Loans and Advances

If the Manager believes that the funds raised through this offering are insufficient for the purposes of the production, he may, but is not required to, advance or borrow on behalf of the LLC whatever additional funds they deem to be necessary. Such Advances or Loans may be required to be repaid prior to the repayment of the Contributions of any Member. Members should note that even if the Motion Picture is completed, placed into distribution and/or otherwise licensed or exploited, such Loans or Advances, if made, might result in a considerable delay in the repayment of Members' contributions or in an extreme situation, a complete loss to the Members, since such Loans or Advances may equal or exceed the revenues from the production.

Unaudited Financial Statements

The financial statements of operations which the Manager has agreed to furnish to the Members no less than annually will be unaudited statements and the Members will be relying on the Manager concerning the accuracy thereof.

Conflicts of Interest

The Manager has the ability to be involved in other business ventures that may create a conflict of interest with their relationship with the LLC. The Manager will have day to day operational and management control of the LLC and, therefore, decisions relating to the LLC will be binding upon the LLC. The Manager may involve himself in other ventures including other motion pictures development projects which may relate or compete with activities of the LLC.

Although the Manager will act in a manner he deems best for the LLC, pursuant to the fiduciary responsibility owed by itself to the LLC, certain decisions, such as the timing of cash distributions, are entirely within its control and at times the interest of any particular Member may conflict with the interest of other Members.

It is possible that, at times, the best interests of the LLC may be inconsistent with those of the Manager or conflicts may arise concerning legal matters as the result of the operation by the Manager. Should a dispute arise between the LLC and the Manager as to the various rights and obligations, the Manager will cause the LLC to retain separate counsel for such matters.

Definitions

Certain terms used in this Memorandum are defined in Article I of the OPERATING AGREEMENT which is attached hereto as Exhibit D.

The LLC

______________, LLC (the "LLC"), will be a California Limited Liability Company formed to arrange for financing, production and licensing for worldwide audiences a feature motion picture tentatively entitled ______________ ______________ (the "Motion Picture"). The Motion Picture will be shot on location in (City, State, Country). The Manager has outlined a production plan which he believes is feasible at the level of minimum capitalization.

The anticipated date of completion is ____________, with an anticipated release date in late ______.

The successful attainment of these objectives has the potential of providing cash distributions to the Members in excess of their Capital Contributions. There is no assurance that all or any of these objectives will be attained.

The Members may be entitled to certain amortization tax benefits on a portion of their investment. Such benefits shall commence upon initial release of the Motion Picture (now intended for late ____). In addition, the LLC will have deductions for ordinary and necessary business expenses and will be entitled to amortize certain organizational costs. However, no representation is being made as to the availability of any particular tax benefits. It is not expected that the LLC will generate federal tax losses in the initial years of the LLC, or thereafter.

Estimated Application of the Capital Contributions

Table I presents the estimated application of the Capital Contributions.

TABLE I

Estimated Application of the Capital Contributions	
Development of the Motion Picture	$740,000
Management Fee to the Manager	None
Organizational Expenses and Legal & Accounting Fees	$ 10,000

Proposed LLC Operations

LLC Objectives

The LLC's objectives are to finance, produce, and release for worldwide audiences a motion picture currently entitled ________________. __________.See "Description of the Motion Picture and Principal Personnel."

Distribution Goals

Over the past fifteen years, a successful strategy for films made outside of Hollywood, is to have your film premiere at one of the major North American film festivals such as New York, Sundance, or Toronto. Festivals are very important, because they let film distributors see the picture in an exhibition context. This allows potential buyers to observe the reactions of the press and the audience, both of which can be critical to a movie's financial success.

Securing a distribution contract for an American theatrical release enhances any movie's potential earning power. U.S. box office receipts become the benchmark of money advanced for ancillary markets such as home video, cable and television broadcast rights.

Another lucrative distribution area is the foreign market. Theatrical and television rights are sold on an individual basis, territory by territory. English-speaking countries generally produce higher licensing fees, though many countries, for example, Germany and France, pay substantial sums for films about the American experience.

To facilitate placement of this film in the domestic and international marketplace, an established producer's representative will be hired, one who has an ongoing relationship with both distributors and film festivals. This producer's representative will professionally present the film to the world entertainment industry.

Estimated Production Budget Summary

The following Table presents a summary of the estimated production budget by which the Manager intends to achieve the proposed LLC operations described above. These figures are subject to change, in the Manager's discretion. Actual expenditures may vary materially. Detailed budget breakdown is available upon request.

PRODUCTION BUDGET SUMMARY OF
(Amounts in U.S. dollars)
Actual expenses will vary.
(Movie title)

Story Rights and Writer	$ 18,500	
Producer	$ 10,000	
Director	$ 15,000	
Cast	$ 42,832	
Extra Talent	$ 10,000	
Total		$ 96,332
Production Staff	$ 23,600	
Meals on Location	$ 29,611	
Set Design/Dressing	$ 47,087	
Property	$ 12,252	
Wardrobe	$ 47,087	
Make-Up & Hairdressing	$ 8,572	
Special Effects	$ 77,000	
Grip & Electrical	$ 39,864	
Camera	$ 26,324	
Film	$ 46,872	
Sound	$ 21,094	
Transportation/PIC Cars	$ 40,933	
Locations	$ 34,809	
Total Production		$ 455,105
Editing	$ 20,673	
Music	$ 15,000	
Post Production Sound	$ 32,400	
Titles	$ 15,000	
Post Production Film & Lab	$ 141,465	
Distribution	$ 11,000	
Total Post Production		$ 235,538
Insurance	$ 20,000	
Business Expenses	$ 24,500	
General Expenses/Post	$ 22,000	
Total Other		$ 66,500

Finders Fee 10.00%	$ 100,000	
Contingency 10.00%	$ 82,051	
Total Above-The-Line	$ 96,332	
Total Below-The-Line	$ 939,194	
Total Above- & Below-The-Line	$1,035,526	
Grand Total		$1,035,526

FINANCING

The Capital Contributions will be used for the purposes set forth under "ESTIMATED APPLICATION OF THE CAPITAL CONTRIBUTIONS," if all the Units are sold. The Manager will continue production when $100,000 is available. In that event, the LLC will require additional cash to pay for the costs to produce the Motion Picture. These costs will be financed primarily through the sale of the remaining Units, and by arranging for deferral of certain production costs. To the extent that the Units sold do not reach 5 Units, or the extent that additional cash in excess of the total Capital Contributions is required by the LLC to meet the costs of production of the Motion Picture, these costs may be financed, among other means, through (i) the use of LLC Revenues otherwise distributable to the Members, (ii) borrowing funds and servicing these loans with LLC assets or income, or (iii) a combination thereof.

Additional Financing for the Further Development, Production and Exploitation of the Motion Picture

After the LLC has expended all the capital for the production of the Motion Picture, the LLC may not be in a position to exploit the Motion Picture. In that event, it is anticipated that the LLC (i) may enter into Agreements with others for the exploitation of the Motion Picture, which may reduce its interest in the Motion Picture or the portion thereof which is subject to the Agreement, or (ii) may sell or otherwise dispose of its interest in the Motion Picture, or (iii) may distribute the Motion Picture itself and pay for the customary costs and expenses of such direct distribution; or (iv) to the extent necessary may borrow funds to pay for the costs of distribution of the Motion Picture and secure such loans with its assets and/or income. If the LLC is unable to pay for and/or finance the cost to distribute the Motion Picture or to enter into such Agreements, the Members may suffer a total loss of their investment in the LLC. Neither the Manager nor the Members are under any obligation to provide capital to the LLC in excess of the amounts of their respective Capital Contributions.

Borrowing

The Manager considers the LLC Capital to be sufficient to complete production of the Motion Picture. The LLC may borrow funds to conduct its business, including the development of the Motion Picture, and may secure these loans with the assets and income of the LLC, with or without recourse to the LLC or the Manager. In no event will any Member be liable for the repayment of such indebtedness unless such Member participates in the management and control of the LLC. There can be no assurance that the LLC will be able to borrow funds on satisfactory terms. The Manager may, but is not required and does not expect to make loans to the LLC. On any such loans, the Manager may not receive interest in excess of the higher of the then prime rate of Bank of America, or the rate of interest actually paid by the Manager to obtain such funds. There can be no assurance that the Manager will obtain such funds. There can be no assurance that the Manager will be able to or elect to make any loan to the LLC.

The LLC will be required to use LLC Revenues to repay any of the borrowing of the LLC, which will reduce the amounts of funds otherwise available for distribution to the Members. Furthermore, these LLC Revenues will constitute taxable income to the Members for federal income tax purposes, even though the Members will not receive such funds.

Management

Manager

The Manager is ____________. ____________ is the writer and will direct and produce the Motion Picture. Please see "PRINCIPAL PERSONNEL" for further description of the Manager. The Manager will devote such time as is reasonably necessary to the production of the Motion Picture and to arranging for its distribution.

Compensation and Fees to the Manager

The following table summarizes the types and estimated amounts of compensation and fees to be paid to the Manager. Some of such compensation and fees will be paid regardless of the success or profitability of the LLC. The compensation and fees were established by the Manager and were not determined by arms-length negotiations.

DESCRIPTION	CONSIDERATION
(a) Fees to (Name) as Producer, Writer & Director	$33,000
(b) Fees to (Name) or other editor as editor	$9,000

NOTE: (Name)'s fees may be deferred if only minimum funding is achieved.

(c) Interest in LLC Profits & Distributions	As set forth in the Operating Agreement. (See "DISTRIBUTION OF CASH FLOW AND ALLOCATIONS OF TAX BENEFITS.")
(d) Reimbursement for advanced funds	To the extent that the Manager advances funds for preproduction and production expenses, he will be entitled to reimbursement upon formation of the Limited Liability Company. As of (Date), the Manager has advanced approximately $5,000 for legal, accounting, script advances and office costs. The Manager estimates that a total of $10,000 will be expended for these and other preproduction expenses related to the Motion Picture prior to Closing.

General Responsibilities of the Manager

The Manager shall be responsible for the management and control of all aspects of the business of the LLC. In the course of such management, the Manager may assign, convey, lease, license, mortgage, or otherwise dispose of or deal with all or any part of the LLC's interest in the Motion Picture and employ such Person(s) either Affiliated or unaffiliated with the Manager as he deems necessary for the operations of the LLC.

Fiduciary Responsibilities of the Manager

Under California law, a Manager is accountable as a fiduciary to the Members and consequently, must exercise good faith and integrity in the administration of LLC affairs. However, the Members will have more limited rights of action against the Manager than they would have absent certain limitations in the Operating Agreement, which provides, for example, that neither the Manager nor his agents or employees will be liable to the LLC or the Members for any good faith act or omission which does not amount to gross negligence or gross or willful misconduct. Furthermore, the Manager will be indemnified and held harmless by the LLC against certain claims or lawsuits arising out of its activities and the operations of the LLC from the Capital Contributions and obtained assets of the LLC (see "RISK FACTORS—INDEMNIFICATION OF MANAGER").

The Offering

$1,000,000 in Limited Liability Company Interests are being offered in Units of $10,000 each (the "Units"). The minimum investment is one Unit ($10,000); however, the Manager may accept subscriptions for less than one Unit.

The Manager of the LLC will be (Name).

The Manager will maintain the LLC's principal business office at (Company Name, Street Address, City, Zip Code, Phone, Fax).

The first ten Units ($100,000) paid in and accepted by the Manager will be deposited in a separate account unless an investor waives the escrow condition. After ten Units have been paid in and accepted by the Manager, the Manager may, in his sole discretion, proceed with production of the Motion Picture. It is anticipated that this amount of LLC Capital will be sufficient to enable the LLC to complete principal photography and a rough cut of the Motion Picture.

If by (Date), or (Date), the Manager in his sole discretion elects to extend the date of closing, offers to purchase ten Units have not been received and accepted, all funds will be returned to the investors without charge, deduction, or interest. The interest earned on the escrow account will be used to pay expenses incurred by the LLC.

The LLC will pay or provide for all organization, legal and accounting costs in connection with the offering, which costs are expected to total $10,000.

The LLC will continue until either ten (10) years from the Closing Date, the sale or other disposition of all its assets, or the occurrence of certain other events set forth in the OPERATING AGREEMENT.

Allocations of Profits, Losses and Distributions

All items of LLC profits and taxable losses, deductions and tax credits will be allocated ninety percent (90%) to the Members in their respective pro-rata Shares and ten percent (10%) to the Manager until the Members have received repayment of one hundred percent (100%) of their initial investments ("Payout"). Thereafter, the Members will receive two thirds of one percent (0.667%) for each Unit owned, with the balance to the Manager, as set forth in the Operating Agreement. All of the foregoing allocations will be subject to adjustment as set forth in the Operating Agreement.

The Units to be sold represent a fifty percent (50%) interest in the Net Profits realized from the Motion Picture's distribution to foreign and domestic theaters and television and to cable and pay TV, as well as video cassettes, music and other copyrights, merchandising rights, and other proprietary interests and rights acquired by the LLC with respect to the Motion Picture after Payout. To the extent the LLC income exceeds the LLC's costs of distribution and advertising of the Motion Picture, and releasing costs, that income will be distributed in the following order of priority: (1) to pay unpaid liabilities incurred in the production of the Motion Picture and to pay loans and/or advances and deferments required to be paid prior to Payout; (2) to the Members until they have received return of their investment ("Payout"); (3) after Payout, to payment of remaining deferments required to be paid after Payout; and (4) thereafter, each Member will receive his or her share of Net Profits as provided in the Operating Agreement.

The Manager currently intends to make semiannual or annual determinations of the cash position of the LLC depending upon the accounting periods from the distributor. At such times, any cash which is available for distribution pursuant to the terms contained in the Offering will be distributed to the Members. The timing or amounts of such distributions (if any) cannot be predicted by the Manager and will most likely not occur at all until the Motion Picture is released and placed in distribution.

No Overcall

None of the Units to be sold are subject to calls for additional Capital Contributions. No Member shall have preemptive rights.

Use of Proceeds

LLC Capital will be used solely in connection with LLC business and is intended by the Manager to be allocated in the manner set forth under "ESTIMATED APPLICATION OF THE CAPITAL CONTRIBUTIONS."

Description of the Motion Picture

The Motion Picture is slated for production in 35mm color film and video format. However, if full funding is not achieved, the Manager may elect to produce the Motion Picture entirely in video.

Synopsis of the Motion Picture

____

____

____

____

____

Principal Personnel

(Your Name), *Director, Writer, Manager.*

____

____

____

____

____

Terms of Offering

Required Capital Contributions

A total of 100 Units are being offered. Each Unit is valued at $10,000. Each Investor will be required to purchase a minimum of one Unit, unless otherwise agreed to by the Manager. The purchase price for each Unit must be paid in cash, certified or bank check.

Prior to the Closing Date, all subscription funds will be deposited and held in an interest bearing escrow account for the benefit of the LLC. Funds deposited in such account will be released from escrow and paid to the LLC only for the purposes described in this Memorandum. If on the Closing Date, offers to purchase a minimum number of the Units totaling $100,000 have not been received and accepted by the Manager and certain other conditions have not been satisfied, all subscription funds will be promptly returned to the investors without charge, deduction or interest.

The Manager may elect to commence production of the Motion Picture at such time as $100,000 in Units have been invested in and agreed to with the LLC. The Manager believes that this amount is sufficient to complete principal photography of the Motion Picture.

To the extent possible deferred amounts will be payable after Payout. The Manager's deferrals will be payable only after Payout. However, the Manager expects that many deferrals will be required to be paid prior to Payout.

Method of Purchasing Units

A prospective Investor may make an offer to purchase Units by completing, signing and returning to the Manager his Purchase Offer, Offeree Information Schedule and Offeree Representative Information Schedule, if applicable, and making payment by cash or certified or bank check payable to the LLC in the amount of the required capital contribution for the total number of Units offered to be purchased. The Manager reserves the right to reject any Purchase Offer in its entirety, to waive the minimum investment requirements or to allocate to any prospective Investor a smaller number of Units than he has offered to purchase. In the former event, the Manager will return to the prospective Investor his subscription funds. In the latter event, the prospective Investor may either withdraw his Purchase Offer or complete, sign and return to the Manager a new Purchase Offer and a new subscription check in the appropriate amount.

Conditions to Closing

The Closing is subject to the satisfaction of the following condition precedent on or before (Date), or (Date) if the Manager in his sole discretion elects to extend the date of closing: a minimum number of the Units totaling $100,000 will have been paid for and accepted by the Manager (the "Closing Conditions"), and the Manager will have assigned the motion picture rights of the screenplay to the LLC.

Following Closing Until Termination Date

In the event the minimum Units have been sold and all other conditions to the Closing have occurred, the funds of all Investors shall be released to the LLC on the Closing Date. Following that date, the Manager may continue to offer Units until the earlier of: (i) sale of all Units; or (ii) __________ (the "Termination Date"). Funds from subscribers to any Units sold during such periods shall be made available to the LLC. Investors purchasing Units during such period shall become and be deemed Members of the LLC as of the date that their cash payments are made available to the LLC.

Distribution of Cash Flow and Allocation of Tax Benefits

Timing of Distributions to the Members

The Manager intends to make either a semi-annual or annual determination of the cash position of the LLC depending upon the reporting practices of the distributor of the Motion Picture. The Manager will distribute Available Cash to the Members. The Manager anticipates that no distribution (if any) will be made until the Motion Picture is released and placed in distribution.

Deferments

At the discretion of the Manager, in lieu of paying cash to Persons, firms or corporations (including without limitation, any Affiliate of the Manager) for rights, services, capital or materials furnished in connection with the Motion Picture, said entities will receive Deferments. Their order of payment shall be solely within the discretion of the Manager except that, Deferments payable to the Manager shall be payable only after Payout.

Division of Cash Distributions Among Members

Subject to the semi-annual or annual determination by the Manager as provided in the Operating Agreement that cash is available for distribution to the Members, and subject to deferments, all LLC Revenues received by the LLC in excess of production and distribution expenses (including expenses incurred in the distributing and advertising of the Motion Picture, and releasing costs) will be distributed in the following order:

(1) to pay unpaid liabilities incurred in the production of the Motion Picture and to pay loans and/or advances and deferments required to be paid prior to Payout;

(2) ninety percent (90%) to the Members and ten percent (10%) to the Manager until the Members have received return of one hundred percent (100%) of their Capital Contributions ("Payout");

(3) after Payout, to payment of remaining deferments required to be paid after Payout; and

(4) thereafter, the Members will receive two thirds of one percent (0.667%) of the Net Profit for each Unit owned, with the balance going to the Manager.

Tax Allocations

Net loss shall be allocated first to the Manager and Members in proportion to their respective positive Capital Account balances until such balances are reduced to zero, and thereafter ninety percent (90%) to the Members (which shall be allocated in proportion to the Members' respective Pro Rata Shares) and ten percent (10%) to the Manager.

Net Income shall be allocated on a quarterly or other basis not less often than annually first to the Manager and Members in proportion to and to the extent of the cumulative Net Losses previously allocated to them and not matched by allocations of Net Income, and second, ten percent (10%) to the Manager and ninety percent (90%) to the Members prior to Payout, and thereafter two thirds of one percent (0.667%) to the Members for each Unit owned, with the balance to the Manager.

The allocation among the Members of the LLC's income, gains, losses, deductions and credits ("Tax Items") will be determined under the Operating Agreement except to the extent an allocation: (i) lacks "substantial economic effect"; and (ii) is not in accordance with the Members' "Interests in the LLC," as determined under all the facts and circumstances. See Code Section 704(b).

Treasury Regulations issued on December 24, 1985, define the term "substantial economic effect" and describe a Member's "Interest in the Partnership" for purposes of Code Section 704(b). Treas. Reg. 1.704-1(b)(2)(3).

The Operating Agreement provides for the maintenance of Capital Accounts in accordance with the regulations and for the distribution of liquidation proceeds in accordance with the Members' respective capital account balances. Although no Member is required to restore a deficit in his capital account balance following the distribution of liquidation proceeds, the Operating Agreement contains a "qualified income offset" provision. Accordingly, the allocations of LLC Tax Items contained in the Operating Agreement should have "economic effect" under the regulations to the extent such allocations do not create or increase a Member's deficit capital account balance. It is not anticipated that the capital account of any Member will become negative. Further, the Operating Agreement does not specially allocate items of income or loss to Members based on their individual tax attributes or provide for disproportionate and offsetting allocations of income and loss from year to year. As a result, the "economic effect" of the allocations contained in the Operating Agreement should also be "substantial." Accordingly, the Manager believes that allocation of LLC Tax Items to investors with positive capital account balances should be respected under existing Treasury Regulations.

Federal Income Tax Consequences

The federal, state and other income tax consequences of an investment in the LLC are uncertain and complex, and will not be the same for all Members.

THE TAX BENEFITS TO BE DERIVED FROM THE PURCHASE, OWNERSHIP OR SALE OF UNITS CANNOT COMPENSATE ANY MEMBER FOR THE TOTAL LOSS OF HIS INVESTMENT. NO PROSPECTIVE INVESTOR SHOULD PURCHASE UNITS UNLESS HE HAS A REASONABLE EXPECTATION OF AN ECONOMIC PROFIT APART FROM THE TAX BENEFITS FROM THE PURCHASE, OWNERSHIP OR SALE OF UNITS. SEE RISK FACTORS—PRINCIPAL TAX RISKS.

Classification as a Partnership

The Manager believes that the LLC will be classified as a partnership for federal income tax purposes, and has attempted to ensure the LLC has more non-corporate characteristics than corporate characteristics as defined in applicable Treasury Regulations.

Under current Treasury Regulations, the classification of an organization as a partnership or an association taxable as a corporation is determined on the basis of the presence or absence of the following corporate characteristics: (i) continuity of life; (ii) centralization of management; (iii) free transferability of interests; and (iv) limited liability, subject further to other "characteristics which are significant" in making such determinations. However, the Manager has not sought an opinion from the Internal Revenue Service, nor an opinion of tax counsel.

General Tax Treatment of the Members

A. *Partnership vs. Corporate Status.* If the LLC is classified as a partnership for federal income tax purposes, it will not be subject to federal income taxation (although it will file an annual information tax return with the Service) and the Members will be deemed to have realized, and will be required to report on their personal income returns, their respective distributive shares of each item if income, gain, loss, deduction, credit and tax preference of the

LLC for the taxable year of the LLC ending with or within each taxable year of the respective Members without regard to whether they have received or will receive any actual distribution from the LLC for such taxable years. Thus, the Members may be required to report as taxable income in a given year an amount in excess of actual distribution to them from the LLC. The characterization of an item of expense, profit or loss will generally be the same for the Members as it is for the LLC; items of loss, deduction and credit may not be deductible by Members.

B. *Tax Reform Act of 1986*. Under the Tax Reform Act of 1986 deductions from business activities in which the taxpayer's participation is passive to the extent that they exceed income from all such activities (exclusive of portfolio income) generally may not be deducted against other income of the taxpayer. Similarly, credits from passive activities are generally limited to the tax allocable to the passive activities. Disallowed losses and credit are carried forward and treated as deductions and credits against income and tax from passive activities in the following taxable year(s). Upon the disposition by taxpayer of his entire interest in a passive activity the suspended losses (but not credits) are allowed in full. Passive activities include trade or business activities in which a taxpayer does not materially participate (e.g., a Limited Liability Company interest is such an activity). This provision is effective for taxable years beginning after December 31, 1986, and accordingly will apply to investments in the LLC.

C. *Deductions*. The LLC will attempt to write off all the deductible items at as early a time as it believes the law permits. However, there are many factual and legal questions involved with respect to the availability and timing of deductions, and there can be no assurance that deductions claimed by the LLC will be accepted by the Internal Revenue Service in any, some or all instances. A Member will not be entitled to deduct any share of LLC losses incurred prior to his admission to the LLC.

D. *Sale or Other Disposition of an LLC Interest*. In general, upon the sale or other disposition of a LLC interest, gain or loss will be recognized by the selling Member to the extent of the difference between the amount realized and the adjusted tax basis of such LLC interest.

E. *Cash Distributions*. Each Member is required to take into account in determining his federal income tax his distributive share of the income, gains, losses, deductions and credits of the LLC, irrespective of any cash distributions made to such Member during the taxable year.

Cash distributions by the LLC to a Member generally will not be taxable as income to a Member to the extent of his adjusted basis in his LLC interest immediately before the distribution, but the amount received will reduce the basis of such interest (but not below zero). Cash distributions in excess of such basis generally will be considered to be gain from the sale or exchange of the Member's LLC interest. Any reduction in a Member's share of LLC liabilities will be treated as a distribution of cash to such Member.

A complete in-depth discussion of the federal income tax consequences of an investment in the LLC is beyond the scope of this Memorandum, and no tax opinion has been requested of counsel. **THEREFORE, EACH PROSPECTIVE INVESTOR IS URGED TO CONSULT WITH HIS OWN TAX ADVISOR WITH RESPECT TO SUCH IMPLICATIONS.**

F. *State and Local Taxes*. The LLC and the Members may be subject to various state and local income business and sales taxes, and estate, inheritance or intangible taxes which may be imposed by jurisdictions in which the LLC may be deemed to be doing business or in which it owns or leases property, including the State of California. A Member may also be subject to various state and local taxes imposed by jurisdictions where he resides or has other contacts.

Litigation

The Manager knows of no litigation, present, threatened or contemplated, or unsatisfied judgments against the Manager or any proceeding in which the Manager is a party.

Financial Statements

There are no financial statements for the LLC, since it will be formed upon the filing of the Certificate of Limited Liability Company.

Access to Information

The Manager will make available to prospective investors any materials reasonably available to the LLC or the Manager. This could include, but not be limited to, information regarding the LLC, the Manager, the LLC's proposed operations, the offering of the units, anything set forth in the Private Placement Memorandum, or any other matter deemed by the prospective Member to be material in his decision to purchase LLC units.

The LLC and the Manager will answer all inquiries from prospective Members and their advisors concerning these matters and will afford prospective Members and their advisors the opportunity to obtain any additional information necessary to verify the accuracy of any representations or information set forth in this Private Placement Memorandum to the extent that the Manager can acquire information without unreasonable effort or expense.

Legal Matters

Legal matters in connection with the Units offered hereby will be passed upon by (Name and Address of Limited Partnership Attorney).

In addition to being counsel to the LLC, Lee is counsel to the Manager.

APPENDIX I

Purchase Offer (Limited Partnership)

By executing this Purchase Offer, the undersigned, a prospective Member of (Production Company Name), LLC, a California Limited Liability Company (the "LLC"), agrees to be bound by the terms of the Operating Agreement of the LLC (the "Operating Agreement"), grants a power of attorney to the Manager of the LLC, agrees to purchase one or more LLC interests in the LLC (the "Units") and makes certain representations and warranties as follows.

1. AGREEMENT TO BE BOUND BY OPERATING AGREEMENT AND GRANT OF POWER OF ATTORNEY TO THE MANAGER OF THE LLC. The undersigned hereby acknowledges that by executing this Purchase Offer, the undersigned agrees that upon becoming a Member in the LLC, the undersigned will be bound by each and every provision of the Operating Agreement. The undersigned hereby constitutes and appoints ____________ (the "Manager"), as the attorney-in-fact for the undersigned with full power of substitution and authority to act in the undersigned's name, place and stead, to make, execute, acknowledge and file documents, including, without limitation, (i) the Operating Agreement and any amendments thereto which are required under the laws of the State of California, or any other state or jurisdiction or by any governmental agency, or which the Manager deems advisable; (ii) any other instruments or documents which may be required under the laws of the State of California, or any other state or jurisdiction or by any governmental agency, or which the Manager deems advisable, including, without limitation, any Articles of Organization and any amendments thereto; (iii) any other instruments or documents which may be required to effect the continuation of the LLC, the admission of additional or substituted Members, or the liquidation and dissolution of the LLC (provided

such continuation, admission or liquidation and dissolution are in accordance with the terms of the Operating Agreement), or to reflect any reduction in the amount of contributions of the Partners, or to reflect any action of the Partners duly taken pursuant to the Operating Agreement, whether or not the undersigned voted in favor of or otherwise approved of the action; (iv) all conveyances and other instruments which the Manager deems appropriate to evidence or reflect any sales, assignments, transfers, exchanges, licenses or other disposition by the LLC; and (v) any production, distribution, exploitation or other agreements with any Person for the purposes of the LLC.

The power of attorney granted herein by the undersigned to the Manager: (i) is a special power of attorney coupled with an interest in favor of the Manager, is irrevocable, will survive the death, retirement, withdrawal, insanity, dissolution or bankruptcy of the undersigned, and is limited to the matters set forth in the Operating Agreement; (ii) may be exercised by the Manager for the undersigned by a facsimile signature of the Manager, or by listing the undersigned executing any instrument with the signature of the Manager acting as attorney-in-fact for the undersigned; and (iii) will survive the delivery of a transfer by the undersigned of all or any portion of the undersigned's Units, provided that where the transferee thereof has been approved by the Manager for admission to the LLC as a Substituted Member, this power of attorney will survive the delivery of such assignment for the sole purpose of enabling the Manager to execute, acknowledge and file any instruments or documents necessary to effect such transfer.

2. LIMITED LLC UNIT PURCHASE OFFER. In consideration of others similarly agreeing and in consideration of the activities of the LLC in connection with the Private Placement Memorandum for the LLC, dated ______ ____, (the "Memorandum"), the undersigned hereby agrees to purchase the number of Units set forth above the undersigned's signature, and for each Unit to pay $10,000 in cash.

3. REPRESENTATIONS AND WARRANTIES. The undersigned hereby represents and warrants that:

a. The undersigned has carefully read and understands the contents of the Operating Agreement, the Memorandum and this Purchase Offer.

b. The undersigned has relied solely upon the Memorandum and investigations made by the undersigned and his Offeree Representatives, if any, in making his decision to purchase Units.

c. No representations or warranties have been made to the undersigned with regard to his purchase of any Units other than those contained in the Memorandum.

d. The undersigned is aware that an investment in the LLC is speculative and involves a high degree of risk and has carefully read and understands that the matters set forth under the captions "RISK FACTORS," "PROPOSED LLC OPERATIONS," "CONFLICTS OF INTEREST," and "FEDERAL INCOME TAX CONSEQUENCES" in the Memorandum.

e. The undersigned is an adult and a legal resident of the state of his residence and acknowledges the Units the undersigned is offering to purchase will be purchased solely for his own account, for investment purposes only, and not with a view to, or for the resale in connection with, any distribution thereof.

f. The undersigned has such knowledge or experience in financial and business matters that he is capable, either alone or together with his offeree representatives, if any, of evaluating the merits and risks of an investment in the LLC as a Member.

g. The undersigned has a net worth (exclusive of home, furnishings and automobiles) of no less than (a) $250,000, without regard to an investment in the LLC, or that he is purchasing Units in a fiduciary capacity for a Person who meets such conditions.

h. The undersigned is able to bear the economic risk of investment in the LLC, which could result in a total loss of that investment.

i. The undersigned, in evaluating the merits and risks of an investment in the LLC, has relied on the advice of his own personal tax and legal counsel.

j. Prior to the sale of the Units, the Manager afforded the undersigned and his offeree representatives, if any, full and complete access to all information with respect to the LLC, the Manager and the LLC's proposed motion picture operations that he and his offeree representatives, if any, deemed necessary to evaluate the merits and risks of an investment in the LLC, to the extent that the Manager possesses such information or could acquire it without unreasonable effort or expense.

k. The undersigned is aware that the Manager reserves the right to reject this Purchase Offer in its entirety or to allocate to the undersigned a smaller number of Units than the undersigned has offered to purchase. In the former event, the Manager will return to the undersigned his subscription funds, and, in the latter event, the undersigned may either withdraw his Purchase Offer or complete, sign and return to the Manager a new Purchase Offer and provide the Manager with a new subscription check.

l. The undersigned is aware that unless offers to purchase at least twenty of the Units have been received and accepted by the Manager and certain other conditions precedent have been satisfied on or before the Closing Date, the LLC will promptly return to the undersigned the subscription funds.

m. The undersigned understands that as a Member he will have no right to participate in the management of the LLC's business or in the decisions of the Manager.

n. The undersigned understands that it is expected that the LLC will be classified as a partnership for federal income tax purposes and as such, the LLC will not be liable to pay federal income taxes but federal income taxes, if any, will be borne by the Members and Manager; any method of reporting income by the LLC, which may limit or exclude federal income taxes of the undersigned in the early years of the LLC, may create substantial federal income tax burdens on the undersigned in later years; the deductibility and/or federal income tax consequences of the transactions anticipated by the LLC are subject to challenge and possible disallowance by the Internal Revenue Service upon an audit of either the LLC's information tax returns or the personal tax returns of the undersigned and federal income tax laws are subject to modification at any time by legislative, judicial and/or administrative action, which modification could be applied on a retroactive basis, all of which may adversely affect the undersigned and reduce or eliminate virtually all the federal income tax benefits, if any, potentially associated with an investment in the LLC.

o. The undersigned has adequate means of providing for his current needs and personal contingencies and has no need for liquidity in his investment.

p. The undersigned is aware that the Units have not been registered under the Securities Act of 1933, that there is no public market for the Units, that the transfer of Units is subject to certain restrictions including obtaining the Manager's approval, compliance with the Securities Act of 1933, as amended, applicable State securities laws and an opinion of counsel satisfactory to the Manager that such transfer is in compliance therewith, and that, as a consequence, it is not likely for the undersigned to be able to liquidate his Units in the event of an emergency.

q. The undersigned is aware that any Member certificates issued by the LLC will bear a legend setting forth the following restrictions on transfer of Units:

"IT IS UNLAWFUL TO CONSUMMATE A SALE OR TRANSFER OF THIS SECURITY, OR ANY INTEREST THEREIN, OR TO RECEIVE ANY CONSIDERATION THEREFORE WITHOUT THE PRIOR WRITTEN CONSENT OF THE COMMISSIONER OF CORPORATIONS OF THE STATE OF CALIFORNIA, EXCEPT AS PERMITTED IN THE COMMISSIONER'S RULES."

"THE SECURITIES REPRESENTED HEREBY HAVE NOT BEEN REGISTERED UNDER THE SECURITIES ACT OF 1933 (THE "ACT") AND MAY NOT BE OFFERED, SOLD OR OTHERWISE TRANSFERRED, PLEDGED OR HYPOTHECATED UNLESS AND UNTIL REGISTERED UNDER THE ACT OR, IN THE OPINION OF COUNSEL IN FORM AND SUBSTANCE SATISFACTORY TO THE MANAGER, SUCH OFFER, SALE OR TRANSFER, PLEDGE OR HYPOTHECATION IS IN COMPLIANCE THEREWITH."

r. The undersigned acknowledges and understands that the LLC will pay the Manager the percentage of net profits set forth in the Operating Agreement, and reasonable compensation for other services rendered to the LLC.

s. The undersigned understands that all documents, records and books pertaining to an investment in the LLC have been made available to the undersigned and his offeree representative (if one is designated in Section 4 below) and that such documents, records and books of the LLC will be available upon reasonable notice, for inspection by the undersigned and his offeree representative during reasonable business hours at the offices of the Manager.

If the undersigned is purchasing the Units in a fiduciary capacity, the above representations and warranties will be deemed to have been made on behalf of the person(s) for whom the undersigned is so purchasing.

If the undersigned is a corporation, the undersigned is authorized and otherwise duly qualified to hold interests in the LLC.

4. OFFEREE REPRESENTATIVE. If the undersigned has designated an offeree representative upon whose expertise and advice the undersigned is relying in analyzing and assessing the risks of an investment in the LLC, his name, address, and telephone number are as set forth below:

NAME: ______________________________

ADDRESS: ______________________________

____

TELEPHONE: (____) __________________________

The undersigned hereby acknowledges that any such offeree representative is acting on behalf of the undersigned in connection with evaluating the merits and risks of an investment in the LLC. If no name is written above, the undersigned represents that the undersigned has no offeree representative (unless such offeree representative is designated by a separate written acknowledgment delivered to the Manager), and the undersigned has sufficient knowledge and experience in financial and business matters for a meaningful evaluation of the merits and risks of an investment in the LLC.

5. COMMISSIONS. In the event any Person, who is an advisor for the undersigned, requests and is entitled to payment of a commission, the undersigned must set forth his name, address and the amount of the agreed commission in the following space.

NAME: ______________________________

ADDRESS: ______________________________

____

AMOUNT OF COMMISSION: $____________

Notwithstanding any of the representations, warranties and acknowledgments contained herein, the undersigned does not hereby or in any manner waive any rights granted to the undersigned under securities laws.

The undersigned agrees to notify the Manager immediately if any of the Statements made herein become untrue.

Purchase Offer for Individual Subscriber

To be fully completed by subscriber, who by executing this Purchase Offer, offers to become a Member in (Company Name), LLC, a California Limited Liability Company (the "LLC"), on the terms provided in the Operating Agreement, grants a power of attorney to the Manager of the LLC as provided in Section 1 of this Purchase Offer, agrees to purchase the number of Units listed below, makes the representations and warranties set forth in Section 3 of this Purchase Offer, designates an offeree representative, if any, by completing Section 4 of this Purchase Offer, and says that the statements and matters set forth in this Purchase Offer are true and correct.

Number of Units Offered to Be Purchased: ____________

Subscription Amount: $____________

Signature(s): ____________________

____

ACKNOWLEDGMENT

State of California)
County of ______________)

On this ____ day of __________, 20__, before me, ______________, the undersigned Notary Public, personally appeared ________________, personally known to me (or proved to me on the basis of satisfactory evidence) to be the person(s) whose name(s) is/are subscribed to the within instrument and acknowledged to me that he/she/they executed the same in his/her/their authorized capacity(ies), and that by his/her/their signature(s) on the instrument the person(s), or the entity upon behalf of which the person(s) acted, executed this instrument.

Witness my hand and official seal.

____
Notary Public in and for said State

Additional Information to Be Furnished by Individual Subscribers: (Please Print or Type) Name(s):

____________________________ ____________________________
(First) (Middle) (Last) Social Security Number

Residence Address: ____________________________
Mailing Address: ____________________________

Purchase Offer for Corporation, Limited Partnership or Trust

To be fully completed by subscriber, who by executing this Purchase Offer, offers to become a Member in (Company Name), LLC, a California Limited Liability Company (the "LLC"), on the terms provided in the Operating Agreement, grants a power of attorney to the Manager of this LLC as provided in Section 1 of this Purchase Offer, agrees to purchase the number of Units listed below, makes the representations and warranties set forth in Section 3 of this Purchase Offer, designates an Offeree Representative, if any, by completing Section 4 of this Purchase Offer, and says that the statements and matters set forth in this Purchase Offer are true and correct.

Attached hereto is an opinion of counsel or other document establishing the subscriber's authority to subscribe for and purchase Units and to execute this Purchase Offer.

Number of Units Offered to Be Purchased: ____________

Subscription Amount: $___________

Name of Limited Partnership,
Corporation or Trust: ____

By: ________________________________

Title: ________________________________

ACKNOWLEDGMENT

State of California)
County of __________________)

On this ____ day of __________, 20__, before me, __________________, the undersigned Notary Public, personally appeared __________________, personally known to me (or proved to me on the basis of satisfactory evidence) to be the person(s) whose name(s) is/are subscribed to the within instrument and acknowledged to me that he/she/they executed the same in his/her/their authorized capacity(ies), and that by his/her/their signature(s) on the instrument the person(s), or the entity upon behalf of which the person(s) acted, executed this instrument.

Witness my hand and official seal.

____
Notary Public in and for said State

Additional Information to Be Furnished by Subscribers:

Name of Subscriber: ______________________________

Federal I.D. No.: ______________________________

Address: ______________________________

____

Mailing Address: ______________________________

If the Units are to be registered in the name(s) of the trustee(s), the date of the trust agreement must be furnished.

Acceptance by the Manager

The Manager of (Company Name), LLC, a California Limited Liability Company, has the right to accept or reject this Purchase Offer in whole or in part.

Accepted:

Date: ____________________, 20__

By: ______________________________

APPENDIX J

Collaborative Agreement (Feature Workshops)

Agreement

RICK SCHMIDT ("Schmidt"), doing business as FEATURE WORKSHOPS, intends to produce and exploit a 16-millimeter motion picture film tentatively entitled ____________________ ("the picture").

The following people named on page 2 will participate in the creation of the 16MM film and upon completion of their services therein as producers, will each receive an equal share of the gross profits derived by Schmidt from the picture and its ancillary rights, in the amount indicated after their name. In exchange for necessary completion costs for the film ($15,000 for conforming, sound mix, answer and release prints) 10% of the gross profits will be reserved for an INVESTOR. FEATURE WORKSHOPS will receive 5% of the gross profits to cover overhead during distribution and sales.

On my own behalf, and on behalf of my heirs, next of kin, executors, administrators, successors and assigns, I hereby release FEATURE WORKSHOPS and RICK SCHMIDT, his agents, licensees, successors and assigns, from any and all claims, liabilities and damages arising out of my participation with the production of this motion picture. This agreement may be executed in several counterparts, each of which shall be deemed an original and such counterparts shall together constitute one and the same agreement, binding all the parties hereto, notwithstanding all of the parties are not signatory to the original on the same counterpart. Profits unclaimed, or not assigned on page 3, will be shared equally among "the Producers" of the film.

Signatures	Date and Place of Execution
______________________	______________________
Investor (10%)	
______________________	______________________
______________________	______________________
______________________	______________________
______________________	______________________
______________________	______________________
______________________	______________________
______________________	______________________
______________________	______________________
______________________	______________________
______________________	______________________

On my own behalf, and on behalf of my heirs, next of kin, executors, administrators, successors and assigns, I hereby release FEATURE WORKSHOPS and RICK SCHMIDT, his agents, licensees, successors and assigns, from any and all claims, liabilities and damages arising out of my participation with the production of this picture. Upon completion of my services as defined below, I will receive one half percent (½%) of the gross profits as derived by Schmidt from the picture and its ancillary rights.

Signatures	Date and Place of Execution
____________________	____________________
____________________	____________________
____________________	____________________
____________________	____________________
____________________	____________________
____________________	____________________
____________________	____________________
____________________	____________________
____________________	____________________
____________________	____________________

Authorized by Rick Schmidt ____________________________

INDEX

Page numbers in *italics* refer to illustrations.